ADVENTURE
TRAVELLERS

SOUTH
AMERICA

AA **World Travel Guides**

ADVENTURE TRAVELLERS

SOUTH AMERICA

Produced by AA Publishing
© The Automobile Association 2000
Maps © The Automobile Association 2000
Coloured maps produced by the Cartographic Department,
The Automobile Association
Black and white maps produced by Advanced Illustration,
Congleton, Cheshire
A CIP catalogue record for this book is available from
the British Library
ISBN 0-7495-2320-4

The contents of this publication are believed correct at the time of print-
ing. Nevertheless, the publishers cannot be held responsible for any errors
or omissions or for changes in the details given in this guide or for the con-
sequences of any reliance on the information provided by the same.
Assessments of sights, accommodation, restaurants and so forth are based
upon the authors' own experience and, therefore, descriptions given in
this guide necessarily contain an element of subjective opinion which may
not reflect the publisher's opinion or dictate a reader's own experience on
another occasion.
We have tried to ensure accuracy in this guide, but things do change and
we would be grateful if readers would advise us of any inaccuracies they
may encounter.
The areas covered in this guide can be subject to political, economic, and
climatic upheaval, readers should consult tour operators, embassies and
consulates, airlines, e.t.c. for current requirements and advice before travelling. The publishers and authors cannot accept responsibility for any
loss, injury, or inconvenience, however caused.

Published by AA Publishing, a trading name of Automobile Association
Developments Limited, whose registered office is Norfolk House, Priestley
Road, Basingstoke, Hampshire RG24 9NY.
Registered number 1878835.

Visit our website at www.theaa.co.uk

Colour separation by Chroma Graphics
Printed and bound in Hong Kong by Dai Nippon

PREVIOUS PAGE Machu Picchu on the Inca Trail, Peru
INSET The Inca Trail below Sayacmarca, Peru

CONTENTS

INTRODUCTION

A continent of excess, South America boasts the largest river in the world, the deepest canyon, the longest mountain range, the most volcanoes, the highest waterfall, one of the driest deserts and the largest area of primeval rain forest. It is different at every point of the compass, with its southernmost point bordering the Antarctic—a land of mountains, massive cliffs and glaciers—and its northern quarter tropical steamy jungle, palm-fringed white-sand beaches, immense river deltas, and mysterious flat-topped mountains hiding secret worlds. Between these two extremities runs the backbone of the snow-capped Andes mountains, laced with active volcanoes, torrential rivers, and crater lakes. To the east are the arid deserts of the Atacama, great salt lakes and the magical, volcanic Galápagos islands: to the west are vast steppes, wetlands with a maze of rivers and dense jungle. Amid this breathtaking geographical diversity lives a huge, uncharted variety of flora and fauna. In the remoter areas are peoples with minimal contact with the outside world and exquisite ruins of long forgotten civilizations which hint at lost wealth and culture. Ancient remains created by stunning feats of engineering vie for the traveller's attentions with beautiful modern cities bustling with ever-growing populations. Each of these areas offers opportunities for adventuring—a chance for clambering in volcanic craters, cycling on precipitous roads, white-water rafting, bird-watching or canoeing through snake-infested jungle. South America is nothing if not exciting and will stretch the adventurous traveller to the limits.

RIGHT The snow-capped Torres del Paine, southern Chile
ABOVE Horseback-riding on the Golondrinas trek, Ecuador

About the Authors

JANE EGGINTON

Jane Egginton is a travel writer and researcher. Jane, a winner in the *Observer* Young Travel Writer of the Year Award, has written for publishers including Reader's Digest and Thomas Cook. She has travelled extensively throughout Britain, Asia, Australasia and the Americas, both for work and for pleasure. Central and South America remain her favourite for their beautiful, varied landscapes and for the adventures they offer. She is currently writing a guide book to Mexico.

GUY MARKS

Now on the committee of the British Guild of Travel Writers (BGTW), Guy Marks first caught the travel bug in the early 80s when he drove from England to Cape Town. On his return to England he worked in finance in the City. In the late 80s he left to spend a few years as an overland tour leader and driver. He worked in Peru and Ecuador, developing an extensive personal knowledge and deep love for South America. Settled in Suffolk since 1992, he has become a well-known travel photographer and travel writer freelancing for national and international publications and the travel industry. He has written *This is Egypt* (New Holland 1998) and *Travel Writing and Photography* (Traveller's Press 1997), and is a course tutor on travel writing and photography.

SIMON RICHMOND

Simon Richmond's first brush with adventure was on the Big Dipper roller-coaster in his hometown of Blackpool, England. He's been in search of the same adrenalin rush ever since. Now based in Sydney, Australia, he's worked as a journalist in London and Tokyo. His features have been published in many U.K. newspapers, the *Sydney Morning Herald*, and *The Australian*. He now spends most of his time travelling and writing guidebooks for the AA, Lonely Planet and Rough Guides.

LEE KAREN STOW

Lee Karen Stow is a full-time travel journalist and photographer, based in Yorkshire, England. A member of BGTW, Lee's work has appeared in a number of publications including *The Times*, the *Express on Sunday*, *In Britain*, *Wanderlust*, and *Travel Weekly* among others. Born with a wandering spirit, Lee travels whenever possible perhaps scuba diving, scrubbing floors, sailing a yacht or teaching English to schoolchildren.

STEVE WATKINS

Photographer and writer Steve Watkins specialises in covering adventure travel, extreme sports and cultural issues, especially in his favourite destinations Latin America and Australia. His work has featured in numerous publications, including *No Limits World*, *Traveller*, *Global Adventure*, *Wanderlust*, *Mountain Biking UK*, *Sunday Express* and various BBC publications. His photographs have been widely exhibited, including a display at London's prestigious Barbican gallery. Now based in South Wales, he has just written *Adventure Sports Europe* (Queensgate Publishing, spring 2000).

How to Use this Book

The book is divided into three distinct sections:

SECTION 1   PAGES 6–17

This comprises the introductory material and some general practical advice to guide you on your travels. We have included an introduction to the writing team. Our authors come from all walks of life and cover a wide age range. What they do have in common, though, is a spirit of adventure and a wealth of travel experience.

The map on pages 10–11 shows the areas covered, and is colour-coded to highlight the regional divides. The 25 adventures are numbered for reference; the contents page will guide you straight to the relevant page numbers.

Pages 12–13 and 16–17 offer practical advice from experienced travellers, complementing information given later.

The seasonal calendar on pages 14–15 gives a guide to the optimum time to visit the areas covered in the adventures. However, there are many factors affecting when you might like to go, and greater details of climate patterns and their effect on activities are given at the end of each chapter. When arranging your trip always seek advice about the conditions you are likely to encounter from a tour operator or country tourist information office.

SECTION 2   PAGES 18–256

The main section of the book contains 25 adventures, chosen to give you a taste of a wide range of activities in a variety of places— some familiar, others not. The first page of each adventure carries a practical information box that gives you an idea of what to expect, plus a grade, numbered according to the relative difficulty of the activity or the level of skill required.

Going it Alone—Each adventure ends with a page of dedicated practical advice for planning that specific adventure yourself. This information should be used in conjunction with the "Blue Pages" at the end of the book (see below).

Any prices mentioned in the book are given in US$ and were the approximate prices current at the time of the trip. Due to variations in inflation and exchange rates these are only meant as guidelines to give an idea of comparative cost.

 Challenge Rating: If you have even thought about booking the trip, you will manage

 Not too difficult but you may need some basic skills

 You will need to be fit, with lots of stamina and may need specialist qualifications

 You need to be fit and determined—not for the faint-hearted*

 This is for the serious adventurer— physically and mentally challenging!*

Sometimes only part of the trip is very hard and there may be an easier option

 Comfort rating: Indicates the degree of hardship you can expect, where 1 is comfortable and 3 is uncomfortable. This category not only covers accommodation, but also factors such as climate and other conditions that may affect your journey.

 Specialist equipment: Advice on any equipment needed for the journey, covering specialist items like diving gear, and also clothing and photographic gear.

SECTION 3   PAGES 257–320

"Blue Pages"—*Contacts* and *A–Z of Activities*—begin with selected contacts specific to the 25 main adventures. Here you'll find names referred to in the main stories, including tour operators, with addresses and contact numbers.

The A–Z lists a wide range of the best activities available in the region, with general information and full contact details of the outfits and organizations able to help you plan your journey. Finally, the book ends with a comprehensive index and gazetteer.

9

SOUTH AMERICA

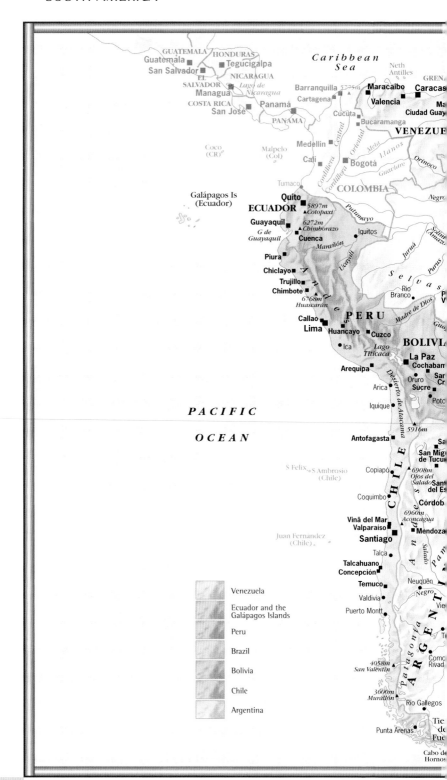

*Caribbean
Sea*

GUATEMALA HONDURAS
Guatemala
San Salvador
Tegucigalpa
EL NICARAGUA
SALVADOR
Managua
*Lago de
Nicaragua*
Neth
Antilles
GREN
COSTA RICA Panamá
San José
PANAMA
Barranquilla
Cartagena
Maracaibo Caracas
Valencia Ma
Ciudad Guay
Cúcuta
Bucaramanga
VENEZUE
Coco
(CR)
Malpelo
(Col)
Medellin
Cali
Bogotá
Meta
Llanos
Orinoco
Guaviare
Negro
VENEZUE

Tumaco
COLOMBIA

Galápagos Is
(Ecuador)
Quito
ECUADOR
5897m
Cotopaxi
Putumayo
Guayaquil
6272m
Chimborazo
Iquitos
*G de
Guayaquil*
Cuenca
Marañón
Juruá
Purus
Solim
Amazo

Piura
Chiclayo
Trujillo
Chimbote
6768m
Huascarán
Ucayali
S e l v a s
Rio
Branco
P
V

Callao
Lima
Huancayo
Cuzco
PERU
Madre de Dios

Ica
Lago
Titicaca
BOLIVIA
La Paz
Cochaban
San
Cr

Arequipa
Oruro
Sucre
Poto

Arica

Iquique
Desierto de Atacama
5916m

PACIFIC

OCEAN

Antofagasta
Sa
San Migu
de Tucu

S Felix S Ambrosio
(Chile)
Copiapó
6908m
Ojos del
Salado San
del Es

Coquimbo
Córdob
6960m
Aconcagua

Viña del Mar
Valparaíso
Santiago
CHILE
Mendoza
Pa

Juan Fernandez
(Chile)
Talca

Talcahuano
Concepción
Neuquén
Negro
Vie

Temuco
Valdivia
Puerto Montt
A
n
d
e
s
Salado
T

	Venezuela
	Ecuador and the Galápagos Islands
	Peru
	Brazil
	Bolivia
	Chile
	Argentina

Patagonia
ARGENTI
Como
Rivad

4058m
San Valentin

3600m
Murallón
Rio Gallegos

Punta Arenas
Tie
de
Fue
Cabo de
Hornos

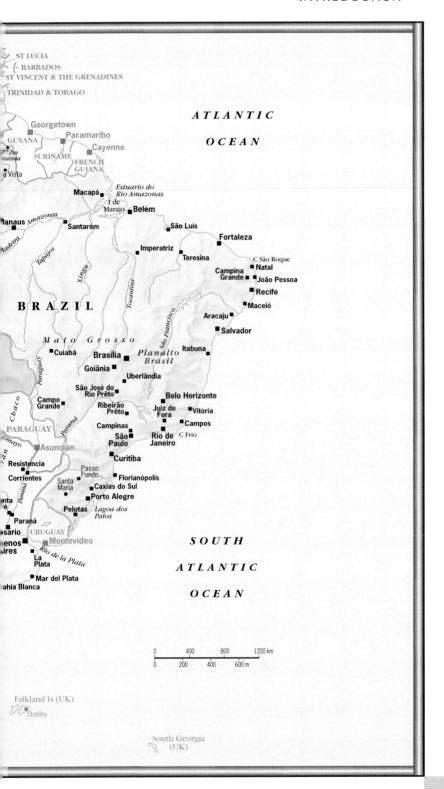

Practical Matters

PREPARATION

To get the best out of your adventure holiday it's worth taking time to plan carefully. Research the areas you are interested in and use the "Blue Pages" to help you find a suitable tour operator. Think about when you will be travelling and what type of activities will be involved. Make sure your chosen tour operator knows the region well and can offer advice and alternative arrangements in case of unforeseen circumstances.

LANGUAGE AND CUSTOMS

Many of the languages spoken in the countries and regions covered will be unfamiliar to visitors. Where there are many local languages or the area is remote, it may prove difficult to communicate. However, there is often a widely used language in any area (such as English or Spanish) of which many locals will have some knowledge. It is generally appreciated if visitors attempt a few words or phrases and and a phrase book or mini-dictionary will be useful. Try to learn something of the local customs and etiquette to minimize the risk of causing offence through inappropriate gestures, body language, or dress.

MOST COMMON LOCAL LANGUAGES

Argentina	Spanish
Bolivia	Spanish, Aymará, Quechua
Brazil	Portuguese,French, German, Tupi-Guaraní, Ge, Carib, Arawak
Chile	Spanish, English
Ecuador	Spanish, Quechua,
Peru	Spanish, Quechua, Aymará, English
Venezuela	Spanish, English, German, Yanomani, Bari

TRAVEL DOCUMENTS

Make sure you have a full, valid passport and that it is valid for much longer than your stay. Check with the embassy or consulate of the countries you might be visiting about visa requirements. These can vary enormously and can change rapidly. If you intend travelling across borders, make sure you have all the relevant documents. Before you go, check the political situation for potential problems, (see below) especially in disputed areas, and try to find out local information before you travel to remoter areas.

CONTACTS:

U.S. State Department
Website: travel.state.gov/travel_warnings.html
Travel warnings and consular information.

Foreign and Commonwealth Office, UK
Tel: 020 727 01500
Website: www.fco.gov.uk
Travellers' advice line for information about potential political risks around the world.

HEALTH MATTERS

Many of the countries covered here are developing areas with relatively basic medical facilities. Check with your doctor or travel clinic and allow plenty of time for any necessary vaccinations. Record your vaccinations on an International Health Certificate and carry it with you.

CONTACTS:

World Health Organization
Website: www.who.ch/
For the latest information on health matters around the world.

U.S. Centers for Disease Control
Tel: (888) 232-3228; faxback: (888) 232-3229
Website: www.cdc.gov
Telephone and fax hotlines offering the latest health information and advice on vaccinations.

LOCAL CURRENCIES

ARGENTINA:	NUEVO PESO CONSISTING OF 100 CENTAVOS
BOLIVIA –	BOLIVIANO = 100 CENTAVOS
BRAZIL –	REAL = 100 CENTAVOS
CHILE –	PESO = 100 CENTAVOS
ECUADOR –	SUCRE = 100 CENTAVOS
PERU –	NUEVO SOL = 100 CÉNTIMOS
VENEZUELA –	BOLÍVAR = 100 CÉNTIMOS

CURRENCY

The safest way to carry currency is by traveller's cheques, preferably in US$, which are readily accepted in most places. Local currencies rates can fluctuate. Carry your money concealed in a money belt and avoid carrying all your valuables and money in the same place.

Please note: Any prices given in this book are in US$ and were the approximate prices current at the time of the trip. Due to variations in inflation and exchange rates these are only guidelines.

INSURANCE

Always make sure you have comprehensive travel and medical insurance before you travel. Check the policy carefully and make sure those arranging the insurance are aware you will be taking part in "dangerous" activities.

Most standard insurances do not cover you for "dangerous" activities such as scuba diving, rock climbing, canoeing e.t.c.—the very type of activities you may wish to tackle.

AT THE BORDER

Local import/export laws vary and you should seek the advice of consuls, border officials or carriers to ensure you are not contravening them. If buying souvenirs, bear in mind that there are universally strict laws against importing items made from some animals, obscene material, offensive weapons and narcotics. Some countries require additional documentation for prescription drugs and in others, alcohol is strictly controlled. Never take risks and always pack your own luggage.

TIME DIFFERENCES

	London, noon = 0 hours (Greenwich Mean Time)	New York Noon local time	San Franicisco Noon local time
ARGENTINA:	-3 HOURS	+2 HOURS	+5 HOURS
(except for North and Andes	-4 HOURS)	+1 HOUR	+4 HOURS
BOLIVIA:	-4 HOURS	+1 HOUR	+4 HOURS
(except around La Paz	-5 HOURS)	0 HOURS	+3 HOURS
BRAZIL:	- 3 HOURS	+2 HOURS	+5 HOURS
(western half,	-4 HOURS	+1 HOUR	+6 HOURS
central and Andes	-5 HOURS	0 HOURS	+3 HOURS
CHILE:	-4 HOURS	+1 HOUR	+4 HOURS
(summertime, October to March	-3 HOURS)	+2 HOURS	+5 HOURS
ECUADOR:	-5 HOURS	0 HOURS	+3 HOURS
GALAPAGOS ISLANDS:	-6 HOURS	-1 HOUR	+2 HOURS
PERU:	-5 HOURS	0 HOURS	+3 HOURS
VENEZUELA:	-4 HOURS	+1 HOUR	+4 HOURS

No account has been taken of daylight saving

When to Go

MARCH	APRIL	MAY	JUNE	JULY	AUGUST

VENEZUELA

RAIDERS OF THE LOST WORLD, SOUTHERN VENEZUELA

WHEELS OF ANDEAN FORTUNE, NORTHWESTERN VENEZUELA

PARADISE ROCKS FROM ABOVE AND BELOW, NORTH COAST

ON AN ALL-TIME HIGH, VENEZUELA

ECUADOR

TREKKING THROUGH CLOUD FOREST, NORTH

LEARNING NEW SKILLS WITH THE CRAFTY OTAVALEÑOS, NORTHERN ECUADOR

CRUISING THE GALÁPAGOS ISLANDS, PACIFIC OCEAN

PERU

A TREK THOUGH TIME ON THE INCA TRAIL, SOUTHERN PERU

EXPLORING THE SECRETS OF THE NAZCA LINES, SOUTHWEST PERU

BOATINGAROUND LAKE TITICACA, SOUTHEAST PERU

HIGHS AND LOWS OF THE COLCA CANYON, SOUTHERN

BRAZIL

THE AMAZON EXPERIENCE, NORTH CENTRAL BRAZIL

FEELING THE FORCE OF IGUAÇU FALLS, SOUTHWEST BRAZIL

RANCHING IN BRAZIL'S GRAND SAVANNAH, THE WEST

BOLIVIA

CORDILLERA RANGE, NORTHWEST BOLIVIA

BOLIVIAN HIGHS AND LOWS, CENTRAL BOLIVIA

CHILE

The ascent of the volcano Villarrica, Chile

BEYOND THE VALLEY OF THE MOON,

IN THE SHADOW OF THE VOLCANO,

ARGENTINA

Riding the Río Mendoza, Argentina

FISHING, CYCLING AND HORSE RIDING IN

WATCHING THE WILDLIFE, CENTRAL COAST

Adventure Planner

SEPTEMBER	OCTOBER	NOVEMBER	DECEMBER	JANUARY	FEBRUARY

BORN TO BE WILD

ECUADOR

Giant vegetation in the subtropical forest, Ecuador.

PERU

The flooded forest on the Río Negro, Brazil

Panoramic views on the trail through the Cani Forest, Chile

NORTH CHILE

CENTRAL SOUTHERN CHILE

THE TOWERS OF CHILE, SOUTH EAST

RAFTING AND HIGH-ALTITUDE HIKING IN MENDOZA

IN THE FOOTSTEPS OF DINOSAURS, CENTRAL COAST

PATAGONIA, SOUTHERN ARGENTINA

ADVENTURES ON ICE, SOUTHWEST ARGENTINA

Travelling Safe

WHAT TO DO BEFORE YOU GO

Confirm in advance of departure as many flights or voyages, and as much accommodation, as possible.

If you have only a limited time available, arrange your "adventures" in advance—some destinations restrict the number of visitors allowed in a particular period. A planned and packaged itinerary, though perhaps more expensive, may prove a wise investment.

❑ Photocopy all important documents and carry them separately from the originals. Keep a copy at home.

❑ Do not pack essential items in your suitcase—carry them in hand luggage.

❑ Give a copy of your itinerary and any contact numbers you have to friends or relatives.

❑ Research thoroughly the places you are visiting to ensure that you are adequately aware of the conditions that await you.

❑ Choose the right seasons.
In some countries election times are best avoided, while public holidays may make travelling difficult.

❑ Check whether you need a visa.

❑ Check with a doctor about vaccinations or prophylactics necessary for the area you are visiting, and obtain an International Health Certificate with your vaccinations recorded on it.

❑ Purchase travel insurance, ensuring it covers your proposed activities—most insurances do not include adventure activities.

WHAT TO TAKE

A soft bag is much better than a hard-frame suitcase. Make sure you have a way of securing the bag, such as a lock or a strap. Pack fewer clothes than you think you will need, and more photographic

---

THE FOLLOWING WILL MAKE ANY TRAVELLING EXPERIENCE MORE COMFORTABLE:

❑ A torch/flashlight and spare batteries.

❑ A first-aid kit to include rehydration tablets and insect repellent. Effective suncream/block. Diarrhoea treatment, antihistamines, aspirin.

❑ Water bottle

❑ Waterproof bag for valuable items

❑ An umbrella

❑ Passport and spare passport photographs

❑ A supply of books to read and/or short-wave radio

❑ A folding walking stick for mountain descents

---

film. If you do not want to be bothered with washing clothes, laundry services can be cheaply and easily obtained in most of the places featured in this book. It is always better to take film than to have to buy it locally. A spare camera battery is also recommended.

Take the RIGHT clothes. It may be sweltering on the coast, but if you are climbing a mountain, it will be very cold at the top. Shorts may be fine on the beach but not in a church. Footwear is especially important if you are tackling a number of contrasting adventures, for example sandals or sneakers for island hopping but boots for hiking. And don't forget your bathing suit.

MONEY

Take US$ travellerscheques and a separate supply of American dollar bills. Don't forget to take note of the numbers. Most major credit cards are widely accepted (although some countries favour one over another), but this cannot be relied on in remoter areas.

What To Avoid

Although you should consider taking a course of anti-malaria tablets, it is better to avoid being bitten by mosquitoes in the first place. Cover all exposed flesh in a good insect repellent.

Avoid offending local sensibilities, whatever your own opinions. Liberal views and open debate may be acceptable at home, but in some countries discussion of religion and politics can be touchy subjects and possibly illegal.

If you are planning to go scuba-diving, or take part in some other instructor-led activity, don't automatically go for the cheapest options unless you are very experienced and competent to judge. A reputable operator may cost more to use, but it may save your life.

Avoid taking things for granted. Local people often presume you know about local conditions or else trivialise or exaggerate possible dangers or irritations, so don't be embarrassed to ask questions.

It is best to be careful about what you eat and drink. Water anywhere may be contaminated so always drink bottled water and avoid ice in drinks, no matter how hot it is. Only eat cooked food and remember, washing food is only helpful if the water used is pure.

Drugs

Do not, under any circumstance, be tempted by offers of drugs—traffickers can face the death penalty. Do not ever carry anything for anyone else, no matter how apparently innocent the request.

PERSONAL SAFETY

Theft

Take only what you really need when out and about—leave as much as possible in a safe at your accommodation. In countries where mugging is a real threat, it is as well to carry a little cash to give away if necessary. Unfortunately, those countries where street theft is a problem, may expect you to carry ID—make a reduced copy of your passport, include a proper passport photograph and enclose the whole thing in a plastic wallet.

Beggars, Sellers and Confidence Tricksters

Difficult though it may be, think twice before you give money to beggars. Sometimes it is a ploy—before long you are surrounded by a sleeve tugging crowd, from among which one member leaps out and snatches your camera or money. Persistent sellers are a nuisance but if you can avoid looking them in the eye and learn the local words for "no thank you" you will find them less troublesome. As for confidence tricksters, do not be taken in by flattery and be deeply suspicious of bargains.

Violence

As a foreigner, you are unlikely to be affected by violent crime. In cities, ask locally if there are areas that are best avoided.

Travelling Alone

The two main things for individuals are to let people know where you are travelling and to carry an absolute minimum of luggage—there will be no one else to watch over it.

Women

It is a tiresome truism that Western women travelling alone may be considered of easy virtue, if only because in some countries women rarely venture anywhere alone. Ignore, with as much dignity as possible, the unwelcome attentions that may come your way. Dress with consideration for local customs (especially completely covering arms and legs when visiting churches or in remote areas). Note that although most toiletries will be available in major towns, they may not be elsewhere.

VENEZUELA

When Christopher Columbus came upon Venezuela during his American wanderings in 1498, he described it as "Paradise on Earth." And yet he saw only the coastal areas. If he had been granted the opportunity to explore further, surely he would never have left. It is a country of extraordinary contrasts. In the west, there are the high, permanent snow peaks of the Andean Mountains. At its heart are the river-laced, wildlife-rich, cowboy lands of Los Llanos. To the east, the lengthy Río Orinoco finally makes it, via an immense delta region, to the ocean. Down south, a weird and mesmerizing landscape of immense, flat-topped mountains borders the deep, deep Amazonian jungle. And all along the extensive Caribbean north coast are the glorious white-sand beaches and idyllic islands that so excited Columbus. Indeed, given that Columbus barely scratched its surface, his description of Venezuela was remarkably apt.

Salto Sapo waterfall, Canaima National Park, Venezuela

Raiders of the Lost World

by Steve Watkins

Southern Venezuela is dominated by tepuis, *the mysterious, flat-topped mountains that inspired Sir Arthur Conan Doyle to write* The Lost World. *One of them, Auyán Tepui, is home to Salto Angel (Angel Falls), the world's highest waterfall. I set off on a three-day tour to fly, hike, and boat to the base of Salto Angel.*

In 1993, Steven Spielberg's block-buster movie *Jurassic Park* became the most successful film in Hollywood history. Millions of people went to see his computer-generated dinosaurs rampaging through "The Lost World," a prehistoric land that modern science had managed to repopulate with clones of its original inhabitants. Its success was primarily owed to the magical yet real-life imagery that fired peoples' imagination of what life on Earth used to be like.

It must have been a similar fascination that in the mid-1880s led Sir Arthur Conan Doyle to attend a lecture in London given by Everard Im Thurn, an eminent botanist. Thurn had just become the first explorer to climb a bizarre table-top mountain called Monte

This adventure involves a flight followed by a short hike to Salto Sapo (Toad Falls), a boat trip through rapids, and a slightly more taxing, hour-long trek up to the Salto Angel lookout point. It is not physically demanding, but requires a moderate level of fitness.

I took a budget-level tour, which included accommodation in attractive, riverside hammock camps. The boat trip to the falls can be quite exciting, but it can also be very wet! More upmarket tours are available at much higher costs.

The essential item is a plastic poncho, which you will need to wear in the boat if you are not to be soaked to the skin. For photographing Salto Angel from the lookout point you need a wide-angle lens, preferably 20mm although 28mm would be sufficient. A water-proof compact camera is ideal for the boat trips and waterfall walks.

Roraima, one of many such peaks in Venezuela's Gran Sabana region. Thurn's account of these isolated, mostly inaccessible peaks, called *tepuis*, sparked Doyle's idea that prehistoric creatures could well be trapped on top of them. In 1912 he published *The Lost World*, a tale of dinosaurs and pterodactyls thriving in isolation on these islands in the sky, which would eventually inspire Spielberg's movie.

When Simón Bolívar was battling for independence against the Caracas-based Spanish forces (see box, page 64), **Angostura**, now known as Ciudad Bolívar, was his major stronghold. These days it is a busy town that retains some grandiose colonial buildings—now, regrettably, in a poor state—from the days when it was a major river port and the centre for the production of Angostura aromatic bitters. At the Ciudad Bolívar airport office of Turi Express I booked a three-day, organized tour to Salto Angel, a trip that would enable me to explore for myself the primordial land where waterfalls seemingly tumble from the heavens, and dinosaurs…well, you never know.

A VIEW FROM THE AIR

Downtown, I joined two people going on the same tour, Jaska and Elena from the United States, for a late-night stroll along the bank of the **Río Orinoco**. Early the following morning we made the flight to Canaima—the village base for visitors to the falls—in a six-seater, twin-engine plane whose limited sitting space was further reduced by our luggage. The pilot nonchalantly jumped in, started the engine, and had us flying so soon afterwards that it felt like a run-of-the-mill taxi ride.

Flying above the city, we could take in the splendid views over the mighty Río Orinoco and the Puente Angostura, the only bridge along the whole river. Banking away to the south, we passed over rolling, bare savannah before seeing the edges of the **Embalse de Guri reservoir**, which was created in 1963 by the damming of the Río Caroní. This is the fourth-largest lake on the continent, and the massive dam's hydroelectric plant supplies an incredible 70 percent of the nation's electricity needs.

There was one thing that we were all waiting to see, though, and as we drew close to Canaima we spied it—the first table-topped mountain poking through the low cloud, its sides made up of the characteristic steep cliffs that make the majority of *tepuis* insurmountable. During the final approach to the airstrip,

ROCK OF ALL AGES

The whole region in the Canaima National Park is part of the ancient granite-rock formation known as the Guyana Shield, one of the largest blocks of granite in the world. It dates back at least to Precambrian times and may be as old as 2 billion years. The huge granite outcrops that form the *tepuis* have an exceptionally high level of plants and animals that are endemic to their summits but, alas, no dinosaurs (well, none that have been found yet). Auyán Tepui is over 2,500m (8,200 feet) high, and around 65 percent of its summit's plants are endemic.

we looked in awe at the golden-brown, tannin-stained waterfalls pounding the edge of Laguna de Canaima (Canaima Lagoon). We knew that Salto Angel is the country's most popular attraction, but it was still disconcerting to encounter hordes of tourists milling around the arrival centre. With a couple of hours to spare before our boat was due to leave for Salto Sapo (Toad Falls), we wandered down to the less-crowded lagoon area and took a walk up the beach. Children from the local Pemón Indian tribe played tag games in the shallow water while their mothers sat on the beach washing clothes in buckets. Past the village's own hydroelectric plant we found a small trail running up through thick bushes to the top of **Salto Ucaima**, the first of the seven waterfalls along the lagoon's edge that we had seen from the plane. Alone now, we watched the thundering, coffee-brown water plunge over the cliff edge, and we began to feel the touch of the wilderness we had hoped to find.

A BITTER LIFESAVER

Angostura, the city now known as Ciudad Bolívar, was the major production centre for Angostura aromatic bitters until around 1875 when the Federal Wars cut supply routes and production moved to Trinidad instead. The bitters are made by combining the aromatic bark of a local tree with other ingredients, although the exact recipe is a well-guarded secret. Originally produced as a cure for stomach problems, Angostura is now used principally as a flavouring and is, perhaps, best known for its use in the making of pink gin. An early recipe, which mixes the bark with honey, is said to have saved the famous German naturalist and explorer, Alexander von Humboldt, from dying in 1800 during his journey down the Río Orinoco.

BEHIND SALTO SAPO'S CASCADE

Canaima village shares its name with the surrounding national park, the Parque

ABOVE A tranquil moment before meeting the Mayaupa rapids on Río Carrao
LEFT At the top of Salto Sapito, and (INSET), our precarious progress en route to it

Nacional Canaima. Protecting almost 3 million hectares (7½ million acres) of the Gran Sabana region, the park is one of the biggest in the world. Although Salto Angel is the best known of its waterfalls, there are scores of others that would be equally lauded in any other country. We boarded a motorized long boat to visit one of them, **Salto Sapo**, over 100m (330 feet) wide and 20m (65 feet) high.

The falls are situated on the far side of the lagoon's boot-shaped island (called Isla de Anatoliy), and they are unique in the national park for the path, hewn from the rock, that tunnels its way behind the cascade from one side to the other. The path was cut by a Peruvian guide called Tomás Bernal, who lived as a hermit in a

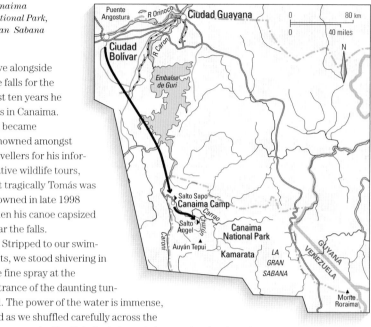

Canaima National Park, Gran Sabana

cave alongside the falls for the first ten years he was in Canaima. He became renowned amongst travellers for his informative wildlife tours, but tragically Tomás was drowned in late 1998 when his canoe capsized near the falls.

Stripped to our swimsuits, we stood shivering in the fine spray at the entrance of the daunting tunnel. The power of the water is immense, and as we shuffled carefully across the slippery rocks the disturbed air gusted around us like a gale-force wind. It was an incredible experience. Halfway along the path, the gushing water reaches maximum power and seems to suck all the air from the walkway, making it difficult to catch a breath. And when I dared to stretch my hand out into the flow I almost had it pulled from its socket. As we emerged from the other end and looked back across the falls, it seemed quite unbelievable that we had just been behind the cascade. The good news was that we would later have to return by this same route in order to continue our journey to Salto Angel.

Having seen the big one from behind, we climbed up a steep dirt-track to see **Salto Sapito** (Little Toad Falls) from above. The views from these falls are outstanding. In the distance, three smaller *tepuis*—Kurún, Kusaris and Kuravaina—rise from the plateau, their broad outlines huddled together as if finalizing an agreement to form one big *tepui*.

After briefly visiting the top of Salto Sapo and hiking back through its wildly exciting tunnel, we walked upriver for

about an hour to meet the outboard-powered, wooden longboat that would take us to our overnight hammock camp. The current of the Río Carrao is very strong, and the boat's engine fought a relentless battle to keep us moving forwards. Negotiating the many rapids calls for great skills from the driver, but at the Mayaupa rapids it was necessary to get out of the boat and walk for half an hour around them. It was slow going, but the increasingly dramatic scenery held our attention. The twisting river played tricks on my sense of direction, and I frequently found myself admiring "new" *tepuis* only to realize later that they were virtually all part of the same one, **Auyán Tepui**.

LAND OF THE SPIRITS

Auyán Tepui rises above the surrounding forest like an immense medieval fortress, its massive standing blocks on top resembling turrets. Auyán Tepui means hell mountain, and it is easy to understand how it acquired its name. The high, sheer cliffs, and the menacing outline of its summit, are often cloaked in dark clouds; and to the Pemón Indians it must have seemed a forbidding place. They believe that bad spirits, called *marawitón*, live on the summit alongside a higher deity called *Tramán-chitá*. If such supernatural beings do live up there, they are not pushed for space: Auyán Tepui's summit area is enormous, and covers 700sq km (252 square miles).

Picking a route up the shallow river became more difficult, but we were lucky to be on it at all: normally, the water is high enough only from June to November, but for our visit unusually heavy and prolonged winter rains meant that it was still navigable as New Year approached. Perhaps the most surprising, and slightly disappointing, aspect of our journey was the distinct lack of wildlife on the river. Our guides put forward the theory that the tannin-stained water is too acidic for many creatures, but I couldn't help feeling that the constant stream of motorized tourist boats may have more to do with it.

After three hours, with dusk beginning to fall, our driver pulled into the riverbank at the tiny Isla La Orquídea (Orchid Island). Unfortunately, the orchids have all gone, and these days the island is a camp with space for 60 hammocks under an open-sided shelter. While the guides erected the sleeping gear, we sat, chatted, and drank a few sodas, with surprisingly little interference from mosquitoes. A romantic candlelit dinner for 22 ensued, and the chat continued into the small hours. Lying in my hammock, I hoped that the weather would improve, for I could see the excitement factor would be significantly reduced if the guides had to explain what Salto Angel *would* look like if the clouds weren't there.

INTO THE RAPIDS

When the guides woke us at half past six the next morning, shafts of golden sunlight were creeping over the treetops. We set off on the next part of the river journey, which became tougher when we turned onto a small tributary, the **Río Churún**, and entered one of Auyán Tepui's canyons.

We had started out in two boats in order to spread the load and so keep them light for tackling the 14 rapids en route, but the going proved too difficult for one of them and it developed engine problems. Despite attempts to repair it on a tiny rocky bank mid-river, we were forced to abandon it and make do with the one remaining boat for the rest of the

THE PÉMON INDIANS

Southeast Venezuela is populated by around 25,000 Pémon Indians, three quarters of whom live within the Parque Nacional Canaima. They migrated to the region relatively recently (about 200 years ago), which is surprising given that many of the area's natural features bear Pémon-related names or are symbols of Pémon myth. "Canaima," for example, is the Pémon word for evil spirits, which the Pémon believe inhabit the *tepuis* and steal the souls of men. But then the people have a very intimate relationship with the landscape, and they attach spiritual significance to waterfalls and *tepuis*.

Traditionally, the Pémon practised subsistence agriculture, hunting and fishing, but more recently many have found work in the growing tourism business and the worryingly burgeoning mining industry. The whole national park area is rich in gold and diamond reserves, and the government has slowly been eroding laws that protect this World Heritage-listed site from exploitation. In 1998, the Pémon Indians became headline news around the world when they attempted to block government-backed efforts to construct a high-voltage power line and several substations right through the park.

Canaima village. On a particularly difficult rapid, the driver raised the engine a little too soon and we failed to make it through. The resulting ride backwards through the turbulent water was even more thrilling than going forwards.

SALTO ANGEL

Throughout the trip, the daunting walls of Auyán Tepui loomed over us and numerous stringy waterfalls cascaded from its summit. It was hard to imagine where so much water came from, and I wondered if dinosaurs ever cried. We were obliged to walk around a few short rapids, but we were aboard when Salto Angel came into

TOP The hammock camp at La Orquídea
LEFT Auyán Tepui rising above the clouds
FAR LEFT The spectacular Salto Angel, the world's highest waterfall, falling from the summit of Auyán Tepui
BELOW Pémon Indian guides

trip. However, the additional weight made the rapids even more fun. At each rapid, water splashed or poured over the sides drenching those who had forgotten to buy one of the cheap, plastic ponchos from

view. Here was the world's highest water-fall, tumbling 807m (2,648 feet) down a rusty-red rock face; and though we were still a good distance from the base it looked mightily impressive. Again we were in luck because, by December, the flow of water from the falls has usually reduced to a trickle.

Eventually, we reached base camp. The clear weather was holding and, although the sun had disappeared, the summit was still visible—something not every group gets to see. Not wanting to waste a moment, we immediately began the hour-long hike through beautiful rain forest to get to the lookout point. Much of the hike involved scrambling up rocks and exposed tree roots before the trail skirted a big boulder and emerged onto a treeless outcrop. High above—so high that it was more comfortable to lie back to look at it—the water begins its long, seemingly slow-motion journey from the top of Auyán Tepui. About halfway down, the flow breaks up into a fine spray that swirls, like light snow buffeted by a winter wind, until finally falling onto the black rocks below.

In 1935, Jimmy Angel, an American pilot, explorer and gold prospector, flew his plane up this very same canyon and saw for the first time this amazing cascade of water. His reports were dismissed as exaggerations, but when Angel found it again two years later he crash-landed his silver Flamingo plane, named Río Caroní, on top of the mountain. It took 11 days for him and the other passengers to make the dangerous descent from the summit to the village of Kamarata, and in recognition of his courageous effort the falls were named after him. More recently, quite a few people have climbed the rockface alongside the fall, and many others have made parachute jumps from the top. It seems that Salto Angel inspires already-crazy adventurers to get just a little crazier.

Our journey was coming to an end. Since the other boat had failed to make it to the base camp we boarded the remaining boat for the journey back to La Orquídia, rather than spend the night at Salto Angel and risk an unfavourable current the next morning. It seemed our driver had been touched by the legend of Jimmy Angel, too, for he raced back downriver, banking the boat around corners and skimming through the shallow rapids.

Back at the base camp, I relaxed. Lulled by the swinging of my hammock, my thoughts drifted to the primordial nature of Auyán Tepui. Starling scenes from *Jurassic Park* seeped into my imagination, and as I looked up at Auyán's faraway summit I was sure that I saw one of the giant blocks move! Canaima may be very commercialized for a "wilderness" area, but the tepuis will surely never be tamed, and it is their mystery and beauty that make this region a very real lost world.

JIMMY ANGEL

Jimmy Angel was born in Missouri in 1889, and was flying planes by the age of 14. Later, during the First World War, he illegally served in the Canadian Flying Corps and became renowned for his aerial stunts. In 1921, Jimmy met a gold prospector in a bar in Panama. The prospector knew of a mountain in South America whose rivers contained gold, and Angel offered to take him there. Without map or compass, they managed to find the mountain and landed the plane nearby. Having successfully paned for gold, Angel left, but for years after he flew around the area trying to relocate the river. In 1935, by chance, he found the waterfall that now bears his name and, two years later, crash-landed on the summit of Auyán Tepui. But he never again found his golden river. True to his life's adventures, Jimmy Angel died after he crashed a plane in Panama in 1956.

GOING IT ALONE

INTERNAL TRAVEL

It is possible to travel to Canaima independently, but the only feasible way to explore the region beyond the village and lagoon, and to go to Salto Angel, is to go with a group tour. Línea Turistica Aerotuy (LTA) runs daily flights to Canaima from Ciudad Bolívar and offers flight-only prices when they are not full with package travellers. There are many independent pilots and other companies, including Rutaca, who also offer spare seats.

WHEN TO GO

Boat tours to the base of Salto Angel normally operate only during the wet season (from May to November) as the rivers are too low throughout the other months. Unusual conditions can change this, so it is worth checking before booking a tour. However, the best time to see a cloud-free Salto Angel is during the dry season, which is from December to April. This is also a good time to take one of the many "waterfall" flights offered by airlines in Canaima.

PLANNING YOUR TRIP

Tours can be arranged at the agencies based at Ciudad Bolívar airport. One such, Turi Express, is a friendly booking agent that uses reputable tour companies based in Canaima, and their all-inclusive 3-day packages are reasonable value.

It is possible to fly down to Canaima independently, and then book a tour with companies such as Kamaracoto Tours and Bernal Tours (now run by Tom's wife). If you decide to do this, negotiate, as prices are flexible. Packages available from Caracas tend to be the much more expensive ones offered by Servivensa, the national airline, which include accommodation in their comfortable but overpriced 115-room Campamento Canaima lodge.

HEALTH AND SAFETY MATTERS

Malaria is present in the region, so precautions should be taken (consult your doctor for the latest information or see Practical. Matters on p.13). Dengue fever, caused by the *Aedes* mosquito, is also a possible problem so use strong repellents, wear long clothing during the evening, and use a good mosquito net on your bed at night.

WHAT TO TAKE

❑ Sun block.
❑ Sun hat.
❑ Sunglasses.
❑ Waterproof jacket or plastic poncho.
❑ Mosquito net.
❑ Hiking footwear.
❑ Torch.

OTHER THINGS TO DO

1. Hike to Cueva Kavac: fly from Canaima to the Pémon Indian village of Kavac in the Valle Kamarata, and take a half-day hike into a beautiful cave system with inner waterfalls. Most flights to Kavac involve a flight over Salto Angel. Day trips can be organized in Canaima.

2. Trek to Roraima: climb to the summit of Monte Roraima *tepui* on a 6- to 9-day trek that takes you through savannah and several forest ecosystems to the vast summit area, covered in bizarre, rock forma-tions. All organized tours include at least one night's camping on the summit.

3. La Gran Sabana by jeep: explore savannah lands, waterfalls, *tepuis*, and the Pémon Indian villages of the Gran Sabana on a 3- or 4-day jeep tour from Ciudad Bolívar—one of the most spectacular routes in the country. The best waterfalls are Salto Yuruan and Salto Aponguao.

TRAVELLERS' TIPS

❑ If you choose to go on a budget tour, take some extra snack foods along as the package includes only main meals with nothing in between. On arrival at Canaima, vegetarians should ensure that the tour company - representative knows of their dietary needs; don't rely on your booking agent to pass on the information.

❑ To stay dry on the boat, you will need a plastic poncho; but you will save money if you buy it before travelling to Canaima as they are more expensive there.

❑ On the hike to Salto Sapo, don't take any valuable items as everything gets drenched, even if it is in a plastic bag.

❑ To sleep well in a hammock, lie diagonally across it and place a rolled-up sweater under your neck, not your head.

VENEZUELA

Wheels of Andean Fortune

by Steve Watkins

Mountains that are ideal for off-road biking surround the Andean city of Mérida. The rides aren't always easy but the rewards are outstanding for those who persist. I joined a two-day tour through beautiful mountain scenery to discover the mountains and villages of the Cordillera de Mérida.

Mérida is a perfect base from which to explore the Andean Mountain region of Venezuela. Many visitors travel around in four-wheel-drive vehicles—the normal, two-wheel-drive ones just can't cope with the terrain found off the beaten track—but since I was unable to afford a four-wheel-drive I opted for pedals and two wheels instead. Contrary to popular belief, mountain bikes are not, merely by definition, capable of going anywhere; but with a rider who has a moderate degree of experience and a spirited nature, the bike can become a more useful and more rewarding form of transport than the big jeeps.

In response to my request for a challenging ride, Tom, the owner of Mérida-based operator Bum Bum Tours, suggested the two-day San José trip, but with a twist. Rather than drive to

 3 This trip needs a good level of fitness and previous, preferably off-road, bike-riding experience. Some of the climbs are tough, but you can always walk, if you find the going too difficult.

★★ A real mix of pain and pleasure, though the latter wins out in the end. The *posada* in Acequias is basic but comfortable, and the food is good.

⚒ Bring a pair of bike shorts and gloves if you have them. Stiff-soled shoes or boots are useful, too. You will need a small daypack or bum-bag in which to carry snacks on the bike. All other equipment—helmets, pumps, repair kits, and so on—is supplied.

ABOVE Our overnight resting place, Acequias village, whose single posada *(INSET RIGHT) offers welcome respite to the weary mountain-biker and magnificent views across the mountains*
RIGHT An easy downhill start on the track from Tierra Negra to Acequias could give no indication of what was to come

VENEZUELA

THE MAKING OF A MOUNTAIN RANGE

If you think it takes a lot of energy to cycle in the Andes, then imagine how much it took to create the mountains in the first place. The Andean chain—the longest mountain system above sea-level in the world—measures almost 8,000km (5,000 miles) in length, and extends along the western coast of the continent from northern Colombia to the southern-most tip of Chile, where it descends into the sea.

The Andes were formed during the Cretaceous Period, from 138 million to 65 million years ago—the period in which the Rocky Mountains emerged and dinosaurs dominated the land. They were created when the South American tec- tonic plate collided violently with the Pacific plate and began to sink below it along the fault line, a process known as subduction. These enormous, conflicting forces lifted sedimentary rock, causing the Earth's crust to rise into a fold. The mountains are volatile, and over the last 20 million years volcanoes and earth- quakes have caused parts of the chain to rise even further.

Many of the peaks—such as Pico Bolívar, in Venezuela—are over 5,000m (16,400 feet); and Aconcagua, in Argentina, is at 6,960m (22,834 feet) the highest mountain in the Andes and, indeed, the western hemisphere.

Acequias (the usual start point for the tour), Alberto, my guide, and I would get a lift to Tierra Negra, a popular paragliding launch point, and bike-ride to Acequias from there. The evil glint in Tom's eye should have been warning enough; but I rather foolishly agreed to the plan, thinking that my previously well-trained, but not recently used,

biking legs would spark back to life.

We loaded our bikes and equipment onto the jeep, and set off from Mérida. Mérida is perched on a narrow shelf high above the Río Chama, and our road out of the city followed the river's course south to the small town of Las Gonzales. The surfaced road from Las Gonzales to Tierra Negra, the usual route, had been closed by a landslide, so we were obliged to follow a spectacular, old dirt-road. To cross the river, we bumped and trundled over the wooden-planked surface of an overbearing metal-girder bridge. On the other side, Tom stopped the jeep to engage the four-wheel drive. This gave us a chance to gaze skywards at the sheer-faced mountains ahead of us. There was no doubting that four-wheel drive was going to be essential.

At times, on the drive up the precipitous track, the gradient became so steep that it was amazing that even four-wheel drive could keep the jeep moving. The route twisted and turned past weird rock formations before straightening out a little as a deep valley opened up to the left. This was our getting-out point, and I consoled myself with the thought that the route to Acequias could not possibly be any steeper than the one we had just come up.

OPPOSITE LOCK

Looking across the valley from Tierra Negra, we were able to make out a faint line angling up the mountainside. This was our track, and although it didn't look too steep from where we stood my lack of recent exercise inclined me to unload the bike and don my helmet and gloves as slowly as possible. When the moment of departure could not be delayed any further, I once again caught sight of the glint in Tom's eyes, before Alberto and I pedalled off in glorious sunshine.

There were no signs of civilization ahead, only mountains—big moun- tains—and I wondered if I had bitten off more than I could chew. After a very brief flat section, we began to descend rapidly down switchback turns. The loose sandy surface made the going fun. And it provided me with an ideal opportunity to get used to the idiosyncrasies of the bike's brakes, which were efficient but set up opposite to those on my own bike back home. This "back-to-front" arrangement is especially noticeable downhill, and it became very apparent when, on one corner, I instinctively pulled on the left lever and was surprised when the front wheel skidded through some gravel. By the end of the descent, I had just about re-trained my reactions.

In the biking world, what goes down must go up, and sure enough, after passing a farmhouse surrounded by brilliant green grass and crossing a small stream, we began the climb that I had seen from our start point. Distance is a great deceiver for the eyes, and the climb proved to be a lung-buster.

Apart from the initial sections it wasn't exceptionally steep, but it was persistent in its rise to the top. My heart pounded away in an attempt to deliver oxygen to my straining body parts, but it was like a one-man courier firm being asked to deliver a nation's telephone directories. I twisted my gear-changer but there was no response—there were no more gears. Standing up on the pedals to add my bodyweight to the cause of reaching the top of the hill seemed to help a little. As I struggled on, Alberto, who was much fitter than I was and accustomed to this terrain, resisted the temptation to laugh at my efforts and instead coaxed me onwards. His encouragement had the required effect. Gradually, my body returned to some kind of equilibrium, and I began to notice the beautiful mountains surrounding us.

The afternoon proved to be just as challenging as the morning, and it was with great relief that I finally caught a glimpse of **Acequias** village up ahead. Acequias is the modern version of an old village called San Antonio Mucuño, known locally as Pueblo Viejo. The original village, whose ruins are about two hours' walk away, was destroyed twice by earthquakes in the 17th and 19th centuries. Acequias is around 2,400m (7,870 feet) above sea-level, so I was able to put at least part of my day's struggles down to the effects of the altitude.

Free-wheeling down the paved road into the village centre, I felt that our efforts deserved a Tour de France-style crowd to welcome us; but the place was almost deserted. Our *posada* was the only one in Acequias and we were the only guests. Set around a rectangular courtyard, the *posada* had what were to my mind two essential features—a kitchen and beds. Exhausted, I fell asleep while Alberto helped the owner cook up a pasta feast.

NIGHT-TIME REPAIRS

As soon as the sun went down, the temperature plummeted, and I was glad to find that I had plenty of blankets for the bed. Sleep can work miracles and,

UP AND DOWN SKILLS

Mountain biking can be made more comfortable and more fun by using good technique when climbing or descending hills. On climbs, you save energy by sitting in your saddle rather than standing on the pedals. Choose a gear that is low enough for you to maintain a constant pace and rhythm rather than pedalling hard in short bursts. Going down, it is better to keep your weight back, and on off-road sections you should stand on the pedals and use your legs like shock absorbers. Don't brake too hard with the front brake, and always apply the back brake first. When riding on steep, rough ground, try not to steer too sharply.

VENEZUELA

despite the strains of the previous day, by morning I was feeling refreshed and ready for the "real" tour to San José.

The views from the posada across the mountains to the north, and down onto the whitewashed walls and red-tiled roofs of the village, were wonderful. A clear dawn sky promised us another sunny day as we set off on a reasonable

RIGHT The climb to San José
BELOW A group of mountain-bikers stops for a short break on the thrilling, downhill ride from Tierra Negra to Las Gonzales

VENEZUELA

climb from the village. Then the track flattened out and began to wind across *paramo*—an open plateau where few trees grow, though there were plenty of the spiky-leaved frailejón (*Espeletia pycnophylla*) plants. Their leaves have a felt-like texture that prevents them from succumbing to the cold at high altitude, and from September until

RIGHT The testing—but exhilarating— descent into the incredibly beautiful, and sparsely inhabited but lush valley of the Tostos river

early December they sprout flowers that turn whole mountainsides a stunning bright yellow.

With the absence of any shade from the sun, I appreciated the cool breeze that was blowing as we rode along narrow paths on the crest of a ridge. Looking back, we could see the snow- and ice-clad summit of **Pico Humboldt**, Venezuela's second highest peak at 4,994m (16,385 feet), in the distant Parque Nacional Sierra Nevada. On another small hill climb we met a young cowboy from Acequias on his way to San José. He makes the journey to San José a couple of times a week throughout the year—even when the trail is covered in snow—in order to buy provisions or find work.

Soon, we began the thrilling descent into the **Valle Tostos**, a lush river valley. The descent was a real test of the strength in my hands, for the going was so consistently steep that they began to ache from the sustained braking. I didn't want to stop, though, because the fun factor was so high. Any lingering memories of the previous day's struggles were instantly wiped out, and by the time I ground to a halt at the bottom my grin was banana-shaped.

The Valle Tostos is largely uninhabited, save for a few farming families living in simple homes, and it is incredibly beautiful. Wildflowers and tall trees line the banks of the river, while the rough track runs gently downhill for miles. Several times we had to cross the river, and both Alberto and I took great delight in seeing how high we could make the water splash while riding through.

A TAME BEAST

It was a pity when the fun was brought to a halt by another uphill climb, the final one before San José. It wasn't as long as some previous ones but the going was tough enough for us to need a couple of rest stops on the way. We felt a real sense of achievement on reaching

the top, because although the end was still a few hours away the most difficult sections were now behind us.

Following a single-track path towards **San José**, we dropped off a grassy ledge down to the village. It was siesta time, so in the recently refurbished plaza every shop, except, thankfully, the most important one, was closed. In the dark, old grocery store, we guzzled down a few bottles of lemonade while the village restaurant owner berated Alberto for not bringing him all his biking clients. To make amends—and since there was room in our bellies for a meal—we called in to his restaurant for a delicious fresh trout dinner.

The road from San José was surfaced and, although it was initially a long, gentle climb, the bitumen made the going enjoyable. The reward for the effort was sensational. The last hour or so back to Tierra Negra was completely downhill, with terrific views of the surrounding mountains and valleys. Tight, hairpin corners added a little extra spice, too, though it was important to keep an eye out for oncoming traffic. This was the sort of freewheeling fun that originally got me hooked on biking and, for the first time in the ride, I was actually ahead of Alberto.

In this last section of the journey we made up so much time that we arrived at the pick-up point over an hour early. Figuring that with the main road out of use, Tom would have to come up the wild, old, dirt-track and would therefore be a while longer, we decided to con- tinue for another hour of off-road thrills down to Las Gonzales. The sandy sur- face made it very tricky in places, particularly on the very steep, inside bends, but we both made it safely.

Celebrating the superb ride with high fives and more lemonade (one great downhill can wipe out the memories of any number of tough uphills!), we agreed that two wheels are certainly better than four for really getting to grips with the Andes.

GOING IT ALONE

WHEN TO GO

Mountain biking in the Andes is possible all year round. The summer months from December to April can be very hot so perhaps the winter months are preferable, though you are more likely to encounter rain or even snow at high altitudes.

PLANNING YOUR TRIP

For independent rides, good-quality mountain bikes can be hired at reasonable daily rates from several of the Mérida tour agencies, including Bum Bum Tours, NaToura, and Guamanchi Expeditions. They provide maps for use on the rides, and can also supply bike pannier bags for carrying equipment.

All these companies offer all-inclusive, guided bike tours ranging from 1 day to 5 days and to suit all levels of experience and ability.

HEALTH AND SAFETY MATTERS

Mountain biking requires a reasonable level of fitness. People with a poor heart or respiratory conditions should consult their doctor for advice.

Always wear your helmet on downhill sections, as the head is usually the first thing to hit the floor in a fall.

Drink plenty of water as water loss is high and dehydration can come on quickly while biking.

Regularly eat carbohydrates, sugars, and salts, to keep energy levels up. This is an important factor in avoiding "The Bonk", a cycling term to describe a condition in which blood sugar levels drop so low that you suddenly can't cycle any more.

WHAT TO TAKE

❏ Bike shorts or shorts with flat seams.

❏ Sunglasses.

❏ Baseball cap worn back to front, or bandanna, to keep sun off your neck.

❏ Bike gloves.

❏ High-factor sunblock.

❏ Warm clothes for cold evenings in mountains.

❏ Torch.

TRAVELLERS' TIPS

❏ For off-road trips take your own riding gloves as they are not available to hire and they make all the difference to your personal comfort.

❏ If you have stiff-soled shoes or boots, bring them as they are ideal for biking.

❏ Use plenty of high-factor sunblock on all exposed skin as the light-coloured sand and dirt reflects the sun's rays, and their effects are particularly intense at high altitude. Wear a baseball cap backwards or use a bandanna to keep the sun off your neck. Drink plenty of water on the way. Check with your guide to see if river water is safe to drink.

❏ Don't give up—every hill has a top!

THREE DIY ANDES RIDES

There are several bike routes around Mérida that can be ridden without guides, and some that do not require the attendance of a support vehicle.

1. **Pico El Aguila:** 75km (46 miles): 80 percent downhill.
   You and the bikes are driven to the highest road pass in Venezuela at Pico El Aguila, 4,100m (13,452 feet). A short climb up to Pinango at 4,300m (14,108 feet), then off-road down to San Rafael de Mucuchíes, is followed by the return via Tabay and two big climbs to Mérida.

2. **Jaji:** 35km (22 miles): mixed terrain, all on-road.
   Drive to Jaji then bike to La Azulita. Along the way are waterfalls, natural swimming pools, and cloud forest. There are some climbs but not big ones.

3. **El Valle Grande:** 45km (28 miles): big climb, big downhill.
   From Mérida, you climb 1,300m (4,265 feet) to La Culata, 2,950m (9,678 feet). After a little off-roading, there is a fast descent back to Mérida. Most of the time you are surrounded by beautiful scenery.

Born to be Wild

by Steve Watkins

Dubbed the Wild West of Venezuela, the vast Los Llanos region is more than just a cowboy sanctuary. Its extensive river network feeds the ever-hungry Río Orinoco and hosts a bewildering array of wildlife. I joined a tour that utilized horses, boats, and tyre tubes, to get closer to nature.

Los Llanos del Orinoco is an incredible flatland region of rivers, swamplands, and savannah, that makes up over one-third of the whole area of Venezuela. It is home to the country's major cattle ranches, known as *hatos*, and a hardy bunch of legendary cowboys, known as *llaneros*; but it is the outstanding diversity of easily spotted wildlife that is attracting increasing numbers of adventure travellers. Strangely, the best place to organize a tour to Los Llanos is from the Andean highland city of Mérida. I chose to go on a five-day, budget-level trip to the Río Apure region, which included tubing (a sort of one-man whitewater rafting), piranha fishing, and an overnight stay in hammocks in the jungle.

Although Mérida does seem like an odd place from which to set off on a trip to the lowlands, there is one distinct advantage: the journey down through the mountains to Barinas is simply spectacular. Our group of nine consisted of five Germans—Kristian, Urma, Hans, Roland and Elizabeth—Roland's French girlfriend, Natalie, and two Dutch guys, Martin and Ravia. Our cheerful guide, Camillo, was Peruvian but had lived in Mérida most of his life. In the cold, dawn air, we loaded ourselves on to the bus for

 This is a very easygoing tour; only the tubing and horse riding require a moderate level of fitness.

★★ I took a budget-level tour with accommodation in hammock camps. More upmarket tours, using ranch hotels, are available.

All specialist equipment is provided for the activities.

TOP RIGHT The leisurely horseback ride from Finca Cielo
RIGHT Tubing in the cool, turbulent waters of the Río Canagua
INSET Venezuela's most photographed church, the stone chapel at San Rafael de Mucuchíes

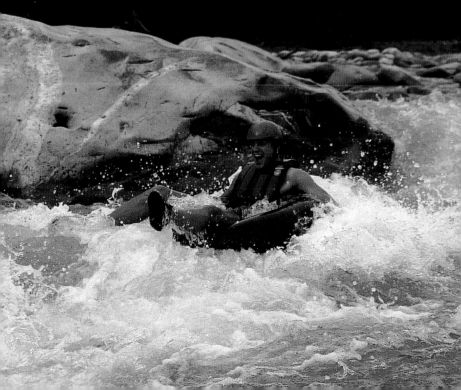

the drive eastwards up through **San Rafael de Mucuchíes**, where we briefly stopped to visit Venezuela's most photographed church. This quirky, quaint stone chapel appears to date from earliest Spanish times, but remarkably it was built in 1984 by local architect Juan Felix Sanchez, then 83 years old.

We were now up in the stark *paramo* region and, after a lake-side stop at the pleasant **Laguna Mucubají**, situated at the northern entrance to the Sierra Nevada National Park, we began the hair-raising switchback descent to the lowlands. It was not a ride for the faint-hearted. For the driver, there was no respite from the sharp, left- and right-hand corners where the penalty for a mistake is a brief flight into a deep, deep valley. For us, the passengers, there was neither respite nor any opportunity to influence our fate. It took four hours to reach Barinas and yet not one of us fell asleep.

A COMMON THREAD

Los Llanos covers around 300,000sq km (116,000 square miles), and yet it contains only ten percent of the country's population. Cattle outnumber people. The whole region is drained by a tangle of rivers that resembles the root system of an ancient tree and have just one destination, the mighty **Río Orinoco**. This remarkable river, which draws water from 70 percent of Venezuela's land area, somehow contrives to keep every single bit of its 2,140-km (1,335-mile) length

within the national boundaries. One of the major feeder rivers is the **Río Apure**, which flows from the Andean foothills south of Barinas via San Fernando de Apure to the Orinoco. The Apure was to be the common thread in our journey around the region.

From Barinas we headed southwest for a further 40 minutes to a small gas station. There, waiting for us, was Grandmother—a battered but charismatic, blue cattle truck. To get to Finca Cielo, the small farm that would serve as a base for the tyre-tubing, and accommodate us for our first night's stay, we had to negotiate a dirt-track too rough for our full bus, so, we all jumped aboard Grandmother. Standing on the back tray, we ducked under the low branches of a small patch of rain forest and soaked up views of the **Río Canagua**, the tributary of the Apure that we would later raft down in tractor-tyre tubes. Finca Cielo is a tiny, family-run farmstead where the undoubted star of the show is a white-faced capuchin monkey (*Cebus capucinus*). Abandoned as a baby, the monkey has adopted the pigs as his surrogate family and is invariably found riding on their backs or leaping from one to the other.

We were to ride rather larger animals, the farm's horses, out through the surrounding ranch lands to the put-in point for the tubing. It was a gentle hour-long ride over rolling hills. Shortly after we arrived at the river, Grandmother faithfully trundled along with our life

COWBOY FIGHTERS, COWBOY SINGERS

The *llaneros* played a central and intriguing role in Venezuela's battles for independence from the Spanish. They fought on both sides! Renowned for their tough spirit, superb horsemanship, and willingness to fight without financial reward, the *llaneros* initially allied themselves to the Spanish royalty. Only towards the end of the wars did they switch to support Simón Bolívar and to play a crucial part in his final victory at the Battle of Carabobo in 1821. These days they are better known for their singing. Accompanied by a mini, four-string guitar, called a *cuatroí* or *guitarraí*, they launch into haunting ballads that tell of the hard-drinking, hard-loving, hard-working life that still characterizes the *llaneros* existence.

jackets, helmets, and tubes. Camillo sat in his tube and took us through the very basic paddling techniques needed for steering downriver, warning us to lift our backsides by lying flat across the tube when going over rocky sections.

TURTLE TRICKS

Under the gaze of a few fascinated local children we carefully lowered ourselves into the water, and the current slowly but inevitably drew us towards the first rapid. By flapping my hands in the water, I manoeuvred the tube easily—too easily in fact, for within seconds I had spun round and entered the rapid backwards with my arms and legs flailing like an upturned turtle desperately trying to right itself. The cool, turbulent water engulfed me, but before panic had any time to set in I had popped out the other end of the rapid and floated towards the rest of the group to compare our equally comical rapid techniques.

The rest of the afternoon was an enjoyable mixture of spinning through rapids and tranquil floating in calm sections where it was possible just to lie back and enjoy the therapeutic sounds of the water and the passing rain forest. Back at Finca Cielo, a fine meal of chicken and pasta was served up and we supped on our self-supplied beers to guarantee that the novel experience of having hammocks for beds wouldn't rob us of sleep.

Early the next morning, we left the farm for the rather monotonous three-hour journey across the flatlands towards **San Vicente**, a tiny village on the banks of the Río Apure. The final section of road was a rough track raised on a causeway to prevent it from flooding during the wet season. Here, we started to see some of the exotic wildlife that the region is famed for. Caiman (*Caiman crocodiilus*), white ibis (*Eudocimus albus*), and even a lone scarlet ibis (*Eudocimus ruber*), were easily seen through the bus windows, and the sights whetted our appetites for what we hoped

PLIGHT OF THE JAGUAR

South America's largest cat, the jaguar (*Panthera onca*), is now a very rare sight indeed—so rare that your best chance of seeing one is to look in the travel brochures, where they frequently and iron- ically appear as the symbol of the wildness of Latin American rain forest. Human destruction of its habitat, and continued hunting—which involves using specially trained dogs to chase the jaguar until it is too exhausted to resist the hunter—have pushed this powerful animal towards the head of the endangered species list. There is only a handful of them left in Los Llanos, so it was especially disturbing to see the skin of a recently killed one stretched on a tree to dry at a house on the Río Paguey. Every part of the jaguar is sold, though no part is put to any worthwhile use, and the hunter can earn around $3,000 for each kill.

would be much closer encounters on the rivers. In San Vicente, an outboard- powered, wooden longboat awaited our arrival to whisk us off for a sunset ride up the wide, coffee-brown waters of the Apure.

The cooling breeze on the boat was a welcome relief from the oppressive lowland heat, but it didn't take long for the wildlife action to hot up. Camillo identified the frequent thuds on the boat's bottom as the sounds of piranha trying to leap out of the water. "They have been known to leap into the boat at times," he said with a big grin, before adding, "Just don't panic and definitely don't try to pick it up." As if we needed further convincing, he displayed the half-moon scar on his little finger where he had once tried to do exactly that. Moments later, with timing to rival the most professional of stage stars, a piranha flew gracefully through the air and landed at the sandal-clad feet of a panic-stricken Ravia. For a while it was mayhem as the piranha flapped

LEFT Getting a good night's sleep in a hammock takes a little practice
BELOW INSET Ravia gets close to a baby caiman. By the time it reaches adulthood, it will have grown to an incredible 1.5–2m (5–6½ feet) in length
BELOW The trip through the swamp to the jungle camp

around in a desperate bid to find water again and Ravia mistook the flapping for premeditated attempts to chew his toes off. The rest of us roared with belly-aching laughter. It seemed to take forever for the fish to lose its energy sufficiently for Camillo once again to risk his digits to throw it back into the river. Only then did he reveal that this particular specimen wasn't a piranha at all but a similar-looking, harmless fish!

A SQUEAKY YOUNG BITER

Further upriver, we observed the unusual feeding technique of the black skimmer bird (*Rynchops nigra*). The red beak of this large, black and white bird is most peculiar in that the lower half is longer than the upper. The purpose of this construction became clear as we watched the bird glide along, just above the water surface, with only the bottom half of its beak submerged to scoop up plankton and small fish. The real highlight of the afternoon, though, was when Camillo spotted a caiman nest on the bank. As we edged towards the back of the boat, Camillo stepped out of the front and picked up one of the six babies scampering along the muddy shore. It was incredible to see it so close up. It was less than a month old, its sharp teeth just forming, and it emitted tiny squeaking barks to inform the other siblings of its whereabouts. Just a couple of minutes later it was back with them as we hurriedly left the scene just in case mum decided to return early.

After another peaceful night in the hammocks, an early start was needed for the three-hour boat trip to the **Hato El Jaguar** ranch. Our route took us briefly back up the Río Apure and then onto one of its smaller tributaries, the Río Paguey. With both banks now so close to the boat, it turned out to be a wildlife extravaganza. The most peculiar bird was the ungainly hoatzin (*Opisthocomus hoatzin*). Easily identified by its elaborate head comb and screeching cry, the hoatzin live in groups of a dozen or so in low trees near the water's edge. The [...] have very strong feet, which is just as [...] because they often appear to be on the [...] verge of falling off their perches. They [...] no more graceful in flight, and they take [...] off like overloaded bomber planes. Along the entire route, iguanas of all colours and sizes—including giant, bright-green common iguanas (*Iguana iguana*)— lazed on small beaches, and one even swam right past the boat.

We had set out on the trip hoping to see one or two caiman. After the twentieth, people stopped screaming and pointing so much. It was incredible. They rarely stayed still on hearing the boat approach, but occasionally we would get close to one hiding behind the mangrove bushes. These armour-plated remnants of the dinosaur era can grow up to 1.8m (6 feet) in length and are renowned for their aggressive nature, particularly when protecting their nests. We knew they were scared of the engine noise and were therefore unlikely to approach, but each time one slipped into the murky water we couldn't help looking nervously around the boat in case it leapt up in a *Jaws*-like manner to eat us.

ANIMAL REFUGE

On reaching the track to the *hato*, we swapped the boat for another old truck for the 40-minute ride to the main house. The 25,000-ha (62,000-acre) ranch is run by Ramon Moser, a wise and charming elderly man from Caracas, who has fallen under the Los Llanos spell. It is a working ranch, but Ramon has effectively turned it into an unofficial wildlife refuge by completely banning hunting on the land.

After eating a delicious lunch in the strictly functional main building, we set up camp in the special, open-air hammock house that offered wonderful views of the savannah. While we lounged around in our hammocks for an hour or so, the ranch hands saddled up the horses for our evening ride around the property. It is hard to judge the nature of a horse solely by looking at it, but I really liked

A GIANT'S TALE

Amongst the swamps and rivers of Los Llanos there lives the world's largest rodent species, the giant guinea pig-like capybara (*Hydrochaeris hydrochaeris*). They are excellent swimmers, partly owing to their webbed back feet, and can dive quite deep in search of aquatic plants (their principal food source). When resting, they often remain half-submerged in the water. They are widely hunted for their meat by the llaneros and, as a result, were once on the verge of extinction. They are also a favourite snack food for caiman.

the alert eyes on mine and it proved to be an excellent choice. South American horses are trained to respond to the rider's bodyweight and just one hand on the reins. A mere flick of the wrist is all that was needed to direct the horses, and they responded well to our inexpert instructions to go faster or slower.

The trail followed a narrow causeway amongst thick undergrowth. Within a few minutes a distracting flash of red through the tall, green grasses caused us to stop. A lone, but nonetheless spectacular, scarlet ibis was feeding in the marshes by prodding its long, curved beak into the water. Its shocking red body and wings transfixed us. It was so red that I wondered if an artist had one night splashed a coat of paint on some of the white variety that we had seen earlier on the river. A little further along the trail, a huge flock of both the scarlet and white ibis exploded from the swamp, soaring upwards like scores of helium balloons being released at a festival. Soon after, Camillo's eyes lit up and he pointed frantically to our right. On the far side of a small pool, four or five female white-tailed deer (*Odocoileus virginianus*) were bouncing off towards the larger bushes in an attempt to hide from us. Their reddish-brown bodies contrasted sharply with the bright-white underside of their tails, which act as a danger warning to the rest of the herd.

WINGED HORSES

At one stage we had to coax the horses down a slope and across a deep, muddy pool, but whatever terrain we encountered the flow of exotic wildlife never ceased. Caiman basked on mudflats or spied on us from the water; scarlet macaws (*Ara macao*) flew overhead emitting their raucous screeches; and huge rufescent tiger herons (*Tigrisoma lineatum*) unflinchingly stood their ground, like camouflaged statue-artists. For once, a wildlife-spotting tour was turning out to be true to its name. We were impressed, even though the normally prevalent anaconda snake (*Eunectes marinus*) had eluded us. As the liquid-gold sun turned rosy red and sank to the horizon, it was time to head back to the ranch. Horses know when it's home time, and mine—with my explicit approval—showed its true colours by galloping all the way. Back at the hammock house, we were joined by some of the *hato*'s *llaneros* who, along with the multi-talented Camillo, entertained us with traditional singing and instrument playing around a campfire.

In the morning, the *llaneros* were back at work herding water buffalo (*Bubalus bubalis*) through a dip. There are around 2,500 water buffalo at the *hato*, and they have proved to be a lucrative business as two-year-olds will fetch in the region of 2,000 US dollars at market. Usually found in the swampy areas of Southeast Asia, these black, horned creatures, which can weigh up to one ton, have made a successful transition to the Los Llanos environment. Ramon has even had some trained so that visitors can ride them into the swamps—a novel experience that is unlikely to be found anywhere else on the continent.

After another, shorter horse trek to the other side of the property, we had a couple of hours to relax in the hammocks and play with the cheeky resident monkey, another White-faced Cappuchin. It took great delight in leaping onto Martin's head, grabbing at his tongue, and occasionally giving him a damn good beating.

FRENZIED SNAPPERS

For our final night's dinner, Ramon sent us out into the wilderness to catch our own. Catching chickens would have been easy enough, but our menu featured piranhas. Surely, it was going to turn into a battle to see who could eat whom first.

Rightly or wrongly, piranhas rank alongside crocodiles and hippopotamus in my own book of creatures that should carry human-health warnings. However, there are several varieties, and they are not all man-eating demons. I recalled a television programme that featured one that is renowned for its blood-thirsty nature, the red-bellied piranha (*Serrasalmus nattereri*). I asked Camillo what type we were trying to catch. "Red-bellied," he replied with a smile. These silver killers, with blood-red stain on their otherwise white bellies, grow up to 30cm (12 inches) in length. Their powerful jaws are filled with sharp teeth that are shaped like those on a saw and used to tear chunks of flesh from their victims. Red-bellied piranha live in large shoals, and when they are particularly hungry their combined efforts have been known to reduce whole cows to a set of bones in around 15 minutes. When the summer sun dries up pools, and competition for food intensifies, their attacks become more frenzied. They will even eat each other.

We set off in the afternoon, riding on another open-backed truck across the savannah to the fishing bridge, where simple lines were baited with sizeable chunks of fresh fish. Casting into the slow-moving flow, I half wanted to catch one and half not. The bridge had no safety railings so we all stood back a little just in case. Martin was the first one to strike lucky, and we all gathered around to watch him land the ugly brute. Its big, forward-placed eyes, hump-shaped back, and jutting bottom jaw, really did match up to its horror-movie image. When it had definitely ceased to function, one of our guides picked it up and opened its jaws to display the razor-sharp teeth. Seven piranhas later, none caught on my line, we had enough to dine on. We would not be eating yet, though.

Our final night was to be spent out in the wilds on a tiny, forest-cloaked island. We boarded a flat-bottomed boat for a brief trip through the swamp. In the late afternoon sunshine, we were fortunate enough to see a family of capybara (*Hydrochaeris hydrochaeris*), the world's largest rodent, which looks like a guinea pig that has overdosed on supplemental growth hormones. By the time we reached the island's lake it was

dark. We swapped the flat-bottomed boat for a distinctly unstable canoe that made the journey across the water a mini-adventure in itself. It was all the more exciting when our flashlights picked up the red, beady eyes of a caiman.

Over an open fire we fried the piranhas and served them up with fresh salad. The thick meat was tasty indeed. Sitting around the fire, we listened to Ramon talk passionately about the eight or so remaining jaguars (*Panthera onca*) on the property, and his dream of turning the hato into an official wildlife reserve. As we slid under the mosquito nets and into our hammocks, and watched a shadowy troop of monkeys eat and play in the trees directly above us, we could only agree with him. Many regions of the world demand recognition as important wildlife centres, but Los Llanos—one that few people will have heard of—served up more than enough proof that it deserves to be right at the top of any such wildlife league. We had thoroughly enjoyed our adventure, and anything that helps to protect the region will be greatly appreciated by generations to come.

LEFT The guinea pig-like capybara
BELOW An adult caiman lurks silently in the water hyacinth

GOING IT ALONE

WHEN TO GO

There are only two seasons in Los Llanos, and they are very, very different. In the wet season, from May to November, torrential rains turn the whole area into a giant lake, and life is easy for the wildlife. However, the best time to see the wildlife is during the completely opposite, dry season from December to April. Hardly a drop of rain falls, and the blistering sun dries up the water to leave cracked and baked mudflats. With water so scarce, the wildlife gathers around the few remaining water sources in astonishing numbers in an attempt—not always successful—to survive until the next rainstorm. The cusp weeks from late November to late December are the best choice between the two extremes. During the wet season, the tubing activity is replaced by Class III/IV whitewater rafting on the same river.

WHAT TO TAKE

❑ Strong insect repellent.
❑ Sun hat.
❑ High-factor sunblock for the boat trips.
❑ Long trousers and long-sleeved shirts for the evening.
❑ Torch.
❑ Beer and rum (there is none available at the *hato*).
❑ Zoom camera lens for shots of wildlife.

PLANNING YOUR TRIP

Mérida is the place to book budget-level, organized tours. Most of the operators there run various trips down into Los Llanos, though Bum Bum Tours are the only company running tours of Hato El Jaguar featured in this book. Four- and 5-day tours are available. More upmarket tours are available in Mérida, from Arrasari Trek (part of Bum Bum Tours), and in Caracas and San Fernando de Apure. Several well-established *hatos* in the region offer tourist facilities, including Hato Piñero and Hato Doña Barbara. Bookings can be made directly with them. Tour package prices normally include all food, accommodation, excursions, and guides.

Whilst it is possible to travel around the region independently with your own vehicle, it is not very practical. The real heart of life in Los Llanos is on the ranches, and it is virtually impossible to travel to these alone. There is a very limited road network, which links only the major towns, and there are no regular boat services on the rivers. It is in any case preferable to have a guide to locate and explain about the abundant wildlife.

HEALTH AND SAFETY MATTERS

You will need to take anti-malarial tablets (consult your doctor for the latest recommendations). These should be used in conjunction with insect repellent, long clothing during the evening, and a mosquito net at night. Suitable protection against the strong sun is necessary, and should include high-factor sunblock on all exposed skin, and a sun hat.

BELOW Frying the catch

TRAVELLERS' TIPS

❑ For the best views on the road from Mérida to Barinas, sit on the left-hand side of the bus.
❑ While on horse-riding or walking tours around the ranches, be as quiet as possible. Try to be at the front of the group as much as possible as much of the wildlife is easily scared off and will probably be gone by the time the last members arrive. When asked by the *hato*'s ride organizer about your riding ability, don't over-rate it as they have horses that can really fly. The ones we rode were all exceptionally well trained.
❑ Check that the tour operator you use has good-quality mosquito nets that are designed to fit over hammocks. The excellent new ones provided by Bum Bum Tours made sleeping out in the jungle a real pleasure.
❑ Adequate vegetarian food options are available but, as you can imagine in the middle of cattle country, they are not that inspired.
❑ Finally, don't get any ideas about playing with the piranhas, in or out of the water. They really do have a nasty bite, even when they have been hooked and appear to be dead.

Paradise Rocks from Above and Below

by Steve Watkins

Off Venezuela's north coast lies the enchanting Archipiélago Los Roques. With over 40 islands offering white sandy beaches, clear blue water, and pristine coral reefs, it is a superb diving destination and a fun place to fly. I shunned the numerous package tours available and organized my own five-day trip to the main island, Gran Roque, to do a spot of diving, walking, and microlighting. And a little sunbathing, too.

On the exquisite Caribbean archipelago of Los Roques, everyone appears to find at least a little bit of paradise, whether it is high above the blue-green waters, at their surface, or far below them.

The archipelago lies some 166km (103 miles) due north of Caracas, and it consists of 42 islands (or *cayos*) that are permanent enough to have names, and over 300 that appear only at low tide. Designated as a national park in 1972, the 225,153-ha (556,353-acre) archipelago was the first—and remains one of the largest—marine reserves in the Caribbean. Of all the islands, only Gran Roque has a significant population (around 1,000) and a surfaced airport runway; almost all the other islands are uninhabited and accessible only by boat. This isolation, the relative expense of visiting it, and the enforcement of national park restrictions on activities, has helped the islands to remain relatively unspoiled.

It was just after New Year, and Caracas airport was packed with holiday-makers. After a little searching I found a small airline, called Vipro, which had space on its afternoon flight to Gran Roque. In the 11-seater, twin-engine plane, ten seats were next to the windows and I got the other one. While I admired the rivets of the fuselage, everyone else used up their holiday ration of superlatives in describing the view as we flew over the islands. On the runway, baggage handlers showed none of their usual determination to carry every personal item for an inflated tip; in fact only two bothered to approach us at all. If the baggage handlers were so laid back, the rest of the island's population was probably functioning on "the day after mañana" time. In a fruitless search for accommodation I strolled past the full *posadas* and brightly coloured houses along the sandy main street. Eventually I found a room at the Posada Terramar, a very pleasant place a couple of streets back.

Although the diving in Los Roques

3 Scuba diving is not a strenuous activity though a reasonable level of fitness is required to cope with the added stresses put on the body under water. Walking on the island is very easy going and microlighting is pure pleasure.

★ Los Roques is an ideal destination for travellers looking to mix adventure with a little bit of self-pampering. Gran Roque has accommodation to suit most budgets, from luxury hotels to free camping for those with tents. Inclusive packages at the recommended *posadas* are generally reported to be good value.

✂ All specialist scuba-diving equipment is available on the island, though it does cost extra to hire it. If you have your own snorkelling gear, i.e., mask, snorkel, and fins, it is worth bringing them, though they too are available for hire.

LIFE AND DEATH OF CORAL

Coral reefs are fragile colonies of living organisms that can live for hundreds of years. They are made up of tiny animals, red algae, and molluscs, and are found only in tropical waters where the temperature remains above 20°C (68°F). Tougher corals, such as brain coral, can survive in turbulent waters, but fans and disc-like corals need calm waters in order to thrive. They all rely on sunlight to grow, so they are found in the upper reaches of the oceans. Threats to their existence are on the increase: ocean pollution, increases in ultraviolet light penetrating the Earth's ozone layer, and commercial activities (including uncontrolled diving and fishing), all damage the coral, often permanently.

VENEZUELA

has gained a reputation for being some of the best in the Caribbean, there is only one dive company, Sesto Continente, operating there. With so many visitors on the island—mainly Italians, whose compatriots first discovered the islands' attractions in the 1960s—and only two dive boats, places on diving expeditions are precious. There was no available space for the next day's diving, and so I turned my attention skywards for entertainment. Hernando Arnal, laid-back owner of the popular Rasquatekey Bar on the main plaza, is a microlight pilot and offers 15- and 30-minute flights over the nearby islands and reefs. Since I had been robbed of my view coming over, I had no hesitation in booking a spot for the following morning. As dusk fell, I wandered down to the beach. From the crooked, wooden pier, local children leapt into the water purely for pleasure, and tens of brown pelicans (*Pelecanus occidentalis*) took off on dramatic missions to dive-bomb fish.

A BIRD'S-EYE VIEW

Microlight construction, maintenance, and pilot training, have advanced significantly since the 1970s when the microlighting pioneers risked life and limb in their delta-winged flying contraptions. And seeing Hernando skilfully swoop in for a smooth landing with another client convinced me that I was in safe hands. The briefing session covered how to get in and out of the tight, rear cockpit seat, and how to locate

the underseat of the never-before-used life jackets. Strapped in, and with my helmet on, I watched as Hernando pulled on the throttle to make the engine buzz rise to a sound like a disturbed hornets' nest, and we taxied out onto the runway.

TRAVELLERS' TIPS

- ❑ Credit cards are accepted at very few places. Sesto Continente, Hernando's microlighting, and a handful of upmarket posadas, will accept them, though even they are reluctant and impose 10 to 15 percent surcharges. It is far better to come with plenty of Bolivares or U.S. dollars, though U.S.-dollar travellers' cheques are widely accepted. There are no banking facilities on the island.
- ❑ Mornings are normally clearer than the evenings for microlight flying.
- ❑ You can save money by getting an accommodation-only deal at a posada and then eating out, but since there are only a few restaurants, the choice is limited. Food at the posadas is generally very good, and they prepare lunch coolboxes for divers. Supplies at the supermarket are very sparse, so campers are advised to bring food over to the island with them. There is a simple bakery on the inland road to Sesto Continente.

Within moments of accelerating, the microlight was airborne, and Hernando banked right and headed south over **Madrizqui**. The view was breathtaking. Down on the island way below us, a row of bright-yellow beach umbrellas looked like pins on a satellite map of the world, while a brilliant-white yacht contrasted sharply against the jade-green waters. Just south of Madrizqui we flew over **Isla Pirata** (Pirate Island), whose name reflects the archipelago's past popularity with the rogues of maritime history who exploited its calm, safe waters and its ideal location for distributing contraband heading for South America. The middle of the island is filled by a tannin-brown lagoon. From Pirata, Hernando turned eastwards towards Cayo Muerto (Death Cay) and Saquisaqui, and continued out over scores of submerged sandbanks to the **Gran Barrera Arrecifal del Este** (Great Eastern Barrier Reef). There, the white battalions of charging Caribbean waves floundered against the defensive coral walls of the archipelago.

Occasionally, Hernando put us through spiralling turns when the trance induced by the scenic overload was broken and the reality of our situation struck home: we were 120m (400 feet) up in the air with just a nylon wing, fibreglass cockpit, and a two-stroke engine to keep us there. The homeward leg took us over the isolated, runner-bean-shaped Nordisqui, formerly Northeast Cay, to Francés Cay, the most popular island for sunbathing and snorkelling day trips. For his grand finale, Hernando swooped down low over Gran Roque's old, Dutch lighthouse, buzzed over the village rooftops, and then executed his trademark, tight-banked turn to take us back to the airstrip and a safe landing.

A GLIMPSE OF THE PAST

In order to wind down, I spent the early afternoon exploring the small hills, mangroves, and more isolated beaches. At only 3km (2 miles) long, and 1km (½ mile) wide, the entire island can easily be walked in a couple of hours.

The archipelago began forming during the Upper Cretaceous period, around 130 million years ago, when igneous, metamorphosed rock, which today makes up the hills and outcrops on Gran Roque, was uplifted. On one of these hills stands the ruined **Dutch lighthouse** I had seen from the air, now a popular place to observe the invariably impressive sunset. Archaeological finds from transient Indian fishing camps on the islands suggest that there were no permanent inhabitants on the archipelago prior to the arrival of the Spanish. Owing to the lack of fresh water, the invaders found little use for the islands and they became bases for pirates operating in the Caribbean Sea. In the early 19th century, Dutch groups from the island colonies of Bonaire, Curacao, and Aruba, began to settle on Gran Roque, exploiting lime from the corals and phosphates from the mangroves. From 1910 onwards, fisherman from the nearby island of Margarita started to arrive, and they remain the backbone of today's population.

From the lighthouse, I wandered down to **North Cliff**, where waves crash against the black rocks, and brown pelicans and fork-tailed magnificent frigatebirds (*Fregata magnificens*) glide on the sea breeze. On the way back to my posada, I called into the Sesto Continente diving headquarters to confirm my place for the following day's diving trip.

INTO THE DEEP

There are eight established dive sites around the archipelago, and our trip was to take us to the one furthest from Gran Roque, the southwestern islands of **Dos Mosquices** (Two Mosquitoes). National park regulations limit the size of diving groups to ten clients plus the instructor or divemaster. Our boat was full and as the 9am departure time beckoned, we

INSET Hernando Arnal prepares for flight
BELOW A view of paradise—Gran Roque from the air

VENEZUELA

loaded our snorkels and fins onto the open-top long boat. Although Sesto Continente run beginners' courses, their daily diving trips are for qualified divers, preferably those with recent experience. The ride out to Dos Mosquices took over an hour, but it gave us the opportunity to see the archipelago's vast central lagoon, **Ensenada de los Corrales**, which covers over 400sq km (154 square miles). The lagoon is full of barely submerged sandbanks, and our driver skilfully wove his way between them.

In calmer water near the beach on Dos Mosquices's southern island, our divemaster, Caroline, asked us to put our equipment on before we moved around the corner to enter rougher water. The first of our two dives was to be a wall dive, in which you descend a vertical face of rock and coral to around 20–30m (65–98 feet) beneath the water surface. It was one of Caroline's favourite spots because of the numerous accessible caves. With everyone, including Peter, my Swiss dive partner (known as a "buddy"), in the water and OK, Caroline gave the thumbs-down signal to descend.

At 25m (80 feet), the big blue—the limitless, featureless view encountered underwater—stretched away to our left, and the big wall loomed over us to the right. Swimming into the first cave, a half-moon shape, Caroline spotted a green moray eel (*Gymnothorax funebris*) poking its head out from a gap in the reef. These mean-looking, snake-like creatures, with strong jaws and sharp teeth, wait motionless for their prey, normally fish, to swim by. Manoeuvring around a couple of large deepwater sea-fans (*Iciligorgia schrammi*), the delicate, vein-like fans that sway gracefully with the current, I followed Caroline in deeper. Our torches lit up purple hollow-tube sponges (*Aplysina archeri*) and spotlighted a bright-blue baby angelfish (*Pomacanthus paru*), a rare sight. Further along the wall, the menacing, rapier-missile-shaped outline of a

barracuda (*Sphyraena barracuda*) lurked amongst some other fans. These silver, underwater pirates, which can grow to almost 1.8m (16 feet) long, are always on the prowl for food, usually alone but sometimes in loose shoals. They investigate anything that moves, including divers, though thankfully humans are usually considered to be way too big even for a main course.

With the bright, midday sun shimmering down from the surface, we swam through a shoal of yellowtail snappers (*Ocyurus chrysurus*), snub-nosed, blue fish with a yellow stripe on their bodies. Shortly afterwards, we came across a spiny lobster (*Panulirus argus*) hiding underneath a craggy coral outcrop, its long antennae waving around in search of potential food. Caroline tried to tempt it from its hideout by gently touching its antennae. After falling for the ruse and momentarily revealing a little more of itself, it quickly realized its mistake and retreated even deeper into its hole. These multi-panelled reddish-brown lobsters are highly prized by fishermen, and over 90 percent of Venezuela's catch comes from Los Roques. No wonder it was scared.

I checked on my air supply to find the tank was getting close to 50 bar, the level at which it is necessary to start returning to the surface. With mutual thumbs-up signs, Peter and I ascended to 5m (16 feet) and waited for a few minutes to allow any excess nitrogen to escape safely from our bodies before surfacing. Safely back in the boat, we all headed off to the stunningly beautiful Dos Mosquices south island for our lunch break.

ENDANGERED TURTLES

Apart from having a superb beach, Dos Mosquices is also home to turtle and shark research projects run by the Fundación Científica Los Roques (Los Roques Scientific Foundation). The main aim of the turtle project is to protect and repopulate endangered turtle species, including the green turtle (*Chelonia mydas*), leatherback turtle (*Dermochelys coriacea*), and loggerhead turtle (*Caretta caretta*). In the main research station, massive water tanks house baby turtles that are allowed to grow before being released back into the ocean. The head start they are given in the tanks significantly increases their chances of survival.

After a two-hour break, we were back in the boat for the very short ride to the day's second dive spot. This was to be shallower dive in more open water, with, Caroline promised, spectacular coral and more fish. Although they were present, visibility was not so good. It was nevertheless a fun dive and we saw plenty of rainbow-coloured parrotfish (*Scarus lepidus*). These fish change colour throughout their lives, but it is only the dominant males that become the brilliant green and blue colour that most people readily identify with the species. With their blunt, beak-like mouths, parrotfish munch on coral and thus play an important part in the recycling of reef nutrients. Perhaps the most fascinating corals we saw were the various species of brain coral, which, as their name suggests, very much resemble huge human brains. The normal growing process is incomplete in these species, and this causes the brain-like furrows. After almost an hour under water, we resurfaced and were soon heading back to Gran Roque.

A CORAL FAIRYLAND

In the morning, both boats were going out to the **Gran Barrera Arrecifal del Sur** (Great Southern Barrier Reef). Another long journey took us back across the central lagoon to the first dive location at Boca de Cote, site of a three-stepped wall that goes down to 60m (200 feet). We were to dive to the second step at around 20–25m (65–80 feet). Underwater conditions were near perfect, with very good visibility and enough sunlight to bring out the plethora of rich colours. But since I had somehow managed to forget

my mask, and was wearing an ill-fitting borrowed one, everyone else enjoyed the dive while I spent most of it with my eyes closed to stop the salt water from stinging them—although I did manage to open them long enough to see a green turtle glide by with the grace of a *Tai Chi* master. Fortunately, the whole day was not lost. With another mask borrowed from the other boat I was once again fully functional for the second dive at Punta Salina, which turned out to be the most impressive dive of the two days.

From start to end, the Punta Salina wall is like a Walt Disney-inspired fairyland grotto. The range of corals on the sloping wall is breathtaking. We saw sheet coral (*Agaricia lamarcki*), which looks like a stack of variously sized poppadoms, boulder star coral (*Motastrea annularis*), a toadstool-shaped, green coral, and three varieties of brain coral. Deeper down, brilliantly coloured, tubular sponges proliferated, including the bright-orange elephant-ear sponge (*Agelas clathrodes*), and the reddish-purple branching tube sponge (*Pseudoceratina crassa*). But the fish weren't going to let the corals and sponges steal the show. Every nook and cranny harboured different coloured fish. My favourites were the cool, yellow and blue blueheads (*Thalassoma*

LEARNING TO DIVE

Learning to dive is relatively easy. There are several qualifying bodies recognized around the world, including PADI and NAUI. Open-water beginners' courses of three to five days are reasonably priced, and lead to a qualification that allows you to dive to 40m (130 feet). You need to pass a simple health test and be able to swim. The course includes classroom instruction and a straightforward multiple-choice exam. One-day taster courses and more advanced courses are also available.

bifasciatum), which seemed content just to hang around watching events unfold on the reef. Other supporting roles in this marine extravaganza were played by a spotted eagle ray (*Aetobatus narinari*), the stealth bomber of the oceans, and shoals of dainty, blue ocean surgeonfish (*Acanthurus coeruleus*). Stars of the show, though, were the two green turtles we saw. This time, I managed to get close to one and swam upwards through the fans alongside it. This was scuba diving at its best, the opportunity to move around freely in a world apart from our own. All too soon, our air gauges reached the red area and we were reluctantly forced to ascend to the surface.

Lying on the beach the next morning, waiting for my afternoon flight back to Caracas, I once again watched pelicans diving deep for fish and magnificent frigatebirds soaring high on the thermals above. They had known about the best ways to see the veritable paradise of Los Roques all along, and I had merely followed their natural lead to find my own little corner of paradise.

GOING IT ALONE

WHEN TO GO

Diving conditions are superb at any time of year, but they are marginally better still during the summer months (May to October). The water temperature ranges from 25°C to 30°C (77°F to 86°F). The air temperature is reasonably constant all year round: it averages 29°C (84°F), and reaches highs of 34°C (93°F) in July. There may be rainfall between September and January but it rarely lasts long as the northeasterly trade winds usually drive any rain clouds away.

PLANNING YOUR TRIP

The most popular way to visit Los Roques is with one of the package tours available, mainly with Línea Turistica Aerotuy (LTA). For divers, they offer both land-based packages, which include accommodation in medium- to high-standard posadas on Gran Roque, and slightly more expensive, live-aboard packages on the

LEFT Microlighting can compete with any modern fun-park ride, and the views are breathtaking
BELOW North Cliff, the place to spot brown pelicans and magnificent frigatebirds

superb dive yacht *Antares III*. Package prices include return flights from Caracas on their large jet, accommodation, food, soft drinks, and three guided dives a day, tanks and weight-belts. BCD (Buoyancy Control Device), regulator, National Park entry fee, and Park Dive fee, are extra. The minimum stay for divers is 3 days because flying 24 hours before or after diving is not recommended.

For independent travellers, there are several airlines that fly daily to and from Gran Roque. They include Vipro, L.T.A. (they offer flight-only deals), Chapi Air, and Aeroejecutivos. In the high season it is wise to secure a return date on booking as flights are usually full. *Posadas* can be reserved directly via fax or telephone, though it would not be a problem finding a room on the spot outside of the peak season, i.e., Christmas, New Year, and Easter. Free camping is permitted at the Inparques office near to Sesto Continente's dive shop.

Diving with Sesto Continente should be reserved at least a day in advance. Multi-dive

discounts are available. Hernando usually flies only during the morning and late afternoon, which are in any case the best times to fly. Reservations should be made the day before at his bar, Rasquatekey.

HEALTH AND SAFETY MATTERS

The biggest threat to health on Los Roques is the sun. There is very little or no shade on many of the islands, and the white sand exacerbates the sun's burning effects. Good sun protection is essential throughout the year. It is not advisable to drink the tap water on Gran Roque. Bottled mineral water is widely available, though large numbers of visitors and a few particularly hot days can cause shortages (it virtually ran out while I was there). Supplies are brought in only once a week. Food at the posadas is prepared with purified water. There are mosquitoes on the island, so precautions are advised, though the constant breeze eases the situation. The sandflies, which occur during the summer months, are probably more irritating, but the evening sea breeze helps to keep bugs at bay.

WHAT TO TAKE

❏ Dive gear, particularly mask, snorkel and fins, if you have your own.
❏ Your diving qualification card.
❏ Plenty of high-factor sunblock.
❏ Sunglasses and sun hat.
❏ Insect repellent.
❏ A good book.

VENEZUELA

On an All-Time High

by Steve Watkins

Western Venezuela is dominated by the Andean Mountains, which are an increasingly popular destination for trekkers in search of a high-altitude challenge. Trek through lush cloud forest and high-altitude paramo, and climb the spectacularly rocky Pico Bolívar, the highest summit in Venezuela, where the burial spot of the legendary liberator himself can be found.

There can be few sensations to match those experienced by a climber upon reaching the summit of a high mountain. The level of self-sufficiency needed to get there, and the uplifting buzz of success that comes with achieving your goal, can make you feel as though you have undergone a complete life-makeover. It is not necessary to climb Mount Everest to enjoy this sense of exhilaration, but there is undoubtedly an extra edge to the experience when you know you are standing at the highest point in a country. In Venezuela, that point is the summit of the 5,007-m (16,427-feet) high Pico Bolívar, so I made for the Andean city of **Mérida** to organize my five-day trek to attempt to reach it.

5 This trek needs a very high level of fitness (reputable tour companies in Mérida suggest alternative treks to people they don't think are fit enough). Most of the trek is not overly steep, though some sections to base camp and the route to the summit are difficult. The altitude affects everyone to some degree, making any effort a challenge.

★★ Your main consideration should be the weight of your backpack, so lightness of load must take priority over any other comfort factors on the Bolívar trek. The high altitude makes it difficult to sleep well, but the food is surprisingly tasty and plentiful. It is normal for clients to carry their own equipment and to share in carrying communal gear and food.

✕ All specialist trekking equipment, including warm and waterproof clothing and sleeping bags, is included in the tour price, but it is worth taking your own if you have it.

Mérida is a very attractive city. It has an agreeable climate and a lively nightlife generated by a 35,000-strong university population, but it is best known for its cable car. It is the highest and longest in the world, reaching 4765m (15,634 feet) in 12.5km (7¾ miles), and offers instant access to the snow peaks of the Sierra Nevada National Park. Why then did we feel the need to hike for three days reach a height that the cable car could attain in just one and a half hours? Tom Evenou, the multilingual owner of Bum Bum Tours, explained that our chances of reaching the summit after alighting at the cable car's end point would be almost zero: the body's inability to adapt quickly to the large gains in altitude that are made during the car's ascent would make it hard to climb a set of steps let alone Pico Bolívar. Walking up would allow our bodies to adapt more successfully to the rarefied air; and in any case, as Tom pointed out, it's a beautiful hike. As a reward for our efforts in getting there, the tour included a ride back down in the cable car.

POSITIVE MENTAL ATTITUDE

At a briefing meeting on the evening before our departure I met the other five members of the trekking group, all Canadians. Peter, Janet, Travis and Joe were on a brief holiday from their teaching jobs in Trinidad, and Sean was taking a break from pulling teeth in Canada. Juan, the head guide, suggested that climbing Bolívar is as much a mental challenge as a physical one, so a positive attitude is very important albeit no guarantee of success. There are no set rules for how altitude affects individuals, however experienced they are, but one thing that does appear to help everyone counteract its effects is water. The process of dehydration accelerates the higher you go, and Tom emphasized the importance of drinking regularly even if we weren't thirsty.

Pico Bolívar is part of the Sierra Nevada de Mérida range of mountains in the northern section of the Andean chain. The peak, and a vast surrounding area that stretches from the Santo Domingo–Mérida road down to the lowland fringes around Barinas, are protected as part of the **Sierra Nevada National Park**. The 276,446-ha (683,098-acre) park, created in 1952, contains Venezuela's five highest peaks, which are collectively known as the Las Cinco Aguilas Blancas (The Five White Eagles). It also has large tracts of cloud forest, hauntingly desolate highland areas, known as *paramo*, and scores of colourful glacial lakes. Our trek would expose us to all these environments.

Loaded up with food and equipment, the backpacks felt heavy as we hoisted them onto a jeep for the hour-long drive up to the ranger station at La Mucuy, entry point to the national park and start point for the trek. As we set off on foot from the ranger station, there was a noticeable lack of chat amongst the group as we focused our minds on the efforts ahead and concentrated on the narrow trail that zigzagged up the mountain. At times, we took steeper shortcuts that had been driven through thick bush, and it was great fun ducking and weaving around the fallen branches, dangling vines, and spiky shrubs.

A LAKE TOO FAR

There were few let-ups in the incessant climb, and we soon passed the 2,500m (8,200 feet) sign at the Mesa de los Piños (Table of the Pines). On crossing the boulder-strewn bed of Quebrada de Oso (Bear Stream), the trail began to ascend more steeply up the left-hand side of Valle de Coromoto (Coromoto Valley). Grey clouds loomed overhead, but thankfully the light drizzle never fulfilled its promise to become a downpour. By late afternoon, the question most repeatedly directed at the guides was "How much further?"—the frequency of the enquiry increasing with the tiredness in our legs. At last we crested a rise and saw the Laguna Coromoto camp. We greeted it as if it were our ancestral home. According to the weather-beaten sign, we were now at exactly 3,000m (9,843 feet), three-fifths of the summit's height.

At dusk, the temperature plummeted, and we donned every piece of available clothing to keep the cold at bay while we waited for the chicken curry and pasta feast to be readied. As delicious as it was, there was no desire to savour it and we quickly finished it off in order to retire to the tents. Everyone seemed to be doing fine with the altitude, but the second day would test our bodies and minds still further as we moved above 3,200m (10,499 feet), the height at which the effects of altitude become more noticeable. Thankfully, it would be a shorter day, and we would probably reach the second camp by early afternoon. Shorter it may have been, but looking upwards from Coromoto at the precipitous wall at the head of the valley we got the feeling that it wouldn't be easy.

Appearances can be deceptive, though, and the path initially angled comfortably up the valley side, only occasionally necessitating a short, steeper detour to skirt big boulders that had tumbled from the cliffs above. The trees and plants of the forest suddenly gave up in their battle to live the high life and were replaced by the hardy, scrubby vegetation of the *paramo*, including the unique frailejón plant (*Espeletia pycnophylla*) with its spiky, felt-textured leaves. Our breathing was starting to become more laboured, and together we sounded like a herd of horses panting after a long, hard gallop, but we pressed on and things improved as our bodies began to adjust to the new conditions.

ICY EXPLORERS

Soon after negotiating a single-plank bridge across a pathless cliff-face, we passed a waterfall and began to trek up steeper, more exposed outcrops of

BELOW The single-plank bridge on the trek from Laguna Coromoto camp (INSET).

grey rock. Occasionally, it was easier to scramble up on all fours than to risk having our heavy packs tip us over backwards. The reward for getting to the top of the outcrops was outstanding. Beyond another waterfall, the large, brilliant-white glacier that cascades down from the summit of **Pico Humboldt** shimmered in the midday sun. Pico Humboldt was originally called La Corona, but the Spanish renamed it after the legendary German explorer and naturalist, Baron Alexander von Humboldt, who came to Venezuela in

1799 to explore the Río Orinoco. And yet he never actually climbed the mountain, nor even visited the Mérida area.

On catching sight of the emerald-green waters of Laguna Verde, our overnight camp, we all felt that our efforts were over. But there was a sting in the tail. To reach the other side of the lake and our camp area, we had to traverse a steep slope on small ledges

and rockflakes. It did not demand a high level of technical skill but, with a sheer drop down to the lake awaiting any slip, it called for a calm head. Every single movement was mentally rehearsed beforehand, and I don't remember breathing too often either! By the time Peter reached the traverse, which is around 3,800m (12,467 feet) high, he was starting to have problems with the altitude. We had already reached the camp, where we sat and watched his slow progress along the rockface, unaware that he was feeling so sick that he had to

VENEZUELA

MÉRIDA'S CABLE CAR

The construction of Mérida's *teleférico*, or cable car—the longest and highest in the world—was a incredible feat of French engineering that utilized 1,300 workers and 500 mules. It opened on October 10, 1958, and takes passengers from Barinitas (in Mérida) at 1,557m (5108 feet) to Pico Espejo at 4,765m (15,633 feet) in just one hour. There are four stages to the journey. At the time of writing, the top section is still closed following an accident in 1991. However, the repair work is now completed, test-runs are underway, and it should have reopened by the time you read this. The journey takes you over the deep Cañon del Río Chama (River Chama Canyon), through beautiful cloud forest and wild paramo, and up to the snow peaks. At each station there is a health centre where bottled oxygen is available for those feeling the effects of the rapid altitude gain.

stop to vomit halfway across. By the time he reached camp, he was exhausted, and we quickly erected his tent so that he could stay warm and rest.

Overnight, the restricted breathing conditions and wacky dreams created by the rarefied air made sleeping difficult, and it was a relief when a fiery-red dawn broke and I could get up. Peter was feeling significantly better and, after a lengthy discussion, decided to carry on up to Pico Bolívar's base camp. Another group at the camp had a sick member, too, and they decided to abandon their trek to Humboldt and head back down to Mérida. For us, the longest, most demanding day of the trek lay ahead, and we packed up quickly to ensure an early departure.

After an easy start through a meadow of golden grass, we skirted a waterfall and followed the stony trail that zigzags steeply up a spur. At the top, we came to another, smaller lake at the foot of Pico Humboldt's west face. At the lakeside, a battered wooden sign, angled awkwardly upwards, appeared to point to the moon. Painted on it in faded red letters were the words La Travesía (The Traverse), our route to base camp. Following the sign's line brought our eyes to a very long and very steep scree slope that was split at the top by a large buttress of black rock. It was a heartbreaking sight. Pico Bolívar was not going to allow us to wander up it unchallenged, and we resigned ourselves to 40 minutes or so of further suffering.

ONE BIG STEP

We filled our water bottles with the deliciously fresh and chilled lake water, tightened our backpack straps, and began the slow plod up the scree. On the loose rocks our boots struggled to gain purchase, and we made frequent stops to grab short, insufficient gasps of air. Around us, the first few pockets of snow appeared and the temperature noticeably dropped. Juan further improved his popularity by pointing out that we didn't need to continue up past the black buttress as our path diverted right onto a wide, flat ledge. There were still more climbs to come, but we felt that we had made a major step towards reaching our goal. The view from this ledge is outstanding, taking in the green waters of **Laguna Verde** back down the valley, Humboldt's glacier, and the seemingly endless folds of mountains and ridges to the northeast. In the warm sun, we relaxed and ate some tasty, dried-fruit snacks.

As we crossed a rock-strewn saddle— a bow-shaped dip in a ridge between two peaks—the wind briefly reached jet force as it funnelled through the gap and buffeted our bodies. Peter was starting to feel poorly again, but now the quickest way down was to continue. Janet was finding the hike hard going too. Sean and I seemed to be coping reasonably well, as were Travis and Joe, both of whom were battling with the additional problem of vertigo. Things seemed to be looking good for at least four of us to make an attempt on the summit.

In the afternoon, grey clouds rolled up from the valleys and dumped sporadic rain and snow showers on us. Our route passed through forests of the weird and prolific frailejón plant. Over 50 varieties occur in the paramo region between 3,000m (9,843 feet) and 4,500m (14,764 feet) above sea-level, and some can grow to over 2m (6½ feet) high. Their spiky, felty leaves help to protect them against the extreme cold, and they are useful for humans too. The leaves of one variety are used to wrap butter, and others are used, amongst many things, as snack foods and mattress fillings.

Despite the spectacular surroundings, it had been a tough day and the final long climb up to the base camp at 4,600m (15,092 feet) almost proved too much for all of us. Peter, however, suffered badly. Completely exhausted, he was moving very slowly, and on arriving at camp he just managed to drink some tea before falling asleep in his tent. Joe was starting to suffer with a headache, and after a day of rock scrambles both he and Travis were unsure about testing further their fear of heights by going for the summit. So it seemed that only Sean and I would be heading that way in the morning. As the sun dipped towards the horizon, I looked out over a rippled carpet of orange cloud in the valleys below. I felt quite good, and Sean was looking strong too. For the first time, I started to feel confident that we would reach the top.

FOUR DOWN, TWO TO GO

We rose at dawn to find that our backpacks had frozen overnight. Whilst I sipped tea, the sun's light crept slowly down the huge rock band towering above us, turning it golden. Above the ridge, the sky was a deep, deep blue, and the clouds in the valley below appeared to be trapped there. It looked as though our luck had held and given us a perfect day for the summit attempt. Peter, Joe, Janet, and Travis decided to head for the cable car with El Burro, one of the guides. It had been a rewarding, worthwhile hike even without going to the summit, and they left happy in the knowledge that they had trekked higher than they had ever been before.

Juan and David, the two remaining guides, and Sean and I packed our gear and focused our minds on the sustained effort that would be required for the next three to five hours of very steep ascent. Despite numerous serious attempts to climb Pico Bolívar in the early 1930s, it wasn't until 1935 that it was conquered. On January 5, Enrique Bourgoin, a doctor

VENEZUELA

ALTITUDE SICKNESS: SYMPTOMS AND REMEDIES

Climbing to altitudes above 3,000m (9,843 feet) has some very strange and noticeable effects on the human body. The most obvious is an increase in breathing and heartbeat rate. This is not caused by a lack of oxygen, which remains constant up until 20,000m (65,620 feet), but is triggered by a reduction in oxygen pressure within the lungs. This is quite normal, but it can lead to more unpleasant effects, especially when you ascend rapidly to high altitude (as you do when you use the cable car to go up to Pico Bolívar). Symptoms of acute mountain sickness, or *Mal de Páramo* as it is known in the Andes, include headache, insomnia (or a feeling of suffocation when sleeping), vertigo, slowing of mental functions, accelerated breathing, nausea, and vomiting. The best treatment for this is rest, water, anti-sickness tablets for the nausea and, where necessary, descent to a lower altitude. In most cases, though, the body acclimatizes in time.

from Mérida, and his guide Domingo Peña finally made it over the then much larger ice and snow fields to stand on the summit.

We expected to find very little snow or ice on the route and so set off with light packs containing only the bare essentials of warm clothing layers, waterproof jackets, food, walking axes, and helmets. Ascending a rocky ledge above the camp, we skirted Laguna Timoncito and began to climb more steeply into a gully. The altitude was now making every movement a challenge, and we stopped every 20 or so steps to suck in more oxygen. It was a good excuse to soak up the marvellous views both down the mountain and up to the jagged peaks above. Soon, we were at the bottom of the first of seven sections (called a pitch in climbing terms) where we needed to use a rope to safe-guard our progress, so we put on our climbing harnesses and helmets, and readied our

walking axes. Juan climbed ahead with one end of the rope and secured himself to a preplaced chain (called a belay point). We then followed him up. This relay system continued as we scrambled and climbed over quite exposed rocks and plodded up snow gullies.

A fresh fall of snow the previous afternoon had made conditions more testing than we had expected. As we ascended further, clouds began to envelop the peak, and the wind picked up, sending temperatures plummeting. In between pitches, we stood on tiny ledges

FAR LEFT The trek to La Travesía took us through scrubby vegetation dotted with frailejón plants—unique to the paramo and, remarkably, a member of the daisy family ABOVE David, one of the guides, pauses for a brief rest during the final ascent. A fresh fall of snow had made condi-tions more testing than expected. In the distance an adjacent, smaller peak is shrouded in cloud LEFT The moment of triumph. David at the summit with the large bronze bust of Venezuela's hero, Simón Bolívar

63

VENEZUELA

PROFILE OF A HERO: SIMÓN BOLÍVAR

No visitor to Venezuela can fail to notice the omnipresent name of Él Libertador (The Liberator), Simón Bolívar. Almost every city, town, and village, has a Plaza Bolívar with a bronze statue of him at its centre. Born in 1783, this short, wiry-figured man led the historic struggle towards the nation's independence from the Spanish in the early 19th century. After several unsuccessful attempts to oust the colonial rulers, his inspired leadership finally paid off in 1821 when a decisive victory at the Battle of Carabobo saw Bolívar enter Caracas to be declared president. In order to fulfil his dream of creating a huge, independent nation called Gran Colombia, he also led the successful liberation struggles in Colombia, Ecuador, and Peru.

one of them we could see the famous, large bronze bust of Simón Bolívar, a rather bizarre sight after the wilderness scenery of the trek to get there. The bust was carried up there (yes, carried!) on April 19, 1951, as a tribute to the great leader—Venezuela's highest-ranked hero on the highest peak.

As if to reward us for our efforts, the clouds briefly cleared, the sun warmed our frozen limbs, and we enjoyed the wonderful views along the ridge. To reach Bolívar's statue, Sean and I took deep breaths and carefully scrambled over the narrow rocks, trying to ignore the big drops on either side. As we reached our goal with a tremendous surge of exhilaration, even Bolívar seemed to smile in recognition of our achievement.

Reaching the summit of any mountain is a great thrill, but getting down again is probably the most dangerous time. As much as we would have enjoyed staying longer on top, limited time (it had taken us five hours to reach the summit) and the increasingly cold temperatures dictated that we should descend. The descent proved to be something of an epic, for cold hands and tired bodies made all the rope work, down-climbing, and abseiling a real challenge. By the time we got back to camp, ten hours had passed since we set out. We were drained of energy, but the feeling of accomplishment was immense, and both Sean and I dug deep to find the tiny bit of energy needed for a big grin.

The following day, it was by no means an easy or short hike to get to the Loma Redonda Teleferico station, though seeing a condor (*Vultur gryphus*) soaring above us certainly lifted our spirits. It was only at the station that we began truly to appreciate the value of the cable-car part of the tour package. The level of self-sufficiency required to summit high mountains may be what makes the experience so enlightening, but a little bit of outside assistance on the way down can prove to be equally welcome.

where there was no option other than to huddle together to stop the cold creeping into our bones as we waited for the belay to be prepared. On one pitch up a steep snow gully, it was necessary to kick steps in the hardening snow to give our boots a chance of holding. Each time I swung my axe, a spray of icy-cold shards would explode into my face. This was turning into a really great adventure.

The last few pitches consisted of short sections of almost vertical rock, and their negotiation required a little bit of thinking and a good dose of courage. After traversing a very exposed ledge, we arrived at the base of the final climb to the summit. My heart was pounding, my mouth was dry, and I had a slight headache, but I knew for sure that we were going to make it.

SUMMIT OR BUST

The knife-edge summit ridge of Pico Bolívar is very dramatic. Sharp, angular plates of rock jut awkwardly upwards. On

GOING IT ALONE

WHEN TO GO

Pico Bolívar is best climbed between December and May when there is little or no snow on the route. From June to November, the mountain is covered in snow, and it becomes a much more technical climb that requires experience as well as specialist snow-climbing equipment.

PLANNING YOUR TRIP

It is strictly not permitted to climb Pico Bolívar alone. Even if you are part of an experienced group it is still advisable to take a guide as the route is far from clear in many places and available maps are poor.

By far the best way to organize a trek to the higher peaks is to use an operator such as Bum Bum Tours. They organize all the paperwork and food supplies, and provide at least two experienced guides and radio communication—all at very reasonable prices indeed. There are several operators, all based around Merida's Plaza Las Heroínas near the cable-car station.

Tours run very regularly throughout the year. If you are travelling alone or in a pair, you should be able just to turn up and leave on a tour within a few days; if you are in a group of four or five then some operators may organize a private tour for you. If possible, arrange things in advance via the internet or fax.

HEALTH AND SAFETY MATTERS

The problem that you are most likely to encounter is some degree of altitude sickness (see box, page 61). Suitable precautions should also be taken to protect exposed skin against the very intense sun, especially on the upper sections of the trek.

HOW TO CHOOSE AN OPERATOR

Many operators in Mérida offer mountain tours, and the vast majority provide an excellent, safe service. However, you should ask these questions before you decide which one to use:

1. Do they maintain round-the-clock radio contact with their guides in the mountains?

2. Is the climbing equipment regularly used?

3. Is there a full safety-briefing on rope and climbing techniques before departure?

4. Do the guides have a set list of climbing equipment needed for various group sizes?

5. Are the guides properly trained in climbing safety systems and rope techniques?

6. What is the guide-to-client ratio? (There should be one guide to every two or three climbers.)

WHAT TO TAKE

For climbing the mountain, bring as much of your own specialist equipment as you can. If this is not possible, the following items are recommended (some are included in the tour price):

- Good walking boots.
- Waterproof jacket.
- Several thin, warm layers, such as Polartec sweaters.
- Warm hat and thick gloves.
- Thermal underwear.
- Large backpack.
- Sunglasses.
- High-factor sunblock.
- Water bottle.
- Torch.

TRAVELLERS' TIPS

- It may not seem like an attractive idea at the time, but it is definitely worth making the effort to get up for sunrise at the Bolívar base camp. It will certainly be freezing but with a little luck you will be treated to a wonderful sight. Ask the guides what time the sun comes up.
- On the trek up, it is a good idea to keep your water bottle handy so you don't have to take your backpack off to get a drink. You will drink more this way, too, which helps to combat altitude sickness.
- Keep a warm layer of clothing handy, and put it on at every rest break to avoid getting cold.
- Credit cards are either not accepted, or only grudgingly accepted (often with a whopping 10–15% surcharge), by the operators in Mérida. They prefer to be paid in Bolívares or U.S. dollars, though they all accept U.S.-dollar travellers' cheques.

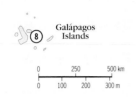

PACIFIC OCEAN

Esmeraldas

6

7

Quito

5897m
Cotopaxi

Guayaquil

Ambato

6272m
Chimborazo

Golfo de
Guayaquil

Cuenca

Galápagos
Islands

8

0	250	500 km
0	100 200 300 m	

ECUADOR

Mainland Ecuador is a lush, tropical country right on the equator. It is a stunning mixture of rolling hills with fertile valleys, snow-capped volcanic peaks, high-altitude plains, and mountains clad in cloud forest. Within a few hours' bus ride of Quito, the capital city, you can be in the heart of the Andean Indian communities, visiting their colourful markets. To the east of Quito, the jungle is accessible in less than a day and, to the west, the Pacific coast offers a tropical setting of sandy beaches and fishing villages. To the west of the mainland are the magical, volcanic islands of the Galápagos, where you can visit the nesting sites and breeding colonies of a host of specialized fauna, snorkel in crystal clear waters, scuba dive in challenging but rewarding dive sites, and even swim with sea lions. Indeed, Equador has so much to offer the visitor that is has become the top destination in South America for newcomers, and an old favourite for experienced travellers.

*View of Villacamba Range from Runquracay
Pass on the Inca Trail*

ECUADOR

Trekking through Cloud Forest

By Guy Marks

In the precious, pristine ecosystems of the Ecuadorian Andes I trekked on foot and on horseback from the high plains of the paramo, *down through the cloud forest of Cerro Golondrinas, to the subtropical forests of the lower elevations.*

El Angel is a quiet highland town in the north of Ecuador, about 20 miles south of the Colombian border. It is typical of a small, South American market town in that it is built on a grid network around a central plaza and has a weekly market on a Monday. The town is not in itself a big tourist attraction but it is a gateway to the paramo, which puts it on the itinerary of walkers and anyone wanting to explore a wilderness environment. The paramo—the high plain from 3,800 to 4,200m (12,500–13,800 feet) above sea-level—has a unique ecosystem. The word is derived from the Quichua Indian language and means a cold, wet place.

I made the 225-km (140-mile) journey from **Quito**, the country's capital, to **El Angel** with Piet Sabbe, a director of the Golondrinas Foundation, and a group of six other people with whom I would trek

Most of this trek is downhill, but a reasonable level of general fitness is required. It can be steep, wet, and slippery; and during the wet season sections of the route are deep with mud, which makes walking very difficult.

Accommodation on the trek is very basic at the village of Morán and at the reserve lodge. Both have dormitory accommodation with simple bunk beds. There is no electricity and only basic facilities. If it is raining you could be uncomfortable, whether you are riding or walking through mud.

Rubber boots, rain gear, and a sleeping bag are essential. Take plastic bags to keep things dry inside your pack. I recommend taking binoculars to view birdlife.

for the next four days. Ellen and Jopie, two Dutch women, had just been down to the jungles of the Amazon basin to the east of the Ecuadorian Andes. Clare had just arrived from England, while Amanda, another Englishwoman, had just flown in from Lima in Peru. We were fortunate in that two of the group, Camillo and Marjolein, who live in Quito and own a travel business, had a large enough vehicle to give us all a lift to El Angel, but it would otherwise have been quite easy to get there using public transport.

From Quito the route north goes through **Otavalo** and then on to Ibarra about half an hour later. From here it is another couple of hours north along the Pan-American highway before you turn west at San Gabriel for the last 20km (12 miles). It was cold and quite late in the evening when we arrived at the Hostería El Angel. They were expecting us, though, and had a fire blazing in the hearth and hot soup, deep-fried pork, and potato cakes cooking for us. In Quito I'd packed my bags in a hurry, so now I took a few moments to sort a few things into a daypack and put the rest into my main pack, wrapping them in plastic bags to keep dry. On this trek the bags go ahead of the walkers, so you need carry only the essentials for the day.

THE ROAD TO THE WILDERNESS

At breakfast our luggage was whisked away by the milkman. The farmers at **Morán**, the remote village where we would spend the first night, produce a small amount of milk but have no road to get it to market. Each day they bring the milk out of their valley by horse and meet up with the milkman and his pick-up vehicle at the end of the track on the paramo. So the milkman had been commandeered to take our bags and give them to the villagers at the rendezvous. If all went to plan the horsemen would get our luggage to the village long before we arrived by foot.

In El Angel we met up with Luis, who was to be our guide and cook, and Armin, a German, who had been travelling non-stop for about a year and was joining our trekking party after taking the Ibarra-to-San Lorenzo train. We boarded a pick-up and headed out of town towards the paramo. To start with the road passed through an agricultural landscape of rolling green pastures, eucalyptus trees, patchwork fields planted with potatoes, corn and vegetables, and farmhouses with red-tiled roofs. But for the fact that the houses were built of mud-brick and adobe, the whole scene could have been plucked from rural Spain.

As the road took us higher the wind grew colder and the vegetation gradually changed until, after about an hour, we were driving through a plain of tufted, brown grasses and tall, weird plants. We had reached the paramo, and the plants were the unmistakable frailejónes (*Espeletia pycnophylla*) for which the area is famed. These plants, which grow only on the paramo and are now quite rare, are a giant relative of the daisy, though they bear very little resemblance to it. They have a trunk topped with a crown of long, furry, light-green leaves with a yellow hue; and as the old leaves die they don't fall but hang in layers forming a sheath of insulation that protects the plant's stem. Some of the varieties can grow up to 6m (20 feet) tall, although most of the ones I saw were about 60–90cm (2–3 feet) with a few at about 1.8m (6 feet).

The road continued upwards and became a gravel track as we passed

through the **Reserva Ecológica El Angel** (El Angel Ecological Reserve). This 15,715-ha (38,833-acre) reserve protects rare frailejónes, which cover 80 percent of the area.

TREKKING ACROSS THE PARAMO

At 10:30 in the morning we reached the end of the track, waved goodbye to the pick-up, and started walking through this wilderness. Clouds closing in around us conjured up a mystical atmosphere as we trudged through wet grass and marshy mosses, surrounded by the strange frailejónes. At 4,000m (13,200 feet), the air was thin and there was a bitter chill in the wind. The cold, wet paramo was aptly named.

At the edge of an escarpment, we took a break. From a sheltered spot beneath the ridge we watched clouds caught in the wind as they swirled across the sky, changing every moment. For brief moments they cleared to reveal a spectacular view. Below us lay a green valley, its cliffs thick with forest; in the distance, where the forest had been cleared, we could just make out the few green fields and small houses that comprise Morán, the village we were heading for. As quickly as the clouds had

THE IBARRA TO SAN LORENZO TRAIN

A railway runs between Ibarra, at 2,210m (7,250 feet), and San Lorenzo on the coast. The day-long journey is popular with travellers, who tend to sit on the roof of the train to get the best views while the locals stay inside the carriages. The scenery changes considerably as you travel from the cool mountains through lush vegetation to the hot, steamy coast. The train is unreliable: it often breaks down, and sometimes it does not run at all. When it is operational it is well worth taking the ride.

ABOVE The waterfall in the cloud forest
LEFT The mystical wilderness of the paramo
at the edge of the escarpment, glimpsed before
the clouds closed in (INSET) as we picked our
way between the remarkable frailejón plants

cleared they closed in again, and it was impossible to see more than a couple of metres in front of the escarpment.

We walked on, picking out a route around the edge of the escarpment, and came to a disused, man-made track overgrown with grass and small shrubs with black berries. It is rare to see wildlife up here, but we saw plenty of evidence. Deer footprints in the soft soil would have been made by white-tailed deer (*Odocoileus virginianius*) or the Soche, while giant bromeliads with their centres ripped out were the leftovers of a feast made by South America's only indigenous bear species, the spectacled bear (*Tremarctoss ornatus*), which comes up from the forest at night to feed.

As the route took us slowly downhill, the frailejónes began to thin out. Finally, we came to the edge of the paramo and a marked change in vegetation. Below us was a tree line, the end of the grasses, and the start of the montane (or cloud) forest. We walked down into it and soon came to a beautiful waterfall where Piet and Luis produced jam sandwiches, cheese, fruit, and nougat, from their daypacks, and lunch was served.

ECUADOR

THROUGH THE FOREST TO MORÁN

The three-hour walk from the waterfall down through the forest to Morán took us along a path that wound its way through a network of small streams and thick vegetation. In these upper elevations of the forest the trees are gnarled and twisted, and their branches hang with mosses. Each tree is like a mini-ecosystem in itself, supporting orchids, bromeliads, and a host of other epiphytes. Clouds often envelop the whole forest in mists, so everything is moist and dripping, and a scent like sweet autumn leaves rises from the forest floor.

Morán is a small settlement located at an altitude of 3,000m (9,850 feet) and set in green fields cleared from the forest. The houses of the 13 families that make up the community are spread out over the farmland. In the centre there's a community building, which acts as a classroom and meeting room; and there's a purpose-built visitors' lodge, which is a wooden shed, with tin roof and concrete floor, furnished with roughly built, wooden bunk beds with thin foam mattresses. There's no electricity in the village, so candles are the only source of light. There is a flushing lavatory outside, but that is the extent of the facilities.

The villagers cooked for us, preparing the local fare of vegetable soup, rice, potatoes, and some fried batter that looks a bit like a doughnut. We were all tired after the long day's walk followed by good hot food, but we nevertheless took the opportunity to get to know each other a little better as we sat and chatted about our various travels.

HORSE TREKKING THROUGH LA CORTADERA

Morning brought a howling gale and torrential rain, which didn't bode well for a day's horse riding. We dug out every piece of waterproof clothing before our bags were secured to pack-horses that once again disappeared ahead of us. It was still raining heavily after breakfast,

DEFINING THE ECOSYSTEMS

There are three distinct ecosystems in this area, each dictated by altitude:

❑ The paramo consists of high-altitude grasslands and wetlands at 3,800–4,200m (2,500–13,800 feet).

❑ Montane forest, or cloud forest, characterized by its high level of condensed moisture, ranges from 1,500–3,800m (4,900–12,500 feet).

❑ The premontane forest is lowland, subtropical forest found at altitudes below 1,500m (4,900 feet).

although the wind had died down. The villagers brought us our mounts, and we set off clad in an array of plastic and gortex. Some of the saddlery was a bit crude, but the horses were good, well looked after, and easy to ride. Two members of the group had never been on a horse before and yet they had no problems, even with the discomfort caused by the wet weather. Thankfully, the rain eased within about half an hour of our setting off.

The narrow path soon left the agricultural lands behind and wound along the mountainside through forest. In the middle of the morning we emerged into grassland dotted with black-and-white cows. There were clumps of tall, white, trumpet-like lilies and the occasional lone Arrayan tree. The Arrayan is such a hard wood that it ruins chainsaws and is rarely cut, but all the rest of the precious cloud forest had been felled. This was **La Cortadera**, and we soon came to the centre of the village where, set either side of a wide green, are a few simple tin-roofed wooden houses, painted with fading, pastel shades of blue, green, and pink. The small community of villagers here, like those at Morán, take an active part in entertaining the few tourists that pass through their lands.

They had been expecting us. It was time for a break, and they had prepared hot vegetable and potato soup as a mid-morning snack. As the soup warmed us the rain stopped and the skies cleared, revealing a distant view of Volcan Chiles on the Colombian border.

We rode on until lunch time, at which point the horses were taken back to Morán by the village guides. From here on we were to proceed on foot, heading for the centre of the **Cerro Golondrinas Reserve**. The walk was quite tough, and we slipped on mud as we picked our way sharply downhill. The forest was now even thicker than before, with clumps of bamboo and tree ferns, wild, flowering fuchsias, rheums (a relative of the rhubarb), vines clinging to trees, and layer upon layer of other green vegetation.

In the centre of the reserve, at about 2,200m (7,200 feet), is a wooden house perched on top of a hill and affording great views out across the forests. El Corazón Lodge is not permanently occupied, being used only by visitors and project workers from the Cerro Golondrinas Foundation. This was our home for the next two nights, and Luis was quick to open the place up, unpack all the kitchen gear, and get a cooking fire going. He looked after us very well and even made fresh popcorn and coffee while he prepared the evening meal.

A day at the lodge is a chance to really make yourself at home in the forest. There is no set plan of activities, but you are free to go birdwatching, explore the area, or just sit back and relax at the lodge. There are all manner of birds to look out for, from the swallow-tailed kite (*Elanoides forficatus*) and colombian screech owl (*Otus columbianus*), to the bright-red cock-of-the-rock (*Rupicola peruviana*), and various talengers, flycatchers, and antpitta (*Grallarina*) species. We saw a quetzal (*Pharomachrus mocinno*), perhaps the most colourful bird in the forest, and a few blue-billed mountain toucans.

Piet and Clare did a bit of tree pruning and forest maintenance, while Ellen and Jopie took the opportunity to relax, spending most of the day sitting in hammocks, reading, and looking out over this wonderful corner of the world.

OUT OF THE WOODS

The vegetation gradually changed as we descended further and came into an area of subtropical or premontane forest. The plants were massive, some with giant leaves as wide as a man is tall. The trees, too, were much bigger here than they are higher up, and some had thick, knobbly, buttress roots sticking out near their base. The huge vines that hung from the upper canopy were thick enough to swing on, and we all had a go at playing Tarzan. At the streams and rivers, clouds of butterflies fed on flowers and sipped at the damp ground. They flitted in the mottled shade, flashing vibrant colours and then vanishing in perfect camouflage as their wings closed.

We crossed the Río Golondrinas and came out of the forest onto grassland. This brought us to Santa Rosa lodge, another of the reserve's centres and the site of a tree nursery where one of the foundation's reforestation projects is

---

MOUNTAIN CEDAR

The mountain cedar tree (*Cedrella montana*), is a slow-growing hardwood found in the cloud forest. Its timber is used for making furniture; it is often referred to as mahogany, although it is not the same as the more familiar mahogany taken from *Sweitenia* species in the lowland rain forests. The tree is a protected species in Ecuador, and permission is needed to cut it. Despite this, large quantities are being felled illegally in unprotected areas, and every day you can see donkeys laden with this rare wood crossing the Golondrinas Reserve from neighbouring land that is fast being deforested.

based. The last hour and a half's walk took us through a mixture of secondary forest—the regrowth after deforestation—and on through agricultural land. The path ended abruptly at the little village of **La Juntas**, where we were plunged back into relative civilization. The village is small, and quite remote, but it has a road.

A pick-up was waiting for us and, after the obligatory bowl of potato soup in one of the village houses, we headed down the road. Our final destination was **Guallupe**, at 1,000m (3,280 feet), on the road and rail track between Ibarra and San Lorenzo. This is where the Cerro Golondrinas Foundation has its main lodge for people working on conservation projects. Looking back across the hills around Guallupe it was obvious just how important the conservation work is. Every hillside was shaved, not a single tree left standing, and huge scars caused by soil erosion were already opening up. Thanks to the foundation, at least some of this forest is preserved and there will be good trekking through fascinating ecosystems for many years to come.

RIGHT En route from Morán to La Cortadera
BELOW A farmhouse on the edge of the forest in the Cerro Golondrinas Reserve
FAR RIGHT Giant vegetation in the subtropical forest.

GOING IT ALONE

WHEN TO GO

The best time to visit the Cerro Golondrinas Reserve is during the dry season from June to September. You can visit at any time of year, but during the wet season (October to May) parts of the trail become extremely muddy.

PLANNING YOUR TRIP

El Angel is served by regular buses from Quito and Ibarra. There is also a bus service between El Angel and Tulcán, which is the border town 6km (3½ miles) from the frontier with Colombia. From Tulcán there are flights to Quito (½ hour) and to Cali in Colombia. You can get to Guallupe on the Ibarra-to-San Lorenzo bus. Ask to be dropped at Guallupe (also called La Carolina, 48km/30 miles from Ibarra), then walk 10 minutes uphill to the foundation's centre, Hostal El Tolondro.

Eliza Manteca, the president of the Golondrinas Foundation, runs a small hostel in Quito. If you are going to tour the country, call in here when you arrive to find out when trips are running. If you have enough people to make up a group, the 4-day trek, or use of the lodges at Santa Rosa and El Corazón, can be arranged at a time to suit you.

Visits to the forest, hiking, and horseback riding can be arranged from the foundation's centre at Guallupe. Visits to the paramo can be organized from El Angel if you enquire at Hostería El Angel.The 4-day trek finishes at Hostal El Tolondro in Guallupe, where you can stay overnight. If you intend to go to Otavalo next you should plan to arrive in Guallupe on a Thursday evening so that you have time to travel to Otavalo on the Friday. Otavalo's main markets are on Saturday, and it is best to be there early in the morning. If you want to go to the coast, Guallupe is on the road and rail track between Ibarra and San Lorenzo. You can take the bus down to San Lorenzo or return the 48km (30 miles) to Ibarra and join the train for the full journey.

FOOD AND DRINK

❑ All meals are provided and included in the trek price.

❑ A cook and guide accompanies the trek and takes care of all lunches and meals at El Corazón Lodge.

❑ Boiled water or tea is brewed up en route to refill your drinking-water bottles.

❑ The villagers en route provide the evening meal and breakfast at Morán, mid-morning refreshments at La Cortadera, and lunch at Las Juntas. These hot meals are local fare, usually potato soups, eggs, rice or bread, yucca (manioc root), plantain (green banana), and plenty of fresh fruit and a variety of vegetables.

VOLUNTARY WORK

The Golondrinas Foundation operates a number of agroforestry projects including reafforestation, education, and scientific research. Volunteers are always needed for these projects. You will be asked to commit to a minimum of three months and to contribute finanically towards your food and lodgings. If you fancy three months of hard work for no pay but all in a good cause, contact the foundation (see Contacts).

ECUADOR

Learning New Skills with the Crafty Otavaleños

By Guy Marks

The people of Otavalo are famed for their skills as craftsmen. On my visit to the markets and the Indian villages I learned about their lifestyle and the local production of textiles, weavings, and a variety of other crafts that have made Otavalo the artisan centre of Ecuador.

Otavalo is 32km (20 miles) north of the equator, in the Imbabura province, at 2,530m (8,300 feet) above sea level. It is set in a picturesque landscape of lakes and hills, overlooked by the magnificent volcanic peaks of Imbabura (4,609m/15,121 feet) to the east, and Cotacachi (4,939m/16,204 feet) to the north. Around the main town of Otavalo, 128 Indian villages make up the Otavalo canton. Of these, 80 are inhabited by true Otavalo Indians, the Otavaleños, while Cayambe Indians predominate in the other villages.

The Otavalo Indian women wear long, straight, dark skirts, white blouses with very little embroidery or colour, dark shawls, and a kind of turban fashioned from a folded scarf. Most of the women wear gold-coloured bead necklaces and red-bead bracelets. The men wear white cotton trousers, dark ponchos, and felt hats, and their black hair is tied in a very distinctive, long, single plait.

The Cayambe Indians from south of Otavalo around San Pablo Lake wear far more colourful clothes, with brighter, more elaborate embroidery on their blouses, and pleated skirts. The men don't wear hats and their facial features are slightly, but noticeably, different from the Otavaleños'. Tradition has it that the Otavaleños are the original inhabitants of the area, and that the Cayambe Indians are Inca colonizers that arrived after a war in the south.

Unlike many of the indigenous groups in other parts of South America, the Otavaleños have managed to maintain their cultural identity while taking an active part in the modern economy. However, despite their ability to adapt to foreign-market demands, their villages are not wealthy, and the communities survive on strong family ties and traditional principles. Each village specializes in particular products, often dictated by local availability of raw materials. This variety of handicrafts and the rich cultural heritage of the villages makes a visit very rewarding.

THE OTAVALO MARKETS

I arrived at Otavalo on a Friday afternoon, on the bus from Ibarra, and settled into the Casa Mojanda, a hacienda-style hotel in the hills just outside the town. Saturday is the main market day in Otavalo, although there is also a smaller crafts market every Thursday. The animal market starts before dawn and is all over by about 9am, so I joined some other guests at Casa Mojanda and took a taxi

This is a cultural experience and does not involve any difficult or challenging activities.

For this itinerary you need to be based in Otavalo, where you can find a range of comfortable hotels to suit your budget.

No specialist equipment is needed, but I would recommend taking a camera with a powerful external flash for taking photographs inside dark workshops.

*Otavalo villages,
Imbabura province*

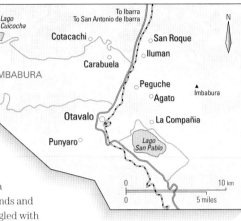

down there before
breakfast. None of
the animals was
tethered or
penned; instead
the owners stood
around holding on
to their prized pig
or cow on the end of a
rope, or they walked through
the crowds herding half a dozen
sheep in front of them. Farmhands and
women in traditional dress mingled with
the crowds and paused at stalls to buy hot
food and chat with neighbours. It seemed
such an informal affair, yet business was
brisk and livestock left the field under
new ownership, crammed into pick-ups
or led by the nose along the road.

After breakfast, back at the hotel, we
set off to browse Ecuador's most famous
market, which attracts a huge number of
national and international visitors. The
main section of this artisan's market is
at **Poncho Plaza**, a central square with
permanent, concrete stalls that look like
giant umbrellas until they are hidden by
a host of hanging garments, blankets,
wall hangings, and textiles. The market's
increasing popularity has resulted in
its outgrowing the square, and it now
spreads in every direction, up the
main street, down side alleys, and
along passageways. Most stalls are run by
local artisans, but the market does attract
traders from outside the region and even
from neighbouring countries. It is the sort
of market that can absorb you all day, and
certainly until mid-afternoon when it
starts to close down. On the edge of the
plaza there's a section selling household
goods and foods, from pottery and
plastics to flour and fresh vegetables.
Elsewhere there are pan pipes and more
pottery, hats, hammocks, and cotton
shirts. The woollen products are the best
local buy, and you can wander for hours
checking out the prices of hand-knitted
jumpers and colourful weavings.

CARABUELA VILLAGE

I spent the next couple of days visiting
the local villages and discovering just
where and how all these market products
are made. For the first day I joined eight
other tourists, from various countries, on
a tour run by a local company called
Zulaytur. I was a bit wary as I thought this
might turn out to be a shopping trip laid
on to coax tourists into parting with their
cash. Nothing could have been further
from the truth, and it turned out to be the
most genuine and comprehensive insight
into the local lifestyle and traditions that I
could possibly have hoped for.

We rattled out of Otavalo in an ancient
minibus driven by Rodrigo Mora, the
owner of the agency, accompanied by
our guide, Jorge Recalde, a local teacher
who speaks very good English. The first
village we stopped at was **Carabuela**,
just outside Otavalo. Here we were
invited into people's homes where families were hard at work, fitting textile
production around their domestic chores.
Every stage of the process—from the
washing of fleece to the completion of the
finished garment—was taking place
somewhere in the village.

The raw wool is bought at other
markets around the country, like
Saquisilí, as well as locally. It is washed
and whitened, then painstakingly carded
by hand, which involves pulling it through
spiky pads to clean it and untangle the

fibres. Little rolls of carded wool are then spun into yarn on a large handpowered spinning wheel. It all looks very easy, but if you take the opportunity to have a go you'll discover just how much strength and skill is needed. The yarn is dyed mainly with natural pigments made from walnuts, cochineal, and indigo, and then the knitting and weaving processes begin.

The old village houses are built of mud bricks, and wooden beams support tiled roofs. Reed mats cover the dirt floors and

LEARNING NEW SKILLS WITH THE CRAFTY OTAVALEÑOS

the planking in upper-storey rooms, and strings of maize cobs hang from the rafters (the driest place to store grain). Inside the dark rooms families sit surrounded by heaps of wool—whether it is raw fleece, balls of yarn, or piles of part-finished jumpers—working steadily at carding fleece, spinning yarn, and knitting jumpers at breakneck speed. The

LEFT Felt-hat making at Iluman
BELOW The artisan market at Poncho Plaza

products are destined to be sold at the market stalls as part of massive export orders met by co-operative wholesalers.

BASKET-MAKERS AND HATTERS

In the little village of **Punyaro** we were introduced to an 88-year-old man who was sitting in the shade on a reed mat outside his house, making traditional baskets just as he has always done. He uses dried mountain bamboo, which

ECUADOR

ECUADOR

first has to be soaked in water to make it flexible enough to work. With all the dexterity of a man a quarter of his age he stripped the bamboo into long flat lengths, holding one end in his lips and using a sharp knife to part the fibres. In a matter of minutes he had woven the flat strips together to produce a small rectangular basket. He makes any number of these to fit perfectly one inside the other, and the resulting sets are used by market traders as measures.

We returned to Otavalo for lunch in a local restaurant. I tried the *ceviche*, a delicious cocktail of raw fish, prawns and other seafood marinated in a piquant sauce made with lime, onion, and fresh chillies. Our tour continued with a visit to **Iluman**. This is a village of hatters, and nearly all the felt hats in the country are produced here.

Once again there was no attempt to sell us anything; we were just shown the family workshops where the hat-making process can be seen. Layer upon layer of carded wool is compressed by hand on a dampened hotplate over glowing coals.

The steam that's produced shrinks the wool fibres; and after constant beating and further shrinking the fibres form felt, which is then shaped over wooden moulds while it's wet and laid out in the sun to dry off.

Finishing the hats is another new skill, which involves brushing the felt and then smoothing it with a hot iron over a damp cloth. The very finest hats take many hours of hard work. Every part of the country has its own style of hat, and all the different types are made here. On this particular day they were producing rough-looking sombreros, like huge Mexican hats, and fine, black, flat-topped hats, like the ones worn by Spanish bullfighters and flamenco dancers, which were destined for Cuenca in the south of the country.

A ROOM WITH A LOOM

In **San Roque**, Iluman's neighbouring village, weaving is the main activity, and it appears that every house has a room with a loom. The first workshop we stopped at was producing sisal sacks. The sisal fibres are produced from a type of agave plant, which has long fleshy leaves like a yucca plant. The extracted fibres are then sold in huge bundles and, like wool, have to be carded and spun to a workable yarn. It is much rougher and tougher than wool, though, so instead of using hand-held carding brushes they pull the bundles through a set of large nail-like spikes sticking out of a fixed wooden block. The first piece of mechanized machinery that we'd seen all day was a crude electric motor, which had been rigged up to run a simple mechanism for spinning the sisal fibres. At the other end of the room there was an upright wooden loom, on which cloth was being woven. This was anything but mechanized—every row of thread was woven by hand. At least there was no pattern to be woven, and the simple cloth was being used purely to make sacks.

Further down the hill, in the same village, the hand looms are put to a more complex use. Here, the decorative wall

PONCHO PLAZA

The first dedicated artisan market in Otavalo started in 1870. At that time it was decreed that only foodstuffs and medicines could be sold on a Sunday, so separate livestock and artisan markets were held on Saturdays. The current structure of the Poncho Plaza was built in 1972 by the Otavalen Institute of Anthropology, and funded by the Dutch government. Because of the recent influx of non-artisan stalls and goods from outside the Otavalo region, plans are now underway to open a new Poncho Plaza, one block northwest of the present location. This will be designated as a museum market, selling only traditional local artisan goods.

BUYING CRAFTS

The Otavaleños are not pushy salesmen. They price their goods at a level that provides them with a fair return for the work, and most items are inexpensive and good value. If you haggle over prices you may find a little leeway, but not much. The prices in the villages are similar to those in the market, but in the villages you are afforded the added pleasure of meeting the craftsmen and seeing the work being produced. The choice may be more limited than it is in the markets.

hangings that I'd seen in the market are made. Using different coloured wool, the weavers produce all manner of intricate patterns, some geometric, others stylized representations of animals or rural scenes. What amazed me was how the weavers, working just from a picture or from memory, know exactly where to place the different threads.

Throughout the tour, Jorge did an expert job of giving us background information on the village lifestyle and traditions, as well as explaining the practical skills that we were watching. By the end of the day we had seen a huge variety of crafts, and yet had sufficient time to drop into **San Antonio de Ibarra**, about 20km (12 miles) north of Otavalo. This village specializes in making decorative carvings from hardwoods. Many of the pieces have a religious theme, while others are abstracts and studies of the human form. We visited several galleries in the main square, many of which incorporate workshops where you can see the carvings being shaped from hunks of solid timber.

A PRIVATE TOUR

There were still some things I wanted to see in the Indian villages, and the next day I headed off with Rodrigo Mora, the owner of Zulaytur. He is a real expert on local culture and anthropology, and has a

deep-rooted desire to see the traditions of the Indian people survive. He sees tourism as one of the ways to maintain interest in hand-production of local goods, and mechanization as a threat to the cultural traditions. His enthusiasm for his subject is overwhelming, but I found it a little difficult to keep up with his torrents of flowing Spanish.

Driving through the village of **Peguche**, Rodrigo suddenly brought the old minibus to a grinding halt. He had spotted two women rolling up miles of cotton thread on the playing field in the centre of the village. Rodrigo was ecstatic, for he had been sure that high-velocity machines had superseded all the hand skills in this village. The woman took us to see the loom that she used and explained that she was weaving braid, which was all due to go to Colombia to make the cross-straps for sandals. A little further up the road, at a village called **La Compañia**, Rodrigo took me to a house where a woman was embroidering a decorative pattern onto a panel of white cotton. This would be used as part of a blouse.

Later in the day he showed me what was going on at the edge of the villages, outside the workshops. There were women down at the river, washing wool and laying it out on the banks to dry, and farmers busy sowing their fields by hand. They were multicropping—placing maize and several different types of beans in the same field. He showed me everything I asked to see, and a whole lot more that I would never have found without a guide. Lastly, at my request, he took me to **Agato**.

WEAVING FOR THE ÉLITE

I had read about Agato, a small village to the east of Peguche, and I was keen to visit it. One of its inhabitants is the very famous Miguel Andrango, who is revered as a master weaver. He is especially notable because he is one of the last craftsmen still to be using the backstrap loom, which originated in the Andes and

pre-dates the upright, wooden-framed loom that was introduced by the Spanish. The backstrap loom consists of an assortment of sticks and strings attached to a post and held taut by a strap that passes around the weaver's back. Weaving with this loom is very slow and tedious, but the results are of extremely fine quality. Andrango uses only natural dyes. His work has found international acclaim, and it is exhibited most years at the folkloric art exhibition at the Smithsonian Institute in Washington, U.S.A. He has used this fame and wealth to set up a co-operative and school for backstrap weaving, and to build a showroom next to his house where you can buy his work. Of course this high-quality work takes a long time to produce so it is considerably more expensive than other locally made weavings.

If you are a real enthusiast for fine weavings, it is impossible to spend time in Otavalo without visiting Andrango's showroom, especially if you are planning to buy fine pieces. If, on the other hand, you want to find out about the lives and traditions of the Otavaleños, be welcomed into their homes, shown their uncomplicated lifestyle, and learn how dozens of different artisans work, then your best bet is to avoid Agato and to rely on people like Rodrigo Mora to take you around these wonderful villages.

GOING IT ALONE

INTERNAL TRAVEL

Otavalo is one of the most easily accessible places in Ecuador. It is 90km (56 miles) north of Quito, the capital, on the country's main road, the Panamericana.

Buses from Quito cost about $3 and the journey takes only a couple of hours. Buses leave at regular intervals all through the day. Buses run regularly between Otavalo and Ibarra, as well as to the outlying villages.

If you want a door-to-door service, or to go directly from Quito's international airport without having to go into the city, you can take a taxi for as little as $30. In Otavalo, taxi rides around town, out to the villages, or to the hacienda accommodation, are inexpensive. There is a central taxi rank in the main plaza at the top of Calle Sucre.

WHEN TO GO

The vast Saturday market means that Otavalo is busiest at the weekend.

Hotels are often fully booked up on a Friday evening so it is advisable to make a booking in advance or to arrive early in the day if you want to stay in a particular hotel.

PLANNING YOUR TRIP

The tour to the villages runs frequently, but not every day: it is dependent on the number of people requiring a tour and the availability of a guide to run it, for the guides who speak English work part-time on a freelance basis. So long as you let Zulaytur know your requirements in advance you will be able to arrange a tour. However, don't expect to walk straight in off the street and to arrange a tour on the same day.

Agencies in Quito offer day trips to the market and can organize transport, accommodation, and excursions for you.

Otavalo is en route from Quito to Ibarra, so it is an ideal stopping point if you are heading for the cloud forest at Golondrinas, or the coastal route to San Lorenzo, or going north to the Colombian border.

ACCOMMODATION

There is a wide choice of accommodation in and around Otavalo. If you are staying in Otavalo for just one night, choose a hotel or hostel in the centre of town as these are convenient for walking to the market and local restaurants. They are mainly budget and mid-range establishments.

If you are planning on a longer stay it is well worth paying the extra money to stay in one of the haciendas, of which there are several within a few miles of town. These places, converted from old farmsteads, have lots of character and large comfortable rooms, and in their rural setting they offer a tranquil retreat from the bustle of the busy town.

You can usually make arrangements for such activities as horse riding and long walks from the haciendas.

LEFT The backstrap loom used by Miguel Andrango, the master weaver whose workshop we visited BELOW The woman in La Campaña embroidering a decorative coloured pattern onto a panel of white cotton

LOCAL WALKS

The area around Otavalo is great walking country. If you have the time, you could walk to the villages rather than taking a tour:

❑ Peguche is less than 3km (2 miles) north from Otavalo. It is Otavalo's nearest village, and takes an hour's walking to reach.

❑ Peguche to Iluman is 3½km (2 miles), and San Roque is a further 2km (1¼ miles).

❑ Peguche to Agato is 3km (1¾ miles).

❑ There is a waterfall 2km (1¼ miles) south of Peguche.

Cruising the Galápagos Islands

By Guy Marks

The Galápagos Islands are like a giant zoo, where you can walk amongst unique wildlife that has no fear of man, and swim with exotic marine life in crystal-clear, azure waters. If you are a nature lover, the Galápagos can offer you one of the most exciting experiences that you are likely to find.

The Galápagos Islands are right on the equator, in the Pacific Ocean, 1,000km (621 miles) west of the Ecuadorian mainland. The volcanic archipelago is made up of 22 main islands and dozens of tiny islets spread over an area of about 50,000sq km (19,300 square miles). Five of these main islands are over 500sq km (193 square miles) and two between 100 and 200sq km (38 and 76 square miles). Nearly 85 percent of the archipelago is a national park. The islands are well controlled and protected, and there are set visitors' sites which you can visit only with an official guide. Only a few islands are inhabited by man, the main towns being Puerto Ayora on Santa Cruz

 The walks organized at all the visitors' sites on the islands are easy. The snorkelling can be challenging if you are not a strong swimmer, and the Galápagos are not a suitable place for inexperienced scuba divers.

★★ On a tourist-class boat or better, you can expect good food and comfortable accommodation. Sailing boats and motor-sailers tend to have more character, but the cabins and facilities are quite small and compact; the motor-yachts may be slightly more roomy.

 Snorkelling gear is often available on the boats, but it is wise to take your own equipment or hire it in Quito. Scuba divers must check what equipment is being supplied on board. Bring the best photographic equipment you can afford as the opportunities for close-up wildlife shots are unparalleled. Bring more film that you could possibly need—you'll use it.

and Puerto Baquerizo Moreno on San Cristóbal.

On an eight-day cruise that followed a fairly typical circuit, I visited a number of sites on ten different islands. From Quito I flew, via Guayaquil, to the archipelago's main airport on Baltra Island. The island is military owned, and when you touch down the place seems bare, hot, and inhospitable. We were met by Monica, our naturalist guide, and the crew from the boat. A short bus journey took us to Baltra's port. Our boat, *The Sulidae*, was a wooden-hulled motor-sailing vessel, shaped like an old galleon, with black and gold paint that made her look more like a pirate ship than a cruise yacht. She certainly had more character than anything else in the bay, and my nine fellow passengers and I immediately felt we had made the right choice.

A NEW WORLD

Soon after we arrived Alejandro, an excellent chef, served us a rich lunch—fish in garlic and coriander, and potatoes in a white sauce with bacon, followed by succulent fresh pineapple. We upped anchor, and motored away, to **Las Bachas Bay** on the north coast of **Santa Cruz Island**, just a half-hour hop from Baltra. The little landing crafts are called *pangas* here, and ours was a small wooden boat in keeping with *The Sulidae*. Some of the sites have small landing platforms so that you can step out of the *panga* onto dry land; at others you have to climb out of the boat in the shallows of a beach. This one was a wet landing, and for those who didn't tackle it properly it was a very wet landing.

We didn't have to go looking for the wildlife; it was immediately all around us. Magnificent frigatebirds (*Frigate magnificens*) were flying overhead, brown pelicans (*Pelecanus occidentalis*) were cruising the beach, gliding just a few centimetres from the ground and dive-bombing the shallows for mouthfuls of fish; and blue-footed boobies (*Sula nebouxii*) flew higher and then plunged at breakneck speed to make their catch. Bright-red crabs, quaintly named Sally Lightfoot crabs (*Grapsus grapsus*), danced on tiptoe along the rocks; the translucent, pale ghost-crabs (*Ocypode* species) gingerly emerged from holes in the sand and disappeared like a shot as they detected the slightest movement. Lava lizards (*Tropidivius* species) darted about, and marine iguanas (*Amblyrhynchus cristatus*) basked in the sun.

In just a couple of hours on Santa Cruz we saw the world's rarest gull, the lava gull (*Larus fuliginosus*); greater flamingos (*Phoenicopterus ruber*) filter-feeding as they wandered through a shallow lagoon, giant opuntia cactus trees (*Opuntia echios*), and stands of black mangrove, whose leaves excrete little crystals of salt as the product of an extraordinary self-desalination process. We even had our first go at snorkelling in the bay to see stingrays (*Urotrygon* species) and other exotic marine species. There was life everywhere, and Monica elaborated on habitats, life cycles, and behaviours, the interaction of species, the plants and algae, and even the geology of the sand on which we stood.

SOUTH PLAZA

The first night was not the best night's sleep I've ever had. It took some time to become accustomed to the rocking of the boat, the noise of the boat's generator working all night, and the chugging of the engines and clank of anchor chains as we left our mooring at four in the morning, destined to arrive at the tiny island of **South Plaza** by breakfast.

A dry landing at seven in the morning brought us face to face with the first of many sea-lion colonies that we would see over the next few days. There were hundreds of these magnificent beasts (a subspecies of the Californian sea lion, *Zalophus californianus*), and this particular island is a great place to observe their social structure.

The females and young lie close together; mothers suckle cute, furry pups; and the dominant males spend all their time defending their territory. These huge bulls swim in the shallows, protecting their young and their harem of females. They are continuously on the move, constantly making a noise to ward off aggressors. "It's their job to bark all day," said Monica. And because this job requires such energy and vigilance, they don't have time to feed, and so they gradually lose condition. This is when other males will come in and challenge them for their territory. The non-dominant bulls live apart from the others in a bachelor colony at the other end of the island. They spend all their time feeding and working out, walking up and down the steep cliff where they've sited their colony. A few months of this and they are then in perfect physical shape, and ready to challenge the dominant bulls.

For visitors, the bachelor-bulls' cliff is a good spot to do a little birdwatching. Swallowtail gulls (*Creagrus furcatus*) and masked boobies (*Sula dactylatra*) fly overhead, and red-billed tropicbirds (*Phaethon aethereus*) with long, white tail plumes nest in the cliff. Also prolific on this island are land iguanas (*Conolophus pallidas*), giant, rather sinister-looking creatures whose light bodies stand out against the pioneering red sesuvium (*Sesuvium portulacastrum*), a short, bushy succulent that covers much of the island.

TOP The Sulidae, *moored in the bay by Sombrero Chino Island, and (INSET RIGHT) sitting down to Alejandro's excellent supper*

ABOVE *A close encounter with a giant Galápagos tortoise at the Charles Darwin Research Station at Puerto Ayora*

Iguanas can spend many hours—or even days—sitting motionless under *Opuntia* species cactus, waiting to feed on their fallen fleshy pads.

PUERTO AYORA AND THE GALÁPAGOS GIANT TORTOISES

Our next destination was **Puerto Ayora**, the main town at the southern tip of Santa Cruz. The crew took the opportunity to stock up on basic supplies, fresh vegetables, and fruit, most of which has to be imported from the Ecuadorian mainland. The town has a few hotels and bars, and shops that seem to survive on T-shirt sales. It is where most people stay if they are not going on a cruise, or if they are flying in and arranging their itinerary once they get to the Galápagos.

Puerto Ayora is also the location of the **Charles Darwin Research Station**, which is just on the edge of town. The station has an information centre for the national park, and puts on displays and slide-shows about the Galápagos in general and the work of the Darwin station in particular. You have to pay a large national park entrance fee when you first arrive at the Galápagos, but, strangely, none of this is allocated to the research station despite its prime functions of conservation and education. The station is a non-profit-making charity, and all their funds have to be raised independently.

The most publicly visible side of the station's work is their captive breeding programme for the Galápagos Giant Tortoise (*Geochelone elephantopos*). These massive beasts can weigh up to 300kg (660 lb). Eleven subspecies still exist, with different-shaped shells relating to the habitats and islands where they evolved. The two main types of shell are categorized as dome-shelled or saddle-back. Some of these subspecies are right on the edge of extinction, notably a single specimen from Isla Pinta famously known as Lonesome George. George is over 100 years old and, unfortunately, no mate can be found for him. A couple of similar females have been introduced, but to no avail.

They have had better luck with some of the other species, and estimate to have released around 1,800 tortoises between the start of their programme in 1965 and the year 2000. You can see the growing-pens where dozens of different tortoises of all stages are being raised for eventual release. One of the larger pens houses half a dozen adult individuals that have been rescued from a life as pets. One of them was found being used for target practice, and his shell carries the scars of several bullet holes. The whole pen is a bit of a sorry sight, but it is the best chance to get close to these animals and appreciate just how big they are. You can see them in the wild in the highland interior of the island except when they go down to the arid regions for the annual breeding season. They leave between January and February; the males return in July, while the females return after their egg-laying in August. They can also

be seen on Isabela Island—especially if you hike the Volcán Alcedo between June and December—but only very long cruises or specially arranged tours include this in the itinerary.

We did go up to the highlands on Santa Cruz the following morning, and it was really quite a different experience seeing these huge, dome-shelled tortoises walking through farmland rather than confined in concrete pens. We also got the chance to visit the pit craters, where huge sections of the Earth's surface have collapsed and sunk, and to visit the Scalesia forest, which is a moss-clad, highland forest full of unusual birds such as the vermilion flycatcher (*Pyrocephalus vubinus*) and the short-eared owl (*Asio flammeus*).

SANTA FE AND GARDNER BAY

We left Puerto Ayora to arrive at **Santa Fe Island** in the late afternoon. Here you'll find an interesting, yellow subspecies of land iguana, which is unique to this island, and rice rats (*Oryzomys bausri*), like overgrown hamsters, which are also endemic. But the main reason for coming to this island is simply that it is en route to **Española** (also known as Hood), one of the most interesting islands in the archipelago.

That evening we dined on fresh prawns in a rich sauce, rice, deep-fried cauliflower, and green bean salad, before sailing for most of the night to reach **Gardner Bay** at Española by morning. We started the day with a walk on the beach, watching and photographing sea lions at close quarters, and observing Hood mockingbirds (*Nesomimus macdonaldi*), which are so friendly that they'll peck at your shoes or land on your head. After a quick return to *The Sulidae*, we headed out in the *panga* to a rock called **turtle rock**. This is a brilliant snorkelling site, and just one of many that we stopped at over the course of the cruise. The marine life is spectacular and can be appreciated even without using scuba equipment. Along the submerged rockface there are hundreds of colourful fish. Amongst the most striking of these were the vividly bright azure parrotfish (*Scarus compressus*), which grow up to 60cm (2 feet) in length, and have beak-like mouths that enable them to bite off pieces of coral. There were large, dense shoals of the yellow-tailed surgeonfish (*Prionurus laticlavius*), and king angel (*Holocanthus passer*) fish, whose bright-orange fins and tail, and white vertical stripe, contrast vividly with the black body. Green turtles (*Chelonia mydas*) swim past, and even the odd shark—like the Galápagos shark or rare hammerhead shark (*Sphyrna lewini*)—can be seen at some sites.

The marine life is certainly as much a part of the attraction of the Galápagos as the terrestrial life is. Indeed it plays a major part in the whole experience, for the crew of the smaller boats cast their fishing lines while cruising in open water, and fish served with rice are frequently on the menu. Of course, it is most likely to be a king fish, jack fish, or tuna, rather than an exotic species, that ends up on the dinner plate, and for this particular day's lunch Alejandro served up grouper in yet another of his excellent sauces.

IGUANAS, ALBATROSS, AND BLUE-FOOTED BOOBIES

On the other side of the island we moored at **Punta Sears** and made a dry landing for what turned out to be the best walk of the trip. Here at the landing site, the bright-red crabs stand out in perfect contrast to jet-black rocks. Marine iguanas (*Amblyrhynchus cristatus*), their black skin mottled with patches of red and green, pile themselves onto the rocks, and onto each other. These iguanas—the only true marine lizards in the world—are about 100cm (40 inches) long and can weigh several kilos. There are different subspecies in the archipelago, but the ones here at Española are the most colourful, for they keep some of their red mottling

POST OFFICE BAY

Post Office Bay on Floreana Island is the most visited site in the Galápagos. And yet it is not the wildlife that attracts such attention, but an old barrel that serves as a postbox. In the past, ships would stop here to leave letters and to pick up any that were destined for a place on their route. This informal mail service is continued today by those who honour the tradition by leaving three-dimensional graffiti—like the name plates from their boats—or depositing postcards in the hope that someone from their country will take it home and deliver it. My own postcard took just six weeks to reach England—not bad without a stamp!

throughout the year while most of the subspecies are black except in the breeding season.

We followed the path away from the iguanas and into the nesting sites of masked boobies and—the Galápagos Islands's most famous inhabitants—the blue-footed boobies. You are not allowed to stray from the path, and the guides make sure that you don't touch the animals or upset them in any way. However, since the birds are not easily disturbed, and often make their nests right in the middle of the path, you can in any case get right up to them for close-up photographs. Of course, you mustn't use a flash, as this may upset them, but if the weather isn't too cloudy there is every chance of getting a good shot of a bird either sitting on her eggs or dancing comically on bright-blue, webbed feet.

As if the boobies weren't interesting enough this is also a massive nesting site for waved albatross (*Diorineda irrorata*). These magnificent birds soar through the air on long, slender wings with an elegance that belies their heavy weight; but then, when it comes to take-off and landing, they are amusingly clumsy. To launch themselves they use

ECUADOR

*LEFT The sinister-looking
land iguana is a frequent
sight on South Plaza
BELOW A view of the
Galápagos from the peak
on Bartolomé Island
RIGHT One of the
vibrantly coloured,
dancing Sally Lightfoot
crabs encountered at Las
Bachas Bay
on the north
coast of Santa
Cruz*

what can only be described as a runway, which is located near the top of a cliff. Along the runway they lumber heavily, gradually picking up speed until they fall off the end and into the air where they can demonstrate their aerial mastery. Landings are equally inelegant and appear to be entirely down to chance: with wings flapping stiffly and bluish legs flailing, they tumble to the ground and lumber to a halt with all the grace of a disabled aircraft.

Their courtship is fascinating, and involves a complex dance of side-stepping and neck-twisting, then meeting face to face with clacking and duelling beaks. Once again, all this activity takes place within a few feet of the path, so there is every opportunity to photograph them; but if the albatross are your priority you should note that the majority leave the site around mid-December and do not return until late March.

ECUADOR

VOLCANOES AND LAND CREATION

Wherever you go in the Galápagos you are always aware of the extraordinary geology. These are volcanic islands, which are constantly changing and still very active. The landmass of the islands is new in both geological terms and real time. This means that it is possible to see how the islands have been created and how the volcanoes have produced strange geological formations and unusual landscapes, and to learn about the various stages of the long process of colonization by plants and animals.

At **Floreana** there are underground lava tunnels that link the sea to an inland lagoon. On **Sombrero Chino**, an island shaped like a Chinese hat, you can see lava tunnels above ground, their flows of solidified magma folded in ropes and knots to form a brittle black crust. On **Santiago**, layers of volcanic ash have compacted to form a soft brown rock called tuff, and subsequent flows of black lava have run across it. At **Bartolomé**, as you climb to a high viewpoint, you pass pioneering plants, such as lava cactus (*Brachycereus nesioticus*), and the spreading *Tiquilia nesiotica* growing out of solid rock. From the top you can look across to **Santiago Island** where you can clearly see a 100-year old lava flow whose path into the ocean engulfed small islets that now stand like isolated chess pieces on a flat black sea.

The view from Bartolomé helped me to put the Galápagos Islands into perspective: as I looked out over the bay and the distant topography, it became fully apparent just how different one island is from the next, which is of course the reason why the Galápagos is able to support such a vast array of animal and plant species.

Before heading back to Baltra airport on the last day, there was time to fit in an early-morning visit to North Seymour Island where there is a nesting colony of magnificent frigatebirds. In a fascinating courtship display, the male frigatebirds

OF THE ORIGIN OF SPECIES

Charles Robert Darwin, the son of a physician, was born in England in 1809. Soon after graduating from Cambridge, he accepted an unpaid position as naturalist to HMS *Beagle*, which was destined for a five-year voyage to chart the Pacific coast of South America. The observations he made about the specialized nature of the species on the different islands of the Galápagos influenced his work and helped him develop his theory of evolution. He recounted his experiences on the expedition in his book, *The Voyage of the Beagle*. Years later, in 1859, he published the controversial work for which he is primarily known, *The Origin of Species by Natural Selection*.

were exhibiting their huge, balloon-like throat pouches to attract the females while, close by, some blue-footed boobies tended to their chicks in nests on the ground. Like so many of the other animals that we'd seen that week, both the boobies and the frigatebirds were completely indifferent to our presence. It is this tolerence of man that makes the islands so very attractive to visitors. In the past, such a lack of fear might have been the animals' downfall; but not so today. For now that these unique islands and their wildlife are so well protected, the interest and revenue that the animals generate by allowing such close observation ensures their continued survival and success.

Just as they were in Darwin's day, the Galápagos are a living laboratory where you can see the principles of evolution at work and the birth of new land in the raw. And you can be sure that whichever islands you are able to visit, at whatever time of year, you are guaranteed an experience of a lifetime and an adventure into a delicate and awe-inspiring ecology.

GOING IT ALONE

INTERNAL TRAVEL

Two airlines operate flights from Quito via Guayaquil to the Galápagos Islands. TAME flies to Baltra island, just off the northern tip of Santa Cruz island. There is a bus service from the airport via a ferry to Puerto Ayora, the main town; the journey takes about 2 hours. SAN-Seata flies to San Cristóbal island. The airport is on the outskirts of the main town, Puerto Baquerizo Moreno.

A passenger ferry operates between Puerto Ayora and Puerto Baquerizo Moreno, but this is not a daily service so you need to check locally for the return schedule.

WHEN TO GO

You can visit the Galápagos at any time of year, but cruise boats offer a slightly less expensive, low-season rate May, June, September, and October. Wildlife can be seen all year round, but since breeding and nesting seasons are different for each species there is no time that is perfect for every-thing, and you should check if you have a particular interest in seeing something specific. The rainy season is from January to May, and the dry season from June to December. There can be heavy downpours in the rainy season, though there should still be sunny periods. In the dry season mists and cloud are common. It is warm all year around, but it is hottest in the rainy season, particularly in February, when temperatures may soar well above 30°C (86°F). If you are not good on boats, you might like to take into consideration that the sea can get very rough between August and October.

CHOOSING A CRUISE

Going to the Galápagos is expensive, but it would be a pity to spoil this wonderful experience by economizing on the cruise. You may come across horror stories about poor service and badly maintained boats, some of which have even been known to sink, so travel with a reputable company, and avoid economy services. I travelled with Angermeyer's on the tourist-class *The Sulidae*, and it was an excel-lent cruise in all respects. Angermeyer's operate a number of other tourist-class and deluxe yachts.

The smaller yachts, with space for 10 to 16 passengers, go to a wider variety of visitors' sites and are more appropriate to the environment than the large cruise ships from which 40 or 80 passengers might land on an island at the same time.

Boats have a fixed itinerary, which is set annually. If you are particular about the islands and the species of wildlife you want to see, you will need to find a boat with a suitable itinerary. If diving is your priority, you must inform your tour operator, as most boats have scuba-diving facilities only on certain departures. Their itinerary for that tour will normally be a specialist diving-orientated cruise.

There are generally 5-day and 8-day trips. The first and last day is taken up almost entirely by travelling to or from the mainland, so take the 8-day cruise if time and money permit.

SCUBA DIVING

Scuba diving around the Galápagos Islands is very exciting and rewarding, for there is a huge variety of spectacular marine life. You have a choice of live-aboard diving boats, or day trips from Puerto Ayora. It is, however, not a suitable place for inexperienced divers. There are dangerous currents and challenging underwater topography. There is no decompression chamber on any of the islands and you are 640km (400 miles) from the mainland.

PLANNING YOUR TRIP

The national park area is so vast, it is impossible to visit all the sites in a single trip. The best way to get a good overview is to take a cruise around the islands, travelling by night and visiting new sites each day. If you base yourself in one of the hotels at Puerto Ayora or Puerto Baquerizo Moreno, you will be able to arrange day trips to various islands. However, you should be aware that the visitors' sites within range of a day trip are very limited, and a lot of time is spent getting to and from the islands. This is not the best way to see the Galápagos, but it is the only option if you can't find a cruise or don't want to sleep on a boat.

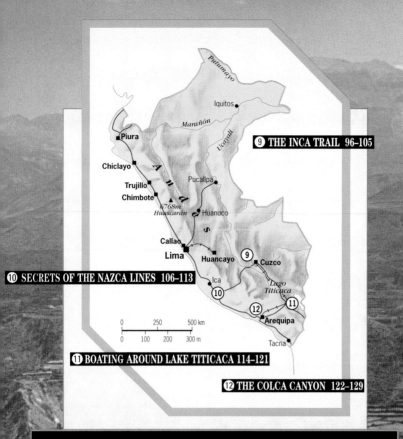

Map labels: Putumayo, Iquitos, Marañón, Ucayali, Piura, Chiclayo, Trujillo, Chimbote, Pucallpa, 6768m Huascarán, Huanuco, Andes, Callao, Lima, Huancayo, ⑨ Cuzco, Ica, ⑩, Lago Titicaca, ⑪, ⑫, Arequipa, Tacna

0 250 500 km
0 100 200 300 m

PERU

Peru has three radically different geographical areas, each with its own climatic conditions. The massive range of the Andes, the backbone of the country, is rich in natural features—rivers and volcanoes, and the world's deepest canyon among them—as well as in cultural interest provided by modern Andean societies, colonial architecture, and the archaeological legacy of the Inca Empire. To the east of the Andes is the jungle of the Amazon Basin, the world's largest tropical rain forest. And to the west, between the mountains and the Pacific Ocean, is the narrow strip of largely desert coastal plains where you'll find today's capital city, Lima, and the extraordinary archaeological sites at Nazca in the south and at Chan Chan in the north. For the adventure traveller, Peru offers a variety of exciting activities on foot, on horseback, and in water, and ample opportunity to gain a fascinating insight into some unique cultures, both ancient and modern.

Terracing near Chivay in the Colca Canyon

PERU

A Trek through Time on the Inca Trail

By Guy Marks

Cusco— founded by a bygone civilization and still rich in Andean traditions— is the cultural centre of Peru, and the Inca Trail is one of the world's most exciting treks. The high-altitude trail takes you through an ever-changing mountain landscape to emerge at the Sun Gate above Machu Picchu, the lost city of the Incas.

Cusco is the most popular destination for visitors in the whole of Peru. It is set high in the Andes in a fertile valley at an altitude of 3,310m (almost 11,000 feet), and surrounded by spectacular mountain scenery. The mountains, and the rivers that run through them, are an idyllic place for walking, horse trekking, and rafting, but it is the area's extraordinary history that makes it such a big attraction.

Cusco was once the seat of the Inca Empire and became the Incas' capital city in A.D. 1438 under their emperor Paracuti. He wasn't the first to settle in the valley (the original town was founded by Manco Capac, the first Inca emperor, in A.D. 1200), and he was almost the last, for the Spanish conquistadors under Pizarro's command arrived in 1533. A year later it

officially became a Spanish colonial city and, though it still had an Inca governor, it was divided among Pizarro's men. Over the following years Cusco and the Inca fortress Sacsayhuaman, located on a hill overlooking the city, were to be the venue for many a battle. These power struggles were not just between the Incas and the Spanish, but between different factions of the Spanish themselves. The most devastating was the battle of 1536: 1,500 Incas were killed, and those that remained—the last members of the Inca civilization—retreated into the jungle at Vilcabamba. They stayed there until the final defeat in 1572, when their leader, Tupac Aymaru, was publicly executed in the centre of Cusco by the Spanish viceroy Toledo.

The Incas were known for their impressive architecture. They developed a system of carving massive, multiangled stone blocks with remarkable precision. Although these were all of irregular shape they interlocked perfectly, and they were used to build incredible walls that would withstand the considerable seismic activity common in the Andes. However, the Spanish had their own ideas about architecture, and in the process of defeating the Incas they dismantled most of their temples, fortresses, and fine buildings, and pilfered the stones for use in new building. The colonial architecture of the 16th and 17th centuries was equally impressive with extravagantly baroque churches, ornate wooden

3 This is quite a tough four-day trek but it can be tackled by anyone of any age who has a reasonable degree of general fitness. The altitude makes the going very slow and tiring, but the days' distances are planned to accommodate even the slowest walkers.

★★ The degree of comfort you experience on this trek will depend on the standard of service you book and the equipment you bring. You can walk the trail unaided, carrying all your own food and equipment, or you can employ a range of services from simple portage to luxury safari-style camping.

 A pair of good walking boots is essential. Carry warm clothes and waterproofs at all times as the weather can turn cold and rainy without warning.

*The Inca Trail to
Machu Picchu*

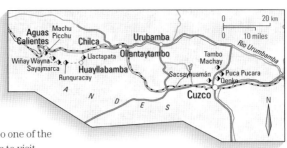

balconies, and
covered walkways
with arched
porticoes flanking
the central square.

This chequered
history has made Cusco one of the
most fascinating places to visit.
Though the Incas have long since gone,
their stonework underpins the colonial
city and their cultural legacy underpins
today's tourist industry.

ARCHAEOLOGICAL SITES

I spent several days in and around
Cusco exploring the cultural heritage
that is in everything from the ancient
archaeological sites to the modern-day
traditional Andean markets. You need at
least a couple of days just to investigate
the narrow alleyways that climb steeply
in every direction from the **Plaza de
Armas**. Architectural gems await you
around every corner: the Cathedral and
La Compañía Church on the Plaza, the
ancient Inca walls in Hatunrumiyoc
Street, and the small, hidden Spanish
courtyards overlooked by balconies
draped with hanging geraniums, which
you will find in residential suburbs such
as San Blas, are only a few.

In every street in the centre of
town, there are artisan shops selling
handcrafted goods—weavings, hats,
Andean musical instruments, pottery,
and the ubiquitous jumpers made from
alpaca wool. The alpaca is a thick-haired
relative of the llama, the local beast of
burden and source of meat. Women in
traditional costumes walk the backstreets
with their laden llamas, still using them
for their daily chores, while the more
commercially minded pose with them for
photos in the Plaza de Armas.

Cusco retains a very genuine Andean
atmosphere while at the same time
managing to cater for tourists' needs.
There is no shortage of good hotels and
restaurants, and bars like the Cross Keys

on the Plaza de Armas are a magnet for
international travellers. In fact this was
the first place I headed for when I arrived
on the train from Puno.

The surrounding area is as fascinating
as the town, and I spent a very pleasant
afternoon on horseback visiting the
archaeological sites. The tour included
the weird ceremonial rock at Qenko, the
natural springs at Tambo Machay, the fort
at Puca Pucara, the hidden inner cave at
the Temple of the Moon, and the fortress
at Sacsayhuaman. This site comes to life
each year on June 24 when thousands of
people gather to watch Inti Raymi, the
annual re-enactment of the Inca winter
solstice festival. These ruins alone would
be reason enough to visit the area, and yet
they proved to be only a taste of what was
to come when I walked the Inca trail to the
most famous of sites, Machu Picchu.

WALKING IN THIN AIR

Walking at altitude is easy if you find the
right balance—the point at which the
oxygen you are inhaling from the air is
equal to the oxygen your body is using for
the level of exercise.

❑ Don't try to keep up with others; walk
for yourself.

❑ Take very small steps at a constant
slow speed rather than spurting ahead
and having to stop to catch your breath.

❑ If you have enough breath to sing, you
could walk faster; if you can't even talk,
you need to walk slower.

PERU

INTO THE SACRED VALLEY

It was raining when I boarded the bus at 7am to join the group going from Cusco to the start of the Inca Trail. But for a couple of nationals who were on holiday from Lima, everyone was European. Within an hour of setting off, we were dropping steeply down towards the river and the fertile land that was once the stronghold of the Inca Empire—a spiritual place known as the **Sacred Valley**.

At the town of Urubamba, we stopped briefly for breakfast before continuing to **Ollantaytambo**, where a huge, terraced Inca fortress and temple site, once used as an Inca stronghold after the fall of Cusco in 1536, clings to the hillside at one end of

LEFT Boarding the bus at Cusco
BELOW The bridge over the Urubamba at the start of the Inca Trail

the town. Here, the Sacred Valley and the main road end. A dirt track continues, past the km 77 marker at Chilca and on to km 82 (see Going it Alone, page 105). Beyond this point is just the end of the track and a narrow suspension bridge across the Urubamba River.

The camping equipment, luggage, and food were unloaded, and the porters started their unenviable task of packing it onto their backs. We started walking at about 10:30, crossing the river to the start of the Inca Trail. For the first hour or so we passed through flat, sparse woodland where traveller's joy, or "old-man's-beard" (*Clematis vitalba*), hangs from twisted limbs of trees. Tall, spindly cactus, as thin as a pencil and with bright, orange and yellow flowers, grows up between the lower branches; and clumps of yellow flowering broom (*Cytisus scopartus*) add to the colour.

Occasionally we came across small dwellings, stone and adobe houses with thatched roofs and the smoke of cooking fires wafting from their glassless windows.

PERU

HORSE TREKKING

Horse trekking is not allowed on the Inca Trail itself, but there are a number of other trails through these mountains. One such is a five-day walking and riding trek that starts at Ollantaytambo and takes you through the Vilcabamba mountains, finishing at Llactapata. From there you pick up the train to reach the final destination of Machu Picchu. Other treks range from a half-day ride around Cusco's outlying archaeological sites, to two- or three-day rides through the Sacred Valley.

By midday we had come upon the first of many upward slopes, a gentle but steady incline as the path wound between low stone walls. It was still drizzling, but the rain held off while we broke for lunch and we never really got soaked that day.

The first Inca site on the trail was **Llactapata**, a vast fortress clinging to the hillside and strategically placed to afford the inhabitants extensive views along the Cusichaca and Urubamba rivers. Agricultural production from the layers of steep, stone terraces may well have kept the population at Machu Picchu in food supplies.

AN UPHILL STRUGGLE

For the next 24 hours the trail took us ever upwards. We left the Urubamba and followed the Cusichaca River until mid-afternoon when we reached a fork in the valley. In true Inca style this, too, was guarded by a fortress, **Huayllabamba** (which means grassy plain). The supporting stone wall of this fortress was restored in the mid-1990s, but little else remains of it. Today there is a village at Huayllabamba, where you can camp and—if you have come ill prepared for the trek—hire the services of a porter.

Our path took us on through a gorge-like valley, always steep, with the river running below us. At about four o'clock we came to a campsite at a place called Yuncachimpa. The Inca Trail is busy and, like most of the camps I saw, a number of different groups were using the same site. While the porters helped put up the tents, the cooks prepared hot soup, rice, and a tasty dish of potatoes, onion, and tomatoes. It had been a tiring day, and we had climbed nearly 545m (1,800 feet) in altitude. I slept well despite rain pelting the tent all night.

By morning, the rain hadn't stopped, and the site was a quagmire. Some unfortunate people I met were walking the trail with a cheap tour company. Their tents were poor and the service was bad. A night spent in inadequate shelter had left them soaking wet and miserable and, despite being on a trek that was a once-in-a-lifetime experience, they turned back and headed for the comfort of Cusco.

The rain eased a little after breakfast, and we set off on the trail once more. We were soon into a forest of twisted, gnarled trees hung with moss and vines, and following a path partly paved with stone steps. The swollen river gushed through the gorge beneath us, while the rain dripped through the canopy and settled on the ferns and orchids on the branches and the forest floor.

We emerged from the forest at another official campsite, Llulluchapama, about an hour and a half's walk from Yuncachimpa. From here the scenery changes to grass-clad hills, and the climb gets ever steeper. This is the approach to the first pass, **Warmiwañusca** (meaning dead woman's pass), which at 4,198m (13,773 feet) is the highest point of the trail. The path is wide, well maintained, and made of compacted gravel with a few sections of stone steps. Despite this, progress is definitely an uphill struggle, and for the last 20 minutes to the top the stone steps seem to go on forever. At the top, the mist was closing in, but on a clear day I know the views from here are spectacular, and the guides will usually point out your route through the mountains.

WARMIWAÑUSCA TO WIÑAYWAYNA

The path down from the pass was even steeper than the one going up, and within an hour we had dropped over 500m (1,600 feet) to the Pacaymayo Valley. Most of this section is paved with stone, and it was the first time that I really felt I was walking on an old Inca road. A great deal of this path has been carefully restored, but it seemed incredible that the Incas had gone to so much trouble to lay a perfect path by hand through remote mountains.

The poor weather had enabled everyone to walk quickly without overheating, but it meant that we had spent very little time sitting looking at the scenery. Our fast progress brought us ahead of schedule, and when we arrived at Pacaymayo it was only the middle of the day. The heavens opened as we had our lunch, and as an afternoon of walking in heavy rain didn't appeal we decided to sit out the storm and set camp at Pacaymayo, which is one of the more developed camp grounds, complete with modern toilet facilities. I'm glad we did, for the following morning brought bright sunshine. There was renewed enthusiasm from everyone as we set off uphill again towards the second pass. More stone steps led to the interesting ruin of a fortress called **Runquracay**. It was easy to understand the Incas' reason for building it in this position, for the ruins afford you a panoramic view of both the valley below and the high pass we had crossed the day before.

The second pass at 3,860m (12,664 feet) brought the best mountain views we'd had on the whole trek. You could see for miles to distant, snow-capped peaks of the awe-inspiring Vilcabamba range.

The rest of the day was mostly downhill in terms of the altitude but certainly not in terms of enjoyment. We visited **Sayamarca** (meaning inaccessible town), and, to my mind, these are the best set of ruins on the trail. The town is precariously perched on a rocky platform, and the stone structures that remain are a jumble of split-level houses, stone steps and twisting walls, and a semi-oval, fortified enclosure with trapezoidal windows that afford magnificent views of the Aobamba Valley. It is accessible only at the one entrance point, which is reached via a steep, narrow, stone staircase that branches off from the Inca Trail.

From the fortress we returned to the trail and walked on through miles of cloud forest. The vegetation had changed radically from exposed, high grassland to forest filled with bamboo, thick shrubs, trees with bromeliads and orchids on their branches, and banks of orange and red mosses that oozed fresh water in a steady trickle.

It was late afternoon when we arrived at **Wiñaywaynan** and were jolted back into a social atmosphere. There is a small hotel here, near another impressive Inca site, but more importantly there is a bar.

PISAC MARKET

One of the best and most colourful Andean markets is at Pisac, 30km (19 miles) from Cusco, in the Sacred Valley. One section of the market is predominantly for the locals, selling cooked food, fresh vegetables, clothes, and household wares, while the other is aimed at the tourists, and sells local handicrafts and textiles. There are small markets every day; but the main market is on a Sunday, when you can also look out for the local ceremonies. The church is attended by an array of village elders, *Varayocs*, who wear distinctive costumes and carry a silver-capped baton of authority. They are accompanied by young boys who also wear colourful traditional costume, and who herald the *Varayocs'* arrival by sounding conch-shell horns.

PERU

PERU

There were dozens of walkers here, some who had walked the Inca Trail, and some who had taken the short cut up from the railway at km 104 that same day. There was a party atmosphere, but not a late night as we were all planning to get to the Sun Gate for dawn.

LEFT Pisac Market, and (RIGHT) one of Pisac's village elders in traditional costume BELOW The culmination of the trek: Machu Picchu, the extraordinary lost city of the Incas, seen from the Sun Gate

P E R U

INTI PUNKU AND MACHU PICCHU

There were already the first signs of daylight as we left Wiñaywayna at just after 5am. I'd been told that it took about two hours to get to **Inti Punku**, the Sun Gate, which meant I'd be hard pushed to get there for dawn. The trail is officially closed before five o'clock, though, and quite rightly so: it's narrow, potentially slippery, and hard work, and it would be dangerous in the dark. I pushed on and was rather surprised to find myself climbing the last few steps to the gate just 50 minutes after setting off. The path is flanked by geometrically cut stones, the remnants of Inca buildings. At the top I joined the many people who had gathered there, sitting silently in the cold of the morning and looking out over this incredible sight. The view was all I could have hoped for. Down below me, perched on a ridge that protrudes into the Urubamba Valley, was **Machu Picchu**. As the sun came up, the long shadows moved and the sun's rays picked out the city's features. Little by little the splendour of the site was revealed.

This extraordinary city was rediscovered by American archaeologist Hiram Bingham in 1911. At that time it was overgrown with jungle, and to all intents and purposes it was lost to the world. Now that it is cleared, the full extent of the city can be seen. Stone-walled terraces tumble away from the cliff sides like giant stairways. Near a central square stand rows of houses with peaked gables that once supported thatched roofs but now sprout wild begonias between their stones. Alleyways lead to split-level temples, sacred stones and altars, and to strange buildings whose twisted structures incorporate the living rock.

No one really knows the story behind this mysterious city—which appears to have been occupied and abandoned within the space of 100 years—but there are many semiscientific, and some fantastical, theories. Some say that Machu Picchu dates from way before the Inca period, and some even attribute its creation to extraterrestrials, but the architectural style of the stonework is late imperial Inca (i.e. after 1438). The purpose of the city and the reason for its decline are not understood. One school of thought suggests that it was a temple occupied by priestesses, the Virgins of the Sun; certainly the high proportion of female skeletons that were unearthed gives credence to this idea, but evidence of death from venereal disease casts a shadow over the notion that they were virgin priestesses. Other theories suggest it was the capital of a breakaway republic that was brutally destroyed by the Incas and erased from oral history, which would explain why the city was "lost" by the time of the Conquest. Hiram Bingham was convinced that the city was a fortress for strategic defence, but it is now generally accepted that it was an administrative, ceremonial and spiritual centre with important links to agricultural production.

We watched the sun rise over Machu Picchu on the morning of the fourth day, and I'm sure that having walked the Inca Trail to get there enhanced every magical moment. It is so overwhelming that by the time you walk down to the ruins from the Sun Gate all you want to do is sit and stare. It takes several hours of exploring the ruined city with a guide to even start to appreciate what you are looking at.

I walked, I watched, and I pondered, and finally I'd seen all that I could take in. I took the minibus that winds its way, via hairpin bends, to the town of **Aguas Calientes** (Hot Baths) in the valley below, 8km (5 miles) from Machu Picchu. After a pizza and a beer I headed for the hot baths that give the town its name. I sat steaming in hot water from the natural thermal springs, soaking away the aches from my long, and sometimes cold, wet walk. I hadn't a care in the world except the one big decision: should I take the four-and-a-half-hour bone-rattling train journey back to Cusco, or jump on the helicopter and be back at the Cross Keys pub in time for happy hour?

GOING IT ALONE

INTERNAL TRAVEL

There are daily direct flights into Cusco from Lima, Arequipa, and La Paz in Bolivia. Since all flights in and out of Cusco are morning flights, connections with other destinations in Peru or international flights often mean an overnight stay in Lima or Arequipa. Aero Continente operate several internal flight routes. LAN Peru also offer a limited number of routes. Be prepared for time changes, delays and cancellations.

Several bus companies operate throughout Peru. The journeys are often long and overnight, but the services are inexpensive and connections can be made with all major towns.

There is a train to Cusco from Puno via Juliaca that runs on Mondays, Wednesdays, Fridays, and Saturdays.

WHEN TO GO

You can walk the Inca Trail at any time of year, but it is best to avoid the wet season from November to March. In the mountains, however, rain is quite likely even during the dry season, and there may be dry days in the wet season.

TRANSPORT BETWEEN MACHU PICCHU AND CUSCO

A railway runs from Cusco to Aguas Calientes, the town below Machu Picchu. It used to continue to Quillabamba but it was washed away in 1998 and is not being replaced. Travel on the local train costs $6 and, although the train is less crowded than it was, there is still no guarantee of a seat for the 4- or 5-hour journey. Pullman coaches, which used to run as a separate tourist train, have now been added to the local train and are worth the extra $12. The *autovagon* is a separate train, providing a first-class service. This train takes about 3½ hours and costs about $55 return. Helicusco operates a 24-seater helicopter from Cusco to Aguas Calientes. The flight takes just 25 minutes and costs $75 one way. A minibus operates between Machu

AVOIDING EXPLOITATION

Most of the porters that work the trail do so to earn some much-needed extra income in between working on the land. They are fit and accustomed to the altitude, so they can carry an astonishing amount of weight. However, there are unscrupulous companies that have little respect for their environment and take advantage of the porters. You can minimize the risk of unwittingly supporting exploitation by using a company that is a member of APTAE, the Peruvian Association of Tour operators of Adventure and Ecological tours. APTAE gives guidelines for the employment of porters, and tackles some of the ecological issues arising from the influx of tourism.

WHERE TO START THE INCA TRAIL

Originally the Inca Trail would have linked Cusco and Machu Picchu, but the trail today starts from the Urubamba Valley. There are starting points at different places along the valley, and these are referred to by their km markers, the number being the distance from Cusco.

❑ Km 77 is in the village of Chilca. It is the most accessible starting point, and both public and private transport can get here on a dirt track. It is, however, the furthest point from Machu Picchu and therefore the longest walk.

❑ Km 82 is 5km (3 miles) further down the dirt track. Many private companies bring their vehicles to start the trail from here, which saves a bit of walking on the first day.

❑ Km 88 is a rail station on the north bank opposite the ruins at Llactapata. You can take the train to this station and then walk across a suspension bridge to join the trail at Llactapata.

❑ Km 104 is just 6km (3½ miles) from Aguas Calientes. An "express Inca Trail" can be done from here in one day. It doesn't follow the conventional path but climbs steeply to Wiñaywayna, where it picks up the Inca Trail for the last couple of hours' walk to Machu Picchu.

PERU

Exploring the Secrets of the Nazca Lines

By Guy Marks

In the southwest of Peru is one of the world's most extraordinary sights. Etched into the desert floor are mysterious designs so vast that an aerial view is necessary if you are to see the shapes that their outlines depict. I took a light plane over the pampa to see these unexplained geoglyphs for myself, and then went on to visit historical sights where I could learn about the ancient civilization that created them.

Nazca is a quiet little town on the edge of a vast, flat, desert plain known as the *pampa*. Here on the pampa are the Nazca Lines, although they might be more accurately called the Nazca ground-drawings or geoglyphs; for along with the thousands of lines, there are geometric shapes, spirals, animals, and anthropomorphic figures, all drawn in giant proportions on the desert floor. Archaeologists have come up with a number of theories about the purpose and origins of the drawings, but since none has found a definitive answer the lines continue to be one of the most baffling enigmas of archaeology.

I approached Nazca from the north along the Pan-American Highway, which runs the length of the Peruvian coast and, indeed, the length of the

South American continent. I'd taken a private vehicle down from Lima; but there are plenty of buses, and you might like to stop at Paracas (see box, Going it Alone, page 113) en route.

About 20km (12½ miles) before the town I stopped at an isolated metal tower

 This is an exciting cultural adventure, and does not require you to do anything more difficult than sit in an aeroplane or walk around historical sites.

★ Your only discomfort on the trip may be motion sickness in the light aircraft, as the pilots tend to swerve and roll the planes to facilitate your viewing the lines.

✕ If you intend to photograph the Nazca Lines from the plane, it is essential that you use fast film in your camera; you will need an ISO rating of at least 200.

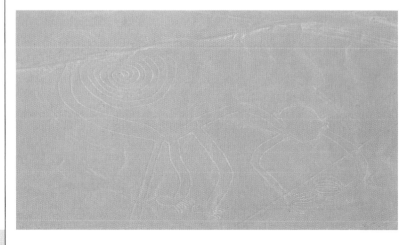

at the side of the road. It is surrounded by bare desert, which stretches away on either side of the road. There appears to be nothing to see, so it is hard to believe that this tower is set in the middle of the Nazca lines.

The tower was erected by Maria Reiche (see box, page 109), who made this noble gesture because she believed that everyone should have an opportunity to view the lines without charge. Contrary to her intentions, the tower has been adopted by a couple of guards who make a nominal charge for using it. The tower is only 14m (46 feet) high, and yet the moment you start to ascend it the desert floor is transformed. It is immediately apparent that you are right in the midst of these famous drawings. In fact the view

LEFT The famous drawing of the monkey
BELOW Ariel view of the mystical spiral at Cantalloc, near Nazca

PERU

from the tower is one of the saddest, for it is apparent that the highway below you cuts right through the centre of one of the figures—a giant lizard about 85m (280 feet) long. Directly in front of the tower there are a couple of more complete figures. One is said to represent a huarango tree, which is a local hardwood whose branches become thickened and twisted as it ages, a bit like a large juniper. The other—a peculiar shape with two large feet—is sometimes described as a frog, and sometimes as a bird.

Two kilometres (1¼ miles) further down the road, a small natural mound has been marked as a mirador. From the top you can see that dozens of straight lines cross the mound and radiate from it. Clearly this point is of some significance, so why the Instituto Nacional de Cultura (National Institute of Culture) allow people to trample all over the delicate lines is perhaps as big a mystery as the lines themselves.

FINDING A PLANE

I arrived in Nazca at about midday and checked into the Alegria Hotel. With this remarkable wonder of the world on its doorstep you would expect Nazca to be thronging, but I found very few tourists, and none of the hotels seemed busy. However, my most immediate concern was to organize a flight over the lines.

Everyone and his brother owns a small plane and offers flights, so competition is high. I made my arrangements with Alegria Tours, or, more precisely, with a man in the Alegria Tours office who seemed to be taking the business elsewhere. I wasn't sure if his involvement was legitimate, and I wondered whether I was about to be ripped off. When I expressed my concern, another character in a beaten-up old car was summoned, and I was taken to the airport just outside of town to inspect the plane. It looked like any other light plane to me, so how would I know if it would fly? I was introduced to the pilot and told

---

PUTTING THE LINES INTO PERSPECTIVE

I met travellers who had been to Nazca and not bothered to take a flight over the lines. Certainly you can see a couple of the drawings from the metal observation tower 20km (12½ miles) north of town, but this is nothing compared with the overall view from the air. This giant drawing board is about 50km (30 miles) long by about 14.5km (9 miles) wide, and there are about 13,000 different lines, trapezoids, spirals, and figures, spread over an area of 700sq km (270 square miles). One of the longest straight lines stretches nearly 14km (8¾ miles) across the pampa. The largest drawings of animals are of a stylized pelican 300m (1,000 feet) across, and a bird with a zigzag neck measuring 285m (935 feet).

---

that for 100 U.S. dollars I could have the plane to myself for the 45-minute flight. This was about twice the going rate for a group flight, which would mean sitting in a plane with three other people vying for the best window space. I made the deal, arranging to fly early the next morning, and parted with my money. Back in town I thought better of it and wondered if I would ever see the man again, but it was too late now.

In the morning my heart sank at the sight of a hazy mist, which would make it difficult to see the lines and would therefore scupper my flight plans. To my relief, though, the old banger rolled up outside my hotel at the appointed time. After some shoulder-shrugging and intuitive assessments of the mist, the flight was rescheduled for mid-morning.

AN AERIAL VIEW

I climbed aboard the single-engined plane, and we were soon rattling along the runway and up into the now-clear sky. Within moments we had cleared the town and the irrigated fields, and reached the barren desert plain. Below me I could see the famous markings, which had been made by removing the top layer of stone to reveal the lighter-coloured ground beneath. At first sight, some of the huge, trapezoid and straight lines crisscrossing the desert look like airport runways, whilst others are seemingly infinite in length as they disappear on the horizon. The co-pilot waved his arms and pointed excitedly at the ground as we approached each of the giant drawings. The circuit took in the most famous of the animals—the spider, the monkey, and the hummingbird—and at first they were difficult to make out as I wasn't sure what angle I was seeing them from. Then the pilot would swerve, banking the plane steeply and circling the drawing, until the right perspective was found and the geoglyphs suddenly came into focus.

As we flew over the observation tower I'd been to the day before, I could clearly see the images I'd struggled to comprehend. At the edge of the pampa, where the flat land reaches the hills, there is a drawing of a man, his outline clearly picked out on a hillside. He has big round eyes and has been nicknamed the owlman. I was so absorbed by the pictures below me that I hardly noticed the potentially unsettling, violent motions of the plane. All too soon the circuit was complete and we were back over Nazca and safely touching down on the little runway.

LOOKING FOR AN EXPLANATION

I was baffled, intrigued. The aerial view was like being let in on a secret, shown a work of art that only the privileged—in this case the airborne—can see. The experience made me more inquisitive about the origins of this masterpiece. I wanted to know how and why such a feat would be undertaken by an ancient culture that wouldn't even be able to view their own handiwork.

There are no answers. The lines have never been adequately explained. In the town, I searched for information. When Maria Reiche was alive, she—and latterly her sister Renate on her behalf—gave free lectures every evening recounting the extraordinary tale of her work on the pampa. Her theory was that the Nazca Lines are an astral calendar: certain lines match the rising sun's rays on solstice days, and she was also able to relate some of the drawings to known constellations. It was her belief that these lines were constructed over a great deal of time, perhaps started by the Paracas culture in 900 B.C. and continued by the Nazcas from A.D. 200 until A.D. 600.

Since Maria's and Renate's death, it has become increasingly difficult to find out about the theories of Nazca, which somehow adds to the great mystery. At the far end of town I found a new museum under construction, so perhaps the situation will soon be rectified. It

MARIA REICHE

Maria Reiche was a German-born mathe-matician and archaeologist who devoted her life to the study and preservation of the Nazca Lines. She can be credited with bringing the lines to the attention of the world, though the lines had first been seen in 1926. Dr. Paul Kosok of Long Island University discovered the ground drawings, introduced Maria to the phenomenon, and handed his work over to her in 1939. After the Second World War, she came to live in Nazca and to start her investigations, which involved plotting out the lines from ground level. No one was more amazed than she was when her first map revealed a 46-m (150-foot) drawing of a spider. Single-handedly, Maria Reiche continued her work right into her senior years. She died in Nazca at the age of 95 on June 8, 1998.

is being built by the municipality in conjunction with Joseppi Orrefice, an Italian archaeologist who has been working on excavations of Cáhuachi, a nearby ceremonial site from a pre-Nazca civilization.

At the other end of town, close to the Pan-American Highway, I followed some signs advertising lectures on the lines. They led me through a tumbledown backstreet to a private house where Viktoria Nikitzki lives. She is an Austrian-born teacher who came to Peru many years ago and ended up working with Maria Reiche in drawing up one of the most comprehensive maps of the pampa yet to be made. In her front room she has a large-scale model of the area, and, by giving lectures, she tries to carry on Maria's work of heightening local and global awareness of the site.

WATERCOURSES AND CEREMONIAL SITES

I spent many hours with Viktoria as she talked me through some of the more recent theories. She explained how David Johnson, an American archaeologist and water-resource expert, has come up with a correlation between the lines and underground watercourses. He suggests that the lines are a chart showing where every underground stream runs. He further suggests that the different shapes have definite identifiable meanings. A

BELOW The cemetery at Chauchilla, and (RIGHT) one of the exposed graves

long triangle, for example, identifies the source of an underground stream, whereas a zigzag pattern means that there is no water below. His work is in the early stages, but perhaps it will one day lead to a full understanding.

I went with Viktoria to see one of the canals that still serves Nazca today. These aqueducts never run dry, and it is clear that the pre-Colombian culture's understanding of water resources is what enabled them to settle and become agriculturists in this desert environment. For $20 I hired a car and driver, and we set out to Cáhuachi on the far western side of the pampa. Covering some 24sq km and (9¼ square miles), Cáhuachi is thought to be the biggest adobe ceremonial site ever found. It dates from about 500 B.C., and its occupation and use

spanned a period up until A.D. 350 when there may have been some natural disaster. The area was abandoned, and the people moved to the present town site where the Nazca culture developed until its demise in about A.D. 800. The excavations carried out over the past 17 years have been extensive but, since there is no finance to preserve the site and keep it open, the archaeologists cover everything up again after each investigation, leaving nothing much to see except windswept mounds and the odd adobe wall.

THE NAZCA GRAVEYARDS

One of the greatest sources of information about the Nazca people has been the gravesites that have been uncovered near the town. I say "uncovered" because they have quite literally been dug up and their contents plundered and left strewn about the desert. The day after my trip to Cáhuachi I joined a tour to one such site at Chauchilla. When the cemetery was discovered in the 1970s it had already been robbed and some 800 mummified corpses left scattered about. Recently a team from the Nazca municipality has tidied the place up, excavated some graves, and returned some of the mummies to their resting places.

It is a very strange experience to see 1,200-year-old corpses sitting in an open pit with their textiles and pottery shards around them. The bodies were originally preserved with lime and cotton, placed in the foetal position, and then dried. The mummies were then wrapped in textiles, put into funerary pots, and placed in the graves in a sitting position facing the rising sun in the east. Now, with the pottery broken and the mummies exposed to the elements, the long braided hair and tattooed skin is falling from the bones, turning to dust, and leaving sun-bleached skeletons.

Originally each grave had three levels: the first was left empty, the second contained the mummies, and the third was kept for the person's possessions. It is these possessions that have revealed so much about the culture, but they have also attracted grave-robbers. Even today this site—a tourist attraction by day—is left wide open by night, unfenced and unguarded. Over the past decade, most of the 2,000 or so mummies that were dug out of the various gravesites around Nazca have disappeared.

NAZCA POTTERY

Luckily not all the ceramics from the graves have gone forever, and that afternoon I got the chance to see some original pieces. My tour itinerary included a visit to a pottery demonstration, where we were given a brief outline of the history of Nazca ceramics. Alberto Segura, the potter, showed us how the pots were made and how the different shapes had evolved over the ages. All the colours were made from mineral dyes, and a gloss effect was achieved by using a pebble to polish the finished piece.

The decoration on the pots reveals much about the Nazcas' culture and their evolution. The earliest examples were decorated with drawings of natural things such as hummingbirds, while the later ones show the introduction of anthropomorphic figures. As Alberto showed us each stage of the process, he would reach for a piece of pot or a complete vessel from the dusty shelf behind him. I was astounded to find out that these demonstration pieces are originals. It is incredible that 1,000-year-old pottery can be knocking around a potter's workshop rather than locked away in a museum. For me, this epitomizes the continuing enigma of the Nazca culture. An ancient civilization creates the most extraordinary geoglyphs in the world, and now the modern civilization busies itself with dissembling and dispersing the last remnants and clues left by a vanished people. I left Nazca with more questions than I'd arrived with, but gratified by the knowledge that I had seen these wonders before they disappear forever.

GOING IT ALONE

GETTING TO NAZCA

A flight over the desert is an important part of the Nazca experience, but actually getting to Nazca by plane is not a good option. The only planes that fly to Nazca are those operating day trips from Lima or Ica, and these run only when they have enough passengers. A day trip isn't enough to do the place justice, and yet no one has thought to operate a one-way flight to allow you to spend longer in Nazca. Most people travel to Nazca by road, and tour companies use their own private transport. Frequent but tedious bus services run from Lima (6 hours), and from Arequipa (10 hours).

WHEN TO GO

Nazca has a desert climate with almost no rain, and it is these conditions that have helped to preserve the lines for so many centuries. The summer months from December to March are the hottest, but the area is never cold. You can therefore plan a visit at any time of year.

ORGANIZING YOUR SIGHTSEEING

It is easy to organize your activities when you arrive at Nazca. Local tour companies offer flights and half-day and full-day tours to the major attractions, and their guides are multi-lingual. If, however, you want to go to Cáhuachi or select your own itinerary, you will need a private guide and transport. Several driver/guides hang around outside the hotels and tour offices. They are inexpensive, but often their English is poor and their knowledge of the sites is limited. It is best to get a recommendation from the hotel, or make private arrangements through a tour company.

FLIGHT PRICES

Many small companies operate planes from Nazca, so competition for business is fierce. The companies undercut each other, bringing prices lower and lower until no one is making a profit. At that point all the prices go back up by mutual agreement and the price war starts again. This can mean dramatic and sudden fluctuations, so you cannot rely on information you may pick up from other travellers. You won't know the current price until you are in Nazca.

TIME TO FLY

It is best not to tie yourself down to a specific time of day for your flights over the lines. For a clear view of the pampa, the early mornings are usually best, before the heat haze builds up. However, there is often an early-morning mist in the months from April to November, and since this doesn't lift until about 10am you need the option of taking a later flight.

HEALTH MATTERS

The Nazca area can be fiercely hot and there is no shade near the gravesites, so you should protect yourself with sunblock and a hat. Drink only bottled water, which is widely available throughout Peru.

WHAT TO DO AND SEE

- ❏ Take a flight over the lines (this is essential).
- ❏ Visit the gravesite at Chauchilla.
- ❏ Drive out to the observation tower (mirador).
- ❏ Visit the Maria Reiche museum.
- ❏ Take a look at the aqueducts and canals.
- ❏ Go to a pottery demonstration.
- ❏ Tour Cáhuachi, the adobe temple complex.
- ❏ Visit the Nazca museum.

MOVING ON

South of Nazca there is very little to see along the coast. Most travellers head for Arequipa as their next port of call. All the buses from Nazca to Arequipa are nightbuses. About 140km (87 miles) north of Nazca is the town of Ica. Here the main attraction is the Museo Regional, which houses a fantastic collection of pre-Columbian textiles, ceramics, and grave artefacts. Another 70km (43 miles) north is the town of Pisco from where it is possible to organize trips to the Paracas Nature Reserve and the Ballestas Islands, where you can view bird and marine life.

PERU

Boating Around Lake Titicaca

By Guy Marks

Lake Titicaca is on the altiplano, *the Andean high plain that straddles the border between Peru and Bolivia. I visited pre-Columbian archaeological sites on the lake's shores, and took a two-day boat trip around its intriguing and culturally independent islands— the floating reed-islands of Uros and the remote islands of Amantaní and Taquile.*

Lake Titicaca is considered to be the highest navigable lake in the world. There are higher lakes, and any lake is navigable, but the fact that an international shipping lane crosses its waters has earned it this recognition. There are two main ports on the lake: Puno on the Peruvian side, and Guaqui on the Bolivian side. There is currently no passenger service from port to port, but the shipping lane is still a major route for cargo vessels, and links landlocked Bolivia to the Pacific coast. Puno's close proximity to the land border with Bolivia has made it commercially important, but it retains all the character of a frontier town. It is the capital of the region, and it was from here that I set out to explore the area. I arrived from Arequipa on the short flight to Juliaca, and from there took a *colectivo* (shared minibus) for the 40-minute ride into town.

Puno was founded in 1668, by the Spanish colonizers, near the site of a settlement that had grown up around a silver mine. A few colonial buildings can be seen in the centre of town, notably the cathedral in the main square and the nearby San Antonio Church. Though the town dates only from the 17th century, the area has a far longer history of human activity. The Incas originated on the islands of Lake Titicaca in A.D. 1440, taking over from the Colla and Lupaka

 This itinerary does not require a great deal of physical activity but, as the lake is at an altitude of 3,820m (12,533 feet), even short walks can be tiring.

★ It is a long, cold journey out to Amantaní Island, and the waters can be rough. The boats are not built for passenger comfort. Accommodation on Amantaní is very basic, with no electricity, and beds usually consist of no more than a thick, reed mat laid on a stone platform.

Bedding is provided at Amantaní, but for comfort and warmth take your own sleeping bag.

ABOVE One of the stone towers that entomb mummified bodies at the ancient burial site of Sillustani
BELOW The bright-green duckweed that floats on the water in Puno Bay makes it seem more like a bowling lawn than a lake

peoples. They in turn had followed the Tiwanaku Empire which ruled until A.D. 1200. Even today the outlying villages are notoriously independent; they have many different lines of tribal heritage, each with its place in the long history of power struggles and superiority.

I would see just how different those cultures were when I got out to the islands. First, though, I wanted to take a look at some of the shoreline's archaeological sites that had stood testament to earlier occupations.

CHUCUITO AND SILLUSTANI

All the tour companies in town offer trips to Chucuito, but I found that they run only occasionally—when there is enough interest to get a group together. They were, however, able to offer me a private trip by taxi with a guide.

The journey to Chucuito village is 18km (11 miles) following the shoreline

PERU

south of Puno. The archaeological site at Chucuito is almost engulfed by the modern village and isn't signposted, so a guide is essential. The site is the remains of a fertility temple that dates from the time of the Lupaka civilization, which ruled the area from A.D.1200 to 1450, prior to the Incas. It consists of a 3-m (10-foot) stone wall enclosing an open courtyard with a single entrance. Inside, the courtyard is completely filled with stone phalluses about 60cm (2 feet) tall and arranged in neat rows, some facing upwards and some apparently burying themselves into the ground. The main altar is an upright phallus about 1.5m (5 feet) tall. Little is known about the ceremonies and rituals of the Lupaka culture, and even the present arrangement of the phalluses is just guesswork by the archaeologists. It is certainly worth a visit, and the old colonial town is picturesque, with a row of archways in front of a church, and the remains of ornately carved, stone doorways to public buildings in the centre of the town.

PRESERVING A CULTURE

The Uros Indians have been criticized for making themselves and their floating reed-islands into a tourist attraction. However, their culture is under threat in a rapidly changing world, and the money that they earn from tourism provides a supplement that helps the population to maintain its traditional lifestyle. For example, with the introduction of large wooden boats and outboard motors, reed boats had almost disappeared from the lake; but when the islanders realized that tourists would pay to ride on a reed boat a few were built for that specific purpose. This may seem a little contrived, but it keeps the art of reed-boat building alive and ensures that the skill is not lost forever.

Far more is known about the history of the ancient burial site at Sillustani, my next port of call on an afternoon tour. Sillustani is perched on a hilltop, 33km (20½ miles) north of Puno, on a peninsula extending into Lake Umayo. The hilltop is covered with stone burial towers, some of which are 12m (40 feet) tall. Mummified bodies wrapped in cloths called *chullpas* were entombed in these towers, and the structures themselves are now referred to as *chullpars*. The site at Sillustani was first established by the Colla civilization—which ruled at the same time as its southern neighbours, the Lupakas—and continued to be used by successive civilizations, each of which adapted and refined the towers to their own style. The progression from crude piles of rock in the early Colla period to the carefully crafted stone masonry of the Inca period can clearly be seen. It was only the arrival of the Spanish conquistadors that put an end to the culture and the use of these extraordinary tombs.

ONTO THE LAKE

At nine o'clock in the morning I joined a group of some 25 travellers for a two-day boat trip to the islands. We had booked individually through a number of different agencies which pool their clients to make up a full boat. We were a mixed group from several different countries in Europe, as well as from Israel, Australia, the Americas, and Peru. Tito, our guide, was an expert linguist. Along with Spanish he was fluent in English and the local Indian dialects of Quechua and Aymara; and when the situation warranted it he even managed to throw in the odd words of Hebrew, German, French, and Italian. The boat was a simple wooden motor launch, with a sheltered cabin and a small open deck at the back where the boatmen clung firmly to the rudder for the entire duration of the trip.

Puno's bay looks more like a bowling lawn than a lake, for it is covered with a layer of bright-green duckweed. The boat chugged out of the harbour, parting the weed and leaving a trail of brown water in its wake. Once out of the immediate area of the harbour, though, the water cleared and we were soon approaching the famous tortora reedbeds. The boat picked its way through the navigation channels that flow through the reedbeds out towards the open water and, about 45 minutes after we had left Puno, we came to the floating reed-islands of Uros. These islands are the home of the Uros Indians, to whom the tortora reeds are an integral part of life. They have built entire islands by matting together layer upon layer of floating reeds, which are anchored to the growing reedbeds by the occasional wooden pole driven into the mud below.

THE UROS CULTURE

The Uros have always been fishermen using boats made from tortora reeds, but tradition has it that they permanently took to the lake centuries ago to avoid persecution during the struggles for power in the time of the Collas. They tied several boats together to form a raft on which they could live; as the boats rotted they added fresh reeds to the surface. Over the years the platforms expanded bit by bit and gradually became small islands. The practice still continues, and even today you can see islands with discarded reed boats incorporated into their foundations.

For many generations the Uros have lived as an independent tribe, making a living by fishing and hunting for birds, and trading their catch with the shore-dwellers. Over the course of time there have been occasions when a rise in water levels has put the substructure of the reedbeds out of reach and forced the Uros to abandon the islands. During their periods on the shore they integrated with the Aymara people who lived there, and it could be said that their ethnic identity was diluted. Some people go so far as to say that there are no longer any true Uros

Indians. Nonetheless there are still some 3,500 people living on 42 islands, and they maintain their traditional way of life by providing fish for the 120,000-strong population in Puno. On the small proportion of islands visited by tourists, the people have capitalized on their artisan skills to earn a good income from selling decorative textiles, pottery, paintings, and ornaments to the visitors.

Our visit to the reed-islands was brief, but it was long enough to gain an insight into the Uros' unique way of life. It was a strange sensation to walk on floating reeds. Rows of women sit with their wares laid out before them, but behind this commercial façade life goes on as normal: there were fish laid out to dry, being smoked over glowing embers; black pots of water boiled over fires contained in pottery hearths; and men and women sat mending their fishing nets.

SETTLING IN ON AMANTANÍ

For the next three hours after our visit to the islands of Uros, we were on the water, slowly making our way to Amantaní island. The lake becomes quite choppy once you pass the peninsulas that protect Puno Bay. Amantaní is a real island made of rock and soil, and has a population of about 4,000. We were to stay with the Incatana people, one of eight communities on the island. On arrival at the little harbour Tito allocated us to different families, making sure that travelling companions were able to stay together. Then we were led off by our eager hosts to their houses on the terraced hillside.

My host was a charming old lady called Venedicta. Her family had grown up and left home, so now she had ample space for visitors. The house consisted of three separate buildings constructed of stone, mud brick, and adobe plaster, set around a small courtyard that was cobbled with a pattern of black and white pebbles, and contained by a mud-brick wall that had a low doorway but no door. Two of the buildings were little more than

prepared some food for us while we inspected our accommodation, which was basic, to say the least. Raised platforms built of stone and adobe, one at either end of the hut, served as beds. There was no electricity supply, and the windows were small openings filled with a translucent-green, corrugated plastic. It was dark and dingy, and the walls were papered with old newspapers and magazine pages.

huts, one with a tin roof and the other with straw thatch, and the third was a two-storey house with access to the upper floor via an outside wooden staircase. The family's main living area was the two-storey building, and one of the smaller huts was used as the guestroom.

In a lean-to kitchen where pots simmered on an open fire and guinea pigs and chickens had free run, Venedicta

A TRANQUIL WAY OF LIFE

The attraction of Amantaní island is the simplicity. There is little to do except enjoy a glimpse of this tranquil, self-sufficient, agricultural lifestyle and learn about the traditions. The women wear layers of skirts and embroidered woollen shawls, and seem to spend every waking moment spinning wool on a hand-held spindle. They even spin while they are

walking along, for their culture has a strong work ethic forbidding idleness.

The hillside has a myriad of small paths winding through stone terraces between houses and fields. There are a few eucalyptus trees and pine trees but most of the land is cultivated or used for grazing sheep. All paths lead to the centre of the village, where there is a small square with an impressive statue of Capac Colla, the last king of the Colla culture. Behind the square a narrow path ascends the hillside, periodically formalized with stone walls and archways. At the top of the hill, at over 4,100m (13,500 feet) are the remains of a pre-Inca stone temple to Pacha Tata, Father Earth. Pachamama, Mother Earth, is a frequently encountered religious figure in much of the Andes and is an all-embracing force encompassing land and life. Only at altitudes above 4,000m (13,000 feet) do people worship

BELOW A guide gives visitors a briefing session on a visit to one of the floating reed islands of Uros
LEFT A Uros Indian women supplements her family's income by selling artisan goods to tourists
INSET BELOW Venedicta, my Incantana host, in the doorway of her two-storey house on the island of Amantaní

Pacha Tata, who is celebrated as the force that fertilizes Mother Earth, and controls the skies and high places where the rain and winds come from. The outer stone walls of the temple are too high to see over, and the entrance is partially blocked with logs. It was difficult to understand what was being protected from visitors, for when I peered over the logs I could see only a sunken courtyard overgrown with grass. But the guide explained that tourists cannot be admitted because the temple is still a sacred site: even today, the islanders hold their religious ceremonies here.

That evening the village band gathered in the community building, and we were invited to dance with the villagers to Andean sounds thrashed out on drums, panpipes, flutes, and *churangos* (Andean stringed instruments that look like small guitars but are traditionally made from an armadillo).

TAQUILE ISLAND

The journey back to Puno was broken by a brief visit over lunch to the neighbouring island of Taquile, which is more developed than Amantaní and more accustomed to visitors. It has basic amenities like limited electricity, and 13 small restaurants, which all serve the same menu at the same price. Despite the increased commercialism it still maintains its tranquillity and has a back-of-beyond feel about it, especially if compared with Puno. The people here are different from the islanders on Amantaní, and even speak a different language. The Amantanís speak Aymara, but the 2,000-strong population of Taquile speaks Quechua, which was introduced by the Incas. The local costume here is unique and perhaps the most interesting aspect of this independent culture. While the women wear clothes that are similar to the Amantanís', the men wear long, floppy woollen caps, like nightcaps, embroidered waistcoats, and braided sashes around their waists. Just like their counterparts in Amantaní, the women and young girls walk around spinning wool as they go; but here the men, too, are involved in textile production. Every man you see is knitting, making the woollen caps that they all wear. And in the centre of town there is a co-operative warehouse where all the islanders bring their textiles to sell.

It took about 45 minutes to walk up the gradual but constant incline from the point where we were dropped off to the town centre. The main harbour, on the other side of the village, is reached by a long, steep, stone stairway, which is fine to go down, but tiring to climb. We spent about three hours on the island, which included the walk, looking around the village and the artisan warehouse, and having lunch. If you want to understand the Taquile culture in greater depth you need to spend much longer here. But as part of a tour that takes in Uros and Amantaní I felt it was a worthwhile visit that neatly introduced me to another Titicaca culture, allowing me to appreciate just how different and independent are the people of the lake. Coupled with the historical interest provided by past civilizations and lost empires, there is enough here to keep the very keenest of cultural adventure travellers occupied for many a visit.

BRINGING GIFTS TO THE ISLANDERS

Your hosts on Amantaní are paid by the tour companies for providing accommodation. However, this is only a minimal amount and many visitors like to take some gifts for the family. They normally have to bring in all their supplies from Puno, so the best things to take are everyday essential items. There is no fruit grown on the island so this is always well received, as are candles, because electricity is either limited or non-existent.

GOING IT ALONE

INTERNAL TRAVEL

There are regular bus services and *colectivos* (shared taxis/minibuses) between Juliaca airport and Puno (45 minutes). Flights from Puno to Arequipa take just 25 minutes, to Lima 2 hours. Unfortunately there is no direct service from Juliaca to Cusco, although you can do this route via Arequipa.

The railway is the best option for transport between Cusco and Puno (10 hours). Trains run on Mondays, Wednesdays, Thursdays, and Saturdays, but it is best to check the current schedule locally. There are different classes of ticket, but I found the middle one, called the executive class, to be reasonably priced and just as good as the more expensive seats. There is an overnight rail service between Puno and Arequipa (11 hours) on Mondays, Wednesdays, Fridays, and Saturdays. The 25-minute flight is a far better option. There are also regular bus services between Puno and Cusco (overnight), Arequipa (10 hours), and other major towns including Copacabana in Bolivia (3 hours).

WHEN TO GO

You can visit Puno and Lake Titicaca at any time of the year, it is best to avoid the wet season, which runs from October to May, with the wettest period being from December to April. It is always cold at night, but from June to August temperatures fall well below freezing.

TOURS AND GUIDES

There are several tour companies in Puno, particularly along the main street, Jirón Lima. All of them offer half-day trips to Sillustani, half-day trips to Chucuito, and 2-day boat trips to the islands with an overnight stay on Amantaní. These tours are the simplest and most economical way to see Sillustani. If there is no Chucuito trip running, you can take a taxi and hire a guide from most agencies.

The standard island trip doesn't give you much time on Taquile, but it is easy to extend your visit by staying an extra night here. You can arrange this once you get to the island, returning with the next day's tour.

ACCOMMODATION

When you arrive in Puno by train or *colectivo*, you will be approached by people offering inexpensive hotels. The facilities in these cheap hotels tend to be poor, and many have infrequently running hot water. Puno lacks good-value, mid-range accommodation, the more

expensive hotels being little better than the budget hostels. Some 5km (3 miles) out of town, there is a 5-star hotel, the Hotel Isla Esteves, which has a fantastic location on an island and views out over the lake.

On both Amantaní and Taquile, there are always families willing to offer overnight accommodation. It is very basic and consequently costs little more than a couple of dollars.

HEALTH AND SAFETY MATTERS

❑ Sanitation is poor on the islands; take toilet paper with you.

❑ Puno Bay is badly polluted, but you needn't worry about eating fresh fish. Why? The pollution is so bad that all the fish have died and so any fish you eat will have come from outside the polluted area.

❑ The effects of altitude can catch you unawares; avoid dehydration by drinking plenty of bottled water.

❑ The sun is extremely strong here, and you can easily get burned even on a cloudy day. Wear a hat and use sunscreen.

❑ Take warm clothes to the islands as night temperatures drop suddenly, and winds on the peaks can be bitter.

ON THE MENU

Expect simple wholesome foods on the islands. On Amantaní you'll be given soup made with potatoes and a local grain called *quinoa*. Eggs and fried potatoes are also a favourite. Very little meat is eaten here, although a family may offer you chicken. The local tea, made with an aromatic herb called *muña*, has a menthol flavour and is excellent for combating the effects of altitude. Food on Taquile island is similar, but here fresh fish is also very popular and usually served in the restaurants on the plaza.

PERU

Highs and Lows of the Colca Canyon

by Guy Marks

High in the Andes in southern Peru is one of the world's deepest canyons. I trekked through spectacular scenery, which took in sheer cliffs and cactus gardens, to remote villages where life follows age-old traditions and condors circle overhead.

Arequipa is the nearest large city to the Colca Canyon, and it was from there that I made the preparations for my trek. The city is famous for its colonial architecture dating from the 16th and 17th centuries when the Spanish conquistadors brought with them baroque and Moorish architectural influences. In between booking a guide and stocking up with provisions for my trek through the canyon, I took time to visit some of these impressive buildings. Possibly the most colourful and aesthetically pleasing example in all of Peru is Arequipa's Santa Catalina Monastery. For nearly 400 years the nuns and the staff who lived here never left the complex, and no outsider was given access. It was finally opened in 1970. Inside, there are hidden plazas and private prayer rooms, and courtyards with fountains, crucifixes and cloistered walkways. The whole complex is brightly decorated in rich sky blue and orange ochres, and every corner is dotted with geraniums. I became so engrossed by it that I quite forgot the time and found myself buying essential high-energy foods late into the evening and reorganizing my luggage late into the night.

Ivan, my guide, had decided that we would take a nightbus to the canyon so that we could start trekking in the morning. Shrouded in darkness, running late, and laden with backpacks, groceries, sleeping bags, and camping gear, Ivan and I clambered aboard a bus at half past two in the morning. I was cold and uncomfortable, and sleep eluded me for the five-hour journey through the Andes. The road climbs past Nevada Chachani and Volcán Misti, whose towering peaks dominate Arequipa's skyline, and then takes you on to the altiplano, the Andean high plain behind. The journey takes you from an altitude of 2,325m (7,629 feet) in

 Steep paths in and out of the canyon, a rapid change in altitude, and intense heat, combine to make this a very challenging trek. You have to carry all your own supplies and camping gear for the trek. You need to be fit and acclimatized to the altitude.

★★ Your degree of comfort is dependent on the standard of your camping gear, but bear in mind that whatever you take needs to be lightweight. Accommodation at Cabanaconde is basic but there are better hotels available in and around Chivay where you can relax at the end of your trek.

 Sturdy walking boots are essential. Bring water-purifying tablets, a tent, a sleeping bag, cooking stove and equipment, and food to last the length of your trek.

RIGHT At the Colca Canyon's trailhead, with views of Coshñihua (right) and Tapay (left)
BELOW Plaza de Armas in Arequipa

PERU

Arequipa, to 4,800m (15,629 feet) on the altiplano, before descending again to 3,650m (almost 12,000 feet) and the sleepy town of Chivay at the head of the Colca Valley.

THROUGH THE VALLEY TO THE TRAILHEAD

Even in the chill of dawn, the Plaza de Armas, Chivay's main square, buzzes with activity. People in this region rely heavily on public transport, and our bus provided an opportunity for them to make their way along the valley to the outlying villages. They loaded the bus with sacks of freshly baked bread and crammed themselves on with bags, bundles, and babes-in-arms wrapped in shawls.

The women here wear hats extravagantly decorated with bows and ribbons, sequins, rosettes, and embroidery. Ivan explained to me that subtle differences in this decoration could identify the wearer's home village, as well as social and even marital status. To me though, they were all colourful, and the only distinction that was discernible to my inexpert eye was between the firm, white straw-hats worn by women from Chivay, and the embroidered floppy hats from further down the valley at Pinchollo village and beyond.

Outside Chivay the Colca River winds through a wide valley of patchwork fields rising to terraced hillsides and a steep mountain backdrop in the distance. We passed through the villages of Yanque, Achoma, Maca, and Pinchollo, frequently stopping to let passengers on and off the bus. All of this area is subject to frequent tremors, and Maca bears the scars of a severe earthquake that took place in 1991: the quaint church next to the road stands derelict, tumbledown, and crumbled; the village square is lower than it was by several metres; and the highway, now reduced to a dirt road, takes on a sinister twisting from this point. The valley narrows, the mountains move in, and whole fields and sections of the road have collapsed and fallen into the valley.

At Cruz del Condor, 9km (5½ miles) past Cabanaconde, the early-morning tour groups were already gathering to watch for Andean condors (*Vultur gryphus*) rising from the canyon (see box). About 6.5km (4 miles) further on, Ivan asked the bus to stop, and we were unceremoniously dumped at the side of the road with all our gear.

A LONG WALK DOWN TO THE RIVER

We started our hike before nine o'clock in the morning, but already the day was warming up. We reorganized our packs, shedding layers of clothing and finding space for groceries. Across a few metres of flat ground is the canyon rim and the trailhead, marked by a small white cross. The view is breathtaking. I looked out across this valley surrounded

THE ANDEAN CONDOR

The Andean condor (*Vultur gryphus*) is a rare and endangered breed, classified on the CITES (Convention on International Trade in Endangered Species) Appendix II list of endangered species. The adult has a wingspan of more than 3m (10 feet), the second-largest in the world (the largest being that of the wandering albatross (*Diomedea exulans*) at 3.2m/10½ feet). Adult plumage is jet black, with white markings on the wings and a white neck ruff. Juvenile birds are dark brown. The male bird has a distinctive grey, fleshy comb on his head. The Colca Canyon is the best place to see these birds, and you are most likely to see them soaring around the cliff sides, the tips of their primary feathers spread out and curving up like long fingers. They can often be seen rising on the morning thermals at a point called Cruz del Condor, halfway between Pinchollo and Cabanaconde.

by magnificent mountains, and my eyes picked out the narrow track that winds its way sharply down the cliff side, but because of the shape of the rocks it disappeared out of sight below us. Somewhere down there was the river, and beyond it the trail back up the other side. You can see across to the remote villages on the north side of the canyon where no roads run, and in the distance, clinging to the side of the Bomboya Mountains, the village of Tapay where we would spend our first night. Alongside it, to the west and at a slightly lower altitude, are the villages of Coshñihua and Malata, where the trail would take us the next day.

We started walking from an altitude of 3,200m (10,500 feet), down to the canyon's river 1,000m (3,280 feet) below us. The vegetation here is sparse, but, in amongst the rocks and sand, tall, cylindrical cactus and spiky yucca plants have taken a foothold. I noticed two different species of hummingbird, feeding alternately from the same sprig of yucca flowers: one (which I couldn't identify) was tiny; and the other—at about 23cm (9 inches) the world's largest—was the giant hummingbird (*Patagona gigas*), which apart from its distinguishing size has a characteristic, swallow-like flight.

As the track went ever downwards, the day grew hotter, the rocks more barren, and my pack ever heavier. My only consolation was that a few people walking up the track, seemed, not surprisingly, even hotter and more tired than I was. Some of them were tackling their trek without a guide and took the opportunity to quiz Ivan about the route ahead. All of them, despite their various states of fitness, said that this was one of the best treks they had ever done. I felt better for seeing the uphill strugglers, but my own exhaustion was soon to be complete. Two and a half hours after we started walking we were still going down and, although the river was now in sight, it didn't seem to come any closer. The last half-hour down lasted forever. We crossed the river on a precarious-looking

THE WORLD'S DEEPEST CANYON

At its deepest point the Colca Canyon is more than twice the depth of the Grand Canyon, Arizona. At the point where the Colca Canyon passes between the mountains Señal Yajirhua, which peaks at 5,226m (17,146 feet), and the Cerro Luceria at 4,257m (13,967 feet), the Colca River runs at 1,051m (3,450 feet), making a depth of 4,175m (13,696 feet). The Grand Canyon's maximum depth is 1,768m (5,800 feet). This deepest part of the Colca Canyon is uninhabitable. Its sheer cliffs run for over 100km (60 miles), and it is not the place for trekking!

suspension bridge and flopped into a corner of shade by the rockface. Despite the shade it was stiflingly hot with the temperature soaring well over 30°C (86°F). We lunched on dry bread, apples, cheese, and some biscuits, and I gulped at my unreplenishable water supply.

THE COCHINEAL TRAIL

The suspension bridge is one of two that cross the river and connect the villages to the outside world via the road we had travelled. Our plan was to walk up to Tapay, along through the other villages, and then back down to the second bridge at San Galle below Cabanaconde.

It was midday, and the sun stole the last few centimetres of shade. I struggled to my feet, knowing there was nowhere to go but up. We were on the outskirts of a little village called San Juan de Chuccho where the path runs between stone walls and small cultivated plots. On one side of the bridge the land is barren, but on this side there were shrubs and cactus, the occasional tree, and pretty orange flowers tumbling over the rocks. A boy with a couple of donkeys appeared out of nowhere and overtook us on the track.

I was now approaching exhaustion, but the sight of the donkeys gave me hope. A little further on we came to a

PERU

stone house where we found the boy tending his donkeys under the watchful gaze of an old woman. Ivan entered into some swift negotiations and we were soon walking unburdened. For a few dollars the lad and one of his donkeys would accompany us and deliver our luggage to Tapay.

Just as the path had gone ever downwards in the morning, so it went ever upwards in the afternoon. Ivan and the donkey driver chatted away as we walked. I, on the other hand, needed every last breath just to keep me going— even without my pack. I realized that my mistake had been to tackle the trek without first acclimatizing myself to the altitude. This, when coupled with the lack of sleep from journeying on nightbuses for two consecutive nights, had rendered me close to useless.

At last we arrived at Tapay where we set up our tent in the schoolyard, much to the interest of the local kids although they are quite accustomed to having visitors camp here. After a few cups of hot tea and a rest I felt fully recovered. In the evening the children went to their dancing classes. I could see them in the

schoolroom dancing away to the sounds of panpipes, flutes, and *churangos* making the classic Andean rhythms from Peru, Bolivia, and Ecuador.

Tapay, perched up here at 2,800m (9,200 feet), is a small village of little more than 300 inhabitants. The houses are made of stone or mud brick, and most are roofed with corrugated iron, although a few still have the traditional grass thatch. In the centre of the village there is a bright-white church with a red doorway, but this and the blue schoolroom are the only buildings that are painted. On the village outskirts—for as far as you can see—there are large cacti with big, round, flat, fleshy pads. I'd noticed these cacti, called tuna, all the way up from the river; but now I realized their importance to the

LEFT The traditional costume of Chivay
ABOVE The tiny town of Cabanaconde, where we came to the end of our trek
BELOW The bridge across the Río Colca at San Galle oasis

PERU

villagers, for they provide the main crop—not the cactus itself, but the cochineal bugs that grow on them. Every cactus is covered in what looks like white-cotton fungus, and within these white patches are large, tick-like scale insects (*Dactylopius coccus*), which feed on the cactus sap. The insects are cropped, dried and then used to produce a natural, deep-red dye.

Morning dawned crisp and clear. The village was calm and quiet, and unpolluted save the litter in the schoolyard. High above us the vast, soaring shapes of three Andean condors circled near the top of the cliffs behind the village. These magnificent birds never flap their huge wings; they just glide on the thermal currents.

We set off on a track that took us along the edge of Tapay to a high point that affords magnificent views along the canyon and down to the neighbouring villages. A cross, decorated with dried, red flowers and palm fronds, marks this vantage point. From here the path winds its way down through a ravine and then up the other side, shortly to emerge in the village of Coshñihua. This is an even smaller place than Tapay, with only about 150 inhabitants. Amongst the sparse buildings are eucalyptus trees, used for firewood and building materials, and Molle trees planted for their shade. Pigs and sheep were tethered to the trees, and the place smelled of hot dust and the rich, sweet aroma of animal dung.

Coshñihua runs into the neighbouring village of Malata, and here the cactus fields begin once more. You could easily spend a day or two in these villages, and then descend once again to cross the second small bridge over the Colca and enter the oasis of San Galle. It is a wonderful place to trek. As we walked from village to village in the remote and peaceful valley, the people we met along the way stopped to wish us well and enquire after our journey. They wanted to know where I'd come from, what my home was like, and what I thought of

theirs. They were charming, proud, welcoming, and cheerful.

SAN GALLE AND THE CLIMB BACK OUT

San Galle is the perfect place to end a day. It is a pocket of lush vegetation served by a hot spring that gushes from the side of the mountain. There are only a few scattered houses, but acres of terraced fields growing an extraordinary variety of plants. Along with the ubiquitous cactus, there are avocado and cotton plants, papayas and bananas, lemon trees and clumps of bamboo, alfalfa, figs, and even palm trees.

As evening fell nature reminded us of her power by shaking a landslide of rocks and dust down the cliff and into the canyon beyond. The villagers live with the constant threat of seismic activity, but these landslides were worrying them as they were becoming more frequent. My own immediate concern, however, was not the landslides but the long climb back out of the canyon next morning.

We decided it was best to tackle the ascent in the cool, so we were on the trail at 4am, long before sunrise. We walked slowly, even though I was now accustomed to the altitude. We got in two hours before the sun rose and another hour before the shadows left the trail. During the last hour it was warming up, but we made it to the top unscathed by 8am. I was elated as I looked back down into the canyon and saw in the distance the tiny villages on the opposite bank. I've walked from there, I thought, and smiled inwardly.

The top of the trail is a walk of about 20 minutes from Cabanaconde town. Although this is only a tiny place it was noisy compared with the villages in the canyon, and the approach was littered with plastic bags, broken glass, batteries, old shoes, and animal bones. We walked into town, dusty and tired, when other tourists were just emerging from sleepy hostels. And I wondered if any of them were lucky enough to be venturing out into this magical canyon.

GOING IT ALONE

GETTING TO THE COLCA CANYON

There are roads from the north across the altiplano connecting Chivay to Cusco and the Titicaca area. However, they are not well served by public transport. Most people get to Chivay from Arequipa. In Arequipa, several buses a day leave from San Juan de Dios for Chivay and Cabanaconde. From Chivay there are taxis and *colectivos* (shared taxis) that travel along the valley to the different villages.

WHEN TO GO

You can visit the Colca Canyon at any time of year, but it is best to avoid the rainy season between October and May. Rains can cause additional landslide hazards and render the roads impassable. If you intend to do some river rafting while you are in the area, bear in mind that this is best done in August.

PLANANING YOUR TRIP

Although it is possible to undertake this trek on your own, it is best to enlist the services of a guide. A good guide does more than just show you the route. He will help you prepare for the trek, and he will introduce you to villagers and explain aspects of the villages' social structure and culture as well as the environment, giving you a far better insight into the area than you will get if you go it alone. Several small companies in Arequipa offer organized treks, but since you have to make your own way to Cabanaconde, take your own food and camping equipment, and carry your own gear, I'm not quite sure what they are

providing for their fee. I would recommend using a private guide who can help you tailor-make your own itinerary. Qualified mountain and trekking guides can be contacted through the agencies in Arequipa.

HEALTH AND SAFETY MATTERS

There are no toilet facilities on this trek, and no drinking water. Water bottles can be filled at the villages and then purified.

OTHER ACTIVITIES

❑ It is well worth spending a morning at Cruz del Condor for the very best sightings of the magnificent birds that have given the place its name.
❑ It is possible to arrange longer treks that take in other areas around the Colca region. These include climbing Mount Mismi to trekking to the most remote contributory source of the Amazon.
❑ Whitewater rafting is available on the Colca at Chivay. There are two grades, and people normally go for 1 to 3 hours. Rafting also takes place on the Río Majes, which is part of the Colca after the dangerous canyon section; this is a 2-day trip arranged from Arequipa or Chivay.
❑ The geothermal hot springs just outside Chivay are an excellent place to relax after a long trek.

COPING WITH ALTITUDE

Your body needs to adjust to the lack of oxygen at high altitudes. Even mild exercise can cause exhaustion if you have not first acclimatized, so a couple of days relaxing at Arequipa at 2,325m (7,629 feet) or Chivay at 3,651 (11,978 feet) is advisable before undertaking any trekking. Once on the trail you need to find a pace that your body can cope with, even if this means walking very, very slowly. Chewing coca leaves or taking homoeopathic coca tablets can relieve the symptoms of breathlessness and tiredness.

ESSENTIAL SUPPLIES

Since the villages in the canyon are not able to offer facilities such as restaurants, it is essential to take sufficient food with you. The trek is strenuous so high-energy foods are important, but the weight of your pack is also a consideration. Stick to basic, dried foods, and maintain a nutritional balance.

❑ Dried mashed potato, pasta, bread, and porridge oats for carbohydrate.
❑ Some proteins, such as tinned meat sauces and peanuts.
❑ Powdered milk, sugar, biscuits.
❑ Chocolate, and fresh and dried fruit.
❑ Don't forget water-purifying tablets.

Negro
Selvas
Amazonas
Belém
São Luís
Selimões
(Amazonas)
⓭
Santarém
Fortaleza
Juruá
Manaus
Teresina
C São Roque
Madeira
Natal
S e l v a s
Tapajós
Xingu
Recife
Pôrto
Velho
Tocantins
São Francisco
Salvador
Mato
Grosso
Cuiabá
Brasília
Planalto
Brasil
Goiânia
Belo
Horizonte
⓯
Ribeirão
Prêto
Vitória
Campo
Grande
Paraná
Campinas
Juiz de Fora
Rio de
Janeiro
São
Paulo
⓮
Curitiba

0   400   800   1200 km
0   200   400   600 m

Porto Alegre
Pelotas

BRAZIL

B razil has long attracted adventurous travellers. The top tourist spots may be well known, but there's still much to discover in this country that covers nearly half of South America. It may not have the mountains of its neighbours, Peru and Bolivia, but it certainly has everything else. There are vast wetlands and enormous jungles that abound with animals, birds and exotic plants, colossal rivers, pounding waterfalls, cool highlands and endless beaches. In Río de Janeiro you'll find one of the world's most visually stunning cities, but equally fascinating is the capital, Brasilia, with its striking modern architecture, and the colonial cities of Salvador and Olinda in the north. The places are wonderful in themselves, but what makes Brazil such a fantastic destination is its people, who must be among the liveliest, friendliest and most fun-loving in the world. It is not for nothing that carnival time in Brazil is legendary, but you don't have to wait until then to join the party.

Iguaçu Falls straddle the boundary between Brazil and Argentina

BRAZIL

The Amazon Experience

by Simon Richmond

Fishing for piranhas, alligator spotting at night, jungle hikes, and all manner of boat rides, can be part of a trip to the Amazon, a river and rain forest of biblical proportions.

It's been called "the last unwritten page of Genesis." The Amazon contains the longest river on Earth and, at over 6 million sq km (2.3 million square miles), the largest rain forest. The entire river basin holds one fifth of our planet's fresh water, and sustains hundreds of thousands of different animal and plant species, many as yet undiscovered by man. It is small wonder that the Amazon is a symbol of the environmental movement, and that it remains an irresistible attraction for explorers and adventurers.

The river itself flows through Brazil for over half the river's total length of 6,500km (4,040 miles), but the jungle and the Amazon's many headwaters are spread across neighbouring Venezuela, Columbia, Peru, and Bolivia. All these countries have jumped on the Amazon ecotourism bandwagon, and many offer unique and interesting trips and activities; but the place that most travellers head for is **Manaus**—the capital of Brazil's largest state, Amazonas, and the transport and commercial heart of the jungle.

With its wealth and former grandeur founded on the rubber boom of the 19th century, Manaus is an unlikely centre for ecotourism. Today it is a sprawling, modern city with a population of over 3 million. With its high-rise towers, a famously ornate opera house, chaotic shopping precincts, and smoothly flowing roads, Manaus can be viewed either as a triumph of man over nature, or as a travesty. What cannot be denied is that in spite of the ever-present, debilitating heat, it's an incredibly lively place from which to start a trip into the jungle.

That trip will comprise either a boat tour or a stay at a jungle lodge. Boat tours generally mean sleeping and eating on board, perhaps with a night or two camping in the jungle. Jungle lodges, which are almost always located on a tributary to the main rivers, range from the very basic to 5-star. Most tours will include activities, such as piranha fishing and alligator spotting, and jungle hikes or canoe rides along the *igarapés* (smaller rivers) and creeks, some of which are navigable only during the high-water season. Either way, if you want to see wildlife and virgin jungle, aim to get as far

2 The very challenging trips, deep into the rain forest, involve learning jungle-survival techniques from army-trained guides. However, most visitors will opt for a lodge stay or a boat trip and do nothing more strenuous than a few day-long hikes or a gentle paddle in a canoe.

★★ Take your pick from facilities ranging from an air-conditioned, luxury cabin to a hammock swinging beneath a mosquito net. Whatever your accommodation, though, the oppressive heat and humidity of the Amazon are draining. You also need to be on guard for mosquitoes, although these are less of a problem in Manaus and along the Río Negro than they are around the Río Solimões.

A mosquito net is essential if you are venturing deep into the jungle. Trekking requires decent boots and loose, long trousers and shirts to protect you from insect bites and scratches from the dense undergrowth. A pair of binoculars is recommended for spotting wildlife, especially along the main rivers where the jungle is likely to be several kilometres from the boat.

away as possible from the noise and bustle of Manaus.

ON THE WATERFRONT

Few scenes are as alive with movement and colour as the daily comings and goings from Manaus's central port, **Escadaria dos Remédios**. Visit in the morning to see the many *barco regional*—the traditional, multi-storey, wooden riverboats that are the main form of Amazon transport—bobbing beside the floating docks on the Río Negro. Hammocks will have been slung across the upper decks by passengers preparing for a voyage.

Sweating stevedores hump cargo off the container ships while vendors of food, drink, hammocks, and lengths of rope to tie up the hammocks, energetically hawk their wares. Like flies buzzing around elephants, smaller ferries and private launches dart around their larger brethren to load and unload passengers at a tiny jetty. And all this activity takes place on one side of a river so broad that it seems more like a giant inland lake.

The docks, built by a British company at the turn of the century, need to float because of the annual rise and fall of the river. The high-water season is from June to July, and on a warehouse wall is painted the levels the Río Negro has reached each year. The heaviest floods were in 1953, when the water rose 29m (95 feet) above sea-level and lapped at the doors of the nearby **Customs House**, a splendid Edwardian creation, which was shipped over from the U.K. in blocks and reconstructed like a giant jigsaw.

The docks are the starting point for long river journeys, as well as for shorter trips to the much-touted "**meeting of the waters**" 10km (6¼ miles) downstream from Manaus. This is where the dark but clear, tannin-stained Río Negro joins the light, silt-carrying Río Solimões (the stretch of the Amazon from Manaus to the Andean border with Peru) and becomes the Río Amazonas.

AMAZON IN A PACKAGE

The most popular day trip is to the meeting of the waters and **Parque Ecológico Janauary** less than an hour from Manaus by boat. As long as you don't mind crowds and are not expecting anything remotely wild or spontaneous, you'll enjoy this trip. On the larger tours, there is a running commentary in English and someone video-recording the entire proceedings for souvenir tapes, which are screened and sold on the return journey.

The typical package starts with a boat journey to the point where the Río Negro joins the Río Solimões. Because of differences in density, temperature, and velocity, the waters from these two rivers run side by side in a caramel-and-cola swirl for 6km (3¾ miles) before combining. Adding some interest to this otherwise mildly intriguing phenomenon is the possibility that you may briefly glimpse pink dolphins—called boutu (*Ima geoffrensis*)—as they break the water.

The 9,000-ha (22,200-acre) Parque Ecológico Janauary is a beautiful place, but it is very commercialized. The first

TRAVELLERS' TIPS

- ❏ The jungle is very dense and although, with patience, it's possible to spot wildlife, especially birds, monkeys, alligators, and dolphins, you'll see much more of this kind of thing in the Pantanal (see page 154).
- ❏ The main rivers are very wide, often well over 20km (12½ miles) in breadth, which can make for very monotonous journeys: most of the time you are surrounded by nothing much other than water. If you want to see the jungle up close you must ensure that your tour includes a trip, preferably by canoe, along the *igarapés*.
- ❏ Note that while perfectly safe during the day, the docks are not somewhere you want to loiter at night.

ABOVE *The multi-storey, wooden riverboats—
the Amazon's main form of transport—
beside the turn-of-the-century, British-built
floating docks of Manuas's central port,
Escadaria dos Remédios, on the Río Negro.
A trip to the famous "meeting of the waters"
will begin here*
LEFT *An exhilarating speedboat ride on the
Río Negro*

stop will be at a giant souvenir stall, next
to the floating restaurant where you'll
later have a mediocre buffet lunch. From
here, a wooden walkway runs through the
jungle, past more souvenir stalls, to a
viewing platform overlooking the famed
Victoria regia water-lilies (*Nymphaea*

135

BRAZIL

amazonica), whose leaves grow to over a metre (3¼ feet) in diameter; the best time to see the flowers, which bloom for only three days, is from February to May.

It is possible to see animals here, but not in natural conditions. You will see sloths, looking like aliens from a *Star Wars* movie, being cuddled in the arms of a small child wanting some money for photographs. More wildlife, including giant jacare alligators, or caiman (*Caiman crocodilus*), various monkeys, and an anaconda (*Eunectes murinus*), is on view beside yet another souvenir shop at the end of the motorized longboat trips through the park. It's straight back to Manaus after lunch.

If you wish to avoid all this hoop-la it's better to arrange a smaller, guided boat trip that will allow you more time to explore the *igapós* (flooded forests) and *igarapés* of the park. It's also possible to strike out independently to view the meeting of the waters: take bus 713 from Manaus to Praca da Matriz and then board the public ferry across the river.

WILDER JUNGLE ADVENTURES

Boats, and the occasional flight, will take you further up the Río Negro from Manaus, past the Anavilhanas archipel- ago, but you'll be going well off the tourist track and into the realms of high adventure. The rivers around the small town of Barcelos, 420km (260 miles) northwest of Manaus, are renowned for their colourful ornamental fish. There are organized trips to view the fish, and also to attend the annual ornamental-fish fes- tival held in January or February. The most challenging trip is the ascent of Brazil's highest peak, the 3,014-m (9,888- foot) Pico da Neblina, on the border with Venezuela. The climb and descent take at least ten days and should not to be attempted without prior training.

And, if you're heading to a jungle lodge downriver, you'll pass the confluence point anyway.

TARZAN'S JUNGLE LODGE

In the opposite direction from the meeting of the waters is the Ariaü Amazon Towers, a top-notch eco-resort some 65km (40 miles) up the Río Negro from Manaus. The starting point for my boat journey there was the Praia Ponta Negra, the popular riverside beach beside the Tropical Hotel, 15km (9½ miles) out of the city.

I was met by Gilberto, one of the Ariaü's team of expert guides, who was there to escort me, and four other guests, to the resort. If there's a large party, the boat journey takes two hours on the resort's barco regional, but since I was in a small group we travelled in the nippier motorboat in half the time. The resort, built on high stilts over a flooded forest, is named after the canal that flows past the entrance and links the Río Negro with the Río Solimões.

The **Ariaü Jungle Tower**, the brainchild of a local environmentally minded lawyer, started in 1984 with just eight rooms and one boat. Today, the only hotel complex in the rain forest with rooms at treetop level has over 200 rooms in seven circular towers, enormous conference rooms and amphitheatres for musical performances, two 41-m (134-foot) high observation towers, two splash pools, an aviary of exotic jungle birds, and around 5km (3 miles) of raised catwalks joining up the complex and running through the jungle. At the end of the longest catwalk, there is even a landing pad for a U.F.O.—this part of the jungle is supposedly a hot spot for extraterrestrial activity.

Gilberto showed us around the resort, pointing out the honeymoon lodge— Tarzan's house, nestling in the uppermost branches of an enormous tree—and one of the ten ultra-luxurious suites occupied by the likes of Bill Gates, Helmut Kohl, and ex-U.S. president Jimmy Carter.

Strolling along the catwalks, high above the jungle floor and surrounded by foliage and birds, I felt that I could have been in the quirkiest and most elaborate treehouse ever built—one that I was sharing with many brightly coloured macaws, and colonies of woolly monkeys (*Lagothrix lagotricha*) and squirrel monkeys (*Saimiri seiureus*), who hang out for scraps beside the restaurant.

BETWEEN SKY AND WATER

Guests are divided into groups according to the languages they speak, and are assigned a guide who'll lead all their activities. I joined a family of Australians, a mother and son from Holland, couples from the Ukraine and Italy, and a nurse from Canada. Our tours were to be led by Charles, a French expat, who knows a thing or two about jungles having guided U.S. troops during the war in Vietnam.

We started at 8am, an hour after breakfast, on a boat trip upriver to the small Caboclo village of **Acajatuba**, on the lake of the same name. The journey to the village even at this early hour is punishing under the harsh equatorial sun, and umbrellas were passed around to provide some shade. Dolphins swam alongside the boat, and dragonflies darted through the humid air. The boat was stopped three degrees south of the equator so that Charles could point out the start of the **Anavilhanas**—a slinky archipelago, 90km (56 miles) long, and consisting of over 400 islands—which in the local language means the place where the sky meets the water. Until recently this river-island archipelago was thought to be the world's largest, but satellite mapping has identified an even larger group further up the Río Negro, near to the Pico da Neblina National Park (see box, page 136).

The Coboclo village has around 40 wooden houses—homes for some 220 people—two churches, four bars, a school, a clinic and a football field, where some youngsters were practising goal shots. Caboclos are of mixed Indian and

THE INDIANS

The chances of meeting any full-blooded Indians on a trip into the jungle are very slim, and potentially fatal—for the Indians, that is—if you do run into any. In the north of Amazonia, on the border with Venezuela, lives one of the largest tribes, the Yanomami, of whom there are thought to be 18,000. Their culture has hardly changed since the Stone Age, and until the 1970s the Yanomami had lived in complete isolation from the modern world.

Despite some protection afforded by reservations, incursions into the jungle by *garimpeiros* (gold prospectors) and the army, keen to encourage settlement along the northern frontier of Brazil, have proved disastrous for the Yanomami, who have no immunity to common diseases. This is an important reason to shun organized trips that offer the possibility of visiting Yanomami reservations. In any case, it is necessary to obtain permission from FUNAI—the government agency looking after Indian affairs—in order to visit Indian reservations, and this is impossible for a tourist to get.

Portuguese or other immigrant heritage (there have been no full-blooded Indians in this part of the Amazon for centuries—see box). They make a living by fishing and farming, growing mainly the manioc root. Since tourists have started dropping by, there's also a gift shop, selling necklaces, the preserved heads of small alligators, and mounted piranha.

FISHING FOR PIRANHA

After the anaconda—the world's largest snake—the most notorious of the Amazon's inhabitants is the piranha. There are 25 different types of these meat-loving fish with razor-sharp teeth. And as we sat in a long canoe in the late afternoon, dangling primitive fishing rods

*ABOVE The flooded forest on the Río Negro
LEFT The piranha is not a large fish, but it
gathers in huge hunting shoals that can
reputedly reduce a large mammal to bones
within minutes. This one, though, was
destined for the dinner plate*

into the water, Charles explained that
despite the gory legends few piranha
would take a bite if we were to fall in. As
long as we were not already bleeding that
is. But from the way the piranha gobbled
up the scraps of meat on the end of our
hooks, it was difficult to believe that they

RIGHT When on the move, the woolly monkey is fast and agile, and swings through the trees hand over hand in typical monkey fashion. But rather than forage for its usual diet of fruit, this one prefers to wait for scraps from diners at the Ariaü Jungle Tower restaurant

would be uninterested in any human foolish enough to go for a quick dip.

To catch them, the trick is to hide the hook in the meat and yank quickly as soon as you feel a tug on the line. Although I managed to land the first piranha of the afternoon, my performance

139

BRAZIL

deteriorated from then on and it was my fellow guests that provided the bulk of the catch, which would later be served up deep fried for dinner.

Having eaten our piranha meal, we returned to the same stretch of river to do some alligator hunting. As the boat slipped along slowly, the guide shining the torch into the reeds and the glassy water, it felt as though we were taking part in a film, or a body-hunt in a swamp. The spotlight picked out the orange eyes of an alligator, looking like the burning tips of cigarettes as they broke the dark surface of the water. The guide suddenly plunged his hands in, yanked out an alligator no more than 1m (3¼ feet) long, and offered it, serrated mouth gaping, for us to hold—an opportunity I had no hesitation declining.

THE WELCOME STORM

The next morning, Mark Aitchison, owner of the jungle and river tour agency Swallows and Amazons, arrived at the Ariaü to transport me to his and his wife Tania's intimate hacienda, the **Overlook Lodge**. It was a bumpy but exhilarating ride in the small steel-hulled motorboat that took us across the Río Negro to the quiet palm-fringed beach where we found the brightly painted lodge. For boat tours, which Mark's company specializes in, one of the barco regional is hired. Itineraries can include both the jungles around the Río Negro and Río Solimões, and the Anavilhanas archipelago, which can be seen from the veranda of the lodge.

Built on the 30,000-ha (74,000-acre) jungle property of Tania's family, the lodge provides an insight into a typical, small landholder's life on the river. There was a genuine Sunday-afternoon outing atmosphere when I joined Tania, family, and friends, on a speedboat trip to a creek with pleasantly cool, natural swimming holes, and waterfalls on the edge of the jungle. Later, Mark led me on a trek through the cultivated fields, and secondary and virgin rain forest behind

HEALTH AND SAFETY MATTERS

- ❏ Yellow fever is endemic in this part of Brazil, and on arrival at Manaus airport and on the boats you'll be asked to show an inoculation certificate; if you haven't been vaccinated, or don't have your certificate (or a copy) to hand, it is likely that you'll be forced to have an inoculation on the spot.

- ❏ There's much debate over whether to take prophylactic pills to protect against malaria. Catching the disease is a risk, but a very small one if you're confining your visit to Manaus and the jungle around the Río Negro, which is generally free of mosquitoes. Consult a doctor before leaving. Take basic precautions in any case, and apply insect repellent liberally and wear long, loose clothing, especially at dusk and during the night.

- ❏ Don't underestimate the strength of the sun, even in the shaded jungle. Drink plenty of liquids throughout the day (botled water is advised), and cover up with a high-factor suncream.

the lodge; along the way he provided a running commentary on the flora and fauna that we came across.

Fresh pineapple was brought back to add to the barbecued fish and plentiful salads for dinner. Sunset was spoiled by too many clouds, which heralded an approaching tropical storm. In the darkness, I swung languidly in a hammock on the veranda, flashes of lightning illuminating the sky. Birds cried, the wind picked up and rustled the trees, and it wasn't until the storm was almost upon us that the thunder chimed in. After three days of relentless heat the refreshing rain was more than welcome, and I listened with relief to the loud clatter of drops on the tin roof.

GOING IT ALONE

INTERNAL TRAVEL

The fastest way into the Amazon rain forest is to fly to Manaus. If you're travelling to other parts of Brazil, such as Río or Iguaçu Falls, it will pay to buy a Varig Brazil Airpass, which is available only outside the country.

Although the roads immediately around Manaus are excellent, road travel from the coast into the jungle along Highway BR230, known as the Transamazonica, is not an option since much of it is now impassable.

For long-distance transport, boats are used by the vast majority of people, and you should have no problem arranging a trip on one. The journey from Belem, on the coast, to Manaus will take between 4 days and a week, depending on the type of vessel and whether you're going up or down the river. The most luxurious boats are catamarans; these have cabins with private bathrooms and air-conditioning, as well as hammock space for 300 passengers. Cheaper and more atmospheric are the 3-deck wooden riverboats of which there are plenty departing daily from major ports along the river. These also offer the choice between cabins with bunk beds, and hammocks on the open decks. The former offer some security for baggage, but the latter are much cooler.

If you don't fancy the long haul, it's worth considering taking a shorter trip between Manaus and, say, Santarem, which also has an airport with connections to major cities.

WHEN TO GO

Expect rain all through the year in the Amazon, but the wettest months are January and February. In December, temperatures regularly soar above 40°C (104°F) and humidity is constantly high.

PLANNING YOUR TRIP

Jungle and boat trips are big business in Manaus, and you'll probably be approached by a tout trying to sell you one within minutes of your arrival at the airport. The best plan is to have a firm idea of exactly what you want to do. Day tours will give you only a taste of what the jungle can offer, but are a good way of finding out whether you might like to venture further.

Typical trips last 3 days or more, with the basic options being camping in the jungle, or a stay at a jungle lodge or on a cruise boat. All can be combined in one trip. Shop around for the best deals, and if a tour operator is charging more than the

going rate (around $60 a day for the most rugged tours), find out why before deciding whether it's worth the extra expense. Build some time into your schedule to investigate all the options. Check what will be included in the itinerary before signing up; and ask to meet the guide before departure, or at least confirm his or her experience and foreign language ability. Whichever tour you choose, it's always a good idea to take extra food provisions, plenty of insect repellent, and sunblock.

ACCOMMODATION AND FOOD

There's a good range of accommodation in Manaus, but because of the constantly high temperatures and humidity it's worth paying for a hotel with decent air-conditioning and, ideally, a swimming pool. The range of restaurants is less impressive, but far from poor. At jungle lodges and on boat tours, it's unlikely you'll be served anything fancy, but there should be plenty of opportunities to try the local fish dishes and exotic fruits.

WHAT TO TAKE

On long-distance boat journeys along the Amazon, you'll be cooped up in a cabin or swinging in a hammock for several days, so some preparation is essential. You'll need:

❑ A hammock and a length of string to tie it up.

❑ Light, loose clothing to protect against mosquitoes at night, and a blanket or sheet.

❑ Plenty of insect repellent.

❑ Lots of bottled water and extra food supplies to supplement what is likely to be poor catering on the boat.

❑ Toilet paper.

❑ The original (or copy) of your yellow fever inoculation certificate.

❑ Optional extras include binoculars for viewing the distant riverbanks, a phrase book or dictionary (if you don't speak Portuguese), a thick book to read, and a Walkman.

BRAZIL

Feeling the Force of Iguaçu Falls

by Simon Richmond

Spanning two countries—Argentina and Brazil—the Iguaçu Falls are one of the world's most awesome sights. From either side you can take a drenching boat ride into the very heart of the falls, or you can explore the beautiful surrounding parkland.

The original inhabitants of this area on the borders of Argentina, Brazil, and Paraguay, came to the falls to perform burial ceremonies, and it is by their name—Iguaçu—that the river and the famous falls are known today. According to a legend of the Guaraní Indians, Iguaçu Falls is where the clouds

were born. The word is spelt differently depending on which side of the border you are—Iguaçu in Brazil, Iguazú in Argentina, and Iguassu in Paraguay—but the meaning remains irrefutably the same: *I* for water and *guaçu* for big.

Summing up Iguaçu Falls in facts and statistics is easy. The falls take the shape of an elongated horseshoe spread across 2.7km (1¾ miles), and plunge at least 60m (197 feet). Depending on the flow of the Iguaçu River, which rises some 600km (370 miles) to the east in the coastal hills

BELOW A view of three of the falls on the Argentine side: the Mitre, the Belgrano, and the Rivadavia
INSET The thundering wall of water called The Three Musketeers

 The walks are very easy and well marked. If you don't like fairground thrill rides then avoid the boat journeys up to the falls.

 Heat and mosquitoes both need to be taken into account. The most comfortable and convenient places to stay are the luxury hotels that are within the national parks. However, it's not difficult travelling into the parks from the nearby towns and using one country as a base from which to visit the other.

 You will need hiking boots for walks in the national parks, binoculars for birdspotting, and a waterproof jacket for walks and boat trips.

BRAZIL

near Curitaba, there are between 150 and 300 separate falls, many with evocative names such as Adam and Eve, Cain and Abel, and the Three Musketeers. Declared a World Heritage Site by UNESCO in 1986, the falls are surrounded by over 230,000ha (570,000 acres) of rain forest protected as a national park.

It's much more difficult, however, to capture in words the total impact of Iguaçu Falls, which surpass both Niagara Falls and Victoria Falls in scope and beauty. Suffice to say that this is one natural wonder that truly is a visual stunner, and you'll want to gaze at it for hours, if not days, and to see it from every conceivable angle. Fortunately, it is possible to do this. There are boat rides allowing views from the water, walking routes to within spray-drenching distance of the falls, and helicopter flights to afford you an overhead panorama. New facilities and activities are continually appearing (see box below) as a result of the ongoing rivalry between Brazil and Argentina to attract visitors to their side of the falls. The fact is, however, that to truly experience Iguaçu a full day in both countries is necessary.

TOAST OF THE TROPICS

I began my acquaintance with the falls on the Brazilian side, staying at the **Tropical das Cataratas Hotel**, a grand, pink and cream edifice, built in the colonial style and opened in 1958. Earlier in the century, this land had been part of the farm of Elfrida Schimmelpfeng, a German immigrant, who grew soya beans. She was visited by the Brazilian aviator Alberto Santos Dumont, who was so impressed by the falls that he persuaded the local state governor to buy the land and make it a national park. Now, the park covers 170,000ha (420,000 acres) on the north bank of the Río Iguaçu, much of which is out of bounds to tourists.

One of the benefits of staying at the Tropical (or the Sheraton International, its modern counterpart on the Argentinian side) is that you'll be able to view the falls and stroll through the parks before they open to the public at 9am and after they close at 7pm. It is well worth making the effort to rise early, for dawn is one of the best times for birdspotting, and from along the road leading to the hotel you might spot the dark-billed cuckoo (*Coccyzus melacoryphus*), hawks, owls, swallows, and five different types of toucan. Also, viewing the falls on the nights of the full moon is said to be an especially memorable experience, for the lunar light makes the spray from the gushing water glow blue.

CHANGES TO THE ARGENTINE NATIONAL PARK

At the time of writing, there are major structural changes in progress on the Argentine side of Iguaçu Falls. A large new visitors' centre, amphitheatre, and interpretive centre, are being constructed at the entrance to the national park, where there'll also be restaurants and shops. Cars and buses will park here, and visitors will then be able to walk to the falls or take the light railway, which will run as far as Puerto Canoas, where a boat can be caught to the lookout directly over the Garganta del Diablo (Devil's Throat). Eventually the boats will be replaced by a new 1.3-km (3¾-mile) bridge linking the lookout with the riverbank.

The train will also stop by the improved walkways beside the old visitors' centre, which is housed in the original resthouse at the falls and being restored as a new home for the park's scientific research offices. The Paseo Inferior walkway, which is currently under construction, will provide the most intimate, forest-surrounded views of the falls, while the upper walkway, Paseo Superior, is being extended to zigzag further through the beguiling series of narrow, forested islands in the flow of the Río Iguazú before it plummets off the Salto Bossetti.

A line of trees blocks out all but the slenderest glimpse of the falls from the Tropical, but the low, rumbling sound of the water is ever present. Just metres from the hotel's front steps is the first dramatic view of the set of falls known as the **Salto Bossetti** (see box, page 148) and the verdant rocky island of San Martín, resolute amid the raging torrents of pink-tinged water cascading around it. The colour comes from the rust-red earth the water flows across.

Hugging the cliffs, and running for about 1.5km (1 mile) up the gorge to the **Florianó Falls**, is a paved walkway. Along here you're likely to see coati (*Nasua nasua nelsoni*), a cute relation of the raccoon, scavenging for scraps left by the tourists. The walkway affords excellent views, especially when it drops down to the level of the falls and you can look straight in the thunderous face of the **Garganta del Diablo** (Devil's Throat), as an average 1,750cu m (62,000 cubic feet) per second of water crashes around you. It's a good idea to take a plastic bag to protect cameras from the spray at this part of the falls. In the sunshine, rainbows arch across the water. Not for nothing do they say that Argentina puts on the show while Brazil charges for the view.

If you don't fancy climbing back up to the road, you can for a small fee use the lift operating at the Florianó Falls. I chose to walk, though, and on the way I spot a large inflatable raft zooming towards the pounding cascades on a seemingly suicidal mission. My next glimpse of the falls will be from inside this very craft.

ADVENTURES WITH POPEYE

The Macuco Safari de Barco (Macuco Boat Safari) combines an hour-long jeep journey and a trek through the rain forest in the company of a bilingual guide, with a thrilling 30-minute boat ride, shooting the rapids up the Iguaçu canyon to the very brink of the falls. I joined six other people in an open-top trolley car that would be hauled along on the

THE ITAIPÚ DAM

The world's largest hydroelectricity scheme is based 10km (6 miles) north of Foz do Iguaçu at Itaipú, where a mammoth dam which generates a staggering 89,200 million kilowatts per hour, spans the Río Paraná. The dam was a joint project between Brazil and Paraguay, and in 1995 it was named one of the seven modern wonders of the world by the American Society of Civil Engineering. Minibus tours to the dam can be arranged from the Tropical das Cataratas Hotel, but they're expensive and it's easy to go independently on one of the local buses that depart hourly from Foz do Iguaçu. There's a visitors' centre at the dam, where you can see a film about its construction. From Monday to Saturday there are also free, guided coach tours across the top of the dam, lasting around one hour.

3-km (1¾-mile) journey through the forest by a camouflage-painted jeep. One of the group, Eduardo, a local law student, was taking the trip for a third time, so much did he enjoy the experience on the previous two occasions.

As we trundled along, our young guide, Valmor, made a bold attempt, in both Portuguese and English, to explain the flora and fauna of the subtropical rain forest. He told us that there are over 1,000 different species of butterfly in the jungle, and dense clusters of yellow ones, known as Jemas (which means egg-yolk), scatter as we approach. The males, Valmor tells us, lick up the salt on the ground to improve their sexual performance.

Big cats, including jaguar (*Pantheon onca*), ocelot (*Leopardus pardalis*) and puma (*Felis concolor*) also prowl the forests, but they are very rarely spotted, even by experienced guides. Birdwatchers are better rewarded with

LEFT On The Sendero Yacaratia trail to Puerto Macuco

ABOVE A view of Iguaçu Falls from the Brazilian side

toucans, swallow-tailed kites (*Elanoides forficatus*), and even hawk eagles. Exotic flora, including some types of orchid, is abundant. Valmor pointed out the chusara, or heart of palm, an edible plant that needs to grow for a decade before it can be harvested.

We were given the choice between riding in the jeep to the steps down to the river, or going for a short trek through the jungle. We decided on the trek, which took us past a 20-m (65-foot) high waterfall; you can bathe in the deep pool at its foot. Much to our consternation, Valmor urged us to watch out for spiders here; to help us identify the ones to avoid, we were told that if the web pattern is geometric the spider that created it won't be dangerous, but if it is irregular then it's time to panic.

At the jetty, we boarded an inflatable raft. At the helm, was a grizzle-faced captain, his white sailor's cap set at a jaunty angle. His nickname is Popeye, and he's famous across Brazil since appearing on TV and in the feature film *Mr Magoo*. There was a mad glint in Popeye's eye as we bumped over the

rapids towards the falls, and a worried fellow passenger, an Italian woman, turned to me and asked, "Is he OK, or is he crazy?"

Herons, perched on rocks in the torrid flow, nonchalantly looked on as we came face to face with the thundering wall of water. Duelling with **The Three Musketeers** takes on a whole new meaning when the musketeers in question are three 60-m (197-foot) tall and 20-m (67-foot) wide, crashing cascades of water, and their opponent is a small boat of screaming adventure tourists. Nevertheless, on the way back we were all yelling for more, including the Italian.

CONTROVERSIAL FLIGHTS

Several years ago, in the scramble to attract visitors, the Brazilians introduced helicopter flights over the falls. Although they provide another perspective on the watery spectacle, and are exciting in themselves, these rides are controversial, not least because of the noise they generate. At peak times, when flights take off nearly every 15 minutes, the disturbance they create can make it seem as though Iguaçu is on the front line of a war zone.

Not surprisingly, the Argentinians have been most vociferous in their condemnation of the helicopter flights, and wildlife experts claim the noise upsets the birds in the forest and is even causing some species to lay defective eggs. In the visitors' centre on the Argentine side there's a petition against the helicopters which has received over 12,000 signatures. Since complaints about the flights were made to UNESCO in November 1997, the helicopters have been flying higher—at 750m (2,500 feet) above the treetops—in an attempt to reduce the problem.

Rather than taking a bird's-eye view of the falls, a worthwhile pastime before leaving the Brazilian side of the falls is to look birds in the eye at the **Parque das Aves**, just outside the park entrance.

HOW THE FALLS WERE FORMED

Some 100,000 years ago a fault developed along the bed of the Río Paraná at the confluence with the Río Iguazú. The Earth shifted, leaving the western (Paraguayan) shore of the river some 30m (100 feet) higher than the eastern shore. The rushing waters of the Paraná further eroded the cracked bed rock and, over millenia, cut 80m (265 feet) deeper, leaving the Iguazú high above to form the waterfalls. Over time, the falls have receded 23km (14 miles) upstream, carving the canyon that now exists. Even today, chunks of basalt very occasionally drop off the rockface of the falls, proof that the process of their evolution continues.

This bird park has huge aviaries with over 60 different species of birds from all around Brazil as well as from overseas. The beauty of this place is that you can watch at incredibly close quarters many beautiful and otherwise shy birds, such as flamingos, the ostrich-like rhea (*Rhea americana*), hyacinth macaws (*Anodorhynchus hyacinthinus*) and toco toucans (*Ramphastoss toco*). Another highlight is walking through the butterfly house, where hummingbirds and fabulous butterflies flit among the exotic blooms.

CROSSING THE RIVER

To reach the Argentine side of the falls from the Brazilian park, I had to make a journey of over 40km (25 miles), which took me through the towns of Foz do Iguaçu and Puerto Iguazú, and across the Río Iguaçu Inferior via the Ponte Trancredo Neves. All this involves getting on and off four different buses. If you're only popping over for a day an organized tour is the better way to go, but if you intend to stay longer or to continue travelling in Argentina then you'll need to go through regular passport formalities on the Argentine side of the bridge.

Argentina's park, at 67,620ha (167,000 acres), is less than half the size of Brazil's, but it is generally more accessible, with several kilometres of walkways and tracks running through the rain forest. The falls here first became known to European settlers in 1541, when Alvar Nuñez Cabeza de Vaca, the second Royal Emissary to the River Plate, stumbled across them while he was making his way to Asunción from the coast. He called them the Santa María Falls, and this was the name the Jesuits gave to the short-lived mission that they established here in the 17th century a few kilometres upstream. The falls were "rediscovered" in 1882 by the Swiss explorer Giaccomo Bové and his Italian immigrant guide Carlos Bossetti (after whom the set of falls called Salto Bossetti is named). In 1934, the area

THE MISSIONS

The falls are in the Argentinian district of Misiones. At the start of the 1986 British film *The Mission*, a Jesuit priest is strapped to a cross and set adrift on the Río Iguaçu, heading for certain doom over the edge of the falls. The film is based on the sad history of South America's Jesuit missions (known as *reducciones*) before 1767 when the religious order was banished from the continent. Some 50 Jesuit garrison settlements—with grand central churches, libraries, and dormitories, and partly built to protect the Indians from raids by slave hunters—dotted the jungle across the Argentina, Brazil, and Paraguay border. Only ruins remain now, but they are worth visiting. Some of the best are at San Ignacio Mini, a mission that once housed 4,356 people and is now a national monument partly maintained by UNESCO. The closest town to San Ignacio Mini is Posadas, 63km (39 miles) to the east, but the ruins can also be visited in a long day trip from Puerto Iguazú.

was declared a national park on the recommendation of the government-commissioned landscape architect Carlos Thays.

With over half a million visitors to the falls each year it's often difficult to escape the crowds at Iguaçu. But if you set off early in the day along the **Macuco Trail**—the start of which is less than a kilometre (½ mile) from the old visitors' centre (see box, page 144)—you're likely to have the rain forest to yourself, save for hens, pheasants, monkeys, butterflies, and the occasional park ranger. The 3-km (1¾-mile) trail ends at the **Salto Arochea**, two small waterfalls plunging into a small pool.

The Paseo Inferior and Paseo Superior, near the old visitors' centre, are made up of metal walkways set above the forest floor and crossing over the many

LEFT *One of the butterflies in the bird park at Iguaçu Falls*
BELOW *Scarlet macaws, the most familiar of the South American parrots, are nevertheless declining in numbers as a result of deforestation and hunting*
RIGHT *The lively squirrel monkey has an exceptionally long prehensile tail, and distinctive facial markings*

BRAZIL

streams and crevasses before the falls. These walkways ensure that the impact visitors make on the plant life is kept to a minimum. Here you'll find some of the best vantage spots to view the **San Martín Falls** behind the island of the same name. From the Paseo Inferior it's possible to reach the river and cross by boat to San Martín island, where a short walkway leads up to **La Ventana** (the window), a rock formation so called because you can view the falls through it.

The most memorable spot in the Argentine park has to be the balcony at the edge of the Garganta del Diablo (Devil's Throat)—the world's single most powerful waterfall in terms of water flow per second. The sight of swifts fearlessly circling in the clouds of spray and darting behind the veils of water to their nests in the rocks is mesmerizing. Most of the walkway here has been washed away by floods, and until the new bridge is completed what's left has to be reached by a short ferry ride from Puerto Canoas, some 3km (1¾ miles) upstream from the park's visitors' centre.

RETURN TO THE DELUGE

Iguazú Jungle Explorer, the main adventure-tour company based in Iguazú National Park, offers five different boat-trip packages around the falls. The most relaxing is the Safari Náutico, a 45-minute trip by inflatable raft through the forested islands along the west bank of the **Río Iguazú Superior**. A guide rows the raft and points out wildlife along the way; you'll be able to spot many birds, such as the emerald-plumed green kingfisher (*Choroceryle americana*) and black cormorants, and turtles sunning themselves on rocks. In such a peaceful spot it's hard to credit that you are so close to the raging falls.

The Safari Náutico can be combined with the boat trip to the Devil's Throat balcony. If you want to make a day of it go for the Pasaporte Verde (Green Pass), which includes a couple of boat rides into

the heart of the falls. The shorter of these trips departs from the jetty on the Paseo Inferior walkway, opposite San Martín Island, and loops past the San Martín, Mbygua, Bosetti and Adam and Eve falls, before ducking under The Three Musketeers. The longer trip, appropriately known as the Grand Adventure, starts 8km (5 miles) down the Río Iguazú Inferior at Puerto Macuco, racing the rapids on the way to the falls. This is the trip that I decided to take.

The Grand Adventure starts at the Iguazú Jungle Explorer offices by the old visitors' centre, where I climbed up into a rugged, open truck, seemingly designed to transport troops into battle. We passed the construction site for the new visitors' centre, and took the muddy **Sendero Yacaratia** trail through the jungle to Puerto Macuco. There was no guided commentary on this trip—as there is on the Macuco Safari on the Brazilian side— but there are plans for an interpretative centre near the boat jetty.

Because the boats are larger and more stable, and because the falls are on the Argentine side of the gorge, we could get much closer to the cascades. At the San Martín Falls we faced the full force of the spray. It was then on for yet another joust with those musketeers. The captain asked if we had enough or if we wanted to go again, and 20 drenched passengers yelled in unison, "Again!"

i

GOING IT ALONE

INTERNAL TRAVEL

There are airports both at Foz do Iguaçu and Puerto Iguazú with connections to major cities in Brazil, Argentina, and Paraguay. If you're travelling around Brazil or to other South American countries it will probably be worth buying a Varig Brazil Airpass or a Mercosur Airpass covering airlines in Argentina, Brazil, Chile, Paraguay, and Uruguay; these passes can only be purchased outside of South America in conjunction with an international flight.

From both Foz do Iguaçu and Puerto Iguazú buses run hourly between 9am and 7pm to the falls. If you're crossing the Ponte Trancredo Neves by bus, keep your ticket so you can board the next local bus to come along after you're through passport control.

Unless you have your own transport (car hire is available at the airports) you'll generally be getting around the parks on foot. Only guests of the Sheraton International Iguazú can hire bikes ($8 a day).

WHEN TO GO

The volume of water passing over the falls is at its greatest during the cold, rainy season (April to July), when some of the catwalks closest to the river may be closed. Although it rains year round, it is warmer during the summer season (November to March), when temperatures and humidity can soar. Weekends, particularly Sunday, are the busiest times for visiting the falls; to see them in peace and quiet, plan your trip for during the week.

PLANNING YOUR TRIP

At least two days are needed to see both sides of the falls. Crossing between Argentina and Brazil by bus or taxi is straightforward, and if you're only visiting either country for a day you won't need a visa. Entrance to the Brazilian park costs 6 Real, payable in local currency only, while the fee for the Argentine park is $5 (likely to rise once the new facilities are in place), payable in either dollars or pesos.

Note that from October to February Argentina is an hour behind Brazil. Take account of this when making your plans, and check on departure times for buses when crossing the border.

PACKAGES AND TOURS

The best accommodation options are the hotels within the national parks, but you can make day trips to either side of the falls from Foz do Iguaçu or Puerto Iguazú. Of the two, Puerto Iguazú has the more relaxed small-town atmosphere.

If you're considering staying at one of the upmarket hotels on either side of the falls, it's worth checking out package deals available

within Brazil and Argentina, since these will certainly work out cheaper than buying flights and accommodation separately. On the Argentine side, it's possible to hire guides who can explain about the rain forest surrounding the falls; this should cost around $35 per group.

Of the two riverboat adventures, the Argentine operation is best if you're at all nervous: their boats are larger and more stable and their drivers are less apt to play daredevil.

For a flight over the falls, a minimum of two people are needed. The 7-minute flight costs $60 per person and circles the falls several times. The 35-minute flight takes in Puerto Iguazú and the Itaipú Dam (see box, page 145), as well as the falls.

ACCOMMODATION AND FOOD

Foz do Iguaçu has the best range of accommodation, including excellent budget options, but avoid its dodgy waterfront area after dark. Very few people who make the day trip to Cuidad del Este in Paraguay have a good word for the place and there's no reason for staying overnight here.

There's a small but fine range of restaurants in both Foz do Iguaçu and Puerto Iguazú. Eating options in the parks are limited and none too thrilling at the budget end; pack a picnic instead. Both Tropical and Sheraton hotels' restaurants are worth splashing out on.

WHAT TO TAKE

❏ Hiking boots.
❏ Binoculars for birdspotting.
❏ A waterproof jacket.
❏ Insect repellent

(see box, page 145)

HEALTH AND SAFETY MATTERS

You are advised to drink bottled water in both Brazil and Argentina. There's no danger of malaria, but there are plenty of mosquitoes so cover up with insect repellent and long-sleeved shirts and trousers, especially when trekking at dusk.

Ranching in Brazil's Grand Savannah

by Simon Richmond

A short stay at a pousada—*preferably one attached to a working ranch—is one of the best ways to experience the Pantanal, a vast and watery landscape in western Brazil, teeming with animal and bird life.*

The Pantanal covers an area larger than France, and yet you don't have to look very hard to spot wildlife. In fact, nothing could be easier. Within seconds of beginning the first afternoon safari of my three-day stay at the working ranch and eco-resort **Refugio Ecológico Caiman**, I was eye-balling a caiman (*Caiman crocodilus*)—the region's native alligator, also called a jacaré—its eyes and the tip of its snout being the only parts of the reptile above water. Near by was the wattled jacana (*Jacana jacana*), also known as the Jesus bird because it appears to walk on water.

A gate opened, and the truck carrying me and my fellow guests, Ton and Mariou from Holland, our young guide and trainee vet Fabio, and the local field guide and

ABOVE Bramah cattle on the savannah
LEFT A Caimaner leads a ride through the coper-
nica palms of the Carandazal lagoon
INSET The caiman absorbs heat through its
mouth, so it will bask in the sun with its jaws
open. This raises its body temperature, and so
provides it with sufficient energy for hunting

 Most activities involve sitting in a jeep or truck, riding on a horse, or walking slowly and watching for wildlife, so they're suitable for just about anyone.

★★ At the upmarket pousadas, the accommodation and food is tip-top, but if you're going budget then expect to rough it, either in a tent, a hut, or a hammock. The Pantanal is very wet during the wet season and sweltering hot during the dry, so come prepared. There are mosquitoes year round.

During the wet season, you'll need at least two pairs of boots because any hike will necessarily involve getting your feet wet. The weather is hot enough for one pair of shoes to dry out while you're wearing the others. A mosquito net will help you get a comfortable night's sleep. Take binoculars for viewing birds and animals. Photographers should invest in the best zoom lens they can afford. If you are going solo into the Pantanal, take everything you could possibly need for a camping trip.

driver Victor, continued its slow progress along the raised dirt road across the flooded savannah, scattering primrose butterflies as it went. We passed herds of Bramah cattle, which were originally imported from India but look more Scandinavian with their Viking-style horns. Fabio frequently asked the driver to stop so he could point out wildlife: in the long grass, there was a capybara (*Hydrochaeris hydrochaeris*), the world's largest rodent, while flying overhead were snail kites (*Rostrhamus sociabilis*) and limpkins (*Aramus guarana*). The occasional roaring sound we heard was, Fabio joked, the extended croak of the "Formula One frog."

Before the end of the afternoon, many, many more birds had been spotted, including the rare hyacinth macaw (*Anodorhynchus hyacinthinus*)—at 100cm (39in) long, the world's largest parrot—which is known in Portuguese as the *arara azul*. The Pantanal is the main habitat for this striking, deep-blue bird with a yellow ring beneath its hawked bill. Hunting and trapping have severely threatened the species, and the *refugio* sponsors a project to monitor the birds' well-being. On a walk across the flooded countryside, the water sloshing around

our shins, we spied a crab-eating fox (*Cerdocyon thous*) and brocket deer hasten into the undergrowth as we approached higher ground, and a large turtle retract into its shell.

We returned to the lodge as the setting sun created silhouettes of the trees against a sky running the gamut of colours from flamingo pink to deep turquoise. Cicadas and macaws were joining in the dusk chorus, as the Formula One frogs did one last lap of the Pantanal Grand Prix circuit.

ECOTOURISM BOOM

The Pantanal is one of the world's richest nature reserves. It is a 140,000-sq km (54,000-square mile) savannah that spreads across the west Brazilian states of Mato Grosso and Mato Grosso do Sol, as well as parts of neighbouring Bolivia and Paraguay. It's not a swamp, but an alluvial plane, where the rivers break their banks each year during the rainy season, flooding into the *baias* (small lakes and ponds) and creating an environment like the Florida Everglades.

Through both wet and dry seasons, the area is home to the largest concentration of wildlife in South America. An estimated 650 species of

BONITO

South of the Pantanal, and five hours by road from Campo Grande, is an alternative ecotourism destination, the small, relaxed town of Bonito. Since it was "discovered" by Brazilian T.V. in the early 1990s, Bonito's surrounding natural attractions have assured it a steady stream of local visitors, who, judging from their enthusiastic recommendations, are rarely disappointed.

The main places to head for are the Gruta do Lago Azul, a giant cave amid protected woodlands, 20km (12½ miles) from Bonito, and the Aquario Natural, a snorkelling spot teeming with fish at the source of the Río Formoso, 7km (4½ miles) from the town. Both places can be visited independently, but in view of the entry regulations it's more convenient, and cheaper, to take an organized tour. Whitewater rafting and scuba diving can be arranged with agents such as Hapankany Tours in Bonito (see Contacts).

There are over 30 hotels, as well as a new 50-bed youth hostel in Bonito, but if you're planning to visit during Christmas or Easter, or between July and August, you'll need to book accommodation well ahead of time. Contact tourist information in Campo Grande (see Contacts) for more details.

bird live here, including egrets, macaws, spoonbills, storks, and toucans, and there are 80 species of mammal and reptile, such as deer, monkeys, lizards, anacondas, and caiman. Migratory birds, such as geese and ducks from Argentina and Central America, also depend on the Pantanal, feeding on the 400 different species of fish that breed in the wetlands. And unlike the Amazon, where thick jungle obscures much of the wildlife, the Pantanal has wide open spaces that make it ideal for safaris.

The animal that you're likely to see most of, though, is the cow. Ranches,

The Panatal of western Brazil

THE TRANSPANTANEIRA

Despite its being pot-holed for most of its 145km (90 miles), and its ending in the middle of nowhere, the Transpantaneira highway—which links Pocone, 100km (62 miles) from Cuiabá, and the outpost of Porto Jofre—is one of the best places in the northern Pantanal for spotting the region's wildlife. The road is raised 2–3m (6–10 feet) above the plain and has some 120 bridges, many of which are very rickety wooden affairs. The original plan was for the highway to cross the Pantanal entirely, but the combined forces of ecological opposition and technical problems put a halt to the project.

There are plenty of tour operators and freelance guides in Cuiabá who can help you to arrange a trip along the Transpantaneira. If you are hiring a vehicle, a four-wheel drive is advisable because it will make the driving easier, but it is not essential. Make sure you have a spare tyre in good condition and keep a full tank of fuel. Hitching along the Transpantaneira is possible but not recommended, not least because of the prospect of sunstroke.

known as *fazendas*, sprang up across the grasslands of the Pantanal at the end of the 19th century, just as a local gold rush was petering out. Today, ranching is on the downturn, and though there are some 23 million head of cattle in the area, the cows are beginning to play second fiddle to the indigenous mammals, birds, and fish, whose commercial importance has become apparent with the increase in ecotourism. The **Refugio Ecológico Caiman**—located on the southern edge of the Pantanal, 236km (146 miles) west of Campo Grande, the capital of Mato Grosso do Sul—has led the way in capitilizing on the ecotourism boom. When owner Roberto Klaibin converted part of his 53,000-ha (130,000-acre) property into an ecotourism venture in the mid-1980s, his neighbours thought he was crazy. He set aside 7,000ha (17,300 acres) as an ecological reserve, vacated the family house (Pousada Caiman, a colonial-style lodge), and built three smaller, more modern lodges around the estate. Some 15 years later, Klaibin's instincts have proved right, and across the Pantanal many other *fazendas* are embracing ecotourism as the means to survive.

INSET *Two of the four* pantaneiros *that we watched in the corral helping to catch the next colt for gelding*

*ABOVE At the Refugio Ecológico Caiman, you
can ride alongside the* pantaneiros *as they
drive the cattle to higher ground*

BRAZIL

COWBOYS AND CAIMAN

Apart from its proximity to abundant nature, the Refugio Ecológico Caiman's main drawcard is its enthusiastic staff of bilingual biologists and naturalists, known as Caimaners, and its local field guides—people who have grown up in the Pantanal and know it and its inhabitants as they would family. Together they lead the hikes, truck safaris, horseback treks, and boat rides around the fazenda, providing the background information and personal touch that can transform a trudge through mosquito-ridden swamps into a fascinating adventure.

A bell is rung at half past six each morning to call guests to breakfast, and 30 minutes later the morning excursions begin, before the scorching sun rises too high in the sky. During the high season, when the lodge is full, there's a number of excursions to choose from, all detailed on a noticeboard in the courtyard beside the swimming pool. Near by hangs a photograph of Harrison Ford with the Caimaners, a memento of Ford's visit in his capacity as a board member of Conservation International.

The Caimaner leading us on this morning was Tilo, a biologist of German descent, accompanied by the field guide Getulio, a burly ex-cowboy. Getulio was carrying a bucket of cattle guts, breakfast for the caiman that hang out by the **Ponte do Paizinho** (Little Father Bridge). The bridge is named after the old man who first fed the reptiles many years ago. On the way there, we passed the cowboys (known in these parts as *pantaneiros*), who were waiting for the vet to arrive to assist them in gelding a herd of colts.

In the gallery forest that runs alongside the edge of the lagoon, capuchin monkeys (*Cebus capusinus*) were swinging in the trees, and an agouti (*Dasyprocta leporina*), a large rodent without a tail, scuffled in the undergrowth. A giant red-throated stork, the jabiru (*Ephippiorhynchus mycteria*), was sunning itself on the opposite side of the pond from the bridge, while cormorants dived for fish in the water, all unafraid of the several caiman that lurked close by. The reason for their bravery soon became obvious: the caiman were waiting for easier pickings. As we arrived, they waddled on to the land to be fed. Clumsy and somewhat blind, the caiman clambered over each other and often missed the meat entirely in their eagerness to eat. Tilo prodded one with a stick, pointing out the cuts of skin that make them prized by poachers. At least 2 million a year are "culled," so many in fact, that the species has become endangered. And although they're frightening to look at, these prehistoric reptiles are harmless if not provoked.

RANCH BUSINESS

The advantage of staying on a cattle-breeding ranch such as Refugio Ecológico Caiman is that you can see the *pantaneiros* at work. Would-be John Waynes are advised to visit between May and November, high season for cattle work. After gathering together the *fazenda*'s 23,000 cows, separating the males and females, and branding the newborn, the *pantaneiros* drive the herd up to higher ground before the rains begin. It's possible to join in these cattle drives and ride alongside the *pantaneiros*, experiencing the heat, humidity, mosquitoes, and fantastic scenery.

In the quieter months, there's work to be done domesticating horses. By the time we reached the corral, the vet was operating on the second colt, its legs trussed up and held down by four *pantaneiros*. At two years old, colts begin to get frisky, and they need to be gelded if the *pantaneiros* are going to train them to do useful work. Blood and iodine stain the muddy floor and the remaining colts huddle nervously by the fence. When it's time for the next one, the horse bolts round the corral, dodging the lasso, as if fully aware that his manhood is about to be cut out and tossed

TIPS FOR RIDING SOUTH AMERICAN STYLE

- ❏ Mount the horse from the left side. Put your left foot in the stirrup, push yourself upwards from your right foot, and swing your right leg over the saddle.
- ❏ Hold the reins in your right hand at a point above and in front of the withers (the base of the horse's neck). If you have the reins too long you will find it difficult to pull them towards you when you want to stop.
- ❏ Keep just your toe in the stirrup.
- ❏ To get the horse going forward, use your legs against his sides to push him on. When you want to stop, pull back smoothly on the reins and lean slightly back.

Pousada Caiman. Two months before, this area had been a dry, dusty plain covered with grass. Now, save for a few *cordilheiras* (islands of dry land that become the wet-season habitat of animals and reptiles) it was all under at least a metre (3¼ feet) of water.

The Dutch couple had never ridden before, but the pace was slow and the horses—all retired after putting in hard service on the ranch—were easy going. Getulio had joined our party again, leading the way and making sure the horses didn't accidentally step on a caiman. The horses don't mind the water at all, and they waded happily through the marsh grasses, as Mauritzio pointed to great black hawks, eared owls, and more hyacinth macaws. My recently dried boots got another thorough soaking.

The sun was setting as we headed back over the bridge to the pousada, but the day's activities were not over yet. After dinner at 8pm, we set off on the night safari led by Fabio. In the spotlight we saw how the caiman do their fishing: jaws are held open at the point where the river rushes into the pond, and the fish are swept into their mouths as they would into a net. We also passed a herd of capybara, looking like giant guinea pigs, feeding on the marsh plants. Most memorable though were the fireflies, flashing around us like stars falling from the heavens, and the incredible soundscape of the wetlands, intensified by the darkness.

BIG CATS AND BIRDS

The morning safari on the third day is led by Tietta, the only female Caimaner of the team, and the field guide Eduardo. We set off by truck to the **Pousada Cordilheira**, 14km (8½ miles) from Pousada Caiman and the most remote of the refugio's accommodation options. The whispering ibis, the ringed kingfisher (*Megaceryle torquata*), the great black hawk (*Buteogallus urubitinga*), and the greater ani (*Crotophaga major*), which

to the dogs that wait near by for an early lunch.

From the sidelines, we sipped *terere* tea through a silver straw-filter out of a hollowed bullock's horn, and watched as the vet, dressed in blue overalls, brandished syringe and scalpel with expertise. The horse struggles and sweats, and then suffers the final indignity of having its empty scrotum dusted with a white disinfectant powder and sprayed with a purple solution to keep away the flies. Before being released to totter off woozily, the colt's tail is clipped—the sign that he has now become a gelding. It's a gory spectacle, but it is also a fascinating insight into the "Rawhide" life of the *pantaneiros*.

HORSEBACK SAFARI

Mauritzio, another in the team of five Caimaners, was our guide for the afternoon's activity, which is a horse ride across the **Carandazal**, a beautiful lagoon sprouting hundreds of lofty copernica palms, beyond the *baia* next to

migrates to the Pantanal in the wet season, were spotted along the route; all were in search of fish across the freshly flooded plains.

One of the perplexing things about the Pantanal is how so many fish so quickly populate the area after the first rains of the wet season. The local legend is that it rains fish, but the less romantic explanation is that they hatch from eggs left in the mud.

If you're interested in going fishing in the Pantanal (see box, page 164), the best places to arrange a trip are Cuiabá and Corumbá, in the north. The ramshackle town of Corumbá, hard against the Bolivian border in the heart of the Pantanal, was a major river port in the 19th century. Now it's the place to head if you want to tour the Pantanal on the cheap. Guides meet all the buses and

trains arriving at the town and hang out in the hotels and restaurants.

From Pousada Cordilheira we continued on foot along a trail through the gallery forest. Tietta pointed out an anthill, and I was impressed to discover that the mighty ant that lives here can carry 30 times its bodyweight—a feat equivalent to that of a human lifting a car—but then Eduardo motioned for us to stop. Ten metres (30 feet) ahead on the path, and hiding in the shadows, is an ocelot (*Leopardus pardalis*), a predator rarely seen at this time of day. For a few seconds, both big cat and humans froze. We stared at each other. Then, in a couple of bounds, the ocelot disappeared into the forest.

Another safari moment awaited as we emerged from the trees. Three gangling rhea (*Rhea americana*),

cousins of the emu and ostrich, and the largest bird in the Americas, were stalking the long grass in the open pasture. According to Tietta, these brown and grey birds can sprint at up to 60km (37 miles) an hour, and they certainly don't hang around once they realize they have company.

ABOVE The guinea-pig-like capybara, the world's largest rodent, can grow up to 1.3m (4 feet) long and weigh up to 50g (110lb). It is a social animal, and an excellent swimmer and diver, so it is found in family groups near water, such as marshes. You are most likely to see capybaras at dawn or dusk, either foraging for food or swimming with only their eyes, nose and ears breaking the surface
LEFT The Refugio da Ilha
BELOW On a trip in a rowing boat to explore the baia beside Pousada Caiman

BRAZIL

FISHING IN THE PANTANAL

With over 400 different species of fish to go after—including the dorado (*Salminus maxillosus*), which can grow up to 30kg (32lb), and many species of piranha—it's not surprising that the Pantanal is considered to be one of the world's top fishing locations. Boats can be hired and fishing trips arranged in Corumbá, 400km (248 miles) west of Campo Grande, and in Cuiabá, the northern gateway to the Pantanal. To fish legally, you must have a licence (which costs $100). If you are planning an independent trip, you'll need to obtain the licence yourself from the IBAMA (Brazilian Environment and Natural Resources Institute), which has offices in both cities. Fishing is not allowed in the breeding season (between November and January).

MESSING ABOUT ON THE WATER

The final afternoon at the refugio was spent in a rowboat exploring the edge of the large *baia* beside Pousada Caiman. We drifted past water hyacinths, watched cormorants on branches, drying their feathers, and were thankful for the dragonflies, which helped to keep the mosquitoes at bay.

I spent an even better day on the water, though, at the **Refugio da Ilha** on the banks of the Río Salobra, some 60km (37 miles) south of the Caiman *fazenda*. I had come to this small and homely *pousada* to sample an alternative to the highly organized ranch and safari experience at Caiman, and immediately I found the relaxed atmosphere very appealing. It's fine just to lie in a hammock or sit in the shade of one of the magnificent fig trees round the *pousada*, but there are plenty of activities, too. The young English-speaking owner, Mauricio, was quick to show me the

16-km (10-mile) walking or mountain biking track that runs along the top of dikes behind the property, as well as the snorkelling spot, and the fishing pond.

The best part of the day—apart from mealtimes when I was treated to fantastic food—was the motorboat trip up the **Río Salobra**, a narrow waterway that meanders wildly through forests bristling with wildlife. The trip took us past several natural aquaria—areas of the river where giant schools of fish gather—and ended at the lush, expansive **Baia Negra**, a body of tannin-stained water that is a magnet for birdlife. Big-billed toco toucans (*Ramphastos toco*) were hanging out in the trees, a couple of jabiru were gliding by, and the quintessential Pantanal scene was completed with the distinctive sound of the one bird of the area whose name you'll never forget: the chaco chachalaca (*Ortalis canicollis*).

CHAPÃDA DOS GUIMARAES

Some 60km (37 miles) northeast of Cuiabá is Chapãda dos Guimaraes—the northern gateway to the Pantanal—a startling, rocky highland and forest that bears more resemblance to the landscape of Arizona than it does to Mato Grosso's lush swamps. Like the North American state this is also a reputed hotspot for UFO activity, although you shouldn't let that put you off visiting. If you don't have your own transport, it's best to organize an excursion out of the town of Chapãda, 73km (45 miles) north of Cuiabá; the agency Eco Turismo has a good reputation. Make sure you visit the area's two premier sights, Véu de Noiva (Bridal Veil), a 60-m (196-foot) high waterfall, and the Mirante, which affords an amazing view all the way back to Cuiabá. Short treks lasting anything up to three days can be arranged in the area, along with cave explorations and horse rides.

GOING IT ALONE

INTERNAL TRAVEL

Both Campo Grande and Cuiabá—the southern and northern points of access respectively to the Pantanal—have airports with connections to other major Brazilian cities. Turbulence from dry-season bushfires and wet-season storms can make landing at these airports a nerve-wracking ordeal; in the worst cases the plane will fly on to Sao Paulo, or another nearby airport and you'll have to wait for conditions to improve. Because Brazil is such a big country, if you're planning to visit more than one place it's well worth buying a Varig Brazil Airpass.

There are few all-weather roads in the Pantanal, but travelling by car or bus is generally the fastest and cheapest way of getting around. However, some *pousadas* are so isolated that they can be reached only by plane, which will add considerably to the expense even if you can split the cost among a group. Boats are another way to go; both budget and luxury cruise trips are best arranged in Corumbá, a small town on the banks of the Río Paraguay and close to the Bolivian border; it's possible to get here by train from Santa Cruz, Bolivia. There's also an airport in Corumbá served by connections from both Campo Grande and Cuiabá; you will not be able to use an airpass for flights to Corumbá, though.

WHEN TO GO

Many guides recommend visiting the Pantanal in the dry season, from April to October, when the weather is more settled and you're guaranteed to see animals. But it is in the rainy season, from December to April, that the Pantanal is at its most characteristic—a vast flooded plain. The hottest months are December to February when temperatures are regularly above 40°C (104°F). If you are interested in seeing the *pantaneiros* at work, go between May and November.

PLANNING YOUR TRIP

The Pantanal is a difficult place to travel through independently. The buses that connect up the main cities of Campo Grande and Cuiabá with settlements inside the wetlands are infrequent and subject to the weather during the wet season. If driving yourself, it's easy to get lost or stuck on one of the many tracks that snake off towards the *fazendas* from the few main roads. You should seriously consider hiring a guide (easily found in Corumba or Cuiaba); and take all your own gear, including food,

tent, first-aid kit, mosquito repellent, torches, and spare batteries.

An organized trip will enable you to avoid such hassles. You'll enter the Pantanal by jeep, truck or boat, and either camp, or stay at one of the more up-market *pousadas*. If time is limited, the best place to head for is Corumbá because it is conveniently situated in the centre of the Pantanal.

If you are on a tight budget, the Pantanal is not really the best place to be travelling in. The most inexpensive option would be to go to Corumbá, where you'll find the highest concentration of backpacker operations offering trips. If money isn't an issue then it's worth forking out to stay in one of the *pousadas*, where the safari excursions will be better organized, and the accommodation—especially after what can be exhausting days in such high temperatures—is likely to be much more comfortable than you'll find elsewhere. Both Campo Grande and Cuiabá have a good selection of hotels and restaurants, and shops in which to stock up on essentials before heading out to the wilds.

WHAT TO TAKE

❏ If visiting during the wet season, you'll need at least two pairs of boots.

❏ A mosquito net is essential.

❏ If striking out solo into the Pantanal, take everything you could possibly need for a camping trip.

❏ Binoculars for the wildlife.

HEALTH AND SAFETY MATTERS

❏ Officially there's no malaria in the Pantanal, but there are plenty of mosquitoes; constantly apply insect repellent and keep covered up, especially during the peak biting hours at dusk.

❏ Drink only bottled water.

❏ Take a first-aid kit.

Madre de Dios

Mamoré

Guaporé

Trinidad

Lago
Titicaca

16 **17**

■ **La Paz**   Cochabamba

Oruro   ■ **Santa Cruz**

Lago de
Poopó   **Sucre**

Salar
de
Uyuni   Potosí

Uyuni

A n d e s

Tarija

▲ 5916m

| 0 | 250 | 500 km |
| 0 | 100 | 200 | 300 m |

BOLIVIA

L andlocked Bolivia might be one of the poorest
countries in South America, but it is rich in natural
beauty, indigenous culture, and adventure-tourism
opportunities. Here you'll find some of the most extreme
landscapes in the world: from the literally breathtaking
heights of the Cordillera Real mountains, to the sultry, lush
jungles of the Yungas and the Amazon Basin there is a
difference in altitude of over 5,000m (16,400 feet).

You'll need plenty of time and a sense of humour to find
your way around this surreal country, where women sell
bizarre potions in the La Paz markets, flamingos strut across
the paint-pot-coloured lakes of the altiplano, and roads and
railways are in a shocking state. But the mountain climbing
and the treks—many along pre-Hispanic, paved roads—and
the trips into the jungle and through off-the-beaten track
national parks, make the effort to get there well worth while.

The trails to the Yungas from La Cumbre, Bolivia

Cordillera Range

by Simon Richmond

The picturesque town of Sorata, fancifully compared to Adam and Eve's Garden of Eden, is paradise found when it comes to hiking and climbing in the northern part of the snow-capped Cordillera Real range.

Flying into La Paz's John F. Kennedy Airport—at 4,058m (13,315 feet) above sea-level the highest commercial airport in the world—is an unnerving experience. Out of the window, I can see the flat plain of the *altiplano*, Lake Titicaca off in the distance, and surrounded by the jagged, snow-capped peaks of the Andes, and the brick, box houses of the city tumbling into a looming canyon below. This is no place to overshoot the runway, but in the thin air at this lofty altitude, planes actually have to accelerate to land safely.

Once on the ground, the altitude affected me and it wasn't so easy to catch my breath. For the next couple of days, I took things easy, acclimatizing myself to the altitude as I strolled slowly up and down the steeply raked streets of the *defacto* capital of Bolivia (the official one is Sucre, some 500km further south). In the bustling atmosphere, I shopped at the colourful street markets and in between stopped for restorative cups of the local brew, *maté de coca*.

By day three, I was ready to head to Sorata, 149km (92½ miles) northwest of La Paz at the gentler altitude of 2,695m (8,840 feet). This tranquil colonial town, perched on a hill amid fertile valleys and fed by sparkling streams, has been compared in Bolivian literature to the Garden of Eden. It's obviously not quite that perfect, but for trekkers and climbers Sorata is an ideal base for excursions into the northern part of the 160-km (99-mile) long Cordillera Real mountain range, the eastern flank of the continent-long Andes range; and for anyone else it rates as one of the best places in Bolivia in which to relax.

I arrived at the start of the rainy season, which put a damper on the possibility of undertaking the longer treks, such as the seven-day circuit of the Illampu-Ancohuma massif, or the infamous Mapiri Trail. But, as long as the weather held, there was no reason why I couldn't aim for Laguna Glaciar, a three-day trip from Sorata, or at the very least knock off a couple of day hikes in an area from which the ancient Tiahuanaco and Inca empires extracted gold.

There are over 500 mountains topping 5,000m (16,400 feet) in the Cordillera Real. Sorata is the base for the northern end of the range, in particular the Ancohuma-Illampu massif. There are plenty of relatively easy day hikes in the foothills, but the longer trails and ascents are tough work. You'll need to have acclimatized in La Paz for around a week before attempting to climb the highest mountains, such as Huayna Potosí and Illampu, and to have sorted out guides, since there are no experienced mountaineering guides in Sorata.

Sorata is a very pleasant, small town, with a few good hotels and restaurants, but nothing approaching top-class international standards. Once out in the mountains, you'll be relying on your own resources for comfort. The less you carry, however, the easier you'll find the going.

Ultraviolet-proof glacier glasses are essential to protect against snow blindness. Bring your own climbing boots, sleeping bag, and ground mat. Virtually all other climbing gear can be hired in La Paz. For cooking, take a multi-fuel stove that can burn the cheap pump petrol available in Bolivia. A pack cover will protect a backpack from dust and the elements while hiking and during the periods it might spend on top of a bus.

JOURNEY TO SORATA

I shared a taxi up to the Cementario district with Pete from England and Cathy from New Zealand. We'd left in plenty of time (time enough to get snarled up in La Paz's traffic), only to find that the bus that would take us from Cementario to Sorata was delayed, giving the hawkers more time to try to sell their stocks of toilet paper, matches, and sweets. Together with a German couple, we were the only "gringos" on a bus full of Aymara men, women, and their children bundled in warm woollies, all heading for the altiplano and beyond.

Eventually we set off, winding up out of the canyon, past graffiti-covered buildings to El Alto, the grungy, urban overspill of La Paz. The sun reflecting off the tin roofs of the houses in the valley below made them twinkle like quartz crystals in a opencast mine. Beyond the police checkpoint (you might need to show your passport), rural Bolivia begins and in another hour we were passing Lake Titicaca. Ever present are the mountains of the Cordillera Real, including Huayna Potosí, a very popular two-day mountain climb out of La Paz (see box, page 172).

Past the small town of Achacachi, the asphalt ends and the road continues as a reasonably good gravel track alongside marshy fields through which cows and sheep wade. Once into the foothills of the cordillera, the ground became rockier and the route more twisting. The hairpin-bend descent into the valley is stomach-churning. The steep hillsides, with their terraced fields, look like they're clothed in corduroy, and the clean scent of eucalyptus trees hangs in the air. As we made a sharp turn by a hill crowned by a statue of Christ, Sorata came into view, a patchwork of cream-, terracotta-, and blue-painted houses across a sloping plateau above the Río San Cristóbal.

A TOWN WITH A VIEW

The fortunes of Sorata have long been tied in with the area's natural wealth. From the end of the Tiahuanaco empire in Bolivia

TRAIL OF BLOOD AND TEARS

The very arduous Mapiri Trail, which links the villages of Ingenio and Mapiri, was originally hacked out of the jungle in the 19th century as a transport route for rubber between Sorata and the Yungas. It takes at least six days to walk, during which time—according to British writer Matthew Parris (author of *Inca Cola*)—you'll have endured worse than the ten plagues, but have been rewarded with spectacular views and as close an encounter with the wilds of Bolivia as you could possibly wish for.

Because of the route's difficulty, which includes sections blocked by rocks, mud and fallen trees, it's recommended that you take an organized tour along the trail, such as those offered by Club Sorata. Be prepared for freezing to tropical temperatures (the trail starts at 4,658m (15,280 feet) and ends in the Yungas jungle), and the full gamut of attacking insects. If you're still not sure whether to do it, the comments book and photos at the Copacabana Hotel will give you a good idea of what you're letting yourself in for.

(around A.D. 1000), the valleys that surround the town were one of the main centres for gold mining in the Andes, and the Incas carted the precious metal to Cusco from here. Sorata was destroyed in a siege during a revolt by the indigenous Indians against the Spanish in 1781, but it recovered a century later to prosper from the trade in quinine, rubber, and coca, fostered by an influx of German migrants.

The now quietly fading mansions that were built during this period of wealth still surround Sorata's Plaza General Peñaranda, a cool square of neatly bordered gardens and tall palm trees. The square is named after Enrique Peñaranda, a local boy made good, who was Bolivia's

president from 1940 to 1943, and whose statue stands at its centre. Cobbled streets run up and down the hill from the square, leading out to the trekking trails that are the prime attraction for visitors today. On clear days it's possible to see the summits of both Illampu and Ancohuma from here—the classic Sorata view of both tropical palms and snowbound peaks.

In one corner of the square is the two-storey mansion built in the mid-19th century as the home of a German rubber baron. When the Günther family bought the house this century, it became known as Casa Günther; but since 1968 it has been a hotel, the Residencial Sorata. Some of the Günther's quirky possessions still decorate the rambling place. In the airy sitting rooms hang stern-looking black and white family portraits. On one wall in the inner courtyard are tacked the scaly hides of enormous snakes, looking for the world like strips of dragon skin. And in the unruly, colourful garden, hook-billed macaws, hopping rabbits and slinky cats vie for the guests' attention.

THE LAND THAT TIME FORGOT

The next morning, I headed to the **San Pedro Caves**, a 24-km (15-mile) round-trip that is one of the most popular day walks from Sorata. You can follow the road, which winds along high above the Río San Cristóbal, or take a track that runs closer to the river. A map in the Residencial Sorata shows the way, and warns that the lower route can be dangerous in places. I opted for the road, and packed plenty of food and water.

Leaving the town, I passed squealing pigs, bleating sheep, and snoozing dogs, as well as kids having a kick-about on the football pitch. Wispy rain clouds hung in the valley, and for the next hour of intermittent showers I pulled my raincoat on and off until the weather finally made up its mind to be sunny. Looking back from this point along the road, I had

PREVIOUS PAGE A woman tends her llamas against a backdrop of Lake Titicaca

CLIMBING HUAYNA POTOSÍ

With a guide and the right equipment, such as ropes, crampons, and ice axes, the inexperienced can scale Huayna Potosí, but it's still not a climb to be approached lightly. To reach the summit at 6,088m (19,9733 feet), involves camping overnight on a glacier at 5,600m (18,370 feet)—higher than the base camp on Everest—and you'll have to negotiate many dangerous crevasses. Also you must have been in La Paz for at least a week to avoid a possible fatal case of altitude sickness.

The trailhead, at the Zongo Pass, is best reached by hired jeep, although it's possible to travel there by public transport from La Paz (go to Plaza Ballivan in El Alto and haggle for ride). The first day's climb to the Campamento Argentino will take around four hours, up scree slopes and across the crevassed glacier. The next day, set off early (before 4am) if you plan to reach the summit—at least another five-hour climb away—and returning to La Paz the same day. A better plan is to camp at the Zongo Pass, next to the house of Miguel, who works with his family as porters on the mountain. Camping elsewhere at the Zongo Pass dam is not recommended because the place is notorious for thieves.

chocolate-box views of Sorata. The hillsides ahead are deeply eroded in places, exposing turquoise and yellow seams of minerals.

It seems that the modern world has completely passed the valley by: the steeply terraced fields of the Incas are still farmed in much the same way as they've always been; an old man passes me, bearing a heavy load of wooden sticks on his back; an ox drags an iron plough through a ridiculously slanted field, while a peasant woman, with a baby strapped to her back in a sling shawl, drops seeds in the fresh furrows. On the entire walk, only a handful of vehicles overtake me.

IN THE BAT CAVE

After two hours I reached the hamlet of San Pedro, where I paused for lunch by the sign pointing up to the entrance to the caves. The locals take it in turns to keep guard and collect the entrance fee of $1. On this day it was the turn of Alansio, accompanied by his playful, honey-coloured dog, Tesero, who sniffed around me for scraps of food. Alansio cranked up the generator and a string of naked bulbs lit the way into the cavern.

The initial section of the passage is low, and I had to crouch down to get through to the lofty, wide chamber. The walls are etched with graffiti, and in the dark recesses bats and owls make their homes. The humidity comes from the shallow lake at the far end of the cavern, impeding further exploration. As soon as I had exited the cave, Alansio and Tesero packed up and returned to the village. I followed on and, after an ill-fated attempt to pick up the lower track, stuck with the more reliable road back to Sorata.

If you have the energy, continue up the track past the cave for about 20 minutes and you'll reach a panoramic viewpoint across the valley, where it's also possible to camp. A similarly spectacular view can be had on the way down to Sorata from the 3,061-m (10,042-foot) summit of Cerro Ulluni Tija, the hill topped by a statue of Christ. An easy way to do this is to take a La Paz-bound bus up the hill (ask to be dropped at El Cristo), and walk back down, following the trail that leads through the village of Atahuallani and across the Río San Cristóbal back up to Sorata.

TWO MEN AND A MULE

For the best views of all—clouds permitting, it's necessary to put in the leg work and climb the mountains. Don't underestimate the possible impact of altitude sickness at these heights; and certainly don't attempt to go unless

there's been a clear run of good weather, for conditions can quickly become very grim as you climb higher. Warm clothes and all-weather gear are essential.

Before undertaking the three-day hike to the **Laguna Glaciar**—at 5,038m (16,528 feet) one of the world's highest lakes—I paid a visit to the Sorata Guides Association, to arrange all the necessary equipment, a guide, and a mule to transport our gear and supplies up the initial section of the climb. I was asked if I wanted to organize my own food, or have the guide do all the shopping for me and himself. I opted for the full-service approach, but decided to take a few snacks of my own for variety.

I was lucky as my guide, Eduardo, spoke a little English; most don't. Despite the threateningly cloudy conditions, Eduardo and mule were waiting for me the next morning at 8am. We headed out of the village, climbing steeply up the northern side of the Río Lakathiya Valley. The mule did the hard work of carrying the packs, leaving me free to admire the verdant scenery which, as you get higher, gives way to a sparser landscape of rocks, gravel, and mosses.

This is the route you must take to start the six-to-seven day circuit of Illampu-Ancohuma massif, an epic trek requiring climbs through three passes over 4,000m (13,100 feet) and one over 5,000m (16,400 feet). You should hire mules and a guide for the start of this trek, too, since the many paths through cultivated fields and to the scattered lowland villages make finding the right way tricky. There are a couple of villages en route in which you may be able to replenish supplies, but it's safer to carry sufficient food for the entire trek.

COLD MOUNTAIN

An hour out of Sorata we crossed the Río Tucsa Jahuira and passed through the hamlet of Conani, not far from which are the ruins of an Inca *marka*, an ancient burial place. It might not look much, but to the locals this is a sacred place and

Eduardo warned me not to touch any of the surrounding litter, much of which is offerings to the Pachamama, the earth deity worshipped by the Aymara Indians.

Late in the day we reached **Laguna Chillata**, at 4,200m (13,780 feet), where we would camp for the next two nights. Witches are said to gather here to invoke the power of the lake to cure illness, and, although the lake is reputed to harbour a fortune in gold, all who have prospected at Chillata have met their doom. After sunset, there's no doubting the chilling power of this desolate spot.

We began the final climb of 800m (2,625 feet) to the Laguna Glaciar at 7am in frigid temperatures after a basic breakfast of porridge and *maté* tea.

ABOVE Taking a break near the summit of Huayna Potosí, Bolivia's most popular mountain for climbers
BELOW Sorata makes an attractive base for exploring the northern Cordillera Real range

I was unlucky in that clouds enfolded the mountains, blocking out what I'm told are fabulous views of Sorata below and, on especially clear days, Lake Titicaca and the snow-capped Cordillera Apolobamba way to the north. I imagined what this would be like, while scrambling slowly behind Eduardo across the gravel slopes towards our goal, which was the gap between Illampu and Ancohuma— mountains that were now so close that they seemed within a hand's grasp.

After four hours of hard leg work, the glacier finally came into view—a wall of white ice between the mountain slopes, plunging into the steely grey waters of the lake, across which mini icebergs float. The altitude was making my head pound, but I was glad to have made it to this remote spot and to have the opportunity to experience something of the untamed beauty of the Cordillera Real.

GOING IT ALONE

INTERNAL TRAVEL

Buses leaving from the Cementario area of the city take four hours to reach Sorata, and they depart at frequent intervals during the day. The cost is around 11 bolivianos. Snacks, water, a portable cassette player (or earplugs), and a good book, are all essential carry-on items. Keep your passport handy as there are checkpoints along the route. For the best views of the mountains, sit on the right-hand side of the bus.

The road to Sorata is generally in a good enough condition to consider driving along it yourself, but there have been fatal accidents, so think twice. If you hire a car, go for a four-wheel drive and check the tyres and brakes before handing over any money.

WHEN TO GO

Bolivia's winter season runs from May to October, but the best time for climbing and trekking, when the weather is almost guaranteed to be fine, is from June to August. The rainy season is between December and March, during which time you should avoid mountain climbing altogether and choose trekking routes with care.

PLANNING YOUR TRIP

Being able to speak Spanish helps immensely, but you won't find things too difficult if you don't.

For long-distance trekking and climbing, get hold of the best maps you can before departing; look for the 1:50,000-scale Deutschen Alpen Verein Cordillera Real Nord, the Illampu and Cordillera Real Sud–Illumani, or similar.

The best guidebooks are *Trekking in Bolivia* and *Bolivia: a climbing guide*, both by Yossi Brain, who is a local climbing guide. They are published in the U.S.A. by The Mountaineers, and in the U.K. by Cordee.

Many tour agencies in La Paz offer organized treks in the Cordillera Real, including guides and equipment; rates and services differ so check out several before deciding. Rates will be more expensive than those in Sorata, especially if you insist on an English-speaking guide, but the guides and organization tend to be more professional.

The going rate for hiring a guide in Sorata is 50 bolivianos a day per group. You'll be expected to pay extra for the guide's food and for any gear you rent. The tours organized by Eduardo at Club Sorata in the Hotel Copacabana are a bit more expensive, but he does have the best information in town on trekking and climbing. Louis Demers, the manager of the Residencial Sorata, can also give advice on trekking.

If you opt to go solo, it's possible to hire equipment such as tents and sleeping bags in La Paz and Sorata, if you haven't brought your own. If you're looking for trekking companions, consider putting a note up at the most popular travellers' hotels.

You'll have no problem finding accommodation to suit your budget in La Paz, which is well served with hotels and restaurants. In Sorata there's a reasonable range of tourist facilities. Out of season it's a quiet place, but at other times it's important to book ahead if you want to be sure of staying at a particular hotel. On the mountains the only option is camping.

HEALTH AND SAFETY MATTERS

Headaches, lethargy, dizziness, loss of appetite, and nausea, are all symptoms of high-altitude sickness, called *soroche* in Bolivia. The best treatment is rest, lots of clear liquids (but not alcohol), non-aspirin painkillers for the headaches, and anti-nausea tablets. *Maté de coca*, an infusion of coca leaves, is the local remedy.

Although food hygiene has improved in recent years, you should remain cautious about where you eat, and avoid uncooked foods. You should drink bottled water; if taking water from streams while hiking and camping, boil it, or use iodine-based purification tablets or a filter. It is also a good idea to carry drugs, such as Tinidazole, to deal with amoebic dysentry or giardia.

Bolivia has no mountain-rescue service, so take extra care when climbing and trekking.

Medical repatriation insurance is essential, as all serious injuries should be dealt with in the U.S.A., Europe, or similar, and not in Bolivia, where medical standards, although improving, are still low.

Bolivian Highs and Lows

by Simon Richmond

Looking for adventure? Try a mountain-bike ride down what is possibly the most dangerous road in the world—the narrow track from high-altitude La Paz to the sultry jungles of the Yungas—followed by a rafting trip along the Río Coroico.

The Aymara women tending the bizarre stalls at the Witches Market in La Paz are not known for being friendly; and they will shoo away inquisitive tourists, especially those with cameras. But Josephina was different, and happy to explain the tricks of her superstitious trade. The dried llama foetus, placed in a bowl of pastel-shaded sugar candies and twists of wool, was an offering to ensure good fortune for a new building. The clay model of an owl was for intelligence, the tortoise for goodbyes; the condor was for safe travels, and this was the one I wanted. Facing a mountain-bike ride down a road claimed to be the most dangerous in Bolivia, if not

4 Neither the bike ride nor the rafting (the river is rated Class III–IV) are for the faint-hearted. Previous rafting experience is recommended before taking a trip down the Río Coroico. The longer treks also require a fair deal of stamina. There are several good, short, but hilly, hikes around Coroico, whose comparatively warm temperature and low altitude make it a pleasant place to relax. The bike ride can be tackled by beginners.

★★ Expect to be coated in grime and shaken to your very core by the end of the bike ride. On the longer treks you'll be camping and will have to carry your own water or find it along the way.

For the bike ride, a thermal jacket or sweater is needed for the chilly start—these can be purchased cheaply in La Paz. Sunglasses and a bandanna to keep grit from eyes and nose. It's also a good idea to have a replacement battery for your camera; the cold at high altitude often causes batteries to stop working. For the treks, get hold of the best map you can and take all the usual camping gear.

the world, followed by a rafting trip through the Class IV rapids of the Río Coroico, I reckoned I needed all the protection I could get. I handed over a few coins, and clutching my talisman, tripped back down Sagárnaga.

In a mountainous country where only 5 percent of the roads have any form of asphalt covering (with the result that the remaining ones frequently turn to mud with the onset of the rainy season), a road that is above all others in awfulness earns itself quite a reputation. Such is the road from La Paz to the Yungas, and in particular the unpaved, narrow section from Unduavi to the pitstop of Yolosa. Anyone who has ever travelled it will be in no doubt that the reputation is well deserved. This is a nerve-wracking route, with vertical drops of over 1km (½ mile) off the side of a poor gravel track that takes you into impenetrable jungle. This so-called road is no wider than 3m (10 feet) in places, and passes under several waterfalls that further erode its already crumbling surface.

In a bus or car the journey is thrilling enough, taking you down, via hairpin bends, 3,600m (11,800 feet) in altitude from snowy mountain peaks shrouded in clouds to sultry jungle. Riding on a mountain bike at speeds of up to 50km (30 miles) per hour, and freewheeling past seemingly suicidal truck drivers and howling dogs, it's nothing short of an adrenaline injection straight to the heart. "You can't do rides like these at home," boasts the publicity leaflet for Gravity Assisted Mountain Biking, run by young New Zealander Alistair Matthews. This is

Routes from La Paz to the remote Yungas region

no hype. The 62-km (38½-mile) ride, which will take between four and five hours depending on the weather, will leave me exhausted, filthy and, Alistair assured me, exhilarated. I just hoped I'd be alive to tell the tale.

A PRAYER FOR THE TRAVELLERS

The only difference between the minibus that pulled up in front of McDonalds on the Prado at 8am, and the scores of others plying the streets of La Paz, was its roof rack stacked with eight mountain bikes. McDonalds was the meeting point, and from here we'd drive the 26km (16 miles) uphill to La Cumbre, the start of the bike ride. On the way we passed through Villa Fátima, from where buses for Coroico depart, and then through the *tranca*, a police checkpoint found on the edge of all Bolivian towns. Aymara women, bundled in their shawls against the chill, sell drinks and snacks; and an unlikely looking priest in a blue boiler suit offers, for a small renumeration, to bless vehicles for a safe journey ahead.

The road to **La Cumbre** (the 4,725-m (15,500-foot) high point of the La Paz–Yungas route) is smooth asphalt passing through a dour landscape of steel-grey rocks, coated with a light dusting of snow, and hardy vegetation reminiscent of the highlands of Scotland. But for the llamas that graze by its side, the reservoir Laguna Inkachata could well be a loch. On a clear day, the icy summit of Huayna Potosí, the most popular mountain to climb in Bolivia, can be glimpsed.

Plenty of stray dogs loiter by the side of the road, waiting for the scraps of food Bolivians always chuck to them. Some

people believe the dogs are the reincarnated souls of those who have perished on the road, but if that's the case there should be hundreds more. Many small tombstones and crosses line the way; in one incident alone in 1983, over 100 *campesinos* (country people) died when the lorry they were hitching a lift in plunged into the jungle. For bikers, these dogs are one more obstacle on the road; if they snap at you, Alistair's advice is to "bark at them madder and meaner than they do."

THE RIDE BEGINS

It had been chilly in La Paz, but at this altitude it's even colder. Leaving the minibus at the desolate La Cumbre plateau, crowned with its statue of Christ, I was glad of the extra layers of clothes I was advised to bring. Between March and May you can expect snow here. Activity is also more of an effort in the thinner air, so it's a good idea to acclimatize in La Paz for several days before undertaking any mountain ventures, such as this, or the classic Choro Trail bike ride to Coroico (see box, page 181), which starts at the same spot.

Before the warm-up ride around the shallow pond at La Cumbre, Alistair gave us a short lecture on how best to ride the bike (see box, page 180), and on some of the obstacles (apart from the dogs) to be aware of on the way down. We were to start on the right side of the road, but would have to move to the left when the asphalt stopped and the gravel began. There's one tunnel, and we were to remove our sunglasses before entering it. When passing through the couple of small villages along the road, we were to slow down: colliding with a chicken or small child would be disastrous.

It was reassuring to know that if any of us had a puncture or worn brake pads—either of which is not unlikely given the punishment the bikes endure during the descent—a guide at the rear of the group carried spares and a repair kit. At two places along the route the brakes and tyre pressure would be checked, and there would be plenty of other breaks to allow

LEFT At the Witches Market in La Paz: the bizarre collections of objects will bring good luck to the purchasers
BELOW On one of several trails that lead down from La Paz into the Yungas Valley

us to have a snack (chocolate is recommended) and take photographs.

The ride began in awe-inspiring fashion. We whizzed down a wide, level road that meanders wildly through a V-shaped valley between jagged spurs of rust-brown mountains. A stream tumbles along the bottom of the valley, electricity pylons marching by its side, and clouds drift in among the spurs. On one slope, a zigzag path leads to a

RIGHT Dizzying precipices and terrifyingly tight bends on the road down from La Paz

B O L I V I A

glacier, down which mules cart ice used to preserve the freshwater fish brought from the rivers beyond the Yungas to La Paz. The low, metal barriers on the curves are crumpled and misshapen from collisions; but I tried not to think about that.

THROUGH THE CLOUD FOREST

An hour later, we were pausing for a late breakfast of coffee and fried-egg sandwiches at one of the refreshment shacks that line the road beside the drugs checkpoint at Unduavi. The lush Yungas is a major producer of coca leaves that can be turned into cocaine, and it's a condition of American aid to Bolivia that this checkpoint inspects all vehicles on the road. Already we'd dropped 1,500m (4,920 feet), and the sharp wind has cut through to the bone. From here to the start of the gravel—roughly 4km (2½

miles)— is a series of small uphills with one 200-m (220-yard) long slope that gets the blood pumping again.

The clouds closed in, creating a wall of fog that shrouds the landscape and provides the damp conditions for the prolific growth of ferns, mosses, and other plants, across the rocky cliffs. At the crest of the hill, the road splits and we took the leg heading to Nor Yungas. Near by we passed the engineering works for the new road to Coroico, which is largely completed save for a major tunnel. This new route is designed to be safer than the one I was using, but it is not expected to be ready for a long while yet. In the meantime, the ugly evidence of its construction is apparent in the broad scars of red mud that blight the forested slopes lower down the road.

Just before we switched, as Alistair put it, to the "scenic side" of the road (i.e. the side on which there are sheer 1,000-m/3,280-foot drops), we stopped for another safety briefing. From here on, downhill traffic passes on the outside of the road. The idea is to get vehicles to slow down and ensure that drivers with the best view of their outside tyres—and the cliff edge—do the risky backing up if faced with oncoming traffic on the narrow patches. Although it would often be possible for us to squeeze past vehicles, we were not to attempt to overtake until Alistair had given the OK signal.

DOWN TO COROICO

The true nature of the road remains hidden in the clouds for several kilometres but, as we emerged into the sunshine, its full beauty—and hideous danger—became immediately apparent. I paused to marvel at the buses, lorries, and cars, slowly making their way along the ledge precariously cut into the hillside; and on one particularly tight corner, I gawped in horror at the twisted remains of a truck scattered across the vegetation hundreds of metres below.

When faced with lorries, swaying along the road like unsteady elephants,

BIKING TIPS

- ❑ Use the back brake as much as possible, and handle the front brake with care. The front brake has **70 percent** of the braking power and, if you're travelling at speed, a sudden squeeze is likely to send you over the handle bars.

- ❑ On the corners, use only the back brake, and go round with outside pedal down, your weight pressing onto it. Lean the bike in a little bit, but keep your body upright.

- ❑ Don't look directly at obstacles but at the point you're aiming for; by doing this you're more likely to skirt obstacles safely.

- ❑ If you sit down the whole way, your bottom will be so sore you won't be able to sit afterwards. On the corners rest on the back of the seat; and on the straight, don't sit at all. Keep knees bent to absorb the shock, and let your thighs grip the seat.

MORE MOUNTAIN BIKING OPTIONS

There are two other main one-day tours offered by Gravity Assisted Mountain Biking. The first takes you 36km (22½ miles) from Chacaltaya to La Paz; the second is a 45-km (28-mile) route from the Zongo Pass to the Sud Yungas jungles. At 5,345m (17,535 feet), Chacaltaya is the site of the world's highest, developed ski-slope, serviced by South America's oldest (dating from 1940) and most dangerous ski-lift. It's been described as the world's only blue ski-run with a black ski-lift. Better to admire the spectacular mountain views of Illimani, Mururata, and Huayna Potosí, and then do the bike ride down the scree slope and along an old mining road back to the city. There are rough sections on this ride that the inexperienced cyclist might feel happier walking, and everyone will have to push the bike up the initial 45 vertical metres (50 yards) from the car park to the start of the ride.

The Zongo Pass ride starts at 4,780m (15,680 feet), on the pass at the access point to the peak of Huayna Potosí. Alongside the dirt road, which has few flat stretches, there is a vertical, 3,500-m (11,480-foot) drop into the steamy jungle. You'll pass llamas and alpacas in the higher reaches, and waterfalls below. Explore Bolivia agency offers similar rides, and—for experienced bikers—more challenging ones such as the one through the jungle on the abandoned old rail-road route to Coroico. If you've not had enough of mountain biking by the time you reach Coroico, there's also a reasonably short, twisting route, which takes you down from Cerro Uchumachi to join the road to Caranavi, and offers panoramic views of the Río Coroico Valley.

their brimming loads of bananas and other produce always topped off with hitching *campesinos*, it's not a difficult decision to give them right of way. By this point in the journey, I was feeling more confident on the bike, but my hands ached from constant braking and I was glad of the opportunities to rest. Now that we'd hit the moist wall of heat rising up from the Yungas, we also paused to strip off layers of clothes.

Streams cascade down the rockface, creating muddy puddles on the road. In one place we actually rode under a large waterfall. By the time we'd reached the end of the ride at Yolosa, at 1,100m (36,000 feet), which is nothing more than a shabby pitstop at the river crossing in the valley, the road had dried and our wheels were throwing up clouds of dust. It was no wonder that Alistair jokingly promised that anyone who finished clean would get their money back.

Filthy, exhausted and exhilarated , we boarded the pick-up trucks that were waiting at Yalosa to transfer us up to **Coroico**, the small town perched on the shoulder of the hill Cerro Uchumachi. It's

no surprise that this picturesque place, with its laid-back community, excellent views of the mountains and the fertile Yungas, and its good accommodation, food, and pleasant year-round temperatures, is a favourite retreat for travellers and locals alike. More importantly for me at the end of my ride, it also had, at the Hotel Esmeralda, perhaps the best hot-water showers in Bolivia.

INTO THE VALLEY

Early the next morning I was collected from town by Luis Fernando Jordan, the owner of the Explore Bolivia agency, his partner Raoul, and Raoul's cousin Daniel. We took the road to Caranavi, heading down into the precipitous valley along which the **Río Coroico** flows, towards the Jordan's hacienda La Cascada. La Cascada is Explore Bolivia's base for rafting trips and other adventure tourism activities in Yungas.

The previous night a violent lightning storm had raged with such power that I was afraid all the dirt roads would be washed away by morning. The skies, however, were now a clear blue and the

ABOVE Preparing for a rafting experience in the Río Coroico
LEFT The treacherous route to Yungas, cut into the side of the mountain: we are given instructions (INSET) on how to handle it

scorching sun was beginning to dry out the muddy patches on roads that Jordan's chunky Chevrolet Suburban jeep would certainly have no trouble coping with.

While Jordan and Daniel prepared for the rafting trip later in the day, I joined Raoul to explore the jungle around La Cascada and to see some of the waterfalls that give the hacienda its name. Jordan's mother, who lives on the estate and looks after the pleasant lodge that guests can stay in, led us to the route, and we were followed by two young boys, Vidal and Manacaros. Their fathers farm what must qualify as some of the steepest fields in the world, terraced patches hacked out of the hillside jungle, yielding small crops of

coffee, avocados, tangerines, bananas, and many other fruits, as well as the ubiquitous coca plant.

The narrow path running along the mountain ridge soon dropped to the first of the falls, a broad swathe of clear water plunging some 20m (65 feet) over a jet-black cliff beside the remains of an Inca-era bridge. It's possible to go rappelling here. The boys splashed in the water holes that reached my waist, while I tried to wade along a rocky creek to the next set of falls. The increased volume of water from the previous night's storm defeated me, but promised an even more exciting rafting trip.

RAFTING THE COROICO

Before hiking down to the riverside I was provided with a helmet, life jacket, and paddle, by Jordan, and given a lecture on rafting safety. Beside the Río Coroico, a sturdy inflatable raft was ready to transport the four of us down the swirling brown river, which flows at terrific speed through towering walls of jungle greenery. The opaqueness of the water lends the river a more threatening quality than is suggested by a clearer river whose obstacles are more readily apparent.

The trip is around 17km (10½ miles), culminating just before the waterfall at Puerto Leon; it lasts just over an hour, but it feels much longer. In such a strong current there's little let-up in the paddling, and I was glad I'd had some previous experience of rafting. At the height of the rainy season, more water would be flowing through the river, which would smooth out the bumps across the rocks, but it would also increase the already considerable current.

Beside the village of Choro, a suspension bridge spans the Río Coroico, and a couple of curious people stood to watch as we negotiated the rapids at this tricky bend in the river. Later, Jordan told me that during a major rafting event six years ago, the weight of spectators on the bridge had caused it to collapse, killing three children. The next set of rapids are called My Brother's Pass: tradition has it that if you fall in and someone saves you, that person will become your brother. Luckily, we didn't have to put this to the test.

By the time we reached the exit point beneath the bridge at Puerto Leon, I was exhausted. Jordan had arranged for the truck to be waiting to transport us and the gear back to base, but first we took off to view the waterfall. As I waded upstream, making my way carefully over slippery rocks to the viewpoint, I could hear its thundering noise; and even from this distance—several hundred metres away—the spray from the powerful falls soaked my face.

I reached into my pocket, and discovered that the condor talisman had broken in two—was this a sign that my good fortune was about to run out? I decided to play safe and turn back. After

a delicious lunch at La Cascada, I headed back to Coroico for more relaxation and pampering. It's the least anyone deserves before braving the journey back to La Paz.

YUNGAS HIKING TRAILS

Three of the main hikes from La Paz to the Yungas are the Choro Trail, the Takesi Trail, and the Yunga Cruz Trail. All follow pre-Hispanic paved roads, commonly known as Inca trails despite expert opinion that their construction predates the Inca conquest of the area.

The Choro Trail begins at La Cumbre, which is easily reached by public transport, and can be comfortably completed in three days. The extremes in weather, vegetation, and landscape make it an appealing route, and there's an opportunity to camp in the remote, beautifully tended garden of Tamiji Hanamura, a longtime Japanese resident of Bolivia.

The shortest of the trails, at just over 30km (18½miles), is the Takesi, which starts at Ventilla, and ends at the mining village of Chojlla; press on to the attractive colonial village of Yanacachi, where there's accommodation and daily, early-morning minibuses back to La Paz, or to Chaco. At Chaco you'll find the recommended hotel El Castillo, a formerly upmarket residence, built by Paraguayan prisoners-of-war in the mid-1930s, that has the feel of a haunted castle. Because it's easily accessible and short, the Takesi Trail attracts plenty of traffic and as a consequence there's a great deal of litter along the way.

The Yunga Cruz Trail is the hardest going, but definitely the most rewarding of the three. The trek takes three or five days, depending on whether you start at Chuñavi or Lambate; it ends in Chulumani, the quiet capital of Sud Yungas province. There are excellent opportunities to spot animal and bird life, including condors. Water is scarce, and non-existent after Cerro Yunga Cruz, so carry at least 2 litres (3½ pints).

GOING IT ALONE

INTERNAL TRAVEL

About the safest way to travel down the appalling road to Coroico is by minibus, unless you are on a bicycle or in your own four-whee-drive vehicle. Minibuses leave regularly from the Villa Fátima area of La Paz; expect to pay around 15 bolivianos. Both Flota Yunguenita and Turbus Totai are reliable bus companies.

If you wish to make the return minibus journey from Coroico at a specific time, it's important to book ahead in the town because the buses quickly fill, especially on Sunday.

Bolivia is not an ideal place to hone your driving skills, but if you're thinking of hiring your own vehicle, go for a four-wheel drive; check the tyres and brakes, and also hire a driver.

WHEN TO GO

The best time for visiting Bolivia is in the dry winter season between April and October, with the most favourable weather between June and August. Between La Paz and Coroico, you should be prepared for temperatures ranging from 4°C (39°F) to 30°C (86°F) and increased humidity in the jungle. The rainy season is between December and March, during which time Gravity Assisted Mountain Biking (see Planning your Trip, below) shuts down its operations; it may be possible to arrange a bike tour during this period with Explore Bolivia, but note that many roads become impassable.

PLANNING YOUR TRIP

For mountain-bike tours the best agencies in La Paz are Gravity Assisted Mountain Biking and Explore Bolivia. The latter is the only reliable outfit for kayaking, canoeing, and rafting adventures.

Many of the other tour agencies in La Paz offer organized treks along the various routes heading into the Yungas, including guides and equipment.

If you want to go solo, it's possible to hire equipment such as tents and sleeping bags in La Paz, if you haven't brought your own. Also consider putting a note up at the most popular travellers' hotels if you're looking for trekking companions.

You'll have no problem finding accommodation to suit your budget in La Paz, which is well served with hotels and restaurants.

In Coroico there a similarly good range of tourist facilities available, but it's important to book ahead if you want to be sure of staying at a particular hotel, especially on a weekend or over major holiday periods.

WHAT TO TAKE

For the bike rides:
❏ A thermal jacket or sweater; these can be purchased cheaply in La Paz.
❏ Sunglasses.
❏ Bandanna.
❏ A replacement battery for your camera; the cold at high altitude often causes batteries to stop working.

For the treks:
❏ A good map.
❏ Camping gear.
❏ For the Chaco Trail, you'll need winter weather clothes for the high-altitude section, and lighter ones for the tropical section.
❏ For the Yunga Cruz Trail, the most important thing to take is water. Be prepared to carry at least 2 litres (3½ pints).

HEALTH AND SAFETY MATTERS

Do not underestimate the strength of the sun in the Yungas. Sunscreen lotion and insect repellent are essential. In the mountains high-altitude sickness, known locally as *soroche* is common among visitors. Headaches, lethargy, dizziness, loss of appetite, and nausea, are all symptoms and it need to be taken seriously. The best treatment is rest, lots of clear liquids (but not alcohol), non-aspirin painkillers for the headaches, and antinausea tablets.. *Maté de coca*—an infusion of coca leaves—is the local remedy..

You should be cautious about where you eat, and you should avoid uncooked foods as food hygiene is rudimentary. You should always drink bottled water, or; if you take water from streams while hiking and camping, boil it, or use iodine solution or iodine-based purification tablets (iodine is the only thing that kills giardia).

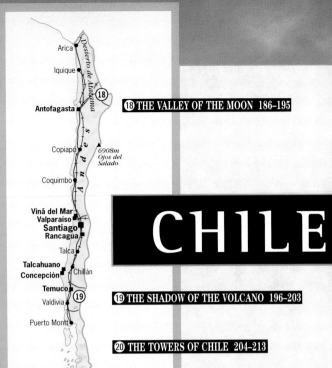

Arica
Iquique

Desierto de Atacama

(18)

Antofagasta

Copiapó   6908m
                 Ojos del
                 Salado
Coquimbo

Andes

Viña del Mar
Valparaiso
Santiago
Rancagua
Talca
Talcahuano
Concepción   Chillán
Temuco
             (19)
Valdivia

Puerto Montt

CHILE

4058m
San Valentín

3600m
Murallón
(20)
                 Tierra
                 del
Punta Arenas   Fuego
Estrecho de
Magallanes   Cabo de
                 Hornos

0   250   1000 km
0   300   600 m

P lastered thinly down
the Pacific coast of
South America,
Chile is a country embracing geographic and climatic
extremes. There's some
4,399km (2,733 miles)
between the Atacama, the
world's driest desert, and
the glaciers and fjords
around Puerto Williams,
Chile's most southern settlement,   closer   to
Antarctica than to the nation's capital, Santiago. In between
you can go mountaineering, trekking, and horseback riding in
the central Andes, and rafting or kayaking on the Maipo and
Bió Bió rivers. In the far northern deserts, a four-wheel-drive
trip will take you across moonlike landscapes and enormous
salt flats to high-altitude lakes and geysers. In total contrast
are the lush valleys and snow-capped volcanoes of the southern Lake District, heartland of the indigenous Mapuche
Indians, and location of Pucón, adrenalin central for adventure travel in Chile. Down in Patagonia is the rugged Torres
del Paine, one of the most visually stunning places in South
America.

Laguna Miscati in the mountains of the Atacama Desert, Chile

CHILE

Beyond the Valley of the Moon

by Simon Richmond

The dramatic desert landscape around San Pedro de Atacama in northern Chile is beaten only by the stark beauty of the multicoloured lakes, teeming with flamingos, that lie en route to Bolivia's dazzling white Salar de Uyuni salt flats.

From one side of the aeroplane I looked down on to the sea, from the other the mountains. I was flying north from Santiago to Calama, on my way to the oasis village of San Pedro de Atacama, and had fully expected to be able to see these physical borders of narrow Chile, plastered like a layer of whipped cream down the western flank of South America. However, little had prepared me for the seemingly endless expanse of the Atacama Desert, a desolate, desiccated landscape as rich in minerals and ores as it is devoid of vegetation.

As I sat in the taxi from the airport, heading along the smooth ribbon of

 Tours out of San Pedro de Atacama are generally well organized and involve little effort beyond getting up early or hiking a short distance in the heat of the day. A knowledge of Spanish is useful as English-speaking guides are not always available. Tours out of Uyuni are more of a hit and miss affair; check out several options thoroughly before handing over any cash.

★★ Be prepared for the dry, dusty, hot atmosphere of the desert, and for chillier evenings. The other major problem you may face—especially when you cross the mountains to Bolivia—is altitude sickness (see Going It Alone, page 195).

A warm sleeping bag is essential if you plan to camp in San Pedro de Atacama (note that camping in the Valley of the Moon is prohibited). Binoculars and/or a camera with telephoto lens will give you the chance of observing shy wildlife in detail.

asphalt through one of the driest places on Earth, I could already feel the arid, dusty air sizzling in my nose and catching at the back of my throat. The view of the sun setting over the burnt red ground and the sand-blasted rocks of the Atacama—a geological masterpiece created over millions of years—was breathtaking. Ahead was the desert's premier landmark, conical Lincancábur, one of highest extinct volcanoes in the Andes at 5,916m (19,409 feet).

As the road dropped steeply, signs of life appeared in the approaching valley. The patch of pale green ahead turned out to be the alfalfa fields and tamarugos trees of **San Pedro de Atacama**, an oasis at 2,440m (8,000 feet) above sea-level, home to 3,000 people and an increasingly popular tourism centre for the Atacama Desert. I was here to explore the nearby Valle de la Luna (Valley of the Moon), the El Tatio geyser field, and the lush Quebrada de Jeria oasis at the village of Toconao. San Pedro would also be the starting point for a four-wheel-drive tour to the Salar de Uyuni salt flats of southern Bolivia, via a string of different-coloured, high-altitude lakes that are havens for flocks of Andean, Chilean, and James' flamingos (see page 192).

INTO THE VALLEY OF DEATH

It's easy to see why San Pedro de Atacama has become so popular with both local and international tourists. The compact village (you can walk across it in ten minutes) has bags of laid-back charm, with traffic-free streets lined with mud-walled adobe huts, and a pleasant central square, the Plaza de Almas, shaded by pimento trees and boasting the white-washed 17th-century Iglesia San Pedro church and Museo Gustavo Le Paige (see box, page 192).

There are a couple of places that rent out mountain bikes in San Pedro (see Contacts), so that you can cycle to the Valle de la Muerte, 3km (2 miles) west of the village, and the Valle de la Luna, some 15km (9 miles) from San Pedro. The most popular mode of transport, however, is a minibus tour (these leave the village every day at 4pm). The first stop is a viewpoint over the Cordillera de la Sal, the low ridge between the Andes and Domeyko ranges. The rugged landscape looks monumental, but Alvaro, the guide on my tour, told us that the mountains are still growing at the rate of 5–7cm (2–3 inches) per year.

Although she wasn't found there, one couldn't imagine a more appropriate

The route from the Atacama Desert, Chile to the Salar de Uyuni, Bolivia

DESERT DANGERS

It goes without saying that for any trip into the desert you should take plenty of water, a hat, and sunscreen lotion. The offroad trails are far from obvious (taking a tour ensures that you won't get lost), and if you are driving your own vehicle, pedalling a mountain bike, or even walking, it's important to stick to the established tracks around San Pedro de Atacama. The Chilean Army once used the area for war games, and there are still many unexploded land-mines scattered across the desert. Unfortunately, the precise location of these mines is no longer known, and some are believed to lie in the vicinity of the Valley of the Moon. For this reason an ascent of Lincancábur is not possible from the Atacama Desert side; if you want to climb this volcano you need to organize the trip from the Bolivian side.

burial ground for the Museo Gustavo's Miss Chile than the parched **Valle de la Muerte** (Valley of Death). Apparently, the valley was originally named after Mars (*Marte* in Spanish), but this was changed when photographs taken of the planet's surface showed just how different it really was. To experience the desert to the full, we took to the ground, walking 20 minutes into the rocky depression under the still-blazing late-afternoon sun before being reunited with the air-conditioned sanctuary of our minibus.

From the Valley of Death we drove along the Valle de la Luna (Valley of the Moon), one of seven different geographical sectors of the Atacama Desert protected within the Reserva Nacional Los Flamencos (Los Flamencos National Reserve). It's not just because of its barren, pockmarked appearance that the valley has been so named, for on nights during the full moon the crystals of salt and gypsum that are scattered across the valley floor twinkle in the lunar light, mirroring the stars above.

The minibus paused by a rock formation known as the Three Marys, a trio of wind-sculpted pillars named by travelling priests in the 1670s. We also inspected a tiny abandoned pit that once served as a salt mine, before heading into the valley proper. The final stop on the tour was at a mammoth sand-dune, which resembled a towering wave frozen in motion. You need to be quite fit to climb the dune, but if you do so you will be rewarded with a magnificent view across the desert. The main viewing point is reached by traversing the slender crest of the dune and then climbing up to a ridge. Some 30 people were gathered there when we arrived, all waiting for the sunset, which promised to be particularly colourful because of the clouds in the sky. We were not disappointed as the light slipped away and the mountains and volcanoes to the east were bathed in tangerine and salmon-pink.

THE FIELD OF STEAM

In total contrast to the sunset over the

BEYOND THE VALLEY OF THE MOON

Valle de la Luna was the eerie dawn I experienced at **El Tatio**, 95km (60 miles) north of San Pedro, the highest geyser field in the world at 4,300m (14,100 feet) above sea-level. I had been warned about possible altitude sickness when I signed up for the trip ("Don't eat red meat or drink alcohol the night before," advised the girl in the tour office). I also had to sign a disclaimer for any injury suffered, including those induced from the scalding waters that bubble up from the ground.

As I waited outside my hotel for the minibus at 4:30am, I spotted a shooting star, surely an auspicious start to this dead-of-night adventure. The journey up into the mountains took nearly two hours. It was pitch-black and there were no roads to speak of, but the driver, Jimmy, knew the way well. Although mine was one of the last of several tour groups to leave San Pedro that day, it was among the first to arrive at the geyser field, just as dawn was beginning to break over the jagged hills and clouds of steam rose in the frigid air. It's the difference in temperature between the frozen earth and the 85°C (185°F) water that creates the billowing clouds of steam and causes columns of liquid, some as high as 20m (65 feet), to shoot out of the geysers. The colder the external temperature, the more dramatic the display. For added effect, tour groups are served a breakfast of eggs boiled in one of the fumaroles, along with geothermally warmed milk for the coffee. I found it worrying that many people wandered idly across this perilously thin crust of earth, even to within spitting distance of the geysers, apparently heedless of the danger.

A safer way to enjoy the geothermally heated waters is in a large bathing pool at the edge of the field. Since most tours leave by 8:30am, when the best of the steam display is over, you can have this pool practically to yourself if you linger. The more attractive local hot springs, however, are the **Termas de Puritama**, 32km (20 miles) from San Pedro, which are usually visited on the return journey

ABOVE LEFT The Valley of the Moon, in the Atacama Desert: salt and gypsum crystals scattered on its floor twinkle in the moonlight LEFT and BELOW Spouts of scalding water and clouds of steam at El Tatio geyser field— best seen at dawn, before the temperature rises

to town. The water in these pools, linked by boardwalks and cascading down a lush gully, is at a pleasant temperature, and the location, amid swaying reeds and mossy stones, cannot be bettered. These hot springs are owned by the luxury Explora resort on the outskirts of San Pedro (there is an entrance fee of about $5; it has toilets and changing rooms).

CANYON OF LIFE

Even more lush than the Termas de Puritama is the **Quebrada de Jeria**, a fertile oasis fed by clear spring water that runs through a narrow canyon just outside Toconao, 38km (24 miles) south of San Pedro. This village makes another ideal cycling excursion from San Pedro, and takes a couple of hours to reach along a partially asphalted road, passing

MUSEO GUSTAVO LE PAIGE

The Museo Gustavo Le Paige, on the northern corner of the Plaza de Almas, is one of Chile's most important archaeological museums, tracing the local history from 10,000 years ago to the time of Spanish colonization and after, when San Pedro was an important pit stop on the cattle drives across the mountains from Argentina. The museum's collection of rocks and artefacts was started by the Belgian priest and archaeologist Gustavo Le Paige during the 1950s, and includes excellent re-creations of the intriguing petroglyphs etched on rocks in the desert. (It's possible to arrange excursions to see the originals.) Also here are the mummified remains of an ancient Indian woman, lanks of hair and patches of dried skin still clinging to her grinning skull. "Miss Chile," as she is known, is one of the most striking examples of how the rarefied air of the Atacama Desert preserves for almost eternity all that is cast into it.

through a planted wood of tamarugos trees and flocks of llamas. In the high-sided canyon—resembling the set in an Indiana Jones movie—the locals grow all manner of fruit and vegetables in small orchards fenced off from one another with low stone walls. It's possible to camp along the grassy banks of the stream, and the water is perfectly safe to drink.

Toconao itself is a sleepy village with a few craft stalls and an old church, its door made of dried cactus. In the graveyard wreaths of crêpe-paper flowers bloom on elaborate pastel-painted tombs in a fabulous garden of pinks, pale blues, and greens set against the monotonous brown backdrop of the desert.

A day-long tour from San Pedro to Laguna Miscati, a sapphire-coloured lake high in the mountains, will take in Toconao as well as Laguna Chaxa—a shallow lake set in the middle of the Salar de Atacama, the largest salt flat in Chile and the habitat for several species of birds, including flamingos and Andean gulls (*Larus serranus*). There are three different species of flamingo found on the altiplano: the Andean flamingo (*Phoenicoparrus andinus*) is over 1m (3 feet) tall, and has pale pink feathers, yellow legs, and a yellow and black bill; the Chilean flamingo (*Phoenicoparrus chilensis*) has a deeper coloured plumage, blue legs with red knees, and a black and white bill; the James' flamingo (*Phoenicoparrus jamesi*), the smallest, has dark red legs.

Impressive though these lakes are, others and many, many more flamingos can be seen on the journey across the altiplano to the Salar de Uyuni, far and away the most remarkable geological feature in the area.

DRIVING WITH DOMINGO

Although most of the three-day tour I took to Uyuni in Bolivia from San Pedro was by four-wheel-drive jeep (essential for this inhospitable terrain), the initial stage from town up into the mountains was completed on board an ancient-looking, green public bus. I was joined on the trip by four Israelis, two Dutch, a Swiss, and an Australian. We assembled at 8am, with our supplies of water and other provisions such as fruit juice and bread rolls (we had been warned the food provided on the tour would be basic).

It took a couple of hours for the bus to rattle up into the mountains to **Laguna Blanca**, a milky white lake beside which Bolivia maintains a tiny immigration control post. Here we exchanged the last of our pesos for bolivianos, and were served breakfast in the neighbouring café by a lady dressed in typical Bolivian style, a brown derby hat perched jauntily on her head. Outside, flocks of flamingos fed in the water of the lake.

A short drive away, at the foot of Lincancábur, we came to **Laguna Verde**, so called because a cocktail of minerals in the water turns it pale green as the day progresses. The colour is best seen after noon, but the lake is remarkable at any time for the fluffy white borax bubbles at the water's edge. Wisps of foam drift in the wind, while the remainder hardens in the sun to leave an outer salt ring.

From Laguna Verde we continued in two Toyota Landcruisers to the **Laguna Salada** salt lake and a rather murky thermal pool where it's possible to bathe. The driver of my Landcruiser was called Placido Domingo, his *chica* Constantina by his side. Disappointingly, he didn't sing opera, and nor did he speak much English, but he was happy to let us play our own music on the tape machine, and he took the tour at a relaxed pace to allow us plenty of time to see each place. Constantina, meanwhile, dozed as he drove, waking to prepare our meals of sandwiches, salads, and fruit for lunch, and soup followed by chicken and potatoes or spaghetti for dinner—all in all much better than we had expected.

A DESERT LAKELAND

By the time the tour reached the **Sol de Manana geyser**, at close to 5,000m (16,400 feet), where fumaroles belched

cement-grey and sludge-brown mud in the most desolate landscape yet, *soroche* (altitude sickness) had me in its grip. The breeze whipping around **Laguna Colorada**—a 60-sq-km (23-square-mile) lake with striking red waters, fringed by white salt rings and green mosses, and inhabited by hundreds of flamingos—failed to clear my throbbing head. When we arrived at the extremely humble lodge beside the lake I was glad that a bed and blanket were ready for me to curl up in.

The next day, with my headache gone and appetite back, I was eager to get on with the tour through the Reserva Eduardo Avaroa, the Bolivian national park that covers the altiplano lakes—especially so after witnessing the early morning slaughter of a llama in the compound outside the lodge. As the dead animal's blood drained from its slit throat into a bowl, we set off to inspect the Arbol de Piedra, "stone trees" crafted by centuries of howling desert winds. Near by, Placido stopped to point out a viscacha (*Lagidium* spp.), a rabbit-like animal with a long tail, and the rare llareta plant. This rock-hard moss, which grows only 1mm (1/25 inch) a year, is protected in the park along with the vicuña (*Vicugna vicugna*), one of South America's cameloids.

As the day progressed we saw more lakes, including Laguna Hedionda (Stinking Lake, after its sulphurous smell), and even more flamingos, and passed Volcán Ollagüe, a 5,870-m (19,260-foot) peak that straddles the Chile–Bolivia border. Before we reached the volcano we saw the weird lava formations of a volcanic mud field that were created before the time of the Incas. From here, the route dropped down to the Salar de Chiguana, a white borax-crusted plain bisected by a railway line. In the rainy season this whole area turns into a giant mud bath. On the far side of the plain, beyond an army barracks consisting of giant camouflaged igloos, was our base for the night—San Juan, a dusty adobe village that would look at home in a spaghetti Western movie.

CHILE

BLINDED BY THE WHITE

On the final day of the tour, dark clouds over San Juan promised a downpour as we headed towards the **Salar de Uyuni**, past terraced hillsides dating from the days of the Inca empire. By the time we reached the 12,000-sq-m (14,350-square-yard) salt pan, the largest in the world and at 3,650m ((11,975 feet) also the highest, the sky had cleared. The contrast of the deep blue sky with the dazzling white surface of the dried-up lake was astounding and utterly surreal, and as I climbed out of the Landcruiser I felt I should be putting on ice-skates rather than sunglasses and suntan lotion.

In the midst of this plain, plastered with 10 billion tonnes of salt, rises a rocky outcrop known as the Isla de Pescado (it's supposed to resemble a fish), to which all tours across the Salar de Uyuni head. The view from the hill, covered with hundreds of spiky, phallic-looking Trichocereus cacti, some of which were blooming with cream and yellow flowers, was truly amazing, and the surrounding sea of salt, tessellated with geometrical crystals, did indeed appear to lap at the rocky shores of the "island."

After lunch at the Isla de Pescado, we drove on to see some small hotels made entirely of salt and to the Ojos, where cold water bubbles through thin patches in the salt crust to form pools. The water is believed to have medicinal properties, and despite the danger that the thin surface may crack underfoot, it's not unusual to see locals soaking their ailing limbs in these pools. At the edge of the salt flat, by the village of Colchani, giant piles of salt lay waiting to be harvested. From here it was another 20km (12 miles) to the railway junction of Uyuni, the end of my journey across one of the continent's most remarkable landscapes.

BELOW and INSET More surreal scenery: the dried-up lake at the Salar de Uyuni, the largest salt pan in the world, and some spectacular cloud formations

GOING IT ALONE

INTERNAL TRAVEL

Unless you have plenty of time (the long-distance bus from Santiago takes 24 hours) flying is the best way to reach the Atacama Desert. The airport is at Calama, 120km (75 miles) northwest of San Pedro de Atacama, and is served by daily flights from Santiago (several go via Antofagasta on the coast). A taxi from the airport to San Pedro will cost around 25,000 pesos; during the day you can take a taxi to Calama's San Pedro Bus Terminal, then board one of the hourly Frontera or Jumar buses on to San Pedro de Atacama. The bus station in San Pedro is within easy walking distance of the rest of the village.

Another way of travelling overland from Chile to Bolivia (or vice versa) is by train. The rail journey from Calama in Chile to Oruro, via Uyuni, in Bolivia gained international fame when it was featured in Michael Palin's T.V. documentary series *Around the World in 80 Days*. Tickets for this absolutely no-frills ride, in ancient carriages across one of the world's most inhospitable high-altitude deserts, cost around $11 to Uyuni and should be booked in advance. The train leaves every Wednesday night around 11pm, but can be boarded a few hours before. Be prepared for long delays during the border crossing at Ollagüe, and for extreme cold at night; take warm clothing, blankets, and plenty of food and water.

WHEN TO GO

Seasonal weather changes are not something you need be overly concerned about when planning a visit to the Atacama Desert, although the temperature plummets at nights, particularly during the winter months (June–September). Winter is the best season to visit the Salar de Uyuni, when the days are cooler and dry. During the rainy season (generally December–March) the salt flat can become flooded and the surrounding land turns to mud; it can be difficult arranging tours of the area during this period.

WHAT TO TAKE

❑ Sleeping bag.

❑ Camera with telephoto lens and/or binoculars.

❑ Sun hat.

❑ Sunscreen lotion.

PLANNING YOUR TRIP

Standards for tour agents in San Pedro are generally high, although it's worth asking around for recommendations and checking out individual itineraries before making a decision. To be sure of getting from San Pedro de Atacama to Uyuni across the altiplano, use the Bolivian agency Colque Tours, which is the only one with offices in both towns. It also offers day trips to Laguna Blanca and Laguna Verde from San Pedro (see Contacts).

In Uyuni, from where tours of the Salar de Uyuni and the altiplano lakes more commonly start, the choice of agencies is bewildering. Sadly, however, there are few that have outstanding reputations, although the competition does keep prices low at around $60 for a 4-day trip. Most Uyuni operators follow the same route as that from San Pedro but in reverse, with an extra night in the desert, diverting via the village of Alota.

HEALTH AND SAFETY MATTERS

Do not drink tap water in San Pedro de Atacama as it contains a high level of arsenic. Be prepared for altitude sickness as you head higher into the altiplano; take plenty of water and headache and anti-nausea tablets to ease the condition. You could also try chewing the local maté leaves (from the shrub *Ilex paraguayensis*) or brewing them into a tea. If you continue to feel ill after a day, return to a lower altitude and rest until you become acclimatized.

HOTELS AND RESTAURANTS

San Pedro de Atacama has much better standards and choices of accommodation and restaurants than Uyuni. In the holiday seasons book hotels in advance. At Laguna Colorada there are two lodges; the better of these is run by the Reserva Eduardo Avaroa national park, but you'll need to specify with the tour agency that this is where you want to stay. The salt hotels in the Salar de Uyuni are not included as part of the standard desert tour either, and will need to be booked separately.

TRAVELLERS' TIP

When booking your tour to the Salar de Uyuni, check out the state of the vehicle and the number of passengers included: six passengers in one car is the maximum for comfort, although some agencies won't run trips without this number.

CHILE

In the Shadow of the Volcano

by Simon Richmond

Pucón is Chile's premier adventure travel destination. Here, you can climb the snow-capped—and active—Volcán Villarrica, go whitewater rafting, hike, or take a horseback ride through beautiful national park countryside.

The Santiago–Puerto Montt railway line is the oldest and longest in Chile, and begins in romantic style under the lofty wrought-iron and glass roof of the capital's Estación Central. I boarded the night train at 8pm bound for Temuco, 675km (420 miles) south of Santiago and the main access point for Chile's "Lake District." My ultimate destination was Pucón, a small town on the black-sand shores of Lake Villarrica, with the symmetrical cone of the smouldering volcano of the same name rising in the background. Despite the volcano's continued activity (recent eruptions occurred in 1971 and 1984), it is southern Chile's most climbed peak. It is just over a century since this part of the

country finally became safe to travel and settle in, after fierce resistance by the Mapuche natives against Spanish colonization. Today, the locals couldn't be more welcoming, and visitors flock to the lakes to enjoy the alpine landscapes of snow-capped volcanoes and mountains, down which pristine rivers flow through ancient forests and lush pastures.

As I heaved my luggage into one of the train's antiquated sleeping carriages, I found the storage area was bursting with bags. Already enjoying the appealingly shabby interior of gold velvet and wood veneer was a contingent of Canadians and a lone German, their boots and backpacks indicating an interest in the great Chilean outdoors similar to mine. I settled down in the Agatha Christie-style splendour as the train pulled out of the city, and we all agreed that this was the perfect way to begin a journey south.

4 Hiking around Pucón is generally easy, along well-marked trails, although people do occasionally get lost and you should always inform someone where you're going and when you plan to return. The volcano climb and white-water rafting need a high level of fitness and/or determination to succeed.

★★ Expect crowds in the peak holiday season (December–April). The warmer weather of late November to April will make outdoor activities more pleasant, but always be prepared for rain and chilly evenings. There are plenty of local hot springs in which to relax at the end of the day.

For the rafting trip you will need a swimsuit and either sandals or shoes that you don't mind getting wet; all other equipment is provided by the operators. If you intend to climb Villarrica, take thermal underwear and a sweater or fleece. Your own climbing boots fitted with crampons will be more comfortable than those provided, but they will get wet.

ADRENALIN CENTRAL

Pucón has enthusiastically embraced adventure tourism like few other places in South America. As well as being the starting point for ascents of Villarrica, it's the base for rafting on the nearby Trancura, a crystal-clear river that gushes over Class IV rapids. Three national parks, the Villarrica, Heurquehue, and Conguillio, as well as the Cañi Forest Sanctuary, a private nature reserve, lie within striking distance of the town and all have excellent hiking trails. There are numerous hot springs, too, warmed by the area's geothermal activity, ideal for easing aching limbs at the end of the day.

I rose at dawn from a fitful sleep

THE BÍO BÍO AND FUTALEUFU

The Bío Bío, Chile's most famous whitewater river, rated Class V on the international scale and often referred to as a "spiritual experience," has had its raftable length cut by the Pangue Dam, and is further threatened by the planned construction of more dams. However, several companies are still running trips down the river, mainly between December to April, when the days are warm and it rains only occasionally. Trips typically last three days, starting from the remote village of Lonquimay near the Argentine border (accessed from the town of Victoria), and involve two nights' camping. The first day's paddling is an easy warm-up. Day two involves six hours' rafting on the middle Bío Bío, negotiating Class II and III rapids, while on the final day you encounter the intense whitewater that rushes through the Ñirreco Canyon along with several Class V rapids.

Even more challenging and dangerous than the Bío Bío is the Futaleufú, south of Chaiten in Patagonia. To tackle this river, which flows through spectacular mountain scenery, requires plenty of previous experience of Class V rapids.

that had been punctuated by the train's rattling progress, and just had time for breakfast before we arrived at Temuco—noticeably chillier than Santiago—at 7am. After a 20-minute walk through the still-slumbering town I reached the bus station, from where regular services head through verdant countryside to Pucón, some 110km (68 miles) to the southeast. It's easy to see why German immigrants settled in this European-looking land in the 19th century, although the few native Indians who boarded the bus with me proved that some of the original inhabitants also remained. There's little that's Mapuche Indian or Chilean about **Pucón**, however, which, with its rustic log-cabin houses, pretty gardens, quaint cafés, and adventure-tour operators, all on a neat grid layout, resembles much more closely a generic Rocky Mountains township. You don't come here so much for native culture as to recharge your spiritual batteries in the beautiful natural surroundings or to tap into the adrenalin rush of such activities as whitewater rafting—something I found myself doing on my first afternoon in Pucón.

RAFTING TIPS

The Trancura's rafting season runs from September to April, although the rockier upper section is really safely runnable only between December and March. Expect to pay around $15 for the two-hour trip or $35 for the four-hour trip. Bring along a swimsuit and either sandals or shoes that you don't mind getting wet as there are usually sections of the river where all but the most experienced of rafters or kayakers will have to walk along the banks. Make sure the raft captain practises with your team, and learn the English and Spanish terms for all the paddling strokes and manoeuvres that may be required during the trip. If you fall out, don't try to stand up or swim; instead, lean back in your life jacket and keep your feet ahead of you so that you can push yourself away from oncoming rocks.

THROUGH THE DEVIL'S THROAT

The rafting trip down the upper section of the **Trancura** is the more challenging of the two classic runs offered by many agencies in Pucón. I joined a couple from Argentina, a Canadian, and two Americans on a trip organized by the long-established Sol y Nieve agency. We headed by van to the put-in point, a calm stretch of the river some 20 minutes' drive from Pucón, where we kitted up in wind-breakers, life jackets, and helmets, and dragged our large rubber raft down to the gently flowing water.

During the practice session, Teo, the captain, seemed especially keen that we responded at lightning speed to the "high side right" command, which demands that everyone jumps over to the right-hand side of the raft. Once in the water we soon came to understand why. The Trancura is a beguiling river, where sparkling waters cascade over smooth rocks, and snow-capped mountains and dense forests form a breathtaking vista in the background, but its tricky rapids demand total attention.

As the raft fell into a savage whirlpool known as the Chuncho, our six bodies lurched, on instruction, instantly to the right, and then we cheered in unison as we realized, to our amazement, that we had survived. The Garganta del Diablo, or Devil's Throat, a precipitous drop in the river that twists around frighteningly large boulders, was even worse, but Teo's skill saw us through.

At the final dramatic set of rapids, the water was too low for us to risk the full run, so we scrambled over rocks along the shore before reboarding the raft to tackle the Ultimo Sondresa, a rapid that indeed produced "the best smile" from us all.

CONQUERING THE VOLCANO

At 7:30am the next day, at Sol y Nieve's office once again, I sat searching for the rigid plastic mountaineering boots I'd been fitted with the previous evening. Trussed up in over-trousers, gaiters, weatherproof jacket, sunglasses, gloves, and two hats (a baseball cap and fleece cap), and carrying a backpack containing crampons and ice axe—all provided by the agency—the 20 other climbers and I felt ready to conquer the 2,840-m (9,318-foot) **Villarrica**, the smoking, snowy peak of which is clearly visible above the rooftops of Pucón.

We split into two groups and headed off in minivans along an unsealed uphill track to the Parque Nacional Villarrica. At the gates the ranger checked through a few of the backpacks to make sure we were carrying crampons before we were allowed to continue to the ski resort, looking somewhat forlorn as the snow melted around the lifts to reveal grey and brown rubble. A few gung-ho types opted to hike from here, but I joined the majority and paid for the ski-lift. The chill wind began to bite through my layers of clothing, and I felt glad that I would soon be starting the climb, which at 1,900m (6,230 feet) was roughly equivalent to a six-hour slog to the summit.

Before we set off, our veteran guide, Joachim, who has led more than 1,000 ascents of the volcano over a decade, adjusted our crampons to fit our boots. We then had a lesson in how to use the ice axe: if you slip, you twist your body so that you are face down in the snow, hold on to the head of the axe, and then dig in with the axe's spike and the tips of your boots. At last we were off, trudging slowly through the crunchy snow along a zigzag route up a slope that averaged between 25 and 35 degrees.

LEFT For those who relish a whitewater challenge, Chile's rivers offer some intensely dramatic runs
RIGHT The ascent of the volcano Villarrica is nothing if not tough; the descent, sliding down on your backside, is more like fun

CLIMBING VILLARRICA

Villarrica can be climbed year round. The ascent takes between six and eight hours, but when you go depends on the weather and volcanic activity; be prepared to hang around for a few days for the right conditions. Although all reputable operators will provide the full set of equipment necessary to make the climb, it's best to check out the quality of this before you hand over your money. Also check that there is at least one guide for every nine people in the group. Thermal underwear and a sweater or fleece will keep you warm, and you're likely to have a more comfortable climb if you use your own boots fitted with crampons—although they will get wet from the snow. At the very least, pack plasters or moleskin to deal with blisters. A handkerchief or some kind of face mask will provide protection from the fumes at the summit. Make sure you also carry a good supply of water and energy-boosting snacks. Finally, take some cash as it's well worth paying the 3,000 pesos for the ski-lift so that you save your energy for later.

THE BEST DESCENT

At 10:15am, we took shelter in an abandoned ski-lift for a snack break. Far below, Lake Villarrica glittered in the sunlight, while above clouds and gusts of sulphurous smoke rose from the bowels of the Earth to obscure our goal. Three Spanish climbers turned back, while an Irish woman abandoned her exhausted Canadian husband at the next rest spot, a bare patch of scree left dry of snow by the thermal heat permeating from below. From here, it would be a steady climb to the summit, which tantalizingly revealed itself periodically against the deep blue sky.

I dropped behind the group, and for most of the next two hours was alone with Joachim, who paused every so often for a nicotine fix while I caught my breath. Then, just when I felt I could go no further, Joachim told me that the crater was only a couple more minutes' climb up the icy rocks. At the summit, the stench of volcanic gases was overpowering, and the smoke was so dense that there was no chance that we would be able to spot bubbling red magma, although apparently this is often possible. We spent no more than a few minutes at this forbidding spot before starting to head back down.

Skiing without skis is called glissading, but I'm not sure what you'd call sledging without a sledge. "Bum-sliding," suggested one member of the group, as we all become kids again, gleefully careering down the slopes on our backsides. If you don't fancy getting a damp bottom, you may like to know that several of the agencies offer the equipment and guides for crosscountry skiing down Villarrica. Either way, the high-speed descent of the volcano may well prove the best part of the trip.

THE CAÑI FOREST

Some 30km (19 miles) east of Pucón is one of Chile's last intact *Araucaria araucana* forests, preserved inside the 500-ha (1,200-acre) **Cañi Forest Sanctuary**. A contemporary of Jurassic-era dinosaurs, the *Araucaria* (known locally as the *pehuen* and internationally as the monkey-puzzle) is one of the Earth's oldest species of tree and is one of Chile's national symbols. Despite this, the spiky tree, which can grow to a height of 50m (160 feet) and live for over 1,500 years, has seen its survival threatened by Chile's forestry practices.

As I studied a baby *Araucaria* in the tree nursery at the Refugio Base Cañi, located in the Liucura Valley village of Pichares, I felt amazed to think that 300 years will pass before it is fully grown. I held this thought in my mind as we drove along a bumpy track to the start of the trail through the forest sanctuary itself.

FUNDACIÓN LAHUEN

This non-governmental organization made up of Chilean and international ecologists was formed in 1991 to help manage the Cañi Forest Sanctuary, and is dedicated to native forest protection and conservation. In addition to maintaining the trails within the sanctuary and training local guides, the Fundación Lahuen has begun a tree and plant nursery, and runs environmental awareness projects with local schools and communities.

If you want to find out more about the organization or wish to assist, you can contact them in Pucón, in the U.S.A, or via e-mail (see Contacts).

Aside from the local guide and two other hikers, I was joined by Rick Klein, a visiting American environmentalist and one of the people responsible for establishing the sanctuary.

Our hike began on the open slopes of the valley, where burnt-out tree trunks—left over from the colonial practice of setting fires to clear pastures for grazing—lay scattered like casualties of war. Inside the sanctuary, "one of the most biologically diverse temperate forests in the world," according to Klein, our route was shaded by lenga, a species of Nothofagus tree with bright green leaves, the darker green coihue, and the bamboo kila. The forest is home to many native birds, foxes, and reptiles, and even puma. Once we started climbing beyond the 1,000-m (3,300-foot) level, the *Araucaria* began to appear in greater numbers. We paused for lunch by Laguna Carpintero (Woodpecker Lagoon), a serene spot I could have lingered at for hours had it not been for the mosquitoes that nibbled us as we nibbled our sandwiches. The nearby Laguna Negra (Black Lagoon) is just as pretty, and is the location of a campsite and basic lodge for those who choose to stay overnight. From here we began the half-hour climb up to the Mirador, a rocky bluff that provides a splendid 360-degree panorama of the surrounding cordillera, forests, and jewel-like lakes, and the climax of the hike. Standing here it was easy to understand why the Mapuche named this area the Cañi, meaning the vision that transforms.

RIDE TO THE HOT SPRINGS

On my last day in Pucón, I decided to return to the **Liucura Valley** to go horse riding. At the Centro de Turismo Ecuestre Huepil, my group of four were greeted warmly by owners Carolina and Rodolfo, their three dogs, Martino, Olivia, and Chocosito, and their two cats, Thelma and Louise, and we were invited into their charming, self-built cottage. Rodolfo, an experienced Argentine showjumper and once trainer of the Spanish Olympic horse-riding team, outlined the proposed route over tea and

LAND OF TERMAS

Hot springs are known as *termas* in Spanish, and Chile's Lake District has plenty of them. From Pucón, head west into the beautiful Liucura Valley, where you'll find the upmarket Termas de Huife and the more rustic (and cheaper) Termas Los Pozones. Both have outdoor pools beside the river, although the Pozones is more naturally designed. Hostería ¡Ecole! organizes transport and discount entrance to Los Pozones most evenings—check their noticeboard for details (see Contacts). You'll need to take along a swimsuit, towel, torch, and something to drink. Also worth checking out are the wacky Termas de Panqui, 58km (36 miles) east of Pucón, where North American Indian tepees have been erected on Mapuche territory to create a New Age centre for ecology and spiritual awareness.

along the dusty mountain road. The only traffic we passed was a farmer in a wooden cart pulled by two oxen.

The style of horse riding in Chile and the rest of South America differs from that generally adopted in Europe. The horse is guided primarily by the rider's body weight, and the reins are held in one hand while the other remains free— a hangover from the days when the conquistadores needed to be ready to use their swords. Rodolfo also told me to keep the reins loose and to point my heels down in the stirrups so that I was ready to give my horse a gentle kick in order to encourage her to move forward.

A hearty picnic lunch was given a touch of class by a bottle of good red wine, all enjoyed while we gazed at the beautiful view across the valley. From this point we rode for a couple more hours, eventually joining the new road, which we followed for a few hundred metres to the hot springs in the riverside grounds of a luxury hotel, the ideal place to unwind after my action-packed four days in Pucón.

biscuits. The weather was too threatening to climb up to the Cañi, so instead we would follow the valley at mid-level, taking the old route to Argentina, to finish at the Termas de Huife hot springs.

Once we had been fitted with leather chaps and spurs, we were taken to the stables and introduced to our horses— mine was a grey and white mare called Chucau. There was the chance to practise in a corral before we set off at a slow pace

GOING IT ALONE

INTERNAL TRAVEL

The airport at Temuco is served by daily flights (1 hour) from Santiago; LanChile may also run occasional flights to a small airfield close to Pucón between December and April—check for details. All long-distance and overnight buses to Pucón go via Temuco, where you'll also need to alight from the overnight train from Santiago. Train tickets ($30–40) are available from the Estación Central, and the sleeping cars (*cama*) provide the choice of upper or lower bunk, or a private compartment. If you travel by bus (faster and cheaper than the train) choose *salón cama* or *executivo* buses as they have roomy reclining seats, blankets, and pillows, serve complimentary drinks and breakfast, and screen a video movie.

WHEN TO GO

Between December and April (the peak season in Chile's Lake District) Pucón can be very busy, especially over holiday periods and weekends. At this time make sure you book accommodation and travel tickets well in advance. The skiing season on Villarrica is from June to October.

PLANNING YOUR TRIP

Competiton between the many tour agents in Pucón is intense; you should check out a few before you book, in particular looking over equipment and confirming itineraries before you hand over any money. The cheapest option is not always the best, or safest, deal. Although the climb up Villarrica is not technically difficult, you'll need plenty of equipment to complete it safely, and you should follow experienced guides who know the route. Conaf, the parks department, does issue special permits to solo climbers, but for all practical purposes it's simpler to join one of the organized tours. If you want to go it alone, solo trekking is a better proposition.

HOTELS AND RESTAURANTS

In Pucón you'll never be more than a few minutes' walk from O'Higgins, the central street along which you'll find most restaurants, shops, and adventure-tour operators. There's a wide range of accommodation in town to suit all budgets and tastes, and the recent boom of building holiday flats and houses might translate into more restaurants and bars staying open outside the peak holiday season. Hiring your own transport (cars can be rented in Temuco) will make it easier to stay at the less busy, more relaxing countryside hotels.

WHAT TO TAKE

❏ Swimsuit.
❏ Sandals or shoes that you don't mind getting wet.
❏ Thermal underwear and a sweater or fleece.
❏ Hiking boots.
❏ First-aid kit, including plasters or moleskin to deal with blisters.
❏ Handkerchief to protect your face from volcanic fumes at Villarrica's summit.
❏ Insect repellent.
❏ Sun hat and sunscreen lotion.
❏ Raincoat.
❏ Sleeping bag and ground mat.
❏ Torch.
❏ Binoculars for bird-spotting.

ABOVE LEFT and LEFT Panoramic views on the trail through the Cani Forest: the Sanctuary preserves the monkey-puzzle tree, Araucaria araucana. *Once threatened by clearance, it is one of the oldest species of tree on Earth and takes 300 years to reach maturity*

TRAVELLERS' TIPS

❏ If you are trekking independently, take a map (Hostería ¡Ecole! may be able to lend you one—see Contacts), and inform someone where you are going and when you expect to return.
❏ Foreign exchange is available in Pucón, but you'll get a better rate (especially for travellers' cheques) in Santiago.

HEALTH AND SAFETY MATTERS

While it is advisable to drink bottled water throughout Chile, the water in Pucón is fresh enough to drink straight from the tap. Also, on hikes you need not be too concerned about drinking untreated river water. It's always a good idea to take a first-aid kit on any long treks.

CHILE

The Towers of Chile

by Lee Karen Stow

The Torres del Paine, rising like skyscrapers over the southeastern tail of the Andes in southern Chile, tower over what is probably South America's finest national park. On foot and by horseback, I skirted shimmering lakes, followed sprawling glaciers, and crossed rushing rivers to stand beneath these granite pinnacles.

The 242,000-ha (59,800-acre) Parque Nacional Torres del Paine straddles the Argentina–Chile border, and is becoming more popular by the year as it offers some of the best trekking on the planet. This World Biosphere Reserve, with snow-capped peaks that disgorge thunderous waterfalls into pools of differing blues surrounded by green-black forests, is roamed by herds of llama-like guanacos (*Lama guanicoe*) and inhabited by over 100 species of birds.

At the end of the last century, European settlers used the land for agriculture. They created one massive sheep station by setting forest fires to clear the way for grazing, a devastating action from which the park is still recovering. That said, the park is wildly glorious, topped by the prime attraction of the Macizo Paine, an awesome four-crowned massif settled by broad glaciers and surrounded by glacial lakes.

The massif is made up of the Cuernos (meaning "horns"), the highest standing at over 2,400m (8,000 feet), and is cut by two rivers, the Río Francés and Río Ascensio. Cerro Paine Grande, soaring 3,248m (10,656 feet) is the tallest peak of all, yet it is often the park's namesake that draws the trekkers. The Torres del Paine consist of one short and three tall towers of hard granite that have become exposed as the softer, surrounding rock has eroded away. Popular with photographers because their colour changes with the light from rose-pink to slate-grey, the towers are frequently challenged by climbers who seem undaunted by the vertical walls of the highest pinnacle, Torre De Agostini, 2,850m (9,351 feet) high.

Most of the trails in the park are easy to follow by map. To venture on the difficult Paine Circuit you need to have experience of orienteering, or should enlist the help of a guide. Apart from the Torres, the most talked about thing in the park is the weather. Ferocious westerly winds blast in from the Pacific and literally take your breath away. Walking into them is tough going and will lengthen your journey, and even when the wind is behind you it can knock you over. In summer it stays light until 10:30pm, so you can trek late into the evening.

Most people spend a few days in the park, staying either at an expensive hotel or a *refugio* (refuge), or in a tent at a designated campsite. About 11 basic refugios are dotted around the park, and for these you need a sleeping bag. On this tour expect the unexpected: boats may not sail, bridges may be out, rivers become unfordable, weather is changeable, and refugios become overbooked or may lack hot water. This is the real outdoors after all.

Quality outdoor wear is essential, including waterproofs, windproof jacket, warm sweater, and walking boots. A headband is a good idea if you have long hair as it will keep it from blowing into your eyes. Maps are available from the park's headquarters or at shops in Puerto Natales, and feature hotels, refugios, campsites, and ranger stations, together with routes and distances given in terms of walking time. Keep cameras in quality waterproof and dustproof bags or containers.

PREPARING FOR THE PARK

Most people travel first to Puerto Natales, 112km (70 miles) from the park,

Parque Nacional Torres del Paine, southern Chile

a corrugated-iron and concrete stop-over town that has grown up around its port on the eastern shore of Ultima Esperenza (Last Hope Sound). Fish restaurants are rated highly here, and there are plenty of provisions stores for fresh supplies. Tents and camping equipment are available for hire, there's a tourist information point, and walking and mountain guides are on hand to accompany you around the Paine Circuit.

From Puerto Natales you can either hire a car or four-wheel drive, or take a bus for the four-hour trip to one of the three entrances to the park—Porteria Lago Sarmiento, Laguna Amarga, and Laguna Azul. At one or other of the entrances, you must register your name and passport number and pay an entrance fee. You can book an organized day excursion, but these give only a fleeting glimpse of the treasures that lie in store; to get a real feel for the park, it's best to stay for at least a couple of days. You can also hire mountain bikes in Puerto Natales and follow the cycleways that are marked on the map of the park, although I must admit that I did not see a single cyclist during my entire five-day stay—perhaps the wind prevented such a venture.

TO THE GLACIER

It is inadvisable to walk alone in the park in case of accident, so to reach my first port of call, Glaciar Grey (I wanted to leave the spectacular Torres until last), I searched for a trekking companion. Seated next to me on the bus on the way to the park was Greg, a marathon runner

from Philadelphia, U.S.A., who planned to set up base camps and run up a few mountains as part of his training. It seemed I would have to seek another walking partner.

The bus dropped some passengers at the ranger station at Laguna Amarga, then proceeded to another stop at Refugio Pudeto. I alighted here, and along with eight others took a boat across the beautifully blue **Lago Pehoe** to the start of a three-hour trek heading northwest to **Glaciar Grey**, a feature every visitor to the park should see. We disembarked on the far shore of Lago Pehoe near a kiosk selling basic provisions. I stocked up with chocolate and joined Kerry and Bryan from England, who had travelled down to Chile from Peru and planned to camp within sight of Glaciar Grey. I, on the other hand, had decided not to bring a tent as I wanted to experience the great

LEFT and INSET The Torres del Paine national park encompasses mountain ranges, lakes, glaciers and waterfalls—as well as the the three tall, granite pinnacles, or towers. Treks vary from easy to very challenging

meeting place of the *refugio*.

The walk warmed up through a grassy valley with shrubs rising to exposed hilltops. The paths in the park are well-trodden and easy to follow, periodically marked by an orange blob on a rock or tree trunk. In some places the walk was quite tough, climbing up shale slopes, but we were rewarded with a vista of icebergs choking the outlet of Lago Grey. The final section consisted of a descent through a sometimes muddy forest, before we reached the shelter of

ABOVE As well as some exotic and colourful flora (above, firebush) you may see guanacos, red foxes, flamingos, eagles, and condors BELOW Glaciar Grey, an ice age formation some 1,500 years old; huge blue icebergs fill the entrance to Lago Grey

Refugio Grey. Along the route, Greg, the marathon runner, passed us twice—once in each direction!

A COSY START

Sweet wrappers and old magazines crackled on the fire in the stove, and I sat as near to the warmth as I could under a clothes-line of drying woolly socks. The *refugio* was a wooden hut perched on the rocky shores of Lago Grey, mere strides away from the snout of the glacier. Kerry and Bryan were somewhat reluctantly pitching their tent outside, and I was happy to be in here rather than out there with them as the wind that had picked up that afternoon was now raging like a bull.

The *refugio*'s Chilean chef was frantically trying to piece together a meal from oddments in the kitchen. Supplies were running short: the last of the bread had been eaten that morning and it looked like dinner would be packet-mix soya chicken and pasta watered down with orange juice. I glanced round to see a dozen other walkers of different nationalities, all reading travel guides, plotting routes on the map, and talking about the

---

THE PAINE CIRCUIT

This classic route, the longest and toughest in the park, is for experienced hikers only and demands a good level of fitness. It circles the Torres and the Macizo Paine, offering tremendous views of the park's central region, and takes at least seven days to complete. Walkers usually begin the 100-km (62-mile) trail at Guardería Laguna Amarga and head anti-clockwise, although you can start from Portería Sarmiento or the administration centre near Posada Río Serrano. Check at the headquarters whether the circuit is completely passable or if there is any change to the route. Take a tent for when you are caught between refugios, and remember to carry sufficient food.

---

weather. Stories abounded of tents blowing away and of walkers leaning into gusts, only to fall flat on their face when the wind suddenly stopped. One girl swore her best buy yet was a headband, which she believed saved her life by keeping her tangled hair out of her eyes. One of the entries in the refugio's visitor's book read: "We came, we tried to conquer, but between the wind, rain, wind, clouds and a bit more rain, we were conquered."

Someone asked if I had arrived here by way of the "W," a popular route from Hostería Las Torres up to the Torres, looping back and up the middle Valle del Francés, then returning to take the left loop to Glaciar Grey. Another asked if I had seen the towers yet, and warned me of the knee-breaking climb involved. Then the door opened. It was as though someone had forgotten to close the refrigerator. A windswept Australian couple clambered in front of the stove and placed their order for soya-chicken mix. They were elated. The night before, they had pitched their tent within sight of Glaciar Francés, and had been woken by the sound of an avalanche. A fantastic sight it was, they said, as ice thundered down and the wind whipped the snow into puffball clouds. They had also "seen the towers." I couldn't wait for the next day.

NO SAILING TODAY

The following day's return walk to Pehoe was a battle through strong winds to the boat launch, only to find that the 11:30am sailing had been cancelled owing to the wind and that the 2:30pm one was fully booked. Refugio Pehoe is in an exceptional spot, set on the grassy banks of the lake and backed by the snow-streaked summit of Cerro Paine Grande. Upland geese (*Chleophaga plata*) nest on the shores, and firebushes (*Embothrium coccineum*) grow in profusion. I decided to stay the night.

The next day, the boat was cancelled yet again, so I decided to head for the

LOCAL BIRD SPECIES

- Andean condor (Vultur gryphus)
- Black-necked swan (Cygnus melancorypus)
- Buff-necked ibis (Theristicus caudatus)
- Chilean flamingo (Phoenicopterus chilensis)
- Great-chested buzzard eagle (Geranoetus melanoleucus)
- Great-horned owl (Bubo virginianus)
- Magellanic oystercatcher (Haematopus leucopodus)
- Magellanic woodpecker (Campephilus magellanicus)
- Patagonian mockingbird (Mimus patagonicus)
- Upland goose (Chleophaga plata)
- White-tufted grebe (Podiceps rolland)

an adventure-tourism establishment in Puerto Natales that sets the scene by hosting a nightly slide show and buffet so you can see the type of pictures you might achieve.

Amerindian's resident photographer ventures out into the known and lesser-known vantage points of the park in all seasons. He says it is ambitious to believe that you can produce perfectly stunning pictures in just a few days (for a start, you may encounter long periods of harsh weather), and suggests that the best thing to do is to stay in and around the park for at least a month. However, reasonable pictures are still easy to come by within a shorter time, and the fun of trying is infectious.

The park's wildlife undoubtedly makes great subject matter. Sightings of guanaco are frequent, along with rhea (known locally as Ñandú), red and grey foxes, and the occasional eagle and

park's administration centre further south at Posada Río Serrano, from where a bus departs to other points in the park. My overall intention was to reach the base of the towers, so I embarked on a five-hour hike along the side of Lago Pehoe and through a thin bush corridor.

The landscape opened out on to shale-scattered hills, and then the well-marked trail continued past deep-blue lagoons, their banks strewn with parched, dead trees bleached by the sun. At the halfway stage I came across a stream flanked by grass and dandelions, a perfect resting place before the final onslaught across a windswept expanse of pampas grass. At the administration centre, everything you need to know about the park is detailed, including the flora, fauna, and landscapes that attract both amateur and professional photographers.

IN THE FRAME
In fact, organized photography tours can be booked through Amerindian Concept,

THE GUANACO
Found mainly on the Patagonian steppes, guanaco are part of the South American camelid family, along with vicuna and the domesticated llama and alpaca. Blessed with beautiful eyelashes, they are the tallest of the Andean land fauna. Guanaco weigh about 120–150kg (260–330lb). They were first hunted by the native Indians, who swung boleadoras (heavy stones held together with a leather strap) at the animal's legs to bring it down. The meat was eaten and the woolly pelt used to make wraps, fur side in and with the skin painted in brightly coloured designs. Now, the guanaco is hunted mainly by puma and, occasionally, red fox, which snatch the young as they graze. Guanaco breed once a year between November and February, and after an 11-week gestation the female gives birth to its young, called a chulengo. The guanaco are not shy of humans, and those in the park in particular are used to people.

condor. To see puma (*Felis concolor patagonica*) you need to stay for a couple of months to learn where they come down from the mountains after winter to fetch food for their young.

The park's scenery is constantly changing as ice melts and pools of water

LEFT Camping on the banks of Lago Pehoe, a base for some of the best trekking in South America, with superb views all the way ABOVE and BELOW The terrain is often tricky but, on mounts born and bred to it, riding is an exciting alternative to trekking

appear. In the summer especially, sunsets are a four-hour show of changing colours, from rose to burnt orange, the mountain peaks becoming silhouetted against the sky. Favourite views include the settled icebergs of Lago Grey and Salto Grande, a crashing waterfall produced as water from Lago Nordenskjöld drains into Lago Pehoe. The cataract is reached via a half-hour hike from the bus drop-off point at Refugio Pudeto. An hour further on is a lookout point over blue Lago Nordenskjöld and the striking Glaciar

Francés opposite. The ideal time to capture the famous Torres on film is sunrise; you can camp at the designated Campamento Torres site at the bottom and rise before 6am. This was where I planned to go, my camera at the ready.

To the towers

I hitched a ride to **Hostería Las Torres**, a luxuriously trim tourist haunt with a campsite set by the side of a babbling river, a decent *refugio*, and an expensive alpine-style hotel that offers horse riding. A thrilling alternative to trekking the 4½-hour route to the base of the Torres is to ride part of the way, tether your horse at Refugio y Campento Chileno, and then hike the final section.

At 8:30am it was completely calm, without a breeze. The Torres peeped between the hills, their tops vague under a veil of mist. It was drizzling, but the glow of sunrise on old snow and a rainbow arching across the sky promised a fine day. Armando, my mountain guide, saddled Tostada, a mottled-fawn Chilean horse wearing a saddle of fancy stitchwork and leather shoes for stirrups. He secured his cowboy hat and led the way along a path that opened into a meadow of cows, crossed a brook, and then followed the course used by walkers. It was early and no one was about, but Armando told me that in the summer months the hillside becomes packed with trekkers who stray from the already numerous snaking paths.

We came to a bridge across the white

water of the Río Ascensio that was too unstable for the horses, and so we forded the depths, the strong legs of our mounts skilfully picking their way over rocks, slipping occasionally but quickly regaining their balance. Armando told me not to worry, reminding me that the horses had been born here. The following ride was memorable indeed. I can still feel the sense of elation as we hugged a ridge high above a river that raged down a steep gorge of layered black shale. We descended to ford the river, and tethered the horses at the Refugio y Campento Chileno, a great place to pause for refreshments or stay the night. Armando swapped his cowboy boots for hiking boots, and before I even had time to order a warming hot chocolate we set off on foot.

Almost there

The hiking trail rose away from the river, curving through forests of lenga, and traversing stepping-stones over streams and fallen tree trunks coated with moss. One punctured trunk bore evidence of the rat-a-tat-tat of a Magellanic woodpecker (*Campephilus magellanicus*). We came to a pause at a tumble of glacial boulders that seemingly led up towards the heavens.

Reaching the Torres viewpoint requires a 45-minute climb over these smooth boulders, putting a strain on the knees. As I'd been warned, the climb was a tough one, and I was glad when the last orange marker fell behind me. Here was what I had spent five days waiting to see: the granite Torres skyscrapers, still magnificent although shrouded in mist. The air was chilly and the atmosphere silent. Another group of walkers reached the top, sat down to rest, and pulled out their cameras, pleased that they had made it. I took my pictures and etched the scene into my memory.

The climb back down passed quickly at the prospect of hot soup at the *refugio* and the chance at last to ask its guests "Have you done the towers yet?"

LOCAL ANIMAL SPECIES

- ❑ Guanaco (*Lama guanicoe*)
- ❑ Hare (*Lepus capensis*)
- ❑ Lesser rhea (*Pterocnemia pennata*)
- ❑ Patagonian fox (*Dusicyon griseus*)
- ❑ Puma (*Felis concolor*)
- ❑ Red fox (*Dusicyon culpaeus*)
- ❑ Skunk (*Conepatus humboldtii*)

GOING IT ALONE

INTERNAL TRAVEL

There is no airport at Puerto Natales; the nearest one is at Punta Arenas, 270km (168 miles) or 3½ hours away. LanChile airline flies from Santiago to Puerto Montt airport, from where a coach to Puerto Natales is available.

There are regular buses from El Calafate in Argentina to Puerto Natales via the border crossings of Chile and Argentina.

There's also a ferry, which runs from Puerto Montt to Puerto Natales, following a spectacular, winding route through fjords and channels. Ferry bookings can be made at the ports.

WHEN TO GO

The main trekking season is from October to March and the peak time is from December to mid-February (the summer months), when *refugios* and camp-sites become full. Note that services may be reduced during the winter period.

In spring and summer the days are long, so you can carry on trekking well into the evening. Winds die down a little during the winter months, although heavy snowfalls are common.

PLANNING YOUR TRIP

The usual way to organize a trip into the Torres del Paine park is from Puerto Natales.

Along Arturo Prat (by the side of the yellow-painted church) and around the corner at Buses Fernández, you can catch early morning buses (8am) to the park; some will even pick you up from your hotel. Prices are around 4,500 pesos one way or 8,000 pesos for a return. Travel in the park is unpre-dictable, and once you are there you may be tempted to stay longer, so remember this before you decide to buy a return ticket.

Take your passport along with you as you have to register at the park entrance, where you also pay a fee of $12.

Camping at designated sites is the least expensive way of spending time in the park. Tents and camping equipment can be hired from Fortaleza Aventura in Puerto Natales. You can also hire guides for the Paine Circuit in Puerta Natales (see Contacts).

Many travel agents in Puerto Natales organize day excursions to the park at a cost of around 15,000 pesos plus the park entrance fee of 6,500 pesos. However, these can offer only a brief glimpse of the attractions and sometimes take in other sights such as the Cueva del Miloden (Cave of the Giant Sloth). Some agencies offer guides. You can hire someone to take you on the Paine Circuit for around $60 per day, although the two trekkers we spoke to said the route was easy.

WHAT TO TAKE

Although most refugios in the park sell basic supplies, it is cheaper to stock up on all necessities before you arrive.

- ❏ Food and drinks.
- ❏ Camping-stove and fuel.
- ❏ Strong tent, if you are camping; just a sleeping bag if you plan to stay at the refugios.
- ❏ Toilet tissue (the refu-gios sometimes run out).
- ❏ Maps.
- ❏ Waterproofs.
- ❏ Windproof jacket.
- ❏ Sweater.
- ❏ Hiking boots.
- ❏ Waterproof and dust-proof bag or container for your camera.
- ❏ Headband if you have long hair.

TRAVELLERS' TIPS

- ❏ You are not allowed to take agricultural products, such as fruit, across the border; if you do it will be confiscated.
- ❏ Trekkers who ignore the restrictions on camping and decide to pitch a tent anywhere are likely to be fined by the park's authorities.

HEALTH AND SAFETY MATTERS

Before you tackle any trek, and especially the Paine Circuit, make sure that you are fit enough to cope with the demands of the route and the volatile weather conditions. If you are at all unsure either of the terrain or your stamina, turn back or head for the nearest refugio and rest. Everyone, no matter where they pitch, is urged not to light fires or cause any damage to the environment.

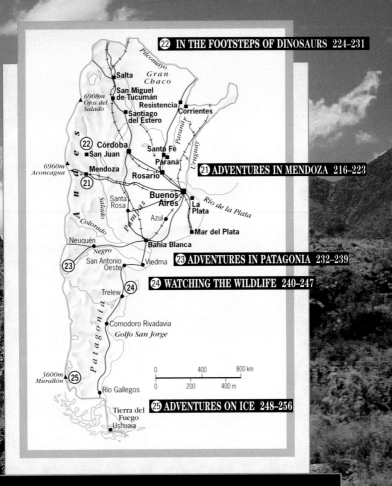

ARGENTINA

A rgentina is different at every angle of the compass. To the south, the windswept scrubland of Patagonia rolls towards Antarctica, while in the north you'll find tropical rain forests and sun-baked deserts. In the east, the Atlantic Ocean, home to a plethora of marine life, crashes on to cliffs; in the west the snow-capped mountain ridge of the Andes separates Argentina from Chile and delivers massive glaciers into waterfalls and vast lakes.

A chain of national parks means boundless activities for the adventure traveller. For the intrepid climber, there is Cerro Aconcagua, South America's highest peak, or the extinct Volcán Lanín. Hiking is a popular pastime on trails or wild back-routes, particularly in the north of Parque Nacional Los Glaciares. There's rafting in canyon rivers, paragliding down hillsides, horse riding on pure-blood Creole horses, fishing for trout, skiing, and endless days of wildlife watching.

The fast-flowing Río Mendoza irrigates the wine-growing region of eastern Argentina

ARGENTINA

Rafting and High-Altitude Hiking in Mendoza

By Lee Karen Stow

In Mendoza, the largest wine-producing region of Argentina, where vineyards grow in the shadow of South America's highest mountain, I get to grips with a paddle on a rushing river, attempt to fly over the vineyards, and even try some of the strong stuff, before reaching high altitude and the view of a lifetime.

Since the first vines were planted in 1556 by the Jesuits, and fed by water channelled from the nearby Andes mountain range, Mendoza has flourished, and now produces up to 30,000 kilolitres (6,600,000 gallons) a year of both red and white wines famous the world over. This is one reason why the province has named itself La Tierra de Buen Vino, meaning land of good wine.

Visiting a winery is the least active pastime on offer here: the only energy you'll spend is that required to lift a glass for the tasting. Far more riveting things to

3 Rafting is a sheer delight, but you do get wet and you may fall in. Beginners can try the basic course: the rapids are moderate and the paddling is not too strenuous. High-altitude hiking requires a degree of fitness, and it's not uncommon for hikers to suffer altitude sickness.

★★ Comfort will depend on your chosen accommodation. There is a wide range of good hotels in Mendoza city. For the day trips, coaches collect you and return you after the activity. On high-altitude hiking excursions, it's usual to stay at least one night in a hostel, or *refugio*, which can be basic (you need to take your own sleeping bag). There are mosquitoes that bite at night in Mendoza but none in the mountains.

⚒ For the rafting, all the necessary equipment (including helmets and life jackets) is provided, but remember to wear an old T-shirt and beach sandals. Specialist mountain equipment is needed for trips to Cerro Aconcagua. If you plan to camp, you will need good camping equipment.

do in this central-western region of Argentina begin in the south at Dique El Nihuil reservoir, a haven for sailing, waterskiing, windsurfing, and fishing, using the city of San Rafael as your base.

If you have the right experience, you can move further north and tackle the region's anchor, Cerro Aconcagua, which, at 6,960m (22,836 feet), is the highest peak in the Americas. Failing that there's a chance to explore beautiful territory in the footsteps of the native Indian tribes that occupied the area before the arrival of the Incas and the Spanish.

Mendoza's year is a calendar of events, from kayak descent competitions to cycling races, mountain survivals, fishing competitions, night marathons, and snow feasts. A refreshing pastime is to hire a mountain bike and ride to the hot thermal spas at Cacheuta, on the outskirts of Mendoza city, and immerse the body in the water's therapeutic properties. In winter, try downhill skiing and snowboarding at the big ski resorts. Rappelling—a form of abseiling down mountain walls or waterfalls—is another option; though for sheer adrenalin-pumping fun, there's nothing to beat rafting through dry-bone canyons.

GET READY TO PADDLE

"Adelante! Adelante! Adelante!" cried Sergio, one of the three brothers Betancourt who run rafting courses in between competing on the world's rapids as the official Argentine rafting team. His

GHOST OF THE ANDES

Does Mendoza's famous El Futre spectre haunt the peaks? A legend from the days of the construction of the railway that crosses the Andes has it that El Futre (slang for an elegant man) was an Englishman wearing a top hat and a poncho who visited the camp on horseback to pay the workers their wages. The story goes that he was mugged and decapitated, and that his spirit accompanies those who walk alone at night in the Andes without harming them.

and it is highly entertaining. It begins at a point in the river past the town of Portrerillos, and follows a 15-km (9-mile) section that, according to Sergio, is ideal for beginners because in rafting terms it is Class I to III (moderate rapids and easy steering).

Altogether, there are 140km (87 miles) of rafting to enjoy on the Río Mendoza, including more difficult levels of Class IV to VI. Two- and three-day expeditions, with overnight camping are organized; these are physically demanding—often requiring four-hour spurts of non-stop paddling—and are not advisable for beginners.

A LIVELY BASE

Most people base themselves in Mendoza city, the administrative, commercial, and cultural capital of the province. It was founded in 1561, and ravaged 300 years later by an earthquake. Today's cosmopolitan scene is of tree-lined streets edged with gutters for irrigation, art galleries, museums, theatres, banks, and cybercafés. Early-morning sweepers brush the pavements with straw brooms, while city folk contemplate *desayuno completo* (a full American breakfast)

order was to paddle forward, fast. I and half a dozen others perched on the inflated edge of a blue raft, plunged our oars into the Río Mendoza and prayed for speed. Surprisingly, the gurgling river is the colour of milky coffee. I'd dreamed of whitewater rafting; this would be better described as brown-water rafting.

Our raft scraped a boulder, slowing us down. Our opponents in the grey raft had been trailing behind, but now, urged on by another Betancourt brother, they were able to gather force and overtake us. They passed us without warning, and then celebrated the victory by using their oars to spoon the murky water over our heads. We were soaked, and the floor of our raft turned into a pond. This meant war.

We cut through the water, swivelling left to right, the nose of the raft inching its way ahead, until we were just clear of the greys. Now it was our turn to drench them. When we thought they'd had enough we raised our oars high in the air, and cheered jubilantly. But the defeated brother wasn't happy: he grabbed Santiago by the life jacket and flung him into the river. The water isn't deep, and the flow here is calm, so we joined him, splashing into the brown water and ruining our clean shirts.

Apparently, this is the normal, everyday rafting trip run by the brothers,

FISHING IN MENDOZA

Río de las Cuevas, Río Mendoza, and their tributaries, are popular fishing areas in the north, while the favoured waters of Malargüe in Mendoza's south include Río Barrancas, Río Saledo, and Río Valenzuela. Other notable spots are Valle Hermoso, with its lagoons of trout, the Río Cobre and Río Tordillo, and Dique El Nihuil reservoir near San Rafael. The fishing season runs from November 1 to April 30 for salmonoids, and from November 1 to July 31 for pejerrey, perch, and carp. Permits and further details area available from the tourist information office.

served in street cafés; and paperboys stand in the middle of a traffic junction, yelling for a sale, as yellow and black taxis speed by.

Nightlife heats up after 9pm when the locals, called *mendocinos*, come out to eat. Trattorias and restaurants lining the main thoroughfare of Ave. San Martín in "downtown" Mendoza spill out to a central area that becomes a makeshift arena: children dress as clowns and balance pigeons on their heads; buskers play. Dancing fountains enliven parks and plazas, the main show being a light and water display at Plaza Independencia. Here, the fashionable young gather to talk, eat ice cream, or browse in the nightly craft market, which sells leather knick-knacks and jewellery by lamplight.

I arrived in Mendoza on a Sunday, when all adventure tour operators were closed. The next day happened to be a

national holiday, and only eating places opened their doors. By the third day things started to happen, though I found it hard to organize my itinerary because people work on the "we'll sort it out tomorrow" principle. They take siestas to escape the heat of the afternoon, and are so laid back you wonder if you should throw in the towel and join them. "We'll collect you at 8am sharp" usually means you'll see them at 8:30, or perhaps even later. That said, I had plenty of adventure. I wasn't able to ski because it was the wrong time of year, so I decided that if I couldn't ski off a mountain, I'd fly off one.

FLY LIKE A KITE

Paragliding (*parapente* in Spanish), differs from hang gliding in that you sit in a harness in front of the instructor or pilot, rather than lie flat out across a steering bar. By gently pulling left and

right on cords, you control the canopy above to keep you sailing on currents of air until you make a gradual but exhilarating descent. No previous experience is needed.

The paragliding take-off point is the top of 700-m (2,297-foot) **Cerro Arco**, which is a ten-minute, uphill drive from downtown Mendoza. The view stretches across the city rooftops to the distant Volcán Tupangato, a volcano that is quiet but not quite extinct. It's up to the instructor to prepare the glider and check the conditions, and it is then that disappointment can set in. Conditions on the morning of my scheduled first course indicated that it was too windy to fly, and any attempt to do so would be dangerous. We tried again in the early evening, but the wind sock, which is used to measure the gusts, was blowing at a right angle: no flying today.

ABOVE Heading, as did the Incas, for the permanently snow-capped peak of Aconcagua LEFT A comparatively easy stretch of white water: others are more dramatic

ACONCAGUA'S BACK GARDEN

Back at Campo Base youth hostel in Mendoza—where I spent a few days because the food is good and I met many adventurous companions—I took up the offer of high-altitude hiking instead. But where? Adrian, the resident mountain guide, nicknamed Roger Rabbit, after the cartoon character because he eats carrots constantly during his ascents, suggested a trip to the mountains around Aconcagua to escape the city heat, traffic fumes, and mosquitoes.

A one-time member of the mountain search and rescue team, Adrian has conquered Aconcagua three times, and

ARGENTINA

SKIING

The 1998 skiing season proved a disaster for Mendoza as there was no snow. Nevertheless, tourism officials are predicting a bumper flurry in future seasons, which here means the months from June/July to early October.

The main resorts are Valle de Las Leñas, Los Penitentes, and Vallecitos. One of the first ski centres in the province, Vallecitos is 79km (49 miles) from Mendoza city and has 12 pistes. Los Penitentes is further, at 160km (99 miles) from the city, on the road to Chile in Las Cuevas valley, and minutes from the border. Its altitude is 2,580m (8,465 feet) at its base and 3,200m (10,499 feet) on high, and there are 28 pistes. Hotels, hostels, and apartments, plus an entertainment centre and sled-riding, complete the package.

The 3-star Las Leñas resort, a venue for international ski competitions and other winter sports such as snowboarding, is 480km (298 miles) south of Mendoza and 200km (124 miles) southwest of San Rafael in the district of Malargüe. It has an altitude of 2,256m (7,402 feet) at base, rising to at 3,430m (11,254 feet) at the top. It is usually surrounded by acres of dry and dust snow, and offers 40 pistes that range from easy to very difficult.

---

he remembers his first summit, on a wonderful evening, when at 9pm he watched a blazing red sun sink into the Pacific Ocean to the east. His stories are gripping, and they help to pass the time on the following morning's bus journey from Mendoza to Las Cuevas (the last settlement before Chile), via the spectacular **Uspallata Valley**.

The mountains are stained ochre or tinged with red. Creamy bands, pigment stripes, and minerals enliven the slopes, which are penetrated by the single, rubble-strewn track of the disused

Argentina to Chile railway line. The thin, brown river seems camouflaged against this monotonous beauty, and I wondered if we'd entered the crust of a huge volcanic crater. It's like another world. In fact, filmgoers would be interested to know that much of *Seven Years in Tibet*, starring Hollywood actor Brad Pitt, was filmed here.

Before reaching Las Cuevas, we stopped off at the entrance to Parque Provincial Aconcagua, which is marked by an aluminium cross similar to the one on the actual Aconcagua summit. Under a skin-scorching sun we walked leisurely for half an hour, passing green meadows and purple wildflowers, to the ranger station. If you are spending longer in the park, hiking or climbing, you have to register at the station and collect a map that shows routes, overnight *refugios*, and base camps. Covering 70,000ha (172,970 acres), and sheltering guanaco (*Lama guanico*), hare (*Lepus capensis*), red fox (*Dusicyon culpaeus*), and the occasional condor, the park is a peaceful sanctuary. It is open all year, though the ranger service for radio, maps, and advice, is available only from November 15 to March 15.

Wherever you are in the park, it's hard to escape the sight of the only snow-covered peak, **Aconcagua**, first climbed by Englishman Edward Fitzgerald over 100 years ago , and first conquered by the Italian-Swiss Mathias Zurbriggen. There's no definite proof that the Incas reached the summit, but evidence that they climbed high was revealed in 1985 when, at 5,200m (17,061 feet), mountaineers discovered the mummified body of a boy, wrapped in sacrificial blankets. The mountain may still hold archaeological secrets, and anyone stumbling across something is asked to leave it untouched and report it to the ranger.

We filled our water bottles and carried on for an hour, passing an emerald lagoon and crossing a bridge to picnic in a circle of rocks. Behind these are strange standing stones, some piled on top of each other and etched with symbols. It's difficult to tell whether the grooves are primitive, a joke, or today's ornate graffiti.

To the border

Back at the park entrance, we waited for the bus to take us the few minutes to **Las Cuevas**. It didn't turn up, so we hitched a ride to the door of Hostería Aconcagua. The hostel is basic and quite grimy, but the prospect of an evening meal—with wine that Adrian had remembered to bring with him—decided us to stay the night.

An earth tremor woke us at 6am the next morning. When the bunk beds in the hostel had ceased rattling, Adrian rushed out to check for avalanches before giving the OK to begin our high-altitude ascent. Wolfgang, a German cyclist riding from Mendoza through the Andes' mountain pass to Santiago in Chile, propped his bike against the wall and decided to join us.

The slope is steep, and deep with shingle and fragments of green rock the colour of emeralds. Every step taken is a slide back down, which makes the going tough. Because the air is thin, we progressed slowly and halted every 15 minutes for long draughts of water or—in Adrian's case—a carrot. Luckily, I experienced no headache, although my breathing felt shallow and I realized I was tiring easily.

After three hours we reached our 3,820-m (12,535-foot) destination, the **Monumento al Cristo Redentor**. This bronze statue of Christ the Redeemer stands on the border with Chile beneath the gathering clouds clutching a staff and raising the other hand as if calming a storm. He is the result of an effort by the mountain people who, at the end of South American-liberator General José San Martín's freedom war of the last century, collected cannons and sent them to Buenos Aires to be melted down and sculpted. The statue was brought here in sections by rail and mule, and erected in 1904.

REGIONAL FOOD AND WINE

Try *humita* (corn in the husk) or *empanadas* (meat turnovers, but sometimes filled with spinach and egg), sold from street bakers and stands. The Argentine diet consists of much beef and other meats, such as *patitas aliñadas* (seasoned pork). A dish of meat stew is a warming meal.

For breakfast, you might try *tortitas raspadas* —baked dough rounds, delicious with coffee—or you could go for *tomaticán* (scrambled eggs with tomato sauce). In southern Mendoza, the climate is perfect for growing olives, fruit, and vegetables, so these feature prominently in the local diet. And goats are everywhere, which is why you'll see barbecued goat and goat's cheese on the menu.

It is no surprise that in this region famous for its vineyards, wine is consumed at lunch and dinner. Brands to look out for include Navarro Correa, Luigi Bosca, and Comte de Beltour, from the Chandon winery, and Saint Felicien. It's cheaper to buy from supermarkets and corner shops, rather than souvenir shops, and a good bottle can cost between $5 and $12.

Opposite, Cerro Tolosa rises with Glaciar Hombre Cojo. Inside the café in the shadow of the statue, hot tea was brewing. Refreshed, we began the descent. The climb down was hilarious as we dug in our heels but could not prevent ourselves from skating on the shale. Soon enough we were back on the main road, busy with rumbling trucks transporting their loads across the border. We were just in time to catch the afternoon bus back to Mendoza.

Site of the Incas

Stay longer and you can see the remains of an Inca road and **Puente del Inca**. The latter is on the site of sulphur springs

ARGENTINA

and boasts one of Argentina's geological wonders, a natural stone bridge the colour of mustard and copper, wet with dripping mineral water. It's a true tourist spot. Coca-Cola cans and children's boots, which have been dipped into the water, are coated with a hard, orange crust and are sold as ornaments. For walkers and

climbers, there are a few refugios and a hotel, plus the possibility of hiring mules to take you to Aconcagua's base camps.

Further along is the **Cementerio de Los Andinistas**, a resting ground for climbers who have perished on Aconcagua. Its centrepiece, a high mound marked by a cross and dated 1903, appears to be the earliest grave. Circling this are the graves of other victims, of all nationalities, with an average age of 20 years. All are decorated with iron or wooden crucifixes, marble tombstones, or plaques.

On my return to Campo Base hostel late that evening, I discovered that the day's wind had dropped, allowing Krista from Chicago to succeed in paragliding. In great detail she described the thrill of running off a mountain, feeling no stomach drop, and being handed the controls to steer the glider down as softly as landing a kite. Her head remained in the clouds all evening.

LEFT The statue of Christ the Redeemer, erected as a symbol of friendship between Chile and Argentina
BELOW and RIGHT Puente del Inca, a natural stone bridge coloured by mineral deposits— which have also been allowed to coat shoes and Coca-Cola cans, making souvenirs

GOING IT ALONE

INTERNAL TRAVEL

Aerolineas Argentinas flies from Buenos Aires and other major destinations to San Rafael and Mendoza. Taxis are available at both airports.

You can also travel by bus (999km/620 miles) from Buenos Aires; the fare varies according to the standard of facilities provided by the different bus companies.

WHEN TO GO

Mendoza is hot and humid in spring and summer, though it's always cooler in the mountains. Rafting is available throughout the year, but December to March—the high season—is best purely because there are more people doing it, which means more fun and more screams. Paragliding can be done throughout the year. The skiing season runs from June/July to October. Look out for San Rafael's Great Fishing Competition in March, and also the Sport Fishing Week in April.

PLANNING YOUR TRIP

Excursions can be booked in Mendoza: many adventure and ski travel agents are located along Ave. Las Heras. Be prepared for the paragliding to be cancelled because of a lack of wind. This can be frustrating, if you allocate a particular day of your holiday for the sport and then find you waste it waiting for the wind to change. Cristo Redentor attractions can be visited on the "Alta Montaña" day excursion, but this entails spending many hours travelling in a bus. It is more rewarding to take a shorter bus journey, and then walk there instead, stopping overnight en route.

Free maps of Parque Provincial Aconcagua and advice on trekking to the base camps are available at the ranger station at the entrance to the park.

Walking, high-altitude trekking, and climbing guides can be booked in Mendoza. See the leaflets at tourist information offices. Many operators can put you in touch with a local guide, and some youth hostels have their own resident guides (see Contacts).Guides and mules to transport your kit to base camps in Parque Provincial Aconcagua can be hired in Puente del Inca.

HEALTH AND SAFETY MATTERS

In the low areas of Mendoza, mosquitoes are a nuisance after sunset. Use repellent or seek relief in the mountains. Altitude sickness and Acute Mountain Sickness (AMS) are the result of insufficient acclimatization to high altitudes; they are serious conditions that should not be ignored. Many climbers and trekkers are reluctant to admit that they are suffering from the classic symptom of shortness of breath. They fear that it may be taken as a sign of weakness and try to hide the signs. However, it is important to recognize altitude sickness and to deal with it at the onset if you are to prevent more serious effects and illness. Look out for headache (particularly one that won't go away with aspirin), nausea and vomiting, giddiness, difficulty in sleeping, intense fatigue, and breathlessness. Rest and take water, but be prepared to descend if the symptoms do not subside.

WHAT TO TAKE

❑ An old T-shirt, shorts, and sandals, for the rafting.

❑ A windproof jacket, warm sweater, and waterproofs, for hiking.

❑ Sunscreen.

❑ A hat or sunglasses.

❑ A daypack for carrying water and snacks. Lots of water and high-calorie snacks are essential for the high-altitude hiking.

❑ Mosquito repellent for use when you are on low ground at night.

❑ Camera film.

❑ Camping equipment, sleeping bag, portable stove, and cooking fuel, if you plan to camp; just a sleeping bag if you plan to stay in *refugios*.

ARGENTINA

In the Footsteps of Dinosaurs

By Lee Karen Stow

Two hundred million years ago giant reptiles thrived in a tropical Argentina that was visibly different from the country we see today. But with a little imagination, inspired by the legacy of petrified forests, ancient rock formations, and fossils, you can travel back in time to the age of the dinosaurs.

At the Museo de Ciencias Naturales in La Plata, two hours' drive southeast of Argentina's capital Buenos Aires, I stood under the bony jaw of an *Iguanadon* and chatted to a member of staff about dinosaurs. An egg laid by a *Titanosaurus* rests round the corner, while a replica of a *Protoceratops* skull livens up displays of more fossils of plants, reptiles, fish, plus the stump of a petrified tree. Meanwhile, at the souvenir shop, the grinning faces of plastic baby dinosaurs pop their heads from cracked plastic shells arranged under a row of *Tyrannosaurus rex* keyrings. The visitors, tourists, and schoolchildren love it.

The museum official told me that since the release of Steven Spielberg's blockbuster movie *Jurassic Park*, in which dinosaurs are brought to life, interest in these extinct creatures has grown phenomenally. Call it a dinosaur renaissance, but over the past ten years in Argentina new museums have opened to accommodate the latest palaeontological finds, schools have increased the study of past life on the planet, and even the country's 75-cent postage stamp features a colourful *Gaspamini saura*.

I was already enthralled, but then I was told that in November 1997 hundreds of dinosaur eggs were found in the area of Auca Mahueva in Neuquín. Nothing unusual in that, some might say— dinosaur eggs are found all over the region of Patagonia—but these eggs

Activities involve only some leisurely walking. No experience is required to search for fossils and archaeological features—just a keen eye. Some experience of horse riding would be useful for the day rides from Hill Station.

★★ There's no hardship on any of the tours, although it can be very hot and humid in this desert area. From San Juan it's a long drive to Parque Provincial Ischigualasto, so you might wish to stay closer to the park.

A camera with a U.V. filter and polarizer is essential for taking pictures of highly photogenic Parque Provincial Ischigualasto and Talampaya. Here, you can get away with slow, colour-saturation film, such as 50ASA, if you use a tripod.

were different, for inside about 40 of them scientists noticed part of the dinosaur's embryonic skin. The skin's texture is so well preserved that to touch the fossil is to actually touch the skin of a real dinosaur.

I was told it might be months, or even years, before the eggs went on view to the public. In the meantime, there is no doubt that Argentina's past will continue to deliver up significant finds. A colossal collection of pottery, arrowheads, and cave paintings left by the early, indigenous Indian tribes, along with a few mummified bodies, have already been found. How many big bones and footprints from a lost age are waiting to be discovered? The answer may lie in the Ischigualasto-Talampaya desert region in the north, where time really has stood still.

INTO THE VALLEY OF THE MOON

For my trip to the region, I based myself in **San Juan**, the capital of the province of the same name. This small town is blessed with sunlight all day long, although the extreme heat slows down the pace of any activity and, particularly during siesta, the swept, tree-lined, marble pavements are empty and all travel agencies are closed. By 5pm the community starts to wake, and that's when I was able to book a trip to Parque Provincial Ischigualasto (pronounced ichy-wulastoo), four hours and a world away from civilization.

I was told by one operator that I was one of only two people that had so far enquired about the next day's excursion into the park, and that since the minimum number for the trip was three we might have to pay for the "missing person." However, by 6am next morning our party had grown to four, including two German travellers and a North American. A car, not a minibus, collected each of us from our hotels, and from there we began the long, monotonous drive north.

Once out of town, the smoothly surfaced road gives way to a straight dirt-track that takes you through a corridor of bare desert sprouting the odd pitiful clump of grass—feeble nourishment for the herds of skinny cattle that occasionally barred our way. Slowly, they mooched across the road, hip bones all but protruding through skin. There are no fences to contain the animals round here, so it was no surprise to see the rotting carcass of a horse on the verge. Then a fox crossed in front of us, a bloodied chicken clasped in its mouth.

A third of the way there we stopped for breakfast at Hostería Valle Fértil in San Agustín del Valle Fértil, still in the province of San Juan, before finally arriving at what I truly believe to be a different planet. **Ischigualasto**—this extraordinary place that attracts archaeologists from around the world—hides between the mountains ranges of the Cerros Colorados in the east, and the Cerro Los Rastros to the west. Flowering cacti, shrubs, dead bark, and the delicate flower of the desert rose, share this vast valley with a few birds and animals, but other than that this is a no-man's land. Without the buzzing insects it would be deathly silent.

Ischigualasto's contribution to global palaeontology is its treasure of fossils, especially those of the great reptiles from Earth's Triassic period when the place was a lush, green swamp. The waters and weather of time have left their marks, and there is incredible beauty in the jumble of eroded rocks, piles of sculpted stones, and enigmatic formations. No wonder the park's other name is Valle de la Lune, meaning valley of the moon.

THE CIRCUIT

Circuito Interno Valle de la Luna is a 40-km (25-mile), three-hour route around the main sights of the park. It starts at the Centro de Interpretación (interpretation centre), where you pay a $5 entrance fee and then, at the nearby cafeteria, stock up on much-needed bottled water for the hot day to come.

If you drive around the circuit yourself, you must be accompanied by a guide (so it's advisable to phone ahead);

THE PETRIFIED FOREST

El Bosques Petrificados is a natural monument in the province of Santa Cruz, 210km (130 miles) south of the port of Caleta Olivia. Around 150 million years ago, during the Jurassic period, this area was covered by dense forests of enormous trees, particularly the *Araucaria*, or monkey-puzzle, before volcanic eruptions buried them. Most of the fossilized trunks and stumps of these trees—some 35m (115 feet) long—still remain in their original place of growth, and visitors are welcome to trail among them.

otherwise, you pay $10 per person to ride in the guide's overland safari truck. The latter sounds expensive, but you do get a *Jurassic Park* experience—without the predators. We decided to drive ourselves round the circuit, following the guide who jumped in the car in front driven by two Argentine tourists.

At intervals we stopped to get out of our cars and walk a few yards to a notable spot. And this is where I was thwarted, for the guide's address was in Spanish and with my limited knowledge of the language I could not understand the scientific terms. My German companion, who spoke fluent Spanish, was also baffled. Luckily, I had done some homework: I had bought an excellent bilingual,

glossy, coffee-table book about the park and its history beforehand (available from the interpretation centre, but priced at a hefty $80), and so I was just about familiar with this complex life zone of the planet and herbivorous reptiles. The guide said that Ischigualasto, which covers some 64,750ha (160,000 acres), has become internationally famous because its layers are a sequence of sedimentation, bearing a wealth of fossils, that encapsulates most of the Triassic period—the age of the dinosaurs from about 250 million years ago.

Water and wind, packed with dust particles, act as a sandblaster, cutting and shaping the region's rock. The process reveals the underlying geology, which in its exposed state is guaranteed to raise the eyebrows of scientists. Such rocks give clues to how dinosaurs lived on Earth, but this in itself is not sufficient to make the region unusual, for grounds from the Triassic period are found in many parts of the world. The reason that Ischigualasto is remarkable is that few other places bear such a vast amount, and such a great variety, of evidence. Almost all of the Triassic period is represented here, without having been obliterated by forests or developments. One palaeontologist—A.S. Rower from Harvard University, who was in charge of an expedition here in 1958— described it in his book *Ischigualasto-TamTalampaya* as "the most extraordinary fossil cemetery ever imagined."

FORGOTTEN LEAVES

At the next stop, we found the ground beneath our feet littered with crushed quartz. You are, however, forbidden to take anything from the park as souvenirs; even the practice of removing fossils for study by professionals from universities has been banned, and all research must be carried out under strict supervision. From here, our guide led us to a boulder the colour of golden beach sand, and pointed to where imprints of fossilized leaves have created a pattern on

the underside of a ledge; these are 150 million years old and yet so clearly defined that they could have been painted on yesterday.

Back in the car we wind leftwards and upwards to the striking vista of Valle Pintado, a gaping canyon whose cone-shaped hills of grey, pale pink and white, ringed by water marks, make it look like a moon crater. Here, in winter, the Río Ischigualasto fills with the park's heavy rainfall, and many roads on the circuit become impassable.

ROLLED STONES

Further down the track we filtered through a corridor of oddly formed, flaking walls with the texture of old skeleton bones. The ground is a crust of clay that in parts is as thin and cracked as broken eggshells, and as dry as our throats, for at midday the valley heats up to scorching point. Before us rose an extraordinary rock formation, the "Sphinx in Egypt," which looks like the crouching figure of the native puma; it is uncannily life-like, with hollows for cat's eyes, pointed ears, and two paws jutting forward into the desert. Behind the Sphinx are 3-m (10-foot) cacti, standing alone or in clusters. At dusk, these tall figures seemed to me to resemble the silhouettes of soldiers standing to attention. We were dumbfounded by the sight. Two of the tourists vowed to come

BELOW LEFT The significance of Parque Provincial Ischigualasto lies in its quite extraordinary wealth and variety of Triassic age fossils
TOP LEFT Concha de Bochas: the spherical concretions have been exposed by erosion
ABOVE Tyrannosaurus rex in replica

back here and be married. But there is more, said our guide.

Concha de Bochas is a unique arrangement of rounded concretions the size of cannon balls. No one has positioned them so; the scene is entirely natural. Near by are more concretions, these ones half-exposed by the erosion of many seasons, and it's only a matter of time before they are fully revealed. We made a further stop to see a large rock sculpted into the shape of a submarine, complete with funnel and nicknamed Submarino. You are allowed to "climb aboard" and gaze across the park's flatness to a distant band of red, sandstone cliffs whose base is a ribbon of blue-green mineral. It's a memorable vision—and if a *Brontosaurus* had reared its head above a rock, I wouldn't have been surprised.

And then, finally, at the site marked **El Hongo Fósiles**, we touched the smooth fossil of a reptile, embedded in the dusty ground where it fell around 220 million years ago. Palaeontologists have left this shiny skeleton where they found it so that visitors like us can imagine what life was like here long ago.

THE MUMMIES

In 1985 the mummified body of a seven-year-old Inca boy was found on Cerro Aconcagua (South America's highest peak) at 5,300m (17,000 feet). Although this mummy is not on show, Mendoza's Arqueológico de la Universidad Nacional de Cuyo displays his sacrificial belongings. These include two pairs of rope sandals, a plume headdress, a tunic, and the blankets in which he was wrapped before being drugged to sleep and left on the mountain. The museum also has a collection of Inca pots and other artefacts. Mummified bodies can also be seen at Museo de Ciencias Naturales in La Plata, near Buenos Aires.

A WORLD OF RED

Too soon, I felt, we returned to our starting point, the interpretation centre. The two Argentines were amazed by what they'd seen, but for them the fossil journey was not yet over. After we had quenched our thirsts with ice-cold Quilmes beers (the local brew) at the park's cafeteria, they decided to venture further north to **Parque Provincial Talampaya**, while we returned to San Juan. I was deeply envious.

Talampaya, which stretches over a slice of the province of La Rioja, is known as Argentina's Grand Canyon. It has 530,000 acres of plains, and its dramatic chasms are walled by red rocks, some etched with petroglyphs, but all in the regular flight paths of eagles, vultures, and condors. Guides accompany you on a two-hour tour of the site, though if you enquire beforehand you may be able to stay longer and even hike. Reluctantly, I bade the two Argentine travellers farewell and headed off to do more fossil hunting of my own, which entailed flying back to Buenos Aires for a meeting with a few old bones.

BONES IN THE CAPITAL

The **Museo Argentino de Ciencias Naturales** in Buenos Aires houses the most important collection of dinosaur bones and finds in Argentina (its main hall is high enough to accommodate the replica of the mightily tall *Patagosaurus*, dated 170 million years ago).

Head of the museum's Vertebrae Palaeontology Division is Dr. Josi Bonaparte, an authority on the subject who has headed many palaeontological expeditions (photos show his team at work extracting bones from the soil). He can be found in his basement office at the end of a long corridor of filing cabinets topped with frightening skulls. Near by, in a brightly lit workshop, staff make replicas of finds; on the back wall is mounted an original *Ictiosaurus*—only the replica is displayed in the main hall , and for good reason. Since visitors began stealing finger bones and teeth from dinosaurs, most of the originals have been locked away and replicas are on show.

But the replicas are just as impressive as the real thing: they include the *Amargasaurus cazaui*, found in the province of Neuquén, a 100-million-year-old *Carnotaurus*; and parts of the winged *Unenlagia comahuensis*—an important one because it marked the turning point between dinosaurs and birds. A prized possession is a whole *Megaraptor namunhuaiqui*, the biggest carnivore found in Argentina, or more precisely Patagonia. This place is undoubtedly a treasure trove.

BONES IN PATAGONIA

It's hard to believe that during the age of the dinosaurs, South America was joined to the west coast of Africa in a huge land mass known as the super-continent of Gondwanaland. But fossils of plants that evolved 280 million years ago have been found in South America and South Africa, and beech forests at the foothills of the Andes mountain range are very similar to those found elsewhere in the southern hemisphere; and from this it can be inferred that there was formerly a land connection.

It's no surprise, then, that fossils of dinosaurs found in Patagonia resemble those found in other parts of the world, and this fact is explored in great depth at the new Museo Paleontológico Egidio Feruglio in Trelew, in the province of Chubut. You may wish to pass by the fossil of the world's largest spider; with an abdomen 38cm (15 inches) long and 20cm (8 inches) wide, it inflicts on your mind a terrifying impression of the actual, living, hairy thing—an image that lingers for many hours afterwards. Far more attractive is a cluster of dinosaur eggs found as a nest. There is also the chance to see technicians working on moulds to build replica dinosaurs, and an artist's impression of how Ischigualasto would have looked when it was roamed by dinosaurs.

MORE ACTIVITIES

San Juan is not just good for fossil hunting; it is the place for adventure tourism at its best, from hang gliding in the lower mountains and trout fishing, to off-road motorcycling, canoeing, windsurfing, and whitewater rafting. *Carrovelismo* is windsurfing on dry land using a three-wheeled cart that can reach speeds of up to 100km (62 miles) per hour. There are also horseback excursions across mountains and desert valleys to see guanaco and the sculpted formations of the landscape.

Trelew is usually the first stop for visitors to Península Valdés, a marine reserve on the coast of the Atlantic Ocean offering whalewatching and wildlife trips. Another favourite excursion is to see fossils of sea urchins and scallop shells as big as your hand embedded in the cliffs and caves. Then from Trelew you can travel to Patagonia's other big town, Río Gallegos. It was while I was there, looking at the few fossils at the Museo Provincial Padre Jesús Molina, that I learned by chance about Hill Station, an *estancia* 64km (40 miles) away.

DOWN ON THE FARM

Hill Station is one of the few remaining working sheep farms run by direct descendants of the original owners, in this case Santiago Eduardo Halliday and his wife Silvino. In the early days, the Halliday children scoured the land to collect the Indian arrowheads and tools that are on display in the dusty Halliday Museum, formerly the cookhouse. Now, Eduardo runs horse riding fossil trails to the nearby cliffs on the coast, where you can see a colony of penguins and comb the beaches for finds. I'd be amazed at what the tide leaves behind, he said.

Hill Station was founded by Eduardo's great grandfather, William Halliday, and his wife, Mary McCall, in 1885. This

ARGENTINA

Scottish couple met and married while William was working in the Islas Malvinas (Falklands Islands). In 1883 the Governor of Santa Cruz province offered land in Patagonia for colonization, and as William's contract was coming to an end he decided to accept and so become the first pioneer sheep farmer to set up here.

Also known by its Spanish name of Los Posoz, meaning The Wells, Eduardo's 24,300-ha (60,000-acre) estancia encircles a charming colonial house. It has polished wood floors, a grandfather clock, English books and rugs, and a garden of poplars and plum trees, goose-

berries and rhubarb. Guanaco, skunk, fox, armadillo, rhea, and, if the lagoons have water, flamingos pay a visit.

I visited in spring, right in the middle of sheepshearing. I watched hired men handclip sheep (they get through an average of 1,000 a day) before sampling Eduardo's mother's breakfast of scrambled eggs from her own chickens and coffee made with fresh cow's milk.

BELOW Rocks have been shaped by the erosive action of wind, water, and dust into weird formations, including (INSET) "The Sphinx" RIGHT Red sandstone cliffs and cactus blooms add a touch of colour to the landscape

GOING IT ALONE

INTERNAL TRAVEL

Aerolineas Argentinas, British Airways, and other major airlines, fly regularly to Buenos Aires.

From Buenos Aires and other parts of the country, you can take internal flights to Mendoza, San Juan, Trelew, and Río Gallegos.

Alternatively, there are efficient and comfortable buses, though you have to remember that Argentina is the world's eighth biggest country and travelling distances can be great.

WHEN TO GO

The best time to visit Parque Provincial Ischigualasto is in the spring, just before Christmas, when visitor numbers are low and your group may be the only visitors to the park. After Christmas, the Argentines tend to spend their Sundays in the park so it is much busier.

Early morning and early evening, when temperatures are much cooler and the light is a vibrant rose-orange, are glorious, particularly for photographers. Midday can be uncomfortably hot, especially in summer.

PLANNING YOUR TRIP

It's not feasible to visit all the sights here in one trip unless you are spending a long time in Argentina.

Most international flights arrive in Buenos Aires, so the two museums can be viewed before heading off to other destinations.

Visits to the museums and fossil trips in Chubut can be combined with wildlife- and whale-watching excursions

to Península Valdés on the Atlantic coast.

A visit to Hill Station could be combined with a trip to Parque Nacional Los Glaciares to see the ancient glaciers.You can stop off at Parque Provincial Ischigualasto during a general visit to the north.

HEALTH AND SAFETY MATTERS

Beware of the sun in the far north, which can be very strong. Drink plenty of water as intense heat can also cause dehydration and fatigue.

Mosquites bite after dark in the north, though there is no malaria risk. In the far north , in rural areas below 1,200m (3,937 feet)—particularly in Salta Province and Jujuy Province—there is a medium risk of malaria between October and May.

WHAT TO TAKE

For a day at Parque Provincial Ischigualasto:

❏ Cool clothing.

❏ Bottled water to help prevent dehydration and to help you cope with the heat.

❏ A camera (see page 224).

❏ High-factor suncream.

For the outdoor activities in the south:

❏ Warm clothing and waterproofs.

For activities in the north:

❏ Shorts.

❏ A sun hat and sunglasses.

❏ Plenty of sunscreen.

❏ Maps. (If you're visiting the various fossil sites by hire car then a good road map, available from major towns, is essential)

TRAVELLERS' TIPS

Visitors are not permitted to collect, or even to pick up, any type of fossil. Official expeditions are generally sponsored by universities and led by one of the professors, whose students form part of the team. It would appear that they do not take volunteers.

Fishing, Cycling, and Horse Riding in Patagonia

By Lee Karen Stow

From the sprawling sheep estancias *around the south, to the volcanoes and sparkling lakes of the north, Patagonia is a treasure trove for the spirited traveller. To cover its vastness you need a lot of time; I could only briefly sample its highlights, sometimes fishing for trout, sometimes feeding the condors, but always on an adventure.*

The region of Patagonia begins south of Buenos Aires, crosses the Río Colorado and Río Negro, and ends at Tierra del Fuego, an area that faces Antarctica and is known to tourists as "the end of the world."

Before the arrival of the Spanish conquerers, the land was occupied by tribes of indigenous Indians. The Portuguese explorer Ferdinand Magellan—the first European to reach Patagonia—described Indians as tall, with large feet, and dressed in guanaco

3 To climb Volcán Lanín you need a degree of climbing experience. Reasonable fitness is a definite requirement for trekking to the base of Monte Tronador. Cycling can be hard or easy, depending on the routes you take, while horse riding and fishing can be enjoyed by anyone.

★ For some of the activities you are based in hotels, ranging from the cosy to the luxurious, and are transported around by the operator. For trekking the mountains, you may decide to stay overnight at a *refugio*; here standards will be adequate, and there are hot meals and drinks, but you do need to bring a sleeping bag. On the cycling tours, the operator drives the bicycles to starting points and over any difficult terrain.

For the fishing, you can buy tackle in the towns, but since this is expensive I would recommend that you bring your own. A camera, with UV and polarizing filters to diffuse glare, is essential if you want to capture the frequently sighted condors and other wildlife. Binoculars are useful.

skins. Much later, during his travels on HMS *Beagle* in 1833, the naturalist Charles Darwin came upon Patagonia and became fascinated by the wildlife and geology of what he saw as boundless, monotonous plains.

Darwin's assessment of the area was understandable, for Patagonia is a colossal area that occupies almost a quarter of Argentina. The scarcely populated plain—sometimes hauntingly quiet, sometimes made noisy by the weather—harbours a diverse range of flora and fauna, including animals in danger of extinction. It is strewn with thorny scrub bushes that grow only to shin height, low enough to avoid the westerly winds so characteristic of this semi-desert. The plain's combined vastness and openness can make you feel that you must be the only one walking there, perhaps even that you are in the midst of something older than time itself.

To the west, Patagonia spans the border between Chile and Argentina. Here, the enormous peaks of the the Andean Cordillera—the longest continuous mountain chain in the world—are waiting to be explored. In Patagonia's southern part is the tremendously popular Parque Nacional Torres del Paine, in Chile (see pages 204–213), and Argentina's Parque Nacional Los Glaciares, whose famous Glaciar Perito Moreno is its centrepiece (see pages 248–256). Here, I cast my attention northwards in search of a catch.

A SPOT OF FISHING

Patagonia's lakes and rivers are a paradise for the keen fisherman, especially the ones in the province of Neuquén, says Jorge Bisso, a Falklands War veteran turned top fishing guide who knows the waters around here like the back of his hand. He lives in Junín de Los Andes, which is regarded by enthusiasts as the fishing capital of the area. When I met him, he was dressed in waterproof khaki pantaloons, and an angler's mesh waistcoat with a selection of flies protruding from his top pocket. It was a hot, sunny morning in spring, and he was to take me fishing in the **Río Chimehuín**, the famed outlet of Lago Huechulafquen.

Neuquén's waters provide the ideal conditions for many different kinds of fish to thrive. Food and shelter is plentiful, and there are areas fit for the spawning of rainbow trout, brown trout, brook trout, landlocked salmon, and perch. The area is good for spinning, trolling, and fly casting. The latter is both the most usual way to fish for trout, and the method considered to be the best.

On the day before my trip to Lago Huechulafquen, I had practised my fly-casting technique by the edge of Lago Paimún, as cattle and horses came down to drink. The trick is to let out a good length of line by whipping the fly at the surface of the water, and then to fling the rod back over your head so that the line makes an "S" shape in the air and a whooshing sound. This allows the reel to release increasing amounts of line, which, when it is cast out again, should reach into the depths where the fat fish lurk.

As fly casting is an expensive form of fishing, I also learnt spinning. You attach a heavier weight to the fly and cast it into the depths. You then instantly spin the reel to bring in the line, and—if all goes well—a fish will follow. On this occasion, however, the fish weren't biting, and I couldn't even claim that one had got away. Which is why I enlisted Jorge's help.

The lakes and mountains of Patagonia, southern Argentina

IN THE SHADOW OF A VOLCANO

Jorge says the best fishing spots are the private areas, and that these are divided into two types: those that do sell fishing rights, and those that don't. Of course, the ones that don't are the better of the two; and if you want to fish on them the only real solution is to become friendly with one of the owners. If that's impossible, Jorge will bring you to this lonely, grassy bank where wild lilac and pink lupins sprout at the edge of the snaking Río Chimehuín. Behind us, in the distance, I could see Volcán Lanín, an extinct plug rising 3,776m (12,389 feet) from the forest and topped with a cap of ice that looked like syrup on an ice cream. It is the dominant feature in **Parque Nacional Lanín**, which is a 170-km (106-mile) strip of lakeland stretching south through the Andes. It is Patagonia's most northerly park, and at its southern

233

ARGENTINA

araucana), also called the Chilean pine. This distinctive, parasol-shaped tree sheds high-protein nuts called *ñulli*, which were once the staple diet of the Mapuche Indians. Today, no one but the Mapuches are allowed to gather them. The park is also home to the northern pudú (*Pudu mephistophiles*)—which at 40cm (16 inches) high is the smallest of the world's deer species—and the Andean deer. Both species are rare, and the pudú is in danger of extinction.

Jorge chose a fishing spot by assessing the water's current, and identifying the calmer spots where the fish rest after an energetic swim. He then observed the colour and kind of fly the fish are feeding on, and matched his artificial flies to these. By today's standards, a 2kg (2¼lb) trout is a big catch in these parts; the record catch 30 years ago weighed in at 11.6kg (25¼lb). We fished and fished. I was struck by the intensity of Jorge's gaze and amazed at his skill in briskly casting

end it borders Parque Nacional Nahuel Huapi, which I was to visit later.

Lanín is visibly different from its southern counterparts. It is primarily southern-beech forest, some of the trees stripped by parasitic mossy plants; but there are also copses of the native monkey puzzle tree (*Araucaria*

the line. But again the fish won, for two got away; one felt like 2.5 kilos—honest.

CYCLING THE LAKES

Many people base themselves either in San Martín de Los Andes—founded in 1883 and the oldest town in the province of Neuquén—or in Junín de Los Andes. San Martín, a pretty town, with cherry-tree lined avenues of pastry shops and alpine houses with lace curtains, sits snugly on the edge of Lago Lácar, and branching from its centre are superbly smooth tracks, perfect for cycling.

Siete Lagos (The Seven Lakes) is a fabulous 187-km (116-mile), easygoing cycle route. It takes you via minimum-traffic roads and back-routes through forests and past lake after glassy lake (more than seven in fact). It is a two-day tour, so you will rest for the night at a Mapuche-run hostel, or wherever Jorge Barcelo of Sendero Sur Patagonia (a local operator who specializes in cycling and walking tours) recommends. One of his favourite overnight resting spots is Villa La Angostura, a villa whose narrow roads, flanked by brilliant-yellow blossom, lead to the banks of the massive Lago Nahuel Huapi.

The route ends in the neighbouring province of Río Negro at San Carlos de Bariloche, a sprawling, commercial tourist resort full of woolly sweaters,

LEFT Jorge demonstrates his skills in the Río Chimehuín
BELOW Spectacular scenery in the Nahuel Huapi national park
RIGHT Cycling through the Cordoba Pass

ARGENTINA

CLIMBING VOLCÁN LANÍN

It takes a fit person two or three days to climb this extinct volcano of 3,776m (12,389 feet), crowned by a 70-m (229-foot) ice cap. The first day's trek of around five hours brings you to an overnight stop at the free *refugio*, which has space for 25 (bookable at the base). The second day's climbing takes seven hours. There is the option of staying for the second night at the *refugio* or continuing the descent. The best time to climb is from November to February, though December and January are busy. Everyone's equipment, including crampons and an ice axe, must be checked with officials at the bottom before climbing. It is advisable to book a guide, which can cost around $250 for two to three days.

cheap cowboy hats, chocolates, and St Bernard dogs attached to a photographer who will take a souvenir picture of you.

STRANGE ROCKS AND PUMAS

For me the best bit of the excursion was cycling back to San Martín de Los Andes through the Cordoba Pass, a slither of a road snaking through weird, weathered rock formations and red mountains that are home to the Patagonian puma (*Felis concolor patagonica*), hare (*lepus capensis*), hawks, and the Andean condor (*Vultur gryphus*). In certain lights the rocks, punctured by caves and perforated by holes, assume the appearance of faces, noses, and beasts.

From here I rode a breathless 32km (20-mile) descent to the shore of Lago Meliquina. I got off my bike and delighted in a bottle of Saint Felipe red wine that Jorge had brought with him and then chilled in the Argentine way, using a length of string to dangle the bottle in the cool water.

As we drank, Jorge had another idea: we would go on an adventure in **Parque**

Nacional Nahuel Huapi to the base of Monte Tronador (The Thunder Mountain) at 3,554m (11,659 feet). But first, he would take me to tea.

TEA WITH THE INDIANS

Dorila is an old Mapuche Indian who lives alone in a wooden cottage on a rise overlooking a lake in Quila Quina, one of two Mapuche reserves in the park. Her horse grazes outside her back door among the flowers. She makes jam from the strawberries in her garden, and rugs and scarves from the wool spun from her flock of 80 sheep, which congregate for the night in a wooden pen, after being brought down from the mountain by a hired boy.

Dorila used to do the spinning herself, but now she's too old and pays someone else to do it for her. She also pays someone to shear the sheep. She is one of 15 children, but now has only one sister remaining. She never married or had children, which she believes must have been what God wanted. Her once-shiny black hair is short and streaked with silver, and her skin is softly olive and oily. Her cottage is a cosy forester's hut, with a

MATÉ TEA

An Argentine tradition followed in many households and gathering places is the drinking of *maté*. It is an elaborate ritual. The tea is made from the dried and chopped leaf of a holly-type plant called yerba maté (*Ilex paraguayensis*). The leaves are spooned into a special drinking vessel—made from wood, clay or even polished silver—and topped with boiling water. When the tea has brewed, the vessel is passed around to every drinker, who sips the tea through a thin pipe called a *bombilla*, which filters the leaves. Maté is an acquired taste, though its bitterness can be reduced with lots of sugar.

log-fired stove and a gas cooker. She doesn't speak any Mapuche, and believes it sounds sad, but knows of people in the reserve that still use the language.

It is believed that the Mapuche (meaning people of the land) existed as early as 500 B.C. They originated in southern Chile, and then migrated eastwards further into Patagonia, following the gaunaco for meat and wool, and finding herbal remedies among the plants. They resisted integration with the Inca people, and fought a bloody war against the invading Spaniards in the 15th and 16th centuries. The Mapuches are skilled at pottery and woodcarving, and at making silver jewellery and woollen items, which today are sold as souvenirs.

Dorila's strawberry jam, spread over freshly baked bread served with tea in a china cup and saucer, was delicious. After saying goodbye, we climbed to the top of a nearby hill called Filo, which means snakes, though there are no snakes in Patagonia. Jorge said that hawks often circle overhead, and sometimes dare to drop closer, but on this occasion there were no encounters. If only I had known of the surprise to follow.

BIRDS OF NAHUEL HUAPI

As I lay on my back, playing dead, six condors—vulture kings of the Andes—swooped low enough to show me their 3-m (10-foot) wingspans before rising as silent as glider planes on currents of air. Condors are not hunting birds. They prefer to feed on dead quarry, and usually of the furry kind, so what they made of me—lying prostrate, zoom lens pointing skywards to snap their underbellies and bald, black heads—I don't know. Soon, the curious scavengers retreated, and Jorge and I picked up our scraps and walked towards **Mount Tronador**.

An extinct volcano standing 3,554m (11,660 feet), Mount Tronador is the gem that makes Parque Nacional Nahuel Huapi Argentina's most popular park. The park is also the country's oldest: the land was donated to the country by Argentine

explorer Francisco Pascasio "Perito" Moreno in 1903, and it was given national-park status in 1934. It stretches for 155km (96 miles) along the Chilean border, and is about 75km (47 miles) at its widest point. The park incorporates both the scrub-dotted desert that is so characteristic of Patagonia, and forests rising up from numerous lakes such as the 45-m (148-foot) deep Lago Nahuel Huapi, the park's largest.

WATCHING THE THUNDER

We planned to ride horseback to the volcano, so that evening we stopped at Hostería Pampa Linda, which has a full view of snow-crowned Tronador. Next morning we hired horses from the neighbouring ranch. I took a chestnut, half-Creole mare called Christina. Accompanied by our guide, a Chilean called Carlos, we forded a rushing river and climbed steep banks of forest, crossing over the walker's normal route and taking short cuts up the mountain.

Our horses sweated profusely, and paused for breath on every corner. Bamboo-like green stalks scraped our shins, and we ducked frequently to avoid overhead branches. Soon the overhead canopy had disappeared, and we found ourselves under a blue sky and in full view of Glacier Castaño Overo, a castle of ice that spreads across the valley top and melts into a spectacular 400-m (1,312-foot) cascade that is often decorated with a rainbow. Ice and water crash to the valley floor in a succession of loud clapping sounds. No wonder Tronador was named thunder.

Having tethered our horses after the tiring three-hour ride (it takes four hours if walking), and fed scraps to the condors, we picked our way over bronze-coloured rocks to the edge of the mountain, and then over crunchy ice fields, dazzling in the sunlight, towards Tronador.

In the distance I could see the flag pole that marks a *refugio* called Otto Meiling, a sheltered base camp for climbers and walkers, named after a

German climber who was the second to summit Tronador. Inside the camp, clothes were drying over a stove burning with wood splinters, and the kettle was on the boil. We sat down to maté tea just as three breathless Argentine climbers plunged through the door, their lips painted white with sunscreen. They had failed in their attempt to summit Tronador, having turned back because of the wind. There wasn't so much as a breeze here, which made me realize just how far away from the mountain I was. The climbers resolved to try again at 2am that morning. It would take them at least seven hours to reach the summit.

We wished them luck, walked back to a refreshed trio of horses, and headed back to Hostería Pampa Linda. But then Jorge had another idea: why not take a short detour to the bottom of Glacier Castaño Overo to see its melting turrets from a different angle? We would have to plough through plants and annoying horseflies, and pick our way over fallen logs, but it would be worth it. And then, he said, the following morning we could visit the Ventisquera Negro, a glacier as brown as chocolate and like nothing you've ever seen before. I nodded my head. All I could do was go with the flow.

GOING IT ALONE

INTERNAL TRAVEL

Aerolineas Argentinas flies from Buenos Aires and other parts of Argentina to Bariloche. A bus, which runs from the main bus station at San Carlos de Bariloche to San Martín de Los Andes and costs $17 one way, takes about 4 hours to travel the wonderfully scenic route. Some operators, particularly those that offer cycling tours, offer a point-to-point luggage service. Alternatively you could hire a car from one of the main towns.

WHEN TO GO

Spring to summer (November to mid-February) is ideal for visiting southern Patagonia: the climate is warmer than in winter, although the winds are still persistent. In the north, temperatures are warmer than they are in the south, although the summer months in the national parks are often the busiest times as many Argentines spend

their holidays here. Spring might be the best option. The time to ski is during the winter months. Bariloche is a good base from which to ski the three-peaked Cerro Catedral (open from June to September), which is about 20km (12 miles) away and has 30 ski-lifts and 52km (32 miles) of slopes. At Cerra Chapelco, which has 29 slopes of 27km (17 miles) and uses San Martín de Los Andes, there is skiing from June to September .

PLANNING YOUR TRIP

Patagonia is so huge that a lot of planning is necessary if you are to make the most of your visit. The best way is to decide where on the map you wish to go and then seek advice from the operators. Finding a local guide is straightforward; and, as long as you have an airpass and enough clothing to see you from cold and wet to hot and dry, it is feasible to visit all the national parks mentioned in this guide in one trip. But if you want a shorter, more concentrated tour, I would recommend visiting both Nahuel Huapi and Lanmn parks, using Bariloche and San Martín de Los Andes as bases. This wil allow you to combine

mountain walking, or even climbing, with leisurely treks, horse riding, and fishing further down on the Patagonian steppe.

HEALTH AND SAFETY MATTERS

When walking or riding through Parque Nacional Nahuel Huapi, watch out for dangerously sharp bamboo stalks, especially where the stalks have been cut to make way for a path. Horseflies can be a nuisance here, so use insect repellent; when the swarms are bad, move upwards above the treeline.

It is safe to drink tap water in the villages, but not in Buenos Aires. Use purifying tablets for river water.

WHAT TO TAKE

Although northern Patagonia is often beautifully warm and sunny, you should be prepared for every eventuality. Take:

- ❏ Shorts, sunhat, and sunscreen.
- ❏ Water- and wind-proofs, warm clothing (moving south, it gets colder).
- ❏ Full camping equipment and cooking fuel, if you plan to camp; just a sleeping bag for the *refugios*.
- ❏ Camera, plenty of film.
- ❏ Binoculars.
- ❏ Detailed maps.

LEFT We climbed Mount Tronador, an extinct volcano, on horseback, with condors (RIGHT) wheeling overhead and a close-up view of the glacier Castaño Overo (TOP LEFT) as it melts into a cascade of ice and water

THE ANDEAN CONDOR

The Andean Condor (*Vultur gryphus*), the "King of the Andes," and the largest American bird, stands 95cm (37½ inches) tall and has a wingspan of 2–3m (6½–10 feet). This vulture, with its black body, bald head, and white collar, lives in the mountains, where it soars silently at high altitude with little effort, and makes its nest on inaccessible high rocks, rather than in trees. It feeds mostly on carrion, though it is known occasionally to hunt small rodents and young, abandoned offspring.

Watching the Wildlife

By Lee Karen Stow

On Patagonia's coast, where the desert meets the Atlantic Ocean, there is one of the world's most important marine wildlife reserves. Here, whales, seals, sea lions, penguins, and seabirds breed and feed in their natural habitat. I took a tour to view the cliffs and then sail out in a catamaran to witness an astonishing aquatic display.

For 2,800 miles, Patagonia's jagged coastline winds in and out of the Atlantic Ocean where the warm Brazilian current from the north meets the cooler current from the Islas Malvinas (Falkland Islands) in the south. Its steep cliffs, sandy like the colour of the pyramids, end abruptly as though sliced from the arid scrubland to tower over rocky ledges, creating the perfect shelter for crowding colonies of marine life.

 It's easy to take part in a wildlife-watching excursion. Coaches collect you from your hotel in Puerto Madryn, the tourist base, and take you within sighting distance of the wildlife. Apart from descending a few flights of steps to the beaches, there's not much walking. For the whalewatching, you board a boat that has an indoor viewing area in case of rain, plus seating, hot drinks and snacks.

★ The degree of comfort you experience on this trip will depend primarily on the weather. It can be windy on the clifftops, and occasional rain may hamper the whalewatching, but with warm and waterproof clothing—including gloves and hats for the boat trips—you should stay dry and comfortable.

 Brightly coloured waterproofs for wearing while on deck of the catamaran are normally provided by the boat operators. Binoculars are essential for spotting distant objects. Take a camera with plenty of film (200ASA speed is best as it's hard to keep the camera stable while sailing) and a long lens for close-up shots of penguins, seals, sea lions, and elephant seals. Salt water and rain can both be hazardous to your camera, so cover everything but the lens end with a plastic, see-through shower cap, like the ones given free in hotel rooms. In spring and summer, sunlight can be strong so remember the sunscreen.

Some say Reserva Provincial Península Valdés, in the province of Chubut, hangs out from this mainland like an axe head, but I like to think it better resembles the barking head of an elephant seal, just one member of this vast, complex food chain that begins with tiny plankton and ends with whales as long as 15m (49 feet). At the turn of the 19th century, the mammals that visited this coastline were still being economically exploited for fat, oil, and fur, a practice that brought many of them close to extinction. Today, wildlife on the entire shoreline is protected, and several reserves have been created, including Punta Norte, Caleta Valdés, Punta Delgada, Puerto Pirámide, Punta Loma, Isla de los Pájaros (Bird Island), and Golfo San José Marine Park.

A SEAL AMONG SEALS

I stood on the windswept cliffs of Caleta Valdés as the surf crashed into foam below me, and gazed aghast at the sheer bulk of the southern elephant seal (*Mirounga leonina*), the largest seal species in the world. The seal's name is derived from the shape of its snout, which looks like an elephant's wrinkled trunk. I watched in awe as one particular bull elephant seal heaved his fat, roly-poly body over the wet pebbles towards a smaller male, and chased him across the shore, growling like an angry dog.

During the breeding season, the bulls become aggressive towards each other, fighting to establish ownership of up to 30 females. The female elephant seal is

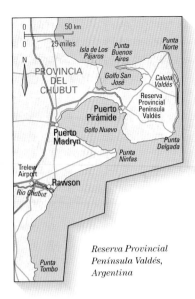

Reserva Provincial Península Valdés, Argentina

Ave. Julio A. Roca and Blvd. Brown are lined with agencies offering all manner of wildlife excursions, and the port is the main haunt for travellers who arrive by air at Trelew airport. It's a bustling place. There are hotels, cafés, and restaurants, and side streets lined with souvenir shops. Look out for knitwear, ceramics, and silver jewellery crafted by the Mapuche Indians, the indigenous people, who inhabited the area long before the area's first European settlers, the Welsh.

On July 28, 1865, 153 Welsh immigrants landed near Puerto Madryn. Disillusioned with England, where they were prohibited from using their own language, the people were granted a patch of Patagonia where no outsiders had settled before. They planned to farm, and to build a happy colony, but they were unskilled at farming and unused to the hardship of the semi-desert. Many had died on the crossing from England, many could not find fresh water on arrival, and all found life tough.

smaller, and her pups brownish black. She nurses her offspring for about a month, during which time she fasts; when her pup is weaned she is free to return to the sea to feed. In April, the killer whale (*Orcinus orca*) rushes to the shallows in a frenzy to snatch a pup in its jaws; then it literally chomps it to death, flesh and blubber flying in its wake. I watched this gruesome sight on the hotel's video, and while I could appreciate it as a fascinating demonstration of the principle that the fittest must survive, I would not have liked to see the real thing.

The bull noticed that I was studying him, and glared at me through my camera lens. Using the zoom, I was able to see the fine down of his fur, drying quickly, and his nostrils flaring. No fear though, for he would have to clamber up a couple of sand-dunes to reach me, and I was forbidden to venture into his territory.

TEA IN THE WELSH VALLEY

Viewing the elephant seals is the first thrilling encounter during a full day's excursion to **Península Valdés**, which I booked through an operator a few doors down from my seafront hotel in the port and seaside resort of Puerto Madryn. Puerto Madryn's main thoroughfares of

OTHER THINGS TO DO

- ❑ Mountain-biking excursions, with or without guides, and trekking along the coast.
- ❑ Sunbathing on the beaches of Playa El Doradillo, which is lined with whale-watching telescopes facing a white-flecked, turquoise ocean.
- ❑ Fishing boats sail 20–40 minutes' distance from the shore, and spend about an hour fishing. Information, prices and times are available from the tourist information.
- ❑ Scuba diving: there are two dive sites, both underwater parks. One is artificial, with sunken cars and ships; the other is a natural reef that offers good opportunities for sighting fish, colourful marine plants, and seals.

Rawson, the Argentine minister who administered the land, gave the settlers seeds to scatter. They waited and waited for the rains, but Patagonia receives an average annual rainfall of only 175mm (6¾ inches), and what water there is quickly evaporates with the westerly winds, so their crop failed. Later, under the guidance of the Mapuche Indians, the Welsh learned how to harness the water from the Río Chubut, which flows from the Andes to the Atlantic Ocean, to create a suitable irrigation system.

The first produce was wheat, and a number of flour mills are still dotted around; next wool, a vast amount of which is today sent to Italy. The Mapuches also taught the Welsh how to cultivate the land and hunt the guanaco (*Lama guanicoe*), a member of the llama family, for meat and fur. In return, the Welsh baked cakes for the Indians.

Soon, towns were established. Gaiman was one of the first, its site chosen because of its proximity to the Río Chubut. The town of Rawson became the provincial capital, and a Welsh valley with stone houses and lace curtains sprang up. The Welsh were Protestant, but since they were of various denominations a number of different chapels were built. Most still host the Gwyl y Glaniad (the

day of the landing), a remembrance ceremony featuring tea in the vestry and hymn singing.

Another traditional event is the Eisteddfod, a Welsh literary and musical festival, when bards, poets, and singers come together to compete. It was first held here in 1875, and now occurs every spring. The festival's name is believed to derive from the Welsh verb *eistedd* (to sit down), and *fod* (to be), probably because the public watch the event sitting down, and the prize for the best poem is a carved, wooden armchair.

Many excursions combine watching

LEFT A colony of sea lions
BELOW Two southern right whales perform for tourists on a whalewatching excursion. The whales come to breed in the peninsula's shallow waters every winter
RIGHT A southern elephant seal and her pup

wildlife with a trip inland to the Welsh valley. This will include a stop for tea, customarily taken in the late afternoon, at one of the teahouses all over town. The whole thing costs around $12 per person, and you can eat as much as you wish from a huge selection of sandwiches, cakes, and scones —all served with a large pot of freshly brewed tea by waitresses in crisp, white, frilly aprons. The Casa de Té in Gaiman, a 100-year-old house with pink tablecloths, teacups and saucers, ticking pendulum clocks, and china display cabinets, is run by descendants of the original owners. The entrance is dedicated to Diana, the late Princess of Wales, who took tea here on November 25, 1995. The cup, saucer, and chair that she used are poignantly reserved.

Delving into the history of the first settlers, whose Welsh language is currently being revived, is an interesting diversion from the main highlights of Península Valdés; but however delicious the buttered scones, they will not keep you away from the creatures of the sea for long.

ON TO THE PENÍNSULA

It is possible to rent a car to the Península, but since, in keeping with the environment, the roads are gravel tracks that seem to go on for ever, I decided to join 15 others in a comfortable bus that collected me from my hotel at 8:30am sharp. In the summer season, groups can be as large as 40, which means extra buses and more tourists clambering to see the wildlife.

The 60-km (37-mile) drive to the Península took us along pin-straight

ARGENTINA

roads, past Puerto Madryn's fish-processing factories and over land privately owned by several sheep ranchers who divide their acres with wire fencing, and past lakes dotted with pink flamingos, ducks, and geese. Sometimes you think you're looking at a lake but it's actually a salt flat, one of the lowest continental depressions in the world at 42m (138 feet) below sea-level.

We stopped at the Centro de Interpretación (interpretation centre), a museum whose exhibits include Welsh farming implements, whale skeletons, and stuffed rheas. You can see the rhea's live counterpart through telescopes perched on top of the observation tower. This bird resembles the ostrich, and the telescopes are powerful enough to enable you to admire its layers of brown-mottled

WILDLIFE TO SEE

Sea mammals:
- ❏ Southern right whale (Eubalaena glacialis)
- ❏ Killer whale (Orcinus orca)
- ❏ Southern elephant seal (Mirounga leonina)
- ❏ Southern sea lion (Otaria byronia)
- ❏ Fitz Roy, or Peale's, dolphin (Lagenorhynchus australis)

Seabirds:
- ❏ Black oystercatcher (Haematopus ater)
- ❏ Blue-eyed cormorant (Phalacrocorax atriceps)
- ❏ Dolphin gull (Leocophaeus scoresbii)
- ❏ Great egret (Egreta alba)
- ❏ Kelp gull (Larus dominicanus)
- ❏ King cormorant (Phalacrocorax albiventer)
- ❏ Magellanic penguin (Spheniscus magellanicus)
- ❏ Plovers (Charadriidae family)
- ❏ Rock cormorant (Phalacrocorax magallanicus)
- ❏ Southern lapwing (Vanellus chilensis)

feathers. The guide told us that since the weather was cold on this particular day it was unlikely that any land wildlife, apart from the odd hare bounding over the scrub, would put in an appearance. However, I could make out the Isla de los Pájaros (Bird Island), and two gulfs on either side of the Península—the Golfo San José and the Golfo Nuevo—though they were too far away for me to see any of the whales that frequent them.

We all boarded the bus again and trundled off to Puerto Pirámide, a shoreside village built among sand-dunes. We climbed steps smelling of seaweed to a wooden platform, which was then pushed out into the shallows to meet the boarding gate of a catamaran.

THERE SHE BLOWS

In the bar of the observation deck, coffee was poured, and we headed out to sea as our guide briefed us on the wildlife that we were about to see. For thousands of winters, southern right whales (*Eubalaena australis*) have swum from their feeding grounds in the high seas to mate, give birth, and nurse their offspring in the calm, shallow waters around the Península. This noble creature, its grey-black body speckled with white spots on its abdomen, stretches between 12 and 15m (40 and 50 feet) and weighs 30–35 tons. Its tail is up to 5m (16 feet) wide; and its head, which takes up a quarter of the massive body, is covered with wart-like crustaceans that differ in shape from one whale to the next and so help identify each individual.

The southern right whale was once the favoured quarry of hunters because when it is dead it floats on the water. The whales were killed for their oil, and also for their baleen (the horny plates that they use instead of teeth to filter food). The latter ended up as clock springs and umbrella ribs. Although the whales are now protected, recuperation of the species is slow, and the whales currently number around 4,500. Females usually give birth once every three years and, during the mating season, copulate with several males a day. The gestation period lasts 12 months and results in a calf over 5m (16 feet) long.

At this point in the talk a southern right whale was sighted, and our boat sped to the site and hovered. But we found only ripples rupturing the surface. Where was the whale? We waited anxiously. Then a female and her calf rose as if in slow motion, blowing spray through holes in their heads to make a sound like that of steam puffing from an engine. The southern right whale does not have a dorsal fin; instead it has side fins, which it lifts to roll itself over. Sometimes, it raises its tail from the water as if posing for that classic picture seen on many wildlife posters. But on my whalewatching trip it was not to be.

Then I caught a fleeting glimpse of something bigger than our boat—a shiny, dark hulk—and I waited, with zoom lens poised. Suddenly it began to rain, then it poured down, churning the sea like cement and obviously dissuading the whale and her young from rising into the air. No leaps today. This was a pity because it was impossible to appreciate the full size of her as she lay submerged like a sandbank. Then she disappeared completely. All was silent, and I was disappointed. But then she was back, moving gracefully through the waves, rain splashing off her back. This may not have been the whalewatching I had dreamed about, but the lady's occasional visits to the surface were the next best thing.

FISH FOR SUPPER

Cold and wet, we disembarked at Puerto Pirámide and filed into the warmth of the Paradise Pub, a brick- and wood-built restaurant where the chef was cooking white salmon and mashed potato, and a large-screen television was showing a guanaco mother giving birth standing up. On the pub's beams and rafters were posters of the local marine wildlife and, yes, superb pictures of a whale's tail disappearing into the blue.

The next day, our proposed trip to Punta Tombo, 120km (74 miles) south of Trelew, to see the Magellanic penguins was cancelled because the previous night's rains had made driving conditions on the gravel roads leading to the site dangerous. Instead, I took a taxi to **Punta Loma** (17km/11 miles away) to see scores of southern sea lions (*Otaria byronia*) wriggling like giant garden slugs as they scrambled for a scrap of bare rock, and barked viciously. This trip turned out to be a good idea: the taxi fare was reasonable ($20), and I had the clifftop platform—and an unobstructed view of the sea lions—to myself.

The southern sea lion was hunted until the 1960s, but now it is protected and its population is increasing as its breeding ground and nurseries on the gravel beaches become more established. The species grows to double the size of its northern hemisphere counterpart, but it is the male especially that catches the eye. He is bigger and heavier than the female; but most notable is his full lion's mane, swept back from his face as though it has been blow-dried by a hairdresser. His antics are entertaining as he prowls on his front fins like a jungle predator, barking, biting, and chasing away any challenging male. This particular male emigrated to this breeding site (called a rookery) in December, gathering up to 15 females in a harem. He will mate with the females who, after fertilization, are free to leave the harem to feed at sea before giving birth to a pup a year later.

HANDICRAFTS

Shops in the streets of Puerto Madryn are stocked with souvenir soft-toy whales, dolphins, seals, and penguins, as well as "save-the-whale" T-shirts and carvings of the marine life in wood and stone. Woollen goods include handknitted jumpers and thick woven scarves, plus Mapuche handicrafts and ornate silver jewellery.

TIME FOR PENGUINS

By the next day, the sun and winds had baked the roads dry and the penguin trip was back on. At 7:30am I boarded a bus whose route took us past more guanaco, and the Punta Loma reserve, before the glorious panorama of the silvery ocean off **Punta Tombo** filled the windscreen.

Even as our coach rolled into the car park, I could see penguins coming from every angle. This is the largest penguin colony outside Antarctica, and these flightless, black and white birds were waddling everywhere, bellyflopping from the rocks, and ducking and diving beneath the waves. Some take a bath on the swell, others reach the shore successfully only to be toppled sideways by an incoming wave that pushes them along on their bellies. Just as they scramble to their webbed feet, another wave washes over them, and knocks them flying. It's a comical performance.

The Magellanic penguin (*Spheniscus magellanicus*) is a small to medium-sized species that stands about 50cm (20 inches) tall, although it can reach 71cm (28 inches). It has a black face, encircled by a white, bonnet-like band, and a white chest broken by a black horseshoe. It swims to Punta Tombo at the end of August, and stays until April,

ABOVE and BELOW Punta Tombo is home to the largest colony of Magellanic penguins outside Antartica

taking advantage of the pebbly beaches and wide sand-dunes for nesting and breeding. First, the male arrives either to build a nest (if it is his first breeding season) or to repair the one used the previous year; then, at the beginning of September, the females arrive. The pairs join for life, mating and laying the first of two eggs towards the end of that month. I arrived in November, when the 40-day egg-incubation period was in full swing, to find penguins snuggled over eggs in rabbit-like burrows holed out of the sand.

If only I could have stayed a few weeks more, until the chicks were born. Then the parents regurgitate fish soup from their stomachs into the crying mouths of their brown, fluffy-haired young, and chase away preying skuas or gulls. December, especially, is a riotous time, when young and old crowd on the beach, tottering to and fro from the sea. The circus goes on until March, when all the chicks leave the nest and the whole colony migrates north, to the waters of Southern Brazil, to return here again the next year.

GOING IT ALONE

INTERNAL TRAVEL

Flights to Trelew, 65km (40 miles) south of Puerto Madryn, leave from Buenos Aires and other major Argentine destinations. There is an airport at Puerto Madryn but it is normally used for private flights. The shuttle from Trelew airport to Puerto Madryn takes 40 minutes, and the price is $10. Hourly buses to and from the airport start at 6:15am (6am from Puerto Madryn), cost $3.70, and take about an hour, but you must tell the driver you wish to be dropped off at the airport. By taxi the journey costs around $8.

You can take a bus from Buenos Aires to Puerto Madryn's Terminal de Omnibus, but the journey covers 1,382 km (859 miles) and takes about 18 hours. There are regular bus services between Puerto Madryn and Trelew.

PLANNING YOUR TRIP

Book organized excursions in Puerto Madryn. For the Península Valdés, typical excursion prices are $25 to $50, plus $5 entrance to the reserve), including whalewatching. Boats vary from small open-top speed-boats to stylish catamarans with an indoor viewing area and snack bars. Trips to the penguin reserve at Punto

Tombo cost $30, plus $5 entrance to the reserve, and include a visit to Trelew and Gaiman. Scuba-diving trips, which are for certified divers only, cost $40 for a 2-hour boat excursion, equipment provided. Diving trips are usually made in the morning to avoid the wind. Book a day in advance.

Hiring a car so that you can drive yourself to the wildlife sites is economical if there are four or five of you in the group, or if you want to stay longer at the sites, avoid the crowds, or photograph the wildlife against a sunrise or sunset. Roads in the Península are no more than gravel tracks, and heavy rain can make them impassable, so when hiring a car, check the spare tyre. Before you set off anywhere, fill up with plenty of petrol and check that the roads on your planned route are open.

Taxis to the sites can be booked from the many excursion offices along Ave. Roca and Blvd. Brown. My round trip to Playa El Doradillo and Punta Loma cost $40.

If money is an issue, there is a local bus to Puerto Pirámide, where you can board a boat trip to see the whales. The bus runs three times a week, leaving the main terminal at Puerto Madryn at 8:55am and

returning at 6pm. A return ticket is 13 Argentine pesos, and you pay just 1 peso for entrance to Península Valdés instead of the 5 asked for during an organized excursion. Whalewatching tours from Puerto Pirámide are all $20 (not negotiable).

Distances from Puerto Madryn to the main tourist sites are: Punta Loma, 17km (11 miles); Punta Tombo, 181km (112 miles); Isla de los Pájaros, 79 km (49 miles); Puerto Pirámide, 104km (65 miles); Punta Norte, 171km (100 miles); Caleta Valdés, 179 km (111 miles).

TRAVELLERS' TIPS

There is a law banning anyone from approaching and/or chasing sea mammals (at any time of year) on the coasts of Chubut. It is also illegal to sail, swim, or scuba dive, with them.

HEALTH AND SAFETY MATTERS

Those who wish to do watersports are asked to let the authorities know. Also, on all tours, it is imperative to listen to the ranger's recommendations and not stray from the designated wildlife-watching platforms.

WHAT TO TAKE

❑ Waterproofs and warm clothing (including hat and gloves) for boat trips and whalewatching tours.

❑ Sunscreen.

❑ Binoculars.

❑ Camera with zoom lens and plenty of film.

❑ A map.

❑ Snacks are served on board the boats, but you may like to take your own (buy supplies in Puerto Pirámide and all the main towns).

WHEN TO GO

TO SEE:

❑ **Birds**—all year.
❑ **Whales**—June to December.
❑ **Sea lions**—all year (pups November to December).
❑ **Elephant seals**—all year (pups in April).
❑ **Penguins**—September to March (chicks from November).

Adventures on Ice

By Lee Karen Stow

Parque Nacional Los Glaciares is a World Heritage Site in the foothills of the Andes in southwest Argentina. I journeyed through forests, passed colonies of flamingos, and wondered at floating icebergs, before reaching Glaciar Perito Moreno—one of the natural wonders of the world—and heading on to the climbing territory of the north.

Parque Nacional Los Glaciares, in the province of Santa Cruz, covers 717,800ha (1,773,700 acres) of land that includes turquoise, iceberg-littered lakes and, for climbers, challenging, snow-dusted peaks around the Fitz Roy range in its far northern corner. The forests sprout clusters of deciduous beech trees, namely lenga

3 Tours to the glaciers are all straightforward and require no physical effort; and once you get used to wearing crampons, the mini ice trekking is easy. You do need a reasonable level of fitness to tackle the mountain trails in the north, which are tricky in parts. Beginners can have a go at the horse riding, which uses mild-mannered local breeds. Saddles are the ones used by the Gauchos, Argentina's celebrated cowboys, and are piled so high with sheepskin they guarantee a comfortable ride.

★★ As long as you wear warm clothing on the glacier tours, you should experience no discomfort on this trip. Coaches ferry you about, and drop you back at your hotel in El Calafate. For hiking in the Fitz Roy range, however, the incessant westerly winds rising to strong blustery gusts can make the going hard, and even in summer the chill factor should not be underestimated, so be prepared.

You will need a camera with polarizing and U.V. filters for taking pictures of glaciers. For the trekking, you need warm, good-quality outdoor wear, including windproof jacket, waterproofs, and hiking boots, plus a daypack for water and snacks. Take camping equipment, sleeping bag, portable stove, and cooking fuel if you plan to camp in the northern part of the park around Fitz Roy; just a sleeping bag if you plan to stay overnight at refugios.

(*Nothofagus pumillo*) and ñirre (*N. antarctica*), and the forest floor's shrubs and green mosses form a backdrop for various orchids and the scarlet petals of the Notro firebush (*Embotrium coccineum*). Sprinting through all this are the Patagonian hare (*Dilochotis patagonum*) and the shy huemel deer (*Hipocamellus bisulcus*), the latter so in danger of extinction that it has been declared a National Monument. Occasionally the mountain lion, or puma, (*Felis concolor*) creeps down from its ledges to attack the young guanaco (*Lama guanicoe*), its main meal.

All this, however, is a mere dress rehearsal for the real stars of the show: a number of glaciers—remnants of the last ice age—plough down mountain valleys like giant icy fingers. Each is fed by the Southern Continental Ice Cap, a sheet of compressed snow that stretches from north to south, packing the troughs of the Andes. One glacier in particular, **Perito Moreno**, is an amazing natural wonder of the world. It advances continuously, cracking and melting under the strain of its own weight. Chunks of ice the size of cars rip free of its face and plunge into the milky waters of Lago Argentina, the third-largest lake in South America, to surface as icebergs.

MEETING THE GLACIER

Perito Moreno is named after Francisco Pascasio "Perito" Moreno, an Argentine explorer of the last century. Moreno covers 257sq km (99 square miles), an area larger than Buenos Aires, rises 180m

A R G E N T I N A

Parque Nacional Los Glaciares, southwest Argentina—a World Heritage Site

second most popular ice mass, Glaciar Upsala, is three times as big—but for its habit of exploding periodically and in a spectacular fashion.

In 1947, for the first time, the surging snout ground to a halt on the opposite bank, Península Magallanes, and blocked the natural drainage of the lake. The ice dam caused the water to rise, flooding the surrounding forest and farms, and drowning sheep (you can still see the stripped tree trunks on a crop of shoreline known as the "tree cemetery"). The pressure of the backed-up water eventually caused the plug of the glacier to rupture, catapulting ice in every direction. From then on the phenomenon occurred intermittently until the last time, in 1988, when it was filmed by T.V. crews (a video is available). I was told that with today's global warming, it's not certain what Moreno will do next. This thought was uppermost in my mind as I actually walked on its crunchy surface.

WALKING ON ICE

Using an ice axe, the mountain guide cut steps into the brilliant white crust of the famous glacier, sending splinters of ice shattering like pieces of a crystal chandelier. Wearing crampons strapped to our walking boots, our group of 12 made its way up slopes, pausing to straddle deep fissures and water-worn holes echoing with the rush of running water beneath.

As the slopes became steeper, we

(590 feet) above sea-level, and is fronted by a snout about 5–6km (3 miles) across. It is famous not for its size—the park's

HOW A GLACIER IS FORMED

Strong westerly winds from the Pacific blow rainclouds high above the Andes. The clouds burst, littering the peaks with snow. Because snow gathers faster than it melts, it accumulates to form the Southern Continental Ice Cap. Season after season, more snow forms, and compresses into ice, until the forces of gravity and the ice mounting up behind push it down the steep mountain slope. Stones are dragged along with the moving ice, scraping out the walls and floors of the valleys. The front of the glacier, known as the snout, is highly visible to the visitor.

ARGENTINA

edged up sideways in crab-like fashion, confidently placing the full crampon and its securing spikes into the crisp surface that looks as if it's never been touched. The extra effort is worth it, for once you are high enough on Moreno, the mountain view is spectacular: a channel of icebergs that have broken free from the glacier sail downstream, melting by the hour. In the distance we hear shotgun fire, thunder, an explosion. But no, it was only Moreno shedding more of its load.

PREPARING FOR THE GLACIER

You can experience Perito Moreno by coach, boat, or on foot. I booked my mini ice trekking in El Calafate, a village growing into a town, on pastures known as the Patagonian steppe just outside the park, facing Lago Argentina. The place takes its name from the commonly seen Calafate bush (*Berberis buxifolia*) which bears a berry used to make marmalade. Local legend says that if you eat the fruit of the Calafate, you will return to the village.

Cattle and horses roam the steppe. Wildfowl wallow in the wetlands, and the Andean condor (*Vultur gryphus*) circles the distant peaks, silent as a glider plane. On the steppe is land belonging to sheep farmers and their *estancias*, many of whom have been so affected by declining wool prices that they have turned to tourism to supplement their income. Estancia Anita, the biggest sheep farm near Los Glaciares, covers 65,000ha (26,300 acres) and is now the 4-star Alta

Vista, asking more than $500 per night for a double room with dinner. At the less expensive Estancia Alice you can watch sheep shearing before gathering round an *asado*, a lamb barbecue (see page 253).

In El Calafate's main street, Ave. del Libertador, and a few side streets off it, there are souvenir shops, delicatessens serving *empanadas* (meat or spinach pastry turnovers), supermarkets where you can stock up on trekking foods and local wine, plus a string of excursion and adventure travel agencies. Perito Moreno is the tour everyone books, and because it's only 85km (53 miles) to the west it makes a great day's outing. The mini ice-trekking is just as popular, though numbers are strictly limited.

THE TRIPS

For the ice-trekking trip you are collected by bus from your hotel and taken to the entrance of the park. Then it's a drive of 30–35km (19–22 miles) to Bajo de la Sombra bay on a winding road that skirts Lago Argentina. The views are stunning: under a cobalt sky laced with angel-hair cloud, forest slopes rise from the blue water of the lake culminating in snow-tipped summits. A curve in the track is nicknamed the Bend of Sighs, because there the first sight of Merino comes into

BELOW Nearing Lago Onelli and its glaciers
RIGHT and INSET Glaciar Perito Moreno
creaks and cracks, continuously on the move.
We take a break for a tot of whisky—served,
bizarrely, with freshly cut ice

view—a brief taster of what is to come.

We arrived at Bajo de la Sombra bay, and boarded a boat for a 20-minute navigation across the Rico Arm. Our route took us within 100m (110 yards) of the side face of Moreno, which rises from the waters like a broken slab of soap the colour of coconut flesh. Its deep cracks are tinged with blue, for the less air the ice has, the stronger the colour.

We disembarked on the opposite shore. There, mountain guides delivered a talk on the park's ecology, and how glaciers are formed, before leading the way through a forest and across a shingle beach to a rack of crampons. Kitted out, we tramped over just a tiny, safe section of the glacier, and yet the two hours flew by. Afterwards, we were treated to a display of ice climbing by the guide, and then led to an amusing sight: a solitary kitchen table standing sheltered by an ice hill. The guide reached into a hole in the hill and pulled out a bottle of whisky, followed by glasses and a chocolate for each trekker. He poured everyone a shot, but before we could lift the warming spirit to our lips he called for us to wait. Out came his ice axe again, and he set upon a block of ice, chopping wildly. Then, with a silver plate, he scooped up a few crystals and asked "Ice anybody?"

We returned across the Rico Arm by boat, and then boarded a coach to take us to Moreno's snout. Here we descended wooden steps to a purpose-built walkway situated 300m (980 feet) away from where splinters of ice were crashing down, causing acute tidal waves before our very eyes. Prior to the construction of this balcony, onlookers could move closer, but waves dragged them into the icy lake and many died. Today, there are warning signs, forbidding anyone to wander from the designated paths.

THE NEXT BEST THING

The tour to **Glaciar Upsala**, the biggest in the park and fed by several smaller glaciers, also begins by bus. On the way we passed by *estancias*, and a ranch with sheepskins hanging over its wooden fences to air, before arriving at the launch 40km (25 miles) away at Punto Bandena. Our catamaran was ultra stylish, with tinted windows, carpets, upholstery, and a hot lunch if you wanted it (it is quite expensive so you may be better to take your own sandwiches). But there is no English-speaking commentary, only Spanish, and I was glad that I had learned earlier what we would be seeing en route.

We were to navigate up the Canal Upsala through a channel of broken icebergs that lengthened into a sculpture gallery of ice formations moulded by melting. In the distance, a cluster of pinnacles towered like New York skyscrapers, and through the heart of one of them water had eroded a perfect archway. Another had melted so far that it looked like a mass of floating soap suds, ready to burst. And some icebergs had clumped together, like wet sugar cubes, while others had disintegrated into fragile skeletons.

Our boat docked for a short stroll through a forest of lenga trees to Lago Onelli and its three glaciers, Onelli, Bolado, and Agassiz. This walk was more of a procession, as tourists spilled from the boats and stopped at intervals to take photos, holding up the line. At the lake, however, there was plenty of room to find an isolated rock on which to sit and stare. Icebergs congregate in the lake against a backdrop of more snow-dusted giants and waterfalls pouring down crevices. Such scenery! Surely nothing can beat this.

ON HORSEBACK TO THE CAVES

For my trip to Punta Walichu Caves, Gustavo Holzmann of Cabalgata en Patagonia picked me up in his battered, four-wheel drive. There were no windows to close, so the wind blew in and coated my skin with a fine caramel-coloured layer of Patagonian dust. Minutes later, we arrived at his horse ranch—the one with the drying sheepskins—which has tremendous views of Lago Argentina.

ASADO

An *asado* is a traditional barbecue in which a lamb is skinned, its carcass cut down the middle, and its intestines removed. The lamb is then stretched, spread-eagled, onto an iron cross, and positioned over hot coals at an angle. Some restaurants display this method of roasting in their window. *Asados* are held regularly at *estancias* for the benefit of tourists, and even cafés off the main road are known to roast a lamb out in the open.

Gustavo wore tatty black pumps, jeans, chaps, checked shirt, neckerchief, and black beret. He is originally from Buenos Aires, but left to work for Parque Nacional Los Glaciares, where he has learned how the natural remedies of the Tehuelche Indians (the original inhabitants of the area) cure his headache after too much whisky. In the summer he leads horse-riding and five-day trails into the mountains.

His 40 horses are a mixed breed, some Creole. Mine was Tornalo, a glossy bay elegantly flicking a shiny, black mane. Tornalo was wearing a typical Gaucho saddle piled high with blankets and a 5-cm (2-inch) thick sheepskin, and designed for endless hours of riding. The bridle, plaited from cow hide, is not so user-friendly, having been baked in the sun to the texture of stiff cardboard.

Accompanied by Gustavo's dogs, we set out towards Lago Argentina's shore of grassy meadows flecked with dandelions and wildflowers, and visited by upland (Magellan) geese (*Chloephaga picta*), and the black-necked swan (*Cygnus melancorypus*). Gustavo searched for goose eggs for breakfast. Finding a cluster of four, cupped in a nest of greying sheep's wool, he picked up two eggs and held them up to the sunlight. "No good—babies, no taste good," he declares.

We continued our journey, which took us across brooks running from the mountains, into hoof-deep muddy bogs,

then to the soft sand at the edge of the lake, and on to Punta Walichu Caves. We dismounted and unsaddled the horses, and then settled down on a blanket for a picnic of cheese, bread, meats, and wine, which we devoured hungrily before exploring the caves.

HANDPRINTS OF THE INDIANS

Discovered by Francisco Pascasio "Perito" Moreno in 1877 (he also found a mummy here wrapped in rhea skin and holding a condor feather), **Punta Walichu Caves** are sandstone rocks decorated with paintings by primitive Indians. The Indians used a mixture of soil, iron oxide, guanaco fat, plant resin, white of egg, and saliva, blown through hollow guanaco bones or rhea feathers, to paint pictures of the guanaco, the puma, hands, man, woman, and their interpretation of the journey to the other world.

Originally, the paintings would have been in striking red, orange, yellow, black, and white, but colours have faded with time, so a series of reproductions that give the visitor a better idea of their original quality has been created.

The horses fully rested, we left the caves and rode back across sand-dunes and through bushland, until Gustavo's dogs were surprised by a hare sprinting over the shrub. Both dogs and rider gave chase and disappeared over a hill. Minutes later, the hunting party returned, and I noticed the dead, bleeding hare tied by its hind legs to Gustavo's saddle. That was dinner. But I wouldn't be joining him; instead I had to make plans for my visit north to see the peak of Fitz Roy.

The 3441-m (11,290-foot) Fitz Roy has been conquered by only a few. It was named Chaltén (Peak of Fire) by local Indian tribes because they believed it to be a volcano. It was Francisco Pascasio "Perito" Moreno (again) who named it Fitz Roy, after Captain Fitzroy of HMS *Beagle*, who sailed with British naturalist Charles Darwin on a well-documented exploration of the area in 1834.

Serious trekking is discouraged in

the southern part of the park around Moreno, and Fitz Roy is where trekkers come to stay and prepare at El Chaltén, a purpose-built staging post not far from the mountain.

THE WAY TO EL CHALTÉN

In El Calafate, a number of adventure travel operators run various excursions to **El Chaltén**. I decided on a two-day trip, which would involve staying overnight at one of the comfortable inns in the

village (there is also a local hostel). In the early morning, I boarded a bus for the four-and-a-half-hour drive through Patagonia's desert to the Fitz Roy Inn.

I found the village deserted—walkers were already out traversing the mountain trails, and at the couple of horse-riding ranches the horses were out for the day too. The wind whistling through shutters made the place seem like a ghost town. Still, it gave me time to explore. I found one or two grocery stores open, one of

which had a skinned puma head dangling from its mailbox. Inside there was bread, fruit, cheese, and basic groceries, and sides of cow and sheep strung up in front of chocolate bars.

I made my way to the park's office to see a display of wildlife relics, and to pick up a map and advice on the various treks. The ranger warned me not to upset the puma: pumas don't usually attack humans, he said, but, if you do encounter one, do not pursue it. Do not crouch down, but make yourself as tall as possible. Above all, do not walk alone. Unfortunately, I was alone, but then I met Maria, an Australian girl on her own who also wanted to hike up through the high beech trees to puma land.

Next day, Maria and I took a leisurely walk to the impressive **Chorrillo del Salto waterfall**. Then we went on to the lookout point at Laguna Torre for a view of Monte Fitzroy and Cerro Poincenot (3,002m/ 9,850 feet), but on that day they were shrouded in thin cloud. Only Cerro Solo (2,248m/7,376 feet) shone out boldly in the foreground.

From here it's another couple of hours

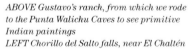

ABOVE Gustavo's ranch, from which we rode to the Punta Walichu Caves to see primitive Indian paintings
LEFT Chorillo del Salto falls, near El Chaltén

along to Mirador Maestri, where there's a lookout over the enormous spread of Glaciar Torre. But since my bus to El Calafate was to leave around 4:30pm, and I dared not risk missing it, I returned through the forest, stopping to take pictures of horses grazing among the wildflowers. Maria walked on with two Japanese, and I never saw her again. I hope she reached a superb view.

I wanted to return— and I'd eaten the Calafate berry, so who knows?

ARGENTINA

GOING IT ALONE

INTERNAL TRAVEL

El Calafate does have its own airport, but the winds often make landing difficult, so flights are unpredictable. The good news is that El Calafate's airport is being reconstructed to accept bigger planes, and will be operational sometime in 1999. The alternative, and usual, way to reach the park is by flying to Río Gallegos, 320km (199 miles) to the east, and taking a bus for the 4- or 5-hour drive to El Calafate.

WHEN TO GO

October to April is high season in the park. Tourist services are currently being expanded and improved with the aim of receiving visitors all year round. The lake doesn't freeze, so boat excursions in the lake can be made all year; the only reason sailings stop for a month in June is the lack of tourists. Spring is a pleasant time because the weather is warm, and the tourist numbers are fairly low. In the Fitz Roy area, in the far north of the park, the trekking season begins around mid-November and lasts until late April or early May. Winds can be strong during the trekking season.

PLANNING YOUR TRIP

Avid walkers usually head straight for the Fitz Roy Mountain range, and spend at least a week following the trails up to the mountains and glaciers. Others base themselves in El Calafate and combine boat and bus trips to Glaciar Perito Moreno with two or three overnight stays in El Chaltén, before moving on to their next destination in Argentina or crossing the border into Chile and to the Torres del Paine Parque Nacional (see pages 204–213). Before you arrive anywhere, work out a rough itinerary to include the areas you wish to see, and use that as a basic structure for your whole trip. If you're on a tight budget, you may prefer to camp. Camping grounds are inexpensive,

WHAT TO TAKE

❑ Plenty of water.
❑ Water and high-energy snacks.
❑ A map.
❑ Good-quality, warm, outdoor wear, including a windproof jacket, waterproofs, hat, gloves and hiking boots.
❑ A camera with U.V and polarizing filters for taking pictures of glaciers.

and there are plenty of food shops in the main towns, particularly El Calafate, selling backpacking and high-energy foods.

Local guides advertise in the tourist information offices. At the National Parks office at the entrance to El Chaltén, you can find details on booking a mountain guide (there are at least five guides, all members of the Association Argentina Guias de Montaqa, who will lead you on various trails through the park or accompany climbers on ascents). Ranger staff here also give an introductory talk about the park and its trails, plus a rather sketchy, photocopied map—not good enough for trekking.

HEALTH AND SAFETY MATTERS

A good basic knowledge of first aid is important for those embarking on long treks. You must also have the confidence to turn back from a trek if the weather turns bad. Take notice of the rangers' advice especially not to trek alone, in case of falls, emergencies, and possible encounters with pumas.

WILDLIFE TO SEE

❑ Andean Condor (*Vultur gryphus*)
❑ Black-necked swan (*Cygnus melencoryphus*)
❑ Chilean flamingo (*Phoenicopterus chilensis*)
❑ Guanaco (*Lama guanicoe*)
❑ Huemul (*Hipocamellus bisulcus*)
❑ Lesser rhea (*Pterocnemia pennata*), known locally as the ñandu.
❑ Magellanic woodpecker (*Campephilus magellanicus*)
❑ Patagonian hare (*Dilochotis patagonum*)
❑ Patagonic skunk (*Conepatus humboldtii*)
❑ Red-backed hawk (*Geranoetus melanoleucus*)
❑ Red fox (*Dusicyon culpaeus*)
❑ Puma or mountain lion (*Felis concolor*)
❑ Upland (Magellan) goose (*Cloephaga picta*)

INTRODUCTION

Contained in the first section of these "Blue Pages" are lists of selected contacts relevant to the 25 adventures related on pages 18–256. Because the adventures are personal accounts, the information provided here will reflect each author's own experience, and therefore details will vary accordingly. Remember also that some contacts are in remote places, so be sure to call or write in advance before setting out. None of the places in the Contacts or the A–Z have been vetted in any way by the publishers and, although some of the companies were used by our writers, this is no guarantee they will still be run by the same people or to the same standard of proficiency.

The Contacts section gives details of companies used by our authors and complements the Activities A–Z in the second part. Below is some general information to help you plan your own adventures.

INTERNATIONAL DIALLING CODES

Telephone and fax numbers given in this section of the book begin with the area code. When dialling from outside the country, prefix this number with the international network access code of the country you are in, followed by the country code.

International Network Access Codes

For calls from the U.K. 00
For calls from the U.S. 011

Country Codes

Argentina 54
Bolivia 591
Brazil 55
Chile 56
Ecuador 593
Peru 51
Venezuela 58

ACCOMMODATION PRICES

Hotels listed in the Contacts and A-Z sections have been split into three price categories. Some parts of the world are generally cheaper than others but a rough guide is as follows:

Expensive = over $85
Moderate = $40–$85
Budget = under $40

EMBASSIES AND CONSULATES
British Embassies
Argentina
Luis Agote 2141-52, corner of
Pueyrredon y Guido
Buenos Aires
☎ (011) 4 803 7070
Fax: (011) 4 803 1731

Bolivia
Ave. Arce 2732-2754
La Paz
☎ (02) 433424
Fax: (02) 431073

Brazil
Praia do Flamengo 284
2nd Floor
Rio de Janeiro
☎ (021) 553 5507
Fax: (021) 553 5976

Chile
El Bosque Norte 0125
Casilla 72 D
Santiago
☎ (02) 231 3737
Fax: (02) 234 2566

Colombia
Edif. Ing. Barings Carrera 9
No. 76-49, 9th Floor
Bogotá
☎ (01) 317 6690
Fax: (01) 317 6265

Bolivia
Ave. Arce 2780
La Paz
☎ (02) 430251
Fax: (02) 433900

Ecuador
Calle González Suárez 111 y 12
de Octubre
Quito
☎ (02) 560 309
Fax: (02) 229 921

Peru
Edif. Pacífico-Washington
Plaza Washington, corner of
Ave. Arequipa y Natalio
Sánchez
Lima
☎ (01) 433 4738
Fax: (01) 433 4735

Venezuela
Torre Las Mercedes
3rd Floor
Ave. La Estancia
Chuao
Caracas
☎ (02) 993 4111
Fax: (02) 993 9989

American Embassies
Argentina
4300 Colombia
Buenos Aires 1425
☎ (011) 4 777 4533
or (011) 4 777 4534
Fax: (011) 4 777 0197

Brazil
Ave. das Nações
Lote 3
Brasilia
☎ (061) 225 2710
Fax: (061) 225 1771

Chile
Ave. Andres Bello 2800
Santiago

☎ (02) 232 2600
Fax: (02) 330 3710

Ecuador
Ave. 12 de Octubre y
Ave. Patria
Quito
☎ (02) 562 890
Fax: (02) 502 052

Peru
Ave. Encalada
Cuadra 17
Monterrico, Lima
☎ (01) 221 1202
Fax: (01) 221 3543

Colombia
Calle 38, No. 8-61
Bogotá

☎ (01) 320 1300
Fax: (01) 288 5687

Venezuela
Calle S. con Calle Suapure
Colinas de Valle Arriba
Caracas
☎ (02) 977 2011
Fax: (02) 977 0843

RAIDERS OF THE LOST WORLD PAGES 20–29

OPERATORS
Bernal Tours
Canaima Airport
Mailing address:
Aptdo. Postal 593
Estado Bolívar
☎/**Fax:** (086) 620 463
email: imel@telcel.net.ve
website: www.worldwander.com/bernal
Runs trips around the Canaima region. A
3-day/2-night package, staying in hotel
accommodation, costs around $350. This
agency was owned and run by Tomás
Bernal, the man who built the tunnel behind
Salto Sapo. Bernal's died 1998, His wife has
taken over the running of the company.

Campamento Canaima
Bookings through Avensa/Servivensa,
Caracas (see Getting There, below)
☎ (02) 907 8130 ext. 34 for Canaima reservations
Fax: (02) 907 8140
Package deals include accommodation in
comfortable double rooms next to the
lagoon, a welcome drink, three meals, a boat
tour on the lagoon, and a flight over Salto
Angel in a DC-3 plane. The 2-day/1-night
option costs about $380 per person (this
does not include flights to/from Canaima or
the entry fee to the national park).

Geodyssey
29 Harburton Rd.
London N19 3JS
U.K.
☎ (020) 7281 7788 **Fax:** (020) 7281 7878
email: enquiries@geodyssey.co.uk
website: www.geodyssey.co.uk
U.K.-based specialists in travel to
Venezuela. Offers a wide variety of tours,
including trips to Canaima and Salto Angel.

Línea Turística Aerotuy (LTA)
Blvd. de Sabana Grande
Edificio Gran Sabana
N-174, Piso 5
Caracas
☎ (02) 761 6231 or (02) 761 6247
Fax: (02) 762 5254
email: tuysales@etheron.net
website: www.tuy.com
LTA offers daily flights to Canaima from
Ciudad Bolívar and Porlamar. Flight-only
deals, or packages starting from $240 for a
1-day trip including a flight over Salto Angel
and hike to Salto Sapo.

Lost World Adventures
112 Church St.
Decatur
GA 30030
U.S.A.
☎ 404/373-5820 or toll-free 1-800/999-0558
Fax: 404/377-1902
email: info@lostworldadventures.com
website: www.lostworldadventures.com
U.S.-based operator, offering a 7-day
package to Salto Angel and Canaima from
$1,295.

Soana Travel
Calle Bolívar #50, con Calle Dalla Costa
Ciudad Bolívar
Mailing address:
Aptdo. Postal 454
Ciudad Bolívar
☎/**Fax:** (085) 22030
A very popular and highly recommended
tour company, run by Martin Haars. Soana
offers various trips throughout the region,
including to Canaima, Salto Angel, the Gran
Sabana, and a unique trip up the Río Caura.
Acts as agents for Bernal Tours (see above).

Southwind Adventures
P.O. Box 621057
Littleton
CO 80162
U.S.A.
☎ 303/972-0701 or toll-free 1-800/377-9463
Fax: 303/972-0708

email: info@southwindadventures.com
website: www.southwindadventures.com
U.S.-based operator, offering a 10-day
package to the Gran Sabana and Salto Angel
from $2,185.

Trips Worldwide
9 Byron Place
Clifton
Bristol BS8 1JT
U.K.
☎ (0117) 987 2626
Fax: (0117) 987 2627
email: post@tripsworldwide.co.uk
website: www.tripsworldwide.co.uk
U.K.-based specialist in tailor-made trips
to South America. The enthusiastic and
knowledgeable staff can organize trips to
suit most budgets.

Turi Express
Entrance hall, Ciudad Bolívar Airport
☎ (085) 29764
or mobile ☎ (016) 685 0405
Run by the efficient and energetic Guillermo
Rodriguez, who organizes trips throughout
the Canaima and Orinoco region, including
3-day tours to Parque Nacional Canaima and
Salto Angel. All-inclusive packages cost
from around $220 in the low season. Very
good value.

GETTING THERE
Venezuela is such a vast country that many
people choose to fly rather than endure the
very long bus journeys that are otherwise
necessary. Internal flights are plentiful and
reasonably reliable, although prices are quite
high, and they are always busy—book ahead
if you can, especially for Friday flights. From
Caracas Maquetía internal airport, many
flights leave from the Gate 5, where mayhem
reigns— the indicator boards may not work,
flights may not be called, and almost all the
flights seem to leave from sub-gate A. Be
pushy, be alert, and direct any questions you
may have to people with radios. The following airlines have offices at all the major
airports in the country.

Aeropostal
☎ 800 28466 (Caracas Airport) for
reservations
Fax: (02) 263 4836
Regular flights to all major domestic
airports.

Avensa/Servivensa
Head office:
Centre Torre Humboldt
Caracas

☎ (02) 907 8000 or for reservations
(02) 561 3366, (02) 562 3366,
or (02) 563 3366
Fax: (02) 907 8053
website: www.avensa.com.ve
This is the national airline, and offers a
many services to most of the country. It also
has an international and domestic air-pass
system; with this pass, domestic flights cost
around $60–$90 each. International flights
cost from $55–$200 per sector, and head as
far afield as Mexico, Miami, Lima, Quito, and
Bogotá. The company usually offers flights
only when you also book accommodation at
Camapamento Canaima. They have daily
flights from Ciudad Bolívar (about $100 one
way). Spaces may be available.

Línea Turística Aerotuy (LTA)
See Operators, above.

Some smaller airlines, such as Rutaca, and
private pilots offer better deals to Canaima.
Talk to them at Ciudad Bolívar Airport.

INFORMATION
Corpoturismo
35 Torre Oeste
Parque Central
Caracas
☎ (02) 507 8815, (02) 507 8607
or (02) 507 8600
Fax: (02) 507 8816
Useful and attractive free brochures on the
various tourism regions of the country,
including Los Roques, Los Llanos, Canaima,
and Mérida. There is also a very helpful
smaller office at the international airport,
whose staff will find and book hotels for you.

ACCOMMODATION
Hotel Laja Real $
Ave. Andrés Bello y Jesús Soto
Ciudad Bolívar
☎ (085) 27911 or (085) 27955
Fax: (085) 28778
Probably the best hotel in Ciudad Bolívar,
and as it is opposite the airport it is ideally
situated for early morning departures to
Canaima. Rooms have air-conditioning,
private bathroom, and T.V. The swimming
pool here is open to the public.

Hotel Unión $
Calle Urica #11 (off Paseo Orinoco)
Ciudad Bolívar
☎ (085) 23374
A reasonably clean, basic hotel with friendly
staff. Rooms have air-conditioning and
private bathroom.

WHEELS OF ANDEAN FORTUNE
PAGES 30–37

OPERATORS
Bum Bum Tours
Final de la Calle 24
No. 8-30
Local "A"
Mérida
☎/Fax: (074) 525 879
email: raquele@bolivar.funmrd.gov.ve
or arassari@telcel.net.ve
website: www.jvm.com/bumbum
Mérida's most popular adventure-tour agency, owned by Tom and Raquel Evenou, and offering a full range of tours throughout the country. The 2-day mountain-bike package to San José includes return transport, all food, the services of a guide, bike hire, helmets, and maintenance equipment (prices are around $50 per person per day). Many other bike tours are available to suit all levels of ability. They can also tailor-make trips for large groups. Bike hire costs around $15 per day. English, French, German, and Spanish are spoken.

If you fancy paragliding, get in touchwith Raul, the area's most experienced paraglider and twice the national champion.He can be cointacted through Bum Bum Tours, and he offers tandem jumps from Tierra Negra into the spectacular Valle Chama (this is an optional extra at the end of the San José bike tour). Prices are around $50 per person. Recommended.

Lost World Adventures
See page 258.
Offers 4- and 5-day mountain-biking packages in the Mérida region, from $660 including air travel from Caracas to Mérida.

Trips Worldwide
See previous page.

GETTING THERE
Aeropostal
See previous page.

Avensa/Servivensa
See previous page.
Offers several flights daily to Mérida from Caracas; tickets cost around $75 one way.

Lai
☎ (031) 552 322 (Caracas Airport) for reservations
Regular flights to all the major domestic airports. Reasonably reliable and slightly less expensive than the other airlines.

INFORMATION
Corpoturismo
See previous page.

ACCOMMODATION
Hospedaje Betania $
Ave. 7
Nos. 20-35 (between Calles 20 & 21)
Mérida
☎ (074) 523 466
A very pleasant, family-run hotel with 10 rooms that have private bathroom and T.V. All rooms are very clean and secure. The owner, Señora Anna, is helpful and will look after baggage while you go on trips. At the time of writing there was no sign on the outside, although the building's numbers (20-35) were visible.

Posada Las Heroinas $
Calle 24
Nos. 8-95 (near Plaza Las Heroinas)
Mérida
☎ (074) 522 665
This hotel, owned by Tom and Raquel from Bum Bum Tours (see Operators, above), is popular with budget travellers. The rooms are basic but good value, bathrooms are shared, and there is the use of a kitchen. Very friendly atmosphere.

BORN TO BE WILD
PAGES 38–47

OPERATORS
Bum Bum Tours
See above.
The 4- or 5-day trips to Los Llanos use exclusive accommodation to ensure that the small groups don't meet up with other tours. All-inclusive tour prices (not including alcoholic drinks) are around $50 per day per person. They also supply hammocks and good mosquito nets. Exceptionally good value, with excellent, knowledgeable guides. English, French, German, and Spanish are spoken.

Geodyssey
See page 158.
U.K.-based specialist in travel to Venezuela. The wide variety of tours on offer include wildlife trips to Los Llanos.

Last Frontiers
Fleet Marston Farm
Aylesbury

Buckinghamshire HP18 0PZ
U.K.
☎ (01296) 658650 **Fax:** (01296) 658651
email: travelinfo@lastfrontiers.co.uk
Organizes tailor-made itineraries to
Venezuela, including Los Llanos.

Lost World Adventures
See page 258.
Offers a 4-day package to Los Llanos from
around $700.

Southwind Adventures
See page 258.
Offers and 11-day package to Los Llanos
from $2,400.

Trips Worldwide
See page 259.

Venezuelan Adventures
P.O. Box 62
Shandaken
NY 12480
U.S.A.
☎ 914/688-7983 or toll-free 1-800/873-9911
email: venadinc@ulster.net
website: www.venz-safari.com
Offers several packages to Los Llanos,
including overnight stays on a *hato* (cattle
ranch).

GETTING THERE
For general domestic air services within
Venezuela, see page 259.

INFORMATION
Corpoturismo
See page 259.

ACCOMMODATION
For places to stay in Mérida, see page 260.

Hato Piñero $$
Near the village of El Baél, between Barinas
and San Fernando de Apure.
Mailing address:
Edificio General de Seguros, 6th Floor
Oficina 6B
Ave. La Estancia
Chuao, Caracas
☎ (02) 991 8935 **Fax:** (02) 991 6668
email: pinero@branger.com
website: www.branger.com
A beautiful nature reserve, *hato* (cattle
ranch), and biological research station with
luxury accommodation. Set in 81,000ha
(200,000 acres) in the Central Llanos, this
was one of the first *hatos* to develop eco-
friendly tourism in the region. Research
scientists come to study the wildlife in the
reserve. Prices per person based on two

people sharing a double room start at
around $120 in the low season, rising to
$150 in the high season. This includes three
meals, soft and national alcoholic drinks,
two tours (one on horseback, the other by
boat), and a bilingual guide. Airport transfers to and from Caracas can be arranged,
either by charter flight or by car.

PARADISE ROCKS FROM ABOVE AND BELOW PAGES 48–55

OPERATORS
Geodyssey
See page 258.
U.K.-based specialists who can arrange
diving trips to Los Roques.

Hernando Arnal
Rasquatekey Bar
Plaza Bolívar
Los Roques
Mailing address:
Ave. Principal de Santa Fe-sur
Residencia Los Jabillos
Piso 9-7F
Caracas
☎ (Caracas): (02) 979 1210 or mobile ☎
(Los Roques) (014) 916 1035
Fax: (02) 979 1805
Hernando is an excellent microlight pilot,
and offers 15-minute flights over Cayo
Frances (about $35) and spectacular 30-
minute flights out over the Gran Barrera
(aboout $50). The latter in particular is
recommended.

Last Frontiers
See facing page.
U.K.-based, offering tailor-made itineraries
to Venezuela, including Los Roques.

Lost World Adventures
See page 259.
Exclusive sailing trips around Los Roques,
with provision for diving and snorkelling.
Three-day trips from $400 plus air fares and
diving.

DIVE OPERATORS
Línea Turística Aerotuy (LTA)
See page 259.
This major tour operator owns *posadas*,
yachts, and lodges, as well as a large fleet
of aircraft. Offers a range of diving and
non-diving package tours to Los Roques.
Land-based dive packages with accommodation in standard *posadas* start from $495

per person for a 3-day/2-night stay, including return flight, all meals, soft drinks, three guided dives per day, and tanks and weight belts. A 5-day/4-night stay costs $759 per person. Yacht-based packages on the luxurious *Antares III* are available only for 7- or 8-day packages. Seven days/6 nights costs $1,295 per person, with the same inclusions as the land-based package. Non-dive packages start from $140 for a day trip, but this is barely worth it. Flight-only prices are $110 return (special offers are sometimes available mid-week). There are two flights daily (early morning and early evening) in each direction, with an extra two flights both ways on Fri.

Sesto Continente

Next to Inparques office and campground at far end of town from airstrip, Los Roques
Mailing address:
Ave. Los Jardines Resid.
Los Girasoles
Local 1
La Florida
Caracas
☎ (02) 749 080 or (02) 731 1507 (Caracas), or (014) 924 1853 (Los Roques)
email: losroques@scdr.com
website: www.scdr.com
The only diving operator on Gran Roque. Very friendly staff. Offers a wide range of diving options and packages, including PADI open-water and advanced courses. All equipment can be hired, but there are discounts if you bring your own buoyancy control device and regulator. Daily boat dives leave at 9am and should be booked at least the day before in high season. A 1-day, 2-tank boat-dive package costs about $90 with all the equipment, or about $70 if you take your own gear. Reasonable discounts are available for multiple-day bookings. The PADI open-water course costs about $350.

GETTING THERE

For general domestic air services within Venezuela, see page 259.

Línea Turística Aerotuy (LTA)

See page 259.

Vipro

Domestic terminal, Caracas Airport
☎ (031) 551 157
or (031) 552 693 for reservations and information
Operates one return flight daily to Gran Roque (about $100 return). Departure time varies depending on the day of the week. Sound airplanes and reliable service.

INFORMATION
Corpoturismo
See page 259.

ACCOMMODATION
Posada de Cigala $$$
Near the airstrip, Los Roques
Mobile ☎ (014) 200 4357
A lovely, friendly place, owned by Liana and Henrique, with four simple, comfortable rooms. Situated right next to the lagoon, so there are always cooling breezes blowing through the rooms—particularly welcome in the summer months. Packages include all meals and daily boat trips. The owners have bought the place next door, which should be open by the time of publication.

Posada La Quigua $$$
Los Roques
☎ (014) 205 1524 or mobile ☎ (014) 373 0040
Fax: (02) 963 4504
email: lharth@yahoo.com
website: www.gis.net/~jcharth
Possibly the nicest *posada* on the island, with a superb atmosphere. Owned, designed, and run by the energetic Alessandra Harth. The rooms are simply decorated and comfortable, and the eating and communal areas are tasteful and homely. Evening meals are cooked in the open kitchen, and are highly recommended. There are single, double, and triple rooms with private bathroom and fan. The package price includes two meals and a picnic lunch, cocktail drinks (national beverages), and a daily boat ride to a different island each day.

Posada Terramar, Posada Arena Blanca, and Posada Arrecife $–$$$
Los Roques
Mailing address:
Ave. Principal de la Carlotta
Edificio Sta. Eulalia
Piso 4
Aptdo. 17
Caracas
☎/**Fax:** (02) 237 1829 or mobile ☎ (014) 373 0303
email: arrecife@cantv.net
website: www.los-roques.com
Three standards of *posada* right next to each other, and all owned by Mauricio. Posada Terramar was due to be renovated at the time of writing, so prices will almost certainly go up, perhaps substantially. Prior to restoration a double room cost $40, with meals extra. There are just three rooms, plus a pleasant sitting area and kitchen, and shared bathrooms.

Arena Blanca is a tastefully decorated, mid-range *posada*. It has simple, comfortable rooms, and the price ($85 per person per night) includes three good meals and boat transfer to nearby islands.

Posada Arrecife is the most upmarket of the three, and has very comfortable rooms with private bathroom. The food is excellent.

FOOD AND DRINK

There are very few restaurants on the island as most people tend to eat at their *posada*.

Aquarena

On the road from the airstrip

A café-deli that serves big, tasty sandwiches, good coffee, and excellent pancakes for breakfast. Tables are set right on the beach. Also sells luxury snack foods.

Madrugadas

On the beach in front of the main plaza

This *posada* is also a popular bar hang-out. You can enjoy the delicious evening meals here even if you are not a guest. Also has a decent selection of wines.

Pizza Bar

On the main plaza

A big open-air bar, popular later on in the evening. Serves up very good, giant pizzas for around $10.

ON AN ALL-TIME HIGH
PAGES 56–65

OPERATORS
Bum Bum Tours

See page 260.

This Mérida-based operator offers a wide range of trekking tours in the Andes. The 5-day trek to Pico Bolívar costs around $200, and includes all food, transport, specialist equipment, guides, and the cable-car ride back down. It is very good value. Other, easier, treks include a 4-day trip to Pico Humboldt and a beautiful 3-day hike in the Sierra Nevadas. There are also several unguided hikes available. English, French, German, and Spanish are spoken.

Southwind Adventures

See page 258.

Offers an 11-day package to ascend the summit of Pico Bolívar. Land-only prices from $2,350.

Trips Worldwide

See page 259.

Venezuelan Adventures

See page 261.

Offers a 6-day trek to the summit of Pico Bolívar. Prices from $1,300.

GETTING THERE
Avensa/Servivensa

See page 259.

Offers several flights daily to Mérida from Caracas; tickets cost around $75 one way.

INFORMATION
Corpoturismo

See page 259.

ACCOMMODATION

For places to stay in Mérida, see page 260.

TREKKING THROUGH
CLOUD FOREST
PAGES 68–75

OPERATORS
Golondrinas Foundation

Gangotena

Quito

☎ (02) 526926

email: manteca@uio.satnet.net

website: www.ecuadorexplorer.com/golondrinas

The organization arranges tours through the Cerro Golondrinas Cloudforest. It is a conservation organization working on re-afforestation projects and has a number of volunteer programmes. The tourist trekking itineraries have been introduced to generate income for the local communities and the work of the foundation.

Tropic Ecological Adventures

Ave. República E7-320 y Almagro

Edificio Taurus, Departamento 1-A

Quito

Ecuador

☎ (593 2) 234 594 / 225 907 **Fax:** 560 756

email: tropic@uio.satnet.net

website: www.tropiceco.com

A small tour operator specialzing in Nature Lodges and Indigenous Community Programmes, whitewater rafting, bird-watching, trekking, photography, scuba diving, and the Galápagos.

Tribes Travel Ltd.

7 The Business Centre

Earl Soham

Woodbridge

Suffolk IP13 7SA

U.K.

ECUADOR

☎ (01728) 685971
Fax: (01728) 685973
email: info@tribes.co.uk
website: www.tribes.co.uk
A Fair Trade company offering a complete range of small group tours and tailor-made itineraries.Culture, wildlife, trekking, and pure relaxation itineraries are offered.Galápagos cruises and jungle trips run in conjunction with indigenous communities, Andean haciendas stays, artisan villages, trekking, and horse riding.

GETTING THERE
Avianca
No. 15–17 Colonnade Walk
151 Buckingham Palace Rd.
London SW1W 9SH
Reservations ☎ (08705) 767747
Fax: (020) 7931 0296
website: www: avianca.com.co
Avianca Airlines offers a 3-month and a 6-month open-dated return. Three flights per week direct from London to Bogota. Two stopovers allowed, the first is free and can be taken in Bogota or Cartagena, the second costs about $100. They have connecting flights to Quito, Lima, Santiago de Chile, Buenos Aries, Sao Paulo, Rio de Janeiro, and Caracas.

INFORMATION
CETUR
CETUR is the national tourist information agency. Their offices are open 9–5, Mon–Fri. They have offices in Quito and at the airport's domestic section.
Eloy Alfaro 1212
Quito
☎ 593 2 225101
Venezuela 914
Quito
☎ 593 2 514 044

ACCOMMODATION
La Casa de Eliza $
Calle Isabel La Católica 1559
Quito
☎ (02) 226602
This very basic guesthouse is owned and run by Eliza, president of the Golondrinas Foundation (see Operators, above).

Hostería El Angel $$
Carretera Panamericana Norte
Ave. Espejo 1302
El Angel
☎ (06) 977584
Comfortable hotel with good food. El Angel is the closest town to Golondrinas; private transport to the reserve can be arranged from here.

FOOD AND DRINK
Hostería El Angel
See Accommodation above.

LEARNING NEW SKILLS WITH THE OTAVALEÑOS PAGES 76–83

OPERATORS
Zulaytur
Colón y Sucre
2nd Floor
Otavalo
☎ (06) 921176 **Fax:** (06) 922969
Run by the very knowledgeable and enthusiastic Rodrigo Mora, who will help you with all your needs. The best of the one-day tours of the Indian villages, taking in all aspects of weaving and local crafts.

South American Experience
47 Causton St.
London SW1P 4AT
☎ (020) 7976 5511
Fax: (020) 7976 6908
website: www.sax.mcmail.com
This specialist in flights throughout South America arranges tailor-made itineraries for individual travel including trekking, white-water rafting, culture, and jungle trips.

Tribes Travel Ltd
See previous page.

GETTING THERE
Avianca
See previous column.

ACCOMMODATION
Casa Mojanda $$
Casilla 160
Otavalo
☎/**Fax:** (06) 731 737
This hotel combines the traditional hacienda style with modern design. Located above Otavalo in the Mojanda foothills, it offers magnificent views of the Andean mountains from each adobe cottage. Price includes breakfast and an evening meal, prepared with homegrown ingredients.

Hostería Hacienda Pinsaquí $$$
5km (3 miles) north of Otavalo on
Panamericana Norte
☎/**Fax:** (06) 946 116
website: www.ecuadorexplorer.com/
pinsaqui/index.html
Originally constructed in 1790 as a textile workshop. Offers 16 suites with fireplaces,

a restaurant and snack bar, and gardens. Arranges horseback-riding, mountain-biking, and hiking trips.

Hotel Coraza $$
Calle Sucre
Otavalo
☎ (06) 921 225
Mid-priced hotel right in the centre of town, handy for the craft market.

FOOD AND DRINK
SISA
Ave. Abdón Calderon 4-09
Otavalo
Good local food and live music most days, including lunch times.

CRUISING THE GALÁPAGOS ISLANDS PAGES 84–93

OPERATORS
Angermeyers
Foch 726 y Ave. Amazonas
P.O. Box 17-1200599
Quito
☎ (02) 569 960
Fax: (02) 569 956
Operates a number of different boats of different classes, all of which have a good reputation; the author's cruise was on the company's *Sulidae*. Experienced divers can be accommodated on certain cruises.

Galápagos Scuba Iguana
Hotel Galápagos
Isla Santa Cruz
Galápagos Islands
☎/**Fax:** (05) 526 330
email: jgallar@ga.pro.ec
website www.scuba-iguana.com
Offers scuba-diving day trips for experienced divers.

Journeys International
107 Aprill Dr., Ste. 3
Ann Arbor
MI 48103
U.S.A.
☎ toll-free 1-800/255-8735
Fax: 734/665-2945
email: info@journeys-intl.com
website: www.journeys-intl.com
The company's Galapagos Wildlife Odyssey is an 8-day tour with accommodationon board comfortable, air-conditioned yachts. Naturalist guide provided. From $2,150, excluding air fare and park fee.

LARC – Latin America Reservation Centre Inc.
P.O. Box 1435
Dundee
FL33838
U.S.A.
Reservations ☎ 1-800 327 3537
fax 1-941 439 2128
email: LARCI@world net.att.net
Theis is the U.S. representative of Angermeyers Enchanted Expeditions (see above), offering tall the the Angermeyer's services.

South American Experience
See facing page.

Tribes Travel Ltd.
See page 263.

Wildlife Worldwide
170 Selsdon Road
South Croydon
Surrey CR2 6PJ
U.K.
☎ (020) 8667 9158 **Fax:** (020) 8667 1960
email: sales@wildlife-ww.co.uk
website: www.wildlife-ww.co.uk
Specializes in wildlife journeys throughout the world. They offer Galápagos cruises on a number of different small vessels.

GETTING THERE
Avianca
See facing page.

TAME
Their Quito offices are at:
Manabí 635 y Venezuela
☎ 593 2 512 988
Avenida Colón 1001 y Rábida
☎ 593 2 554 905
10 de Agosto 239 y La Parque Alameda
☎ 593 2 583 939 or 510 305
TAME flies to Baltra Island. There is a bus service, taking about 2 hours, from the airport via a ferry to Puerto Ayora, the main town.

SAN-Seata
Guayaquil 1228 y Olmedo
Quito
☎ 593 2 211 431
Santa Mariá y Amazonas
Quito
☎ 593 2 502 706 or 564 969
Flies to San Cristóbal island.

INFORMATION
CETUR
Ave. Charles Darwin
Puerto Ayora

Santa Cruz
Galápagos

The Charles Darwin Foundation
CDF Secretary General Office
Casilla 17-01-3891
Quito
Ecuador
☎ 593 2 244 803
Fax: 593 2 443 935
email: cdrs@fcdarwin.org.ec
website: www.galapagos.org

Galapagos Conservation Trust
P.O. Box 50
Shaftesbuty
Dorset SP7 8SB
U.K.

ACCOMMODATION
If you are cruising the islands, as
recommended, accommodation will be on
board the yacht. However, there are several
hotels at Puerto Ayora.

Hotel Galápagos $$$
By the Charles Darwin Research Station
Puerto Ayora
Santa Cruz
Galapagos
☎ 593 5 526330
Fax: 593 5 526 296
A smart hotel with 14 sea view cabins. The
restaurant also has a good reputation.

A TREK THROUGH TIME ON THE INCA TRAIL PAGES 96–105

OPERATORS
Adventure Specialists
Bear Basin Ranch
Westcliffe
Colorado 81252
U.S.A.
☎ 719 783 2519 or 630 7687
Fax: 719 783 2076
email: discovery@ris.net
website: www.gorp.com/adventur
This climbing specialist organizes several
adventure programs in the Andes with a
trekking, exploration, or climbing theme.

Amazonas Explorer
P.O. Box 722
Cusco
☎/**Fax:** (84) 225284
email: info@amazonas-explorer.com
website: www.amazonas-explorer.com

This competant operator runs a number of
rafting and mountain-biking programmes,
and can also arrange tours on the Inca Trail.

Expediciones Manu
Ave. Prado 894
Cusco
☎ (84) 223896
APTE members, operating weekly
departures on the Inca Trail.
Comprehensive, first-class service. The
company is also the best operator for jungle
trips, and specializes in the Manu National
Park in the Amazon Basin.

South American Experience
See page 264.

Tribes Travel Ltd.
See page 263.

GETTING THERE
Avianca
See page 264.

Aero Continente
Ave. Francisco Masias 544
Eighth Floor
San Isidro
☎ 51 1 442 6458
Operates between Lima and Cusco.

INFORMATION
The dozens of travel operators in Cusco all
act as tourist information centres. They are
keen to tell you about the various trips they
organize, and can also offer information on
flights and trains for onward travel.

Tourist Information Office
Mantas 188
Cusco
Located just off the Plaza de Armas, and
open Mon–Sat 9am–noon, 3–6pm.

Tourist Ticket Office
Casa de Garcilaso
Heladeros
Cusco
☎ (84) 263176
This is the place to buy a tourist ticket,
which covers the archaeological sites in and
around Cusco, and is valid for 5 or 10 days.
Open Mon–Fri 7:45am–6pm; Sat
8:30am–1pm.

ACCOMMODATION
El Balcón $$
Calle Tambo de Montero 222
Cusco
☎ (84) 236738 **Fax:** (84) 225253
email: balcon@peru.itele.com.pe

Stylish, mid-priced hotel near the centre of town. There are views across Cusco's rooftops from the bar.

Pension Alemana $$
Tandapata 260
San Blas
Cusco
☎/**Fax:** (84) 226861
email: avendano@peru.itele.com.pe
Small, friendly, mid-priced hostel within walking distance of the town centre.

FOOD AND DRINK
Bagdad Café
1st Floor
Portal de Carnes 216
Cusco
Popular travellers' café, with a balcony overlooking the Plaza de Armas.

Cross Keys Pub
1st Floor
Portal Confiturias 233
Plaza de Armas
Cusco
This English-owned pub has become *the* travellers' bar, and is a great place to meet people. Happy hours 6–7pm and 9–9:30pm.

Kusikuy
Calle Plateros 348-B
Cusco
☎ (84) 262870
Local and traditional foods, including guinea pig.

Pucará
Plateros 309
Cusco
☎ (84) 222027
An excellent restaurant located right on the corner of the Plaza de Armas. Offers the best-value set meal in town.

EXPLORING THE SECRETS OF THE NAZCA LINES PAGES 106–113

OPERATORS
Alegría Tours
Jirón Lima 168
Nazca
☎/**Fax:** (34) 522444
email: alegríatours@hotmail.com
A small company, neither good nor bad, but the only one offering a comprehensive service apart from those offered by the expensive hotels. Offers half-day and one-

day tours of all the local sites, including Nazca flights, the lines viewing platform, the Maria Reiche museum, the graveyards, the ceramic and crafts centres, and aqueducts.

GETTING THERE
See also page 113.

Avianca
See page 264.

AeroCondor
Juan de Arona 781
San Isidro
Lima
☎ 51 1 442 5663
If there are enough passengers, this airline runs flights from Lima to Nazca and back, as a daytrip.

INFORMATION
L. Alberto Segura C.
Ceramic Artesan Center Lasc.
Panamericana sur altura Km 445
Nazca
☎ (34) 521418
Talks on Nazca ceramics. Reproductions of archaeological objects are also on sale.

Viktoria Nikitzki
Calle Bastidas 218
Nazca
Lectures about the Nazca Lines, illustrated with the use of a scale model.

ACCOMMODATION
Hostal El Sol $
Jirón Tacna 476
Nazca
☎ (34) 522064
Basic accommodation on the square in the centre of town.

Hotel Alegría $
Jirón Lima 166
Nazca
☎ (34) 522702 **Fax:** (34) 522444
Clean, comfortable, and reasonably priced.

Hotel Nazca Lines $$$
Jirón Bolognesi
Nazca
☎ (34) 522293
This is a luxury hotel set right in the middle of town. The German researcher Maria Reiche lived here in her latter years.

FOOD AND DRINK
La Cañada
Calle Lima 160
Nazca
Specializes in fish and seafood.

La Encantada
Jirón Callao 529
Nazca
☎ (34) 522930
Not only does this restaurant serve excellent food, but its décor includes some of the finest examples of original pre-Columbian ceramics and textiles in town.

La Taberna
Calle Lima 321
Nazca
☎ (34) 521411
Popular with travellers, and with tour groups in particular. Serves reasonably priced local dishes.

BOATING AROUND LAKE TITICACA
PAGES 114–121

OPERATORS
Alina Tours
Pasaje Lima 343
Puno
☎/Fax: (54) 357139 or (54) 353986
This helpful agency can arrange private tours and guides, in addition to standard boat trips and excursions. Also arranges onward travel.

Crillon Tours
Ave. Camacho 1223
P.O. Box 4785
La Paz
Bolivia
☎ (02) 350363 **Fax:** (02) 364072
email: titicaca@caoba.entelnet.bo
An upmarket agency offering a full range of expensive, individually guided tours around Bolivia. Specializes in packages to Lake Titicaca, where the company operates the comfortable Inca Utama Hotel (see Accommodation, below) and small, intriguing Altiplano Museum at Huatajata; a hydrofoil service across the lake to Copacabana, Isla del Sol, and Isla del Luna; and the exclusive La Posada del Inca hotel on Isla del Sol (see Accommodation, below). The archaeological tour to the Tiwanacu ruins can be combined with the above, but it is expensive for what it offers—the services of English-speaking guides can be secured cheaper elsewhere.

Nomad Travel Planners
3200 W. 88th Ave.
Ste. 1 Anchorage
Alaska 99502

☎ (907) 243 0313 / (888) 345 0313
Fax: (907) 243 0333
website: www.nomad-travel.com
This company specializes in organizing small group travel.

South American Experience
See page 264.

Tribes Travel Ltd
See page 263.

ACCOMMODATION
For details of Lake Titicaca accommodation across the border in Bolivia, see pages 276–277.

La Cúpula $
Calle Michel Pérez 1-3
Copacabana
Bolivia
☎ (0862) 2029
Delightful hotel, with a Mediterranean feel created by cupolas and whitewashed walls. Run by a friendly German couple. Facilities include hot showers, a kitchen, a book exchange, and a video lounge. The vegetarian restaurant (open 7:30am–3pm, 6–9:30pm) has a lovely view from its balcony, and there are painting, sculpting, and acrobatic courses on offer.

Hostal Italia $$
Valcarcel 122
Puno
☎ (54) 352131
Fax: (54) 352521
Reasonably priced, with clean, hot water.

Hotel Isla Esteves $$$
Puno
☎ (54) 353870
Five-star accommodation, with a fantastic island location and lake views.

Hotel Rosario del Lago $$
Rigoberto Paredes (near Ave. Costanera)
Copacabana
Bolivia
☎ (0862) 2141
Fax: (0862) 2140
Stylish lake-view hotel similar to its La Paz cousin, the Residencial Rosario (see below). Rates include breakfast.

Inca Utama Hotel $$$
Huatajata
Bolivia
(Book through: Crillon Tours, La Paz, see Operators, above).A comfortable upmarket hotel on the shores of Lake Titicaca, although rooms are small. The restaurant

serves excellent food, and aside from the nearby Andean-roots cultural complex there are live performances of traditional music in the evenings.

FOOD AND DRINK
Apu Salcantay
Jirón Lima
Puno
A popular travellers' restaurant with a good selection of local specialities.

Huanchaco
Jirón Lima 345
Puno
Quick service, and tasty local food.

Sujna Wasi
Calle Jauregui 1276
Copacabana
Bolivia
A stylish café, restaurant, and bar set around a quiet courtyard. Excellent range of drinks and food, including many vegetarian dishes and fish caught in the lake. Check out the adjoining mini-library for maps, books, and videos on the surrounding area and other parts of Bolivia.

HIGHS AND LOWS OF THE COLCA CANYON PAGES 122–129

OPERATORS
Colca Rafting
Calle Puente Inc.
Chivay
Arranges local river rafting around Chivay.

Eco Tours
Jerusalén 402-A
Arequipa
☎ (54) 200516
Offer 3- and 4-day treks to the Colca Canyon, plus a range of rafting trips lasting from 1½ hours (on the Río Chili) to 2 days (on the Río Majes).

Giardino Tours
Jerusalén 604-A
Arequipa
☎ (54) 226414 or (54) 241206
Fax: (54) 242761
Arranges onward travel and bus, rail, and air tickets. Also rafting and trekking, and tours to the Colca Canyon (1, 2, and 3 days), Valley of the Volcanoes, and Cotahuasi Canyon.

Ivan Bedregal Alpaca
Prolongacion Ave. Ejercito No. 629
Cerro Colorado
Arequipa
☎ (54) 255541
Ivan is a qualified member of the Peruvian Mountain Guide Association (see below). He speaks some English and is an expert mountain and trekking guide, although inot strong on identifying flora and fauna.

Peruvian Mountain Guide Association
House of Guides
Desaguadero 126 Barrio San Lazaro
Arequipa
☎ (54) 263167 **Fax:** (54) 218406
Can recommend guides, and provides routes, maps, and books.

ACCOMMODATION
La Casa de Mi Abuela $$
Jerusalén 606
Arequipa
☎ (54) 241206 **Fax:** (54) 242761
Fairly basic rooms but set in a pleasant garden just up hill from the city centre. Owned by the same people as Giardino Tours, which has its office in the grounds.

Hostal Valle del Fuego Rancho del Sol $
Calle Simon Bolívar
Cabanaconde
This is a very basic hostel in a tiny village. Don't expect too much and you won't be disappointed.

Posada del Inca $
Ave. Salaverry 325
Chivay
☎ (54) 521032
Clean and comfortable; used by many of the tour groups from Arequipa. Restaurant.

THE AMAZON EXPERIENCE PAGES 132–141

OPERATORS
Amazon Explorers
Rua Nhamundá 21
Manaus
☎ (092) 633 3319 **Fax:** (092) 234 5753
Also at:
Municipal tourism booth
Praça Adalberto Valle
Manaus

☎ (092) 232 3052 **Fax:** (092) 234 6767
Apart from organizing regular day tours to the meeting of the waters and the Janauary Ecological Park, this reputable company has its own lodge (the Acajatuba), runs river cruises, hires out boats, and arranges fishing trips, as well as acting as agent for a wide range of other jungle lodges. The director, Iralcy Barros, speaks English.

Amazon Nut Safaris
Ave. Beira Mar 43
Manaus
☎ (092) 671 3525
Fax: (092) 671 1415.
Owner Miguel Rocha runs upmarket cruises to his small floating lodge, Apurissara, on the Rio Cueiras, near the Anavilhanas archipelago. A range of other river trips is offered, and boats can be hired by the day.

Amazonas Indian Turismo
Rua dos Andradas 311
Manaus
☎/**Fax:** (092) 633 5578
A budget tour operator with a solid reputation. Not all its guides speak English, but you can always negotiate on the price. The company's lodge, a compound of cabanas with hammocks on the Rio Urubu, some 180km (110 miles) from Manaus, is basic but has access to virgin jungle and canoe rides along the narrow *igapó* and *igarapés*. Transportation to the lodge is mainly by bus, and finally by speedboat.

Fontur
Tropical Hotel
Estrada da Ponta Negra
Manaus
☎ (092) 658 3052
Fax: (092) 658 3512
email: fontur@manaus.br
website: www.fontur.com.br
This agency runs daily boat tours past the city to the meeting of the waters and Janauary Ecological Park, including lunch. More expensive private speedboat trips to the Anavilhanas archipelago and the Rio Negro can also be arranged, as can fishing jaunts and night cruises to spot alligators.

Jungle Experience
Hotel Ideal
Rua dos Andradas 491
Manaus
☎/**Fax:** (092) 233 9423 or (092) 645 4101 after 7pm
This budget agency, run by English-speakng Chris Gomes, has a sound reputation, although its tours to the small lodge on the Parana do Mamori (a channel leading from the Rio Solimões, south of Manaus) are sometimes fully booked.

Swallows and Amazons
Rua Quintino Bocaiuva 189
1st Floor, Manaus
☎/**Fax:** (092) 622 1246
email: swallows@internext.com.br
website: www.overlookin.com
Mark and Tania Aitchison run this small company, which specializes in more personal tours that are worth paying a bit extra for. Unlike the big operators, its day tour to the meeting of the waters and Janauary Ecological Park really does last a full day, and includes piranha fishing and alligator spotting as well as lunch and dinner. The 3- and 4-day tours up the Rio Negro to the Anavilhanas archipelago might include jungle treks or kayaking trips depending on the season. Accommodation is both on the boat and at its Overlook Lodge.

GETTING THERE
Aeroporto de Eduardo Gomes
Ave. Santos Dumont
Manaus
☎ (092) 621 1210 or (092) 654 2044
Situated 17km (11 miles) north of the city. Facilities include 24-hour tourist information, foreign exchange (daytime only), shops, restaurants, and car hire.

INFORMATION
EMANTUR
Ave. 7 de Setembro 1546
Manaus
☎ (092) 633 3041
Fax: (092) 233 9973
The main tourist office; located next to the Palácio da Cultura. An English-speaker is usually on hand, and staff can provide a lot of information on the various tourist options around Manaus, including a list of jungle lodges. Open Mon–Fri 7:30am–6pm. The EMANTUR booth at the airport (see Getting There, above) is open around the clock.

ACCOMMODATION
Acajatuba Jungle Lodge $$
Anaconda Turismo
Rua Dr. Almínio 36
Manaus
☎/**Fax:** (092) 233 7642
Large (60-bed), standard jungle lodge built on stilts beside a wide stretch of the Rio Negro, some 60km (37 miles) upriver from Manaus. Packages are offered by Amazon Explorers (see Operators, page 270), and include alligator spotting and piranha fishing.

Amazon Ecopark $$$
Praça Auxiliadora 4
Manaus
☎/Fax: (092) 234 0027
This upmarket hotel and nature reserve,
just 20km (12 miles) from Manaus
on Igarapé do Tarumã-Açu, has air-
conditioned rooms with private bathroom in
brick bungalows. There's a programme of
jungle treks, alligator spotting, and canoe
excursions. You are guaranteed to see
wildlife at the attached Amazon Monkey
Jungle park, and there's also an orchid
house, medicinal-plant garden, and Amazon
fruit plantation. Day trips can also be
arranged, and it's sometimes possible to
organize a camping trip.

Ariaü Amazon Towers $$$
Rio Amazonas Turismo (opposite the Hotel
Monaco)
Rua Silva Ramos 41
Manaus
☎ (092) 234 7308 **Fax:** (092) 233 5615
email: treetop@internext.com.br or
ariau@uol.com.br
website: www.ariautowers.com.br
This quirky resort hotel is the largest and
most professional of the jungle lodges,
offering both fan-cooled and air-conditioned
rooms of a high standard in multi-level
towers built over a swamp. Packages (which
start from about $330 for 3 days/2 nights)
cover all meals and activities, including
jungle hikes, boat trips, piranha fishing, and
alligator spotting. The complex, with several
kilometres of walkways through the jungle,
provides plenty of opportunity to explore.

Boa Vida Jungle Resort $$$
Rua Rio Ituxi 68
Manaus
☎ (092) 633 2501 **Fax:** (092) 232 2482
email: boavida@internext.com.br
website: www.internext.com.br/boavida
Some 50km (30 miles) east of Manaus in the
heart of the jungle and reached by road, this
is a large, luxury lodge, with a library, video
room, and children's playroom. Fishing
trips, alligator spotting, jungle trekking, and
canoe rides are offered.

Hospedaria Turistica $
Rua 10 de Julho
Manaus
☎/Fax: (092) 232 6280
Hostel run by a friendly woman. The
rooms lack light, but are clean and have
air-conditioning and T.V. Very convenient
for the Opera House, and rates include
breakfast. Luggage storage and laundry
services are also available.

Hotel Ecológico Terra Verde $$$
Ave. Getulio Vargas 657
Manaus
☎ (092) 234 0148 **Fax:** (092) 238 1742
On the Rio Tiririca, 50km (30 miles) upriver
from Manaus. A jungle lodge consisting of a
complex of comfortable, upmarket wooden
huts with a riverside floating swimming
pool. All the usual jungle activities plus
horseback riding.

Hotel Ideal $
Rua dos Andradas 491
Manaus
☎/Fax: (092) 233 9423
A standard backpackers' hotel, with a view
of the river from its top-floor rooms. Popular
with organized tour groups. Chris Gomez,
owner of Jungle Experience (see page 270),
can arrange trips to jungle lodges. Rates
include a simple breakfast.

Taj Mahal $$$
Ave. Getúlio Vargas 741
Manaus
☎ (092) 633 1010 **Fax:** (092) 233 0068
email: tajmahal@internext.com.br
The rooms of this hotel are large, simply furnished, and have air-conditioning and T.V.
There is a small rooftop pool and a revolving
restaurant that provides excellent views.

Tropical Hotel $$$
Estrada da Ponta Negra
Manaus
☎ (092) 658 5000 **Fax:** (092) 658 5026
email: dcrsao@tropicalhotel.com.br
website: www.tropicalhotel.com.br
This huge luxury hotel has large iron
chandeliers and heavy wooden banisters,
with comfortable rooms, two good pools,
tennis courts, and several restaurants.
Located 15km (9 miles) from Manaus beside
the Rio Negro's most popular beach.

FOOD AND DRINK
Chez Charofe Grill
Estrada de Ponta Negra
Manaus
Located in the cluster of beachside
restaurants near the Tropical Hotel bus
stop. Friendly service complements the
food (mainly set menus of grilled beef and
chicken) at this alfresco restaurant. Good
for watching the action below on the beach.

Churrascaria Búfalo
Ave. Joaquim Nabuco 628a
Manaus
The best all-you-can-eat barbecue in town,
with huge portions of skewered meat.

BRAZIL

Mercado Municipal
Rua dos Bares
Manaus
After admiring the cast-iron reworking of Paris's Les Halles market, pop around the back to the strip of lively cafés, which serve up an enticing range of lunch dishes. The hearty *caldeirada de tambaqui* fish stew will set you up for the day.

FEELING THE FORCE OF IGUACU FALLS PAGES 142–153

OPERATORS
Iguazú Jungle Explorer
Sheraton International Iguazú, Argentina (see Accommodation, below)
The two main programmes you can opt for (neither of which takes up a full day as advertised) both include a boat ride out to the bridge at the edge of the Devil's Throat Falls and a pleasant raft ride along the edge of the Río Iguazú Superior. The "Nautical Adventure" includes a soaking boat ride into the heart of the falls from opposite Isla San Martin, while the "Great Adventure" sees participants shooting the rapids in a long-boat to the falls from farther downriver. The boats are more stable than the Brazilian ones. There are no English-speaking guides, but there are plans to create an interpretive centre on the Yacaratia Trail.

Macuco Safari de Barco
Mailing address:
Caixa Postal 509
85851-000 Foz do Iguaçu
☎ (045) 574 4244
Fax: (045) 574 4717
The office is located 25km (16 miles) out of town along the Cataratas Highway, 3km (2 miles) from the Iguaçu Falls. Arranges a 1½-hour boat safari, including travel in open wagons along the Macuco Jungle Trail in the company of bilingual guides, a short hike down the Iguaçu Canyon Trail, past the small Macuco Falls, and then a boat ride, shooting the rapids to come face to face with the Iguaçu Falls. Departures are daily, roughly every 15 minutes between 8am and 5:30pm. Special expeditions for bird-watchers, botanists, and photographers can also be arranged.

GETTING THERE
Aeroporto Iguaçu International
Foz do Iguaçu
☎ (045) 523 4244
Situated 18km (11 miles) south of town. Facilities include tourist information (see Information, below), foreign exchange, shops, and a café.

Puerto Iguazú Airport
Puerto Iguazú
Argentina
Situated 25km (16 miles) southeast of town, and 50km (31 miles) from Foz do Iguaçu across the border. Facilities include tourist information, shops, and a café.

INFORMATION
Tourist Information Office
Rua Almirante Barroso 1300
Foz do Iguaçu
☎/Fax: (045) 574 2196
email: foztur@pr.gov.br
website: www.foztur.pr.gov.br or www.iguassufalls.com.br
Open Mon–Fri 9am–5pm. There's also a desk at the airport (see Getting There, above), open daily 9am–11pm.

ACCOMMODATION
Hotel Pousada Evelina Navarrete $
Rua Irlan Kalicheski
171 Vila Yolanda
Foz do Iguaçu
☎/Fax: (045) 574 3817
The ideal budget place to stay, this is run by a Polish woman. There is air-conditioning, a lounge area with cable T.V. and a hammock, a laundry area, and kitchen facilities. A good breakfast is included in the rate, and the Navarretes will provide all the information you need to see both sides of the falls.

International Youth Hostel $
Romasa Grande Km 12 (Mile 7)
Foz do Iguaçu
☎ (045) 574 5503
Fax: (045) 572 2430.
Both dormitories and private rooms are available at this modern hostel. Facilities include a swimming pool. Located between the airport and Foz do Iguaçu town (if you are taking the bus, get off by the San Juan Hotel and walk towards the youth hostel sign). Rates include breakfast, and the manager speaks English.

Sheraton International Iguazú $$$
Parque Nacional Iguazú
3370 Iguazú
Argentina
☎/Fax: (0757) 21600 or (0757) 21605
Fax: (0757) 20311
The only hotel within the national park on

the Argentine side of the falls, and recently taken over by the Sheraton group. The white, wedge-like building is out of sympathy with the surrounding lush parkland, but the interior is contemporary in style and the bedrooms, many of which have excellent views of the falls, are studies in 1970s minimalist chic. The restaurant serves tasty, well-presented food. The pool is too small to swim in properly, but is fine for a cooling dip. Bikes are available for hire.

Tropical das Cataratas $$$
Parque Nacional do Iguaçu
☎ (045) 523 2266
Fax: (045) 574 1688
email: resctr@tropicalhotel.com.br
This hotel has a pink colonial façade and elegant interior, and offers views of the falls, a relaxing pool area, landscaped grounds, and a travel agency that can arrange tours across to Argentina and to local sights. Discounts of up to 40 per cent on room rates (which include a buffet breakfast) are available if you have a Brazilian airline ticket, and up to 30 per cent if you do not.

FOOD AND DRINK
On the Argentine side, the Sheraton (see Accommodation, above) has a coffee-shop and à la carte restaurant, Fortin Cataratas (near the old visitors' centre) offers a *tenedorelibre* (eat-all-you-can) barbecue; the visitors' centre sells a good range of snacks.

Cantina Santino Pezzi
Rua Almirante Barroso 1717
Foz do Iguaçu
Known for a hearty dish made from the freshwater fish surubi, and its Italian food.

Churrascaria Tropicana
Ave. Juscelino Kubitschek
Foz do Iguaçu
A recommended, cheap, eat-all-you-can, beef-barbecue buffet, with an even cheaper pizza and salad option. Open daily 6–10pm.

Tropical das Cataratas
See Accommodation, above.
The buffet at the Tropical includes a wide range of barbecued meats, salads, and sweets, and so is worth splurging out on. There is a cheaper café near by (halfway along the walk to the Devil's Throat) that serves sandwiches and simple meals ; it also has a fine view of the Argentine falls.

RANCHING IN BRAZIL'S GRAND SAVANNAH PAGES 154–165

OPERATORS
BR Online Travel
1110 Brickell Ave., Suite 404
Miami
FL 33131
U.S.A.
☎ 305/379-0005 or toll-free 1-888/527-2745
Fax: 305/379-9397
email: brol@brol.com
website: www.brol.com
This U.S.-based operator specializes in travel to Brazil.

Impacto Tourism
Rua Padre João Crippa 686
Campo Grande
☎/**Fax:** (067) 725 1333
email: impactotour@alanet.com.br
The agent for many of the upmarket lodges in the Pantanal (see Accommodation, below). Adenesio Jr. speaks English and is very helpful. Open Mon–Fri 8am–6pm; Sat 8am–noon.

Perola do Pantanal
Rua Manoel Cavassa 255
Corumbá
☎ (067) 231 1460 **Fax:** (067) 231 6585
email: perola@pantanalnet.com.br
website: www.misinternet.com.br/perola
The agent for several of the upmarket river cruises through the Pantanal that depart from Corumbá, including those on the *Kalypso*, a small floating hotel with air-conditioning, bunk rooms, restaurant, and swimming pool.

GETTING THERE
Aeroporto International Antonio Joao
Campo Grande
☎ (067) 763 2444
Situated 7km (4 miles) west of the city. Facilities include tourist information (see Information, below), car hire, shops, a café.

INFORMATION
Tourist Information Office
Morada dos Bais, corner of Ave. Noroeste and Ave. Afonso Pena
Campo Grande
☎/**Fax:** (067) 724 5830
email: pensao@ms.sebrae.com.br
This is the main office, and has very helpful English-speaking assistants who can

provide lots of information on lodges and hotels in the Pantanal and on the eco-tourism destination of Bonito. Open Tue–Sat 9am–8pm; Sun 9am–noon. Closed Mon. A booth at the airport (open daily 10am–6pm) also has maps of the town and makes hotel bookings.

ACCOMMODATION
Baia Bonita $$$
Nhecolandia
☎/Fax: (067) 231 9600
email: apollo@pantanalnet.com.br
website: www.members.xoom.com/baiabonita
An isolated lodge, 200km (125 miles) east of Corumbá, which offers 3- and 4-day packages, including all meals. Transfers to the lodge are by jeep or monoplane. Guided jeep and horseback tours around the Pantanal are available.

Fazenda Rio Negro $$$
Mailing address:
Rua Antonio Correa 1161
Bairro Monte Libano
Campo Grande
☎/Fax: (067) 724 9345 or in Campo Grande
☎ (067) 725 7853
One of the oldest ranches in the Pantanal, with accommodation in a traditional hacienda that was built beside the Rio Negro in 1920. Daily trekking, horse riding, and boat and jeep trips are available, along with flights to the lodge from Campo Grande Airport, or boat transfers from Aquidauana. Rates are inclusive of meals and activities.

Hotel International $$
Rua Allan Kardek 223
Campo Grande
☎ (067) 784 4677
Fax: (067) 721 2729
The cheaper rooms are a real bargain at this high-standard hotel, located close to the main bus station (buffet breakfast included in the price). There's a small outdoor pool.

Hotel Recanto Barra Mansa $$$
c/o Impacto Tourism (see Operators, above)
☎ (067) 725 6807
Fax: (067) 383 5088
email: bmansa@gold.alanet.com.br
website: www.hotelbarramansa.com.br
This intimate, luxury lodge, set in the middle of the Pantanal, is accessible by plane from either Campo Grande or Aquidauana. The lodge is surrounded by water and is therefore an ideal spot for fishing trips along the Rio Negro. Rooms have ceiling fans and mosquito nets. There is a restaurant and telephone.

Réfugio Ecológico Caiman $$$
Rio Aquidauana
São Paulo booking contact:
☎ (011) 246 5016
Fax: (011) 521 9082
U.S. booking contact:
B.R. Online Travel
☎ 305/379-0005
Fax: 305/379-9397
email: brol@brol.com
website: www.brol.com
Can also be booked through operators in Campo Grande and Corumbá. The Réfugio Ecológico Caiman, 36km (22 miles) north of Miranda, is an authentic eco-tourism experience. A team of enthusiastic English-speaking professional naturalists lead hikes, jeep safaris, horseback treks, and boat rides across the Pantanal in 4-day programmes. There are four lodges, all with swimming pools, and the food is excellent. You also have the chance to observe a working ranch, and you can ride out with the cowboys during the herding season.

Réfugio da Ilha $$
Rua Uberlandia 111
79004-500 Campo Grande
☎ (067) 988 2085 or in Campo Grande
☎/Fax (067) 784 3270
A small, homely lodge in a picturesque spot beside the Rio Salobra, around half an hour from Miranda. The rooms are comfortable, and the home cooking is excellent. Day trips include speedboat tours along the meandering river to lagoons teeming with fish. Mountain biking, trekking, fishing, and swimming are also possible. The owner's son speaks English, Italian, and Portuguese.

FOOD AND DRINK
Feira Central
Rua Abrao Julio Rahe (off Ave. Mato Grosso)
Campo Grande
This colourful, twice-weekly market (Wed and Sat) is also well worth visiting in the evening for the buzzing atmosphere of its sit-down stalls, which serve Japanese-style noodles, barbecued beef, and beer.

Parks
Rua Itacuru 140
Campo Grande
☎ (067) 382 6829
A breezy outdoor bar and restaurant, with a buzzing atmosphere and live bossa nova music on most nights. Ask the taxi to take you to Parque Itanhanga.

Viva a Vida
Rua Dom Aquino 1354
1st Floor
Campo Grande
The more central of the two branches of this
excellent self-service vegetarian restaurant
and shop. Payment for the food is by the
kilogram, including drinks. Open Sun–Fri
10:30am–2pm.

CORDILLERA RANGE
PAGES 168–175

OPERATORS
America Tours
Ave. 16 de Julio 1490
Edificio Avenida
Ground floor, Office 9
La Paz
☎ (02) 374204 **Fax:** (02) 328584
email: americatour@usa.net
Trekking and mountaineering trips,
mountain-biking adventures (via Gravity
Assisted Mountain Biking—see page 277),
and four-wheel-drive tours in the remote
Sajama National Park (a day's drive west of
Oruro) and to the salt lakes of Uyuni. Also
the agent for Chalalan, an admirable eco-
tourism venture supported by Conservation
International, in the Madidi National Park
near Rurrenabaque. English-, German-,
French-, and Spanish-speaking guides.

Club Andino Boliviano
Calle México 1638
La Paz
☎/**Fax:** (02) 324682
The main function of the national
mountaineering club (established in 1939)
is to run the skiing facilities at Chacaltaya,
Get information here about climbing. The
office has a noticeboard where climbers
advertise used gear for sale.

Club Sorata
Copacabana Hotel, Sorata (see
Accommodation, below)
The best place in Sorata for information
about hiking and climbing in the Cordillera
Real. The fully organized trips, lasting 3–4
days, include all gear, guides, and mules.
Their Cln. Fawcet Trek extends the chal-
lenging Mapiri Trail to the jungle town of
Rurrenabaque. Gear can also be hired for
independent trips.

Colibri
Calle Sagárnaga 309
P.O. Box 7456
La Paz

☎ (02) 371936 **Fax:** (02) 355043
email: acrolibri@ceibo.entelnet.bo
A friendly and reputable agency that hires
out gear for independent treks and climbs.
Also organizes guides for all the major treks
in the Cordillera Real and down into the
Yungas, including the Takesi and Choro
Trails, and around Titicaca and Isla del Sol.
Guided ascents of the main mountains,
including Huayan Potosí, Illimani, and
Illampu. The company's Amazonia treks and
rafting adventures use the Chalalan project
as a base (see America Tours, above).

Condoriri
Office 8
Galería Sagarnaga
Calle Sagárnaga 339
La Paz
☎/**Fax:** (02) 319369
The best place to buy or rent climbing and
hiking gear. A repair service is also available.

Fremen
Pedro Salazar 537 (near Plaza Avaroa)
La Paz
☎ (02) 416336
Fax: (02) 417327
email: vtfremen@caoba.entelnet.bo
website: www.andes-amazonia.com
A respected agency that specializes in tours
across the *altiplano* and around Lake
Titicaca into Peru, and in the Bolivian
Amazon region around Trinidad, where it
operates the *Flotel Reina de Enin*, a luxury
cruiseship. Can also arrange packages for
the El Puente Jungle Lodge near Carrasco
National Park, one of Bolivia's best bird-
watching sites. Tours to other parts of the
country, including the Salar de Uyuni, can
be arranged. Canadian Michel Livet in the
La Paz office speaks English.

Ozono
Calle Pedro Salazar 2485
La Paz
☎ (02) 322101
Fax: (02) 433202
email: bolivia@ozono.bo or yossibrain@hot-
mail.com
One of the best agencies for mountaineering
and trekking. Yossi Brain, the gung-ho
British author of *Trekking in Bolivia*
and *Bolivia—A Climbing Guide* (both
published by Cordee), is the company's
guide. Can also arrange other adventure-
tourism options such as four-wheel-drive
trips and skiing expeditions.

Sorata Guides Association
c/o Residencial Sorata, Sorata (see
Accommodation, below)

Guides and porters are available for a range of day hikes and longer expeditions, including the 3-day trek up to Laguna Glacial and the 7-day Mapiri Trail. Few of the guides speak English, but if you need help ask for Eduardo or speak to Louis at the Residencial Sorata. All camping gear is available for hire, but you'll need to provide food for both yourself and your guide.

GETTING THERE
Aeropuerto John F. Kennedy
El Alto
La Paz
☎ (02) 810122
Commonly known as Aeropuerto El Alto, and situated 10km (6 miles) from the city centre. Facilities include a small tourist office (not always staffed), banks, a café, and duty-free shops.

INFORMATION
Senatur
Calle Mercado No. 1328
Edificio Mariscal Ballivan
Piso 18
La Paz
☎ (02) 367441 **Fax:** (02) 374630
The country's main tourist information office, located at the foot of the Prado, is open Mon–Fri 8:30am–6pm; Sat 8:30am–1pm. Brochures and maps are available, and you should be able to get information in English and French. There is also a small branch at the airport (see Getting There, above).

ACCOMMODATION
For details of Lake Titicaca accommodation across the border in Peru, see page 268.

Copacabana $
Ave. 9 de Abril
Sorata
☎/**Fax:** (0811) 8115042
email: agsorata@bo.net
Bright and cheerfully decorated modern hotel run by a German expat. There are pleasant gardens and the restaurant's T.V. constantly screens videos. Trekking and climbing information is available from the Club Sorata agency, based in the hotel (see Operators, above).

El Rey Palace Hotel $$
Ave. 20 de Octubre 1947
La Paz
☎ (02) 393016 or (02) 393018
Fax: (02) 367759
email: hotelrey@wara.bolnet.bo
Good-value boutique hotel that comes highly recommended. Rooms have cable

T.V., daily newspapers are provided, and there's a business centre. You can prepare your own food in their kitchen or be assisted there by the chef. Rates include breakfast.

Ex-Prefectural Sorata $$$
Ave. Samuel Tejerina
Sorata
☎/**Fax:** (0811) 5201
email: meetingpoint@mpoint.com.bo
website: www.mpoint.com.bo
Large and impressively renovated ex-government hotel, with wooden fixtures and stained-glass windows. There are gardens, a swimming pool, and good views of the valley, but the place lacks people and atmosphere.

Hostal República $
Calle Comercio 1455
La Paz
☎ (02) 357966
A recommended colonial-era hotel. There are two charming courtyards, complete with vine-covered balconies, where you can eat breakfast from the adjoining café. Luggage storage and a laundry service are available.

Hotel Panchito $
Corner of Calle Fernando Guachalla, facing Plaza Enrique Penaranda
Sorata
☎ (0811) 8700
This basic, but clean, small hotel, overlooks the central plaza. A comfortable lounge with T.V. Note that the doors are locked at 11pm.

Residencial Rosario $$
Illampu 704
La Paz
☎ (02) 369542 or (02) 316156
Fax: (02) 375532
Highly popular colonial-style hotel in a good location, close to the Witches Market and the shopping street of Sagárnaga. Facilities include a good restaurant and a travel agency.

Residencial Sorata $$
Calle Sucre y Villa Vicencio
Sorata
☎ (0811) 5044 **Fax:** (0811) 5218
email: resorata@ceibo.entelnet.bo
The main building, a decaying colonial mansion on the corner of Plaza Enrique Penaranda, has lots of atmosphere, with ramshackle courtyard gardens. Some rooms are damp and the service is often poor, although the restaurant's food is good and videos are shown. The Canadian manager speaks English, French, and Spanish, and can help arrange treks with the Sorata Guides Association (see Operators, above).

FOOD AND DRINK

Altai
Plaza Enrique Penaranda 221
Sorata
The town's best restaurant, run by an English couple. The set lunch and dinner is amazing value and always includes a vegetarian option. There is a reasonable wine list, too. Opening hours are somewhat flexible, but generally daily except Mon.

Andromeda
Ave. Arce 2116
La Paz
Small, top-notch vegetarian restaurant, best visited for its good-value lunch. Closed Sun.

Angelo Colonial Cafetería
Linares 922
La Paz
Funky internet café, with a jumble-sale/antique interior design. Set around a small courtyard just off the shopping street of Sagárnaga. Good range of drinks, snacks, and light meals.

Mongo's Rock Bottom Café
Hermanos Machengo 2444
La Paz
☎ (02) 353914
The primary hangout for La Paz's expat community and trendy locals alike. A lively bar/restaurant that serves American diner-style food and shows sports programmes on big-screen T.Vs. Open daily till late.

Restaurant Pizzeria Italiana
Calle Villamil de Rada
Sorata
This authentic pizzeria and pasta restaurant has a great view across the Río San Cristobal Valley, although to reach it requires a hike up the hill. Slow service.

The Spider
Sorata
Beside the Hotel El Mirador south of Plaza Enrique Penaranda. An expat-run café-bar open only during the climbing season.

Vienna
Federico Zuazo 1905
La Paz
☎ (02) 391660
Excellent European cuisine with an emphasis on hearty meat and fish dishes. Frequently cited as the best restaurant in the city by locals, and yet surprisingly reasonably priced, especially for lunch.

BOLIVIAN HIGHS AND LOWS PAGES 176-185

OPERATORS
For general operators based in La Paz, see page 275.

Explore Bolivia
Galería Sagarnaga
1st Floor, Office 3
La Paz
☎/**Fax:** (02) 391810
email: explobol@ceibo.entelnet.bo
Run by the enthusiastic, English-speaking Luis Fernando Jordan, this all-round adventure-tourism agency specializes in rafting and kayaking adventures in the Yungas and along the Tuichi, Bolivia's premier whitewater river. Some unique trekking and mountain-bike excursions, as well as the usual routes along ancient Inca trails. (Readers should note that the U.S.-based agency also called Explore Bolivia, which can be visited on the Internet at www.explorebolivia.com, was once a partner of the Bolivian company but is now a separate enterprise.)

Gravity Assisted Mountain Biking
c/o America Tours (see page 275) or contact Alistair:
☎ (02) 415530
email: Alistairm@hotmail.com
This mountain-biking operation organizes rides down Bolivia's most dangerous road, from La Cumbre to Coroico, which drops 3,500m (11,500 feet). Transfers to La Cumbre and full support for the 7-hour ride are included, with the option of staying over in Coroico at the end. Trips generally run twice a week (Wed and Sun). Other options include the Zongo Valley and Chacaltaya to La Paz, butyou must acclimatize first.

GETTING THERE
Aeropuerto John F. Kennedy
See facing page.

INFORMATION
Senatur
See facing page.

ACCOMMODATION
For accommodation in La Paz, see facing page. For other towns see over:

La Casa Colonial $
Calle Pando
Coroico
Near the town's central square is this cheap, clean hotel set around a pretty, white-washed courtyard. It has simply furnished rooms and communal bathrooms.

El Cafetal $
Coroico
Located 1km (½ mile) east of Plaza 27 de Mayo next to the hospital. There are fine views from this small guesthouse, which is run by a French couple. Also renowned for its French home cooking.

El Viejo Molino $$$
Coroico
☎/Fax: (0811) 6004, or book through Valmar Tour in La Paz:
☎ (02) 361076 Fax: (02) 352279
A smart hotel, 1km (½ mile) from the centre of Coroico on the road to Caranavi. Comfortable rooms with private bathroom and T.V. Facilities include a pool, sauna, jacuzzi, and gym.

Hostal Sol y Luna $–$$
Coroico
☎ mobile (015) 61626
Book through Chuquiago Turismo:
Ave. Mariscal Santa Cruz 1364
La Paz
☎ (02) 362099 Fax: (02) 359227
A delightful hillside compound run by a genial German expat, with dormitories, a restaurant, three self-catering cabanas, and a campsite. Delightful gardens. Also information on hikes (including overnight trips to nearby villages), shiatzu massages, and massage and meditation workshops.

Hotel Esmeralda $$
Coroico
Mailing address:
P.O. Box-Casilla 9225
La Paz
☎ (0811) 6017
email: esmeralda@latinwide.com
This deservedly popular travellers' haunt overlooks Coroico from the hills above the town; book ahead to be sure of a room with a view. The rooms are large and have power-fully hot showers, there's a sizeable swimming pool set in pleasant gardens, the restaurant is good, and there is a wide choice of videos. The owner speaks and English, German, and Spanish, and can arrange topick you up from the town centre.

FOOD AND DRINK
For eating in La Paz, see previous page.

Back-Stube
Calle Kennedy (west of Plaza 27 de Mayo)
Coroico
Friendly café, next to the Hotel Kory, run by a German/Chilean couple. There is delicious homemade bread for breakfast, and a good-value set meal of two vegetarian dishes, plus bread and coffee all day.

La Casa
La Casa Hotel
Coroico
☎ (0811) 6024
Another German-run operation, where the speciality is tasty fonduesfor a minimum of two people. Served with four salads and plenty of dips.

BEYOND THE VALLEY OF THE MOON PAGES 188–195

OPERATORS
For operators in La Paz, Bolivia, who offer tours to Uyuni, see pages 275–276.

Corvatsch Expediciones Florida
Calle Tocopilla
San Pedro de Atacama
☎ (055) 851087
The standard day tours to Geiser del Tatio, Valle de la Luna, Salar de Atacama, and the *altiplano* lagoons are supplemented by an interesting overnight horseback trip to the Valle de Catarpe to see the remains of an Inca fortress. The owner, Brigitte, speaks English, French, German, and Spanish; the tour guides don't speak English.

Cosmo Andino
Calle Caracoles
San Pedro de Atacama
☎ (055) 851069 Fax: (055) 319834
A reliable agency run by a very know-ledgeable Dutch expat. Apart from the regular tours, he also offers full-day trips to view ancient rock art in the desert, plus 3-day or longer trekking trips around the *altiplano* or up Volcán Lascar. Alvaro, the company's English-speaking guide, is also very knowledgeable and leads most trips.

Desert Adventure
Calle Caracoles
San Pedro de Atacama
☎/Fax: (055) 851067
email: desertadventure@hotmail.com
Another long-established and reputable agency. The Tatio trip arrives earlier than

CHILE

the competition because of better vehicles. Archaeological expeditions and tours up the nearby Lascar and Sairecabur volcanoes are also offered.

Pangea Expediciones
Calle Tocopilla
San Pedro de Atacama
☎/Fax: (055) 851111
Professional mountain-bike-hire shop. There is a range of bike-frame sizes, and all bikes come with panniers and lights. Clear maps are provided for the self-directed tours of the surrounding attractions, including the Valley of the Moon and the oasis town of Toconao.

Turismo Colque
Corner of Calle Caracoles and Calle Calama
San Pedro de Atacama
☎ (055) 851109
Also has a branch in Uyuni, Bolivia:
Ave. Potosi 56 **☎** (0693) 2199
This tour agency is the only reliable operation for the 3-day cross-border four-wheel-drive trip between San Pedro de Atacama and Uyuni since it has offices in both towns.

GETTING THERE
Aeropuerto El Loa
Calama
☎ (055) 312348
Located 2km (1 mile) south of town. No facilities.

INFORMATION
Sernatur
Ave. Providencia 1550, between Manuel Montt and Pedro de Valdivia Metro stations
Santiago
☎ (02) 236 1420
The main tourist information office, with maps and general information on Santiago and the rest of the country (open Mon–Fri 9am–6pm; Sat 9:30am–1:30pm). The airport branch (**☎** (02) 601 9320) has a desk manned by English-speaking staff (open daily 9am–9pm).

ACCOMMODATION
Café Sonchek $
Calle Calama
San Pedro de Atacama
There is no phone at this basic, but delightful, hostel, which has kitchen and laundry facilities and an excellent café (see Food and Drink, below). The friendly owners speak English and French.

Casa Corvatsch $
Calle Antofagasta
San Pedro de Atacama

☎ (055) 851101
website: www.casa-corvatsch.cl
Popular, cheap hotel run by a Chilean/Swiss couple, who also offer desert expeditions via Corvatsch Expediciones Florida (see Operators, above). The cheaper rooms have no air-conditioning and share a communal bathroom, but are clean and simply furnished. Meals are not provided.

Explora en Atacama $$$
San Pedro de Atacama
Mailing address:
Ave. Américo Vespucia Sur 80
Piso 5
Santiago
☎ (02) 206 6060 or (02) 208 0664
Fax: (02) 228 4555
email: explora@entelchile.net
website: www.interknowledge.com/chile/explora
A sister lodge to the Explora en Patagonia (see page 283), this whitewashed, low-rise modern complex lies on the outskirts of San Pedro de Atacama. At the resort everything is included in the price, from transfers to all meals, drinks, and activities. The comfortable, air-conditioned rooms have excellent bathrooms with whirlpool baths. There are 25 different 4-day packages available, including treks, horseback rides, and four-wheel-drive trips.

Hotel de Sal and Hotel Playa Blanca $$
Salar de Uyuni
Bolivia
Book through main La Paz agencies or Hidalgo Tours:
Junin y Bolívar 19
Potosi
Bolivia
☎ (062) 28293 **Fax:** (062) 22985
These two small, novelty hotels, facing each other on the Salar de Uyuni some 34km (21 miles) from the town of Uyuni, are, save for their roofs, made entirely of salt—including the furniture and statues.

Hotel Terrantai $$
P.O. Box 10
Calle Tocopilla 19
San Pedro de Atacama
☎ (055) 851140 **Fax:** (055) 851037
email: atacamadesert@adex.cl
website: www.atacamadesert.cl
A discreetly upmarket hotel, with local arts used in the décor. Rates include buffet breakfast. Also runs Atacama Desert Expeditions, which offers individually guided tours of the area.

FOOD AND DRINK

Virtually all of San Pedro's restaurants and bars are located along the main street, Calle Caracoles, which is about 10 minutes' walk from end to end.

Adobe Café

Calle Caracoles
San Pedro de Atacama
The breakfast fruit juices are highly recommended, along with the pisco sours and the fine selection of evening meals. Fairly pricey, but there is a open campfire and striking petroglyphs. Open till late.

Café Sonchek

Calle Calama
San Pedro de Atacama
Good-value vegetarian options abound at this pleasant café, a minute's walk north of Calle Caracoles and in the hostel of the same name (see Accommodation, above). Has a covered courtyard and funky furniture.

La Estanka

Calle Caracoles
San Pedro de Atacama
A popular, atmospheric bar and restaurant, with live music most nights. The set menu is on the expensive side, but the portions are huge and there's always a vegetarian option. Open till late.

IN THE SHADOW OF THE VOLCANO PAGES 196–203

OPERATORS

Cascada Expediciones

Orrego Luco 054
Piso 2
Providencia
Santiago
☎ (02) 234 2274 or (02) 232 7214
Fax: (02) 233 9768
email: cascada@ibm.net
website: www.cascada-expediciones.com
A top-notch company that organizes trips around Chile, with a strong emphasis on adventure, discovering nature, and local culture. It specializes in kayaking, rafting, horseback riding, mountaineering, and hiking tours, with locations ranging from the Atacama Desert in the north (and across to Bolivia over the *altiplano*) to southern Patagonia and Easter Island. There is a range of day trips on offer from Santiago to the private nature reserve of Cascada de las Animas in the Cajon del Maipo (including

treks, rafting and kayaking, and horse riding). From Dec to Apr the company also operates an office in Pucón, for hikes up Villarrica, mountain biking, trekking in the Cani Forest Reserve,rafting the Río Trancura, as well as a 2-day kayak course.

Centro de Turismo Ecuestre Huepil

Casilla 16
Pucón
☎ (09) 453 4212
Rodolfo Coombs, a professional showjumper from Argentina, and his partner, Carolina Pumpin, run this homely equestrian centre in the beautiful Liucura Valley, some 30km (19 miles) from Pucón. Half-day and full-day trips can be arranged via Hostería ¡Ecole! (see Accommodation, below). In summer they also offer a 3-day ride across the mountains into Argentina and back.

Fundacion Lahuen

General Urrutia 477
Pucón
☎/**Fax:** (045) 441660
email: lahuen@interaccess.cl
U.S. contact:
Ancient Forest International
P.O. Box 1850
Redway
CA 95560
U.S.A.
☎ 707/923-3015 **email:** afi@igc.org
A non-governmental organization set up to manage the Cani Forest Sanctuary. Contact them for more information or if you would like to assist.

Politur

O'Higgins 635
Pucón
☎/**Fax:** (045) 441373
email: agencia@politur.com
One of the more reputable agencies in Pucón, offering the usual range of adventure trips, including the ascent of Villarrica, rafting on the Trancura, and trekking in the Huerquehue National Park, plus mountain biking, fishing, and horse riding.

Sol y Nieve

O'Higgins/Esquina Lincoyán
Pucón
☎/**Fax:** (045) 441070
email: solnieve@entelchile.net
The oldest and most reliable adventure-tourism operation in Pucón, run by Colombian/American Willie Hatcher. Professional guides lead climbs up Villarrica, as well as rafting trips on the Río Trancura and the challenging Río Futaleufú

in Patagonia. Fishing trips on the Río Liucura, horseback riding with the German-run Rancho de Caballos, and treks in the Huerquehue National Park are also offered.

GETTING THERE
Aeropuerto International Arturo Merino Benitez
Pudahuel
Santiago
☎ (02) 601 9001
Located 26km (16 miles) west of the capital. There are separate terminals for international and domestic flights, and facilities include tourist information (see Information, below), foreign exchange, restaurants, shops, and car hire.

Aeropuerto Maquehue
Temuco
Located 2km (1 mile) south of town. No facilities.

INFORMATION
Sernatur
See page 279.

ACCOMMODATION
Gran Hotel Pucón $$$
Clemente Holzapfel 190
Pucón
☎/Fax: (045) 441001
email: ghp_ski@entelchile.net
Some of the rooms in this brash hotel, set on the black-sand shores of Lake Villarrica, lack finishing touches, but the staff are friendly and the views pleasant.

Hostería ¡Ecole! $
General Urrutia 592
Pucón
☎/Fax: (045) 441675
email: trek@ecole.mic.cl
Run by hospitable and environmentally minded Americans and locals, ¡Ecole! is one of Chile's most delightful hotels. The quirky wooden building also houses an excellent vegetarian restaurant.The best place to arrange hiking and camping tours to the serene Cani Forest Sanctuary near Pucón or to the El Arco Alercal, an ancient forest near Puerto Montt to the south.

Hotel Antumalal $$$
Pucón
☎ (045) 441012 Fax: (045) 441013
email: antumalal@entelchile.net
Just outside Pucón, overlooking Lake Villarrica. An intimate luxury hotel that pays homage to the 1950s through Frank Lloyd Wright-style architecture, superb interiors, and splendid gardens. Rooms are mini-

logcabins with their own fireplaces and lake-side views.

Hotel Orly $$$
Pedro de Valdivia 027
Providencia
Santiago
☎ (02) 231 8947
Fax: (02) 252 0051
Small, chic boutique hotel in the trendy Providencia area of the city. All rooms are air-conditioned with ensuite bathroom, cable T.V., and mini-bar. The rates include a buffet breakfast.

Hotel Paris $
Calle Paris 809-813
Santiago
☎ (02) 639 4037
Popular budget choice with independent travellers and tour companies. The small rooms are clean, with ensuite bathrooms.

Hotel and Spa Araucarias $$
Caupolican 243
Casilla 103
Pucón
☎/Fax: (045) 441286 or (045) 441963
email: araucari@cepri.cl
A good, standard hotel, close by Lake Villarrica and the centre of Pucón. Rooms have T.V. and other amenities, and there's a spa bath and sauna. Rates include breakfast.

Sheraton Santiago $$$
Ave. Santa Maria 1742
Santiago
☎ (02) 233 5000
Fax: (02) 234 1729 or (02)234 1732
email: guest@stgo.sheraton.cl
An impressive luxury hotel with good views of the city and surrounding mountains. In a central, yet quiet, location.

Termas de Panqui $$
Mailing address:
O'Higgins 615
Pucón
☎ (45) 442039
Fax: (045) 442040
A remote hot spring resort, 58km (36 miles) northeast of Pucón, which styles itself as a North American Indian reservation, complete with Sioux-style tepees. There is also a small hotel. It also offers a range of New Age therapies and courses. Transportation from Pucón can be arranged.

La Tetera $
General Urrutia 580
Pucón
☎/Fax: (045) 441462

Run by a Swiss/Chilean couple, this excellent-value guesthouse also has a popular café that serves a wide range of herbal infusions. There's a book exchange, and the owners can arrange horseriding trips and reservations for boat passages to Puerto Natales and Laguna San Rafael to the south.

FOOD AND DRINK

O'Higgins, Pucón's main street, has a good range of restaurants and bars, but many only open Dec–Apr for the summer season. There's a well-stocked supermarket here, where you can also change money.

Holzapfel Bäckerei

Clemente Holzapfel
Pucón
Located in the whitewashed wooden building near the casino, this café, bakery, and chocolate shop serves good snacks and more substantial dishes. There is an outdoor dining patio.

Mercado Central

San Pablo and Puente
Santiago
This elegant old produce market has a range of food stalls. Many tourists settle on Donde Augusto, with good view of the action and serves a great seafood soup. The cheaper cafés in the outer halls serve good food too.

La Terraza

O'Higgins 323
Pucón
☎ (045) 441361
Seves a reasonable range of Italian, seafood, and steak dishes, as well as local favourites such as *pastel de choclo* stew. Choice of indoor or outdoor dining.

La Tetera

See Accommodation on previous page.

THE TOWERS OF CHILE
PAGES 204–213

OPERATORS
Amerindia Concept

Ladrilleros 105
Puerto Natales
☎ (061) 410678 **Fax:** (061) 410169
email: amerindi@entelchile.net
website: www.chilnet.cl/amerindia
This independent expedition company organizes trekking in the park along traditional routes, or glacier crossings and technical hikes off the main pathways with qualified and bilingual guides. On ice hikes

(around $85) the lodge provides tents, ice and rock climbing gear, stoves, and food. It offers courses in climbing, beginning on a practice wall (1 day costs around $90, 2 days $165), sea-kayaking classes on the channels that weave between the mountains, and a 1-day photography course covering the park's scenery and wildlife (around $120 per person). Accommodation is in the company's lodge, and there is a vegetarian restaurant (see Accommodation and Food and Drink, below).

G.A.P. Adventures

266 Dupont St.
Toronto
Ontario M5R 1V7
Canada
☎ 416/922-8899 or toll-free 1-800/465-5600
Fax: 416/922-0822
U.K. contact:
Guerba Expeditions
Wessex House
40 Station Rd.
Westbury, Wiltshire BA13 3JN
U.K.
☎ (01373) 826611 **Fax:** (01373) 858351
Escorted adventure travel to Patagonia, staying in mountain cabins, including boat trips to view marine wildlife and a 5-day hike through the Torres del Paine National Park.

Hostería Las Torres

Parque Nacional Torres del Paine
Mailing address:
Magallenes 960
Punta Arenas
☎ (061) 226054 **Fax:** (061) 222641
email: lastorres@chileaustral.com
website: www.chileaustral.com/lastorres
Three 6–8-hour guided horse-riding tours run from Hostería Las Torres: the Torres (; Los Cuernos; and Valle Encantado (. All cost between $30-$70 including picnic lunch). There's also a 2–3-hour ride to Lago Nordenskjold.

Journey Latin America

12–13 Heathfield Terrace
Chiswick
London W4 4JE
U.K.
☎ (0181) 747 8315 **Fax:** (0181) 742 131
email: tours@journeyatinamerica.co.uk
Organizes customized itineraries and escorted group tours to Torres del Paine and Península Valdés, plus skiing at Bariloche.

Patagonian Brothers Expeditions

Damian and Willie Benegas
P.O. Box 400018

Berkeley
CA 94704
U.S.A.
☎/Fax: 510/843-6805
email: thetwins@slip.net
The Benegas brothers are mountain guides
who specialize in hikes and climbs in the
Andes, including Torres del Paine.

Travelbag Adventures
15 Turk St.
Alton
Hampshire GU34 1AG
U.K.
☎ (01420) 541007 **Fax:** (01420) 541022
email: info@travelbag-adventures.co.uk
website: www.travelbag-adventures.co.uk
Arranges small group trips, including the
Patagonian Explorer, which covers mountain walks in Torres del Paine, Los Glaciares,
the Fitzroy range, and Tierra del Fuego.
There is also a Península Valdés extension.

GETTING THERE
Aeropuerto International Arturo Merino Benitez
See page 281.

Aeropuerto Maquehue
See page 281.

INFORMATION
Servicio Nacional de Turismo (Sernatur)
Pedro Montt 19 esquina Phillip
Puerto Natales
☎/Fax: (061) 412125
The tourist information office.
Maps detailing routes, lodgings, and camp-
sites are available at the park entrances or in
shops in Puerto Natales. Alternatively, you
can order one beforehand from:

Zaiger & Urruty Publications
P.O. Box 94
Suc. 19
1419 Buenos Aires
Argentina
☎ (011) 4 572 1050 **Fax:** (011) 4 572 5766

ACCOMMODATION
There are many clean and comfortable
family-run hostels in Puerto Natales for
under $10 a night, including breakfast, and
some can even organize excursions to the
park. In the park itself, options include
campsites, *refugios*, and *hosterías*.

Amerindian Concept $
See Operators, above.
A brightly painted and artistically decorated
lodge facing the sea, with private rooms

(shared bathroom) that offer views of the
waterfront and mountains (from $15,
including breakfast). Facilities include a
laundry, vegetarian restaurant (see Food
and Drink, below), and email. There is a
welcome buffet and slide show at 8–11pm
every night. Also acts as an independent
expedition operator (see Operators, above).

Andescape $
Mailing address:
Pedro Montt 308
Puerto Natales
☎/Fax: (061) 412592
Andescape runs more than 20 campsites,
plus four *refugios* at Lago Grey, Lago
Pehoé, Lago Dickson, and Los Perros. The
refugios offer bunk beds, showers, break-
fast, lunch, and evening meal, basic
groceries, first aid, and a radio service. In
the summer it's best to book ahead.

Explora en Patagonia $$$
Parque Nacional Torres del Paine
Mailing address:
Ave. Américo Vespucia Sur 80
Piso 5
Santiago
☎ (02) 206 6060 or (02) 208 0664
Fax: (02) 228 4555
email: explora@entelchile.net
website: www.interknowledge.com/chile/
explora
A sister hotel to the Explora en Atacama
(see page 280), this eco-lodge lies on Lago
Pehoé. The rates are high, but include
everything: deluxe accommodation in one of
30 rooms, all transfers, four meals per day,
and daily excursions into the park with
guides and equipment. A gym, a restaurant
and bar, a games room, and a laundry.

Fantástico Sur $
Near Hostería Las Torres
Parque Nacional Torres del Paine
☎ (061) 226054 **Fax:** (061) 222641
email: lastorres@chileaustral.com
A well-run *refugio* with bunk beds,
showers, and a communal dining room. It's
best to book ahead to ensure a bed. There's
also an attractive campsite with a view of
the tops of the Torres. Sleeping bags, tents,
mats, and a stove can be rented.

"Maria" Casa de Familie $
Chorrillos 771
Puerto Natales
☎ (061) 413033
Bed-and-breakfast accommodation with hot
showers, bag storage, a kitchen, and a dining room. Excursions to Torres del Paine
and Glaciar Perito Moreno can be arranged.

FOOD AND DRINK
Amerindian Concept
See Operators on previous page.
A superb, bohemian restaurant with views over the water, distant mountains, and the odd sailing boat. The food is vegetarian and . there are herbal teas and coffees, plus beer and wine. The popular evening buffe is followed by a slide show about the park.

La Tranquera
Bulnes 579
Puerto Natales
☎ (061) 411039
Puerto Natales' position on the sea has led to the establishment of a cluster of fish restaurants, including this one. Salmon is a speciality, and stuffed mussels make an appetizing starter.

RAFTING AND HIGH-ALTITUDE HIKING IN MENDOZA
PAGES 216–223

OPERATORS
Adrian (Roger Rabbit) Cangiani
c/o Cafayate 3033
Bo Judicial
Godoy Cruz
Mendoza
☎ (0261) 4 272181
High-altitude hiking and climbing guide for Cerro Aconcagua, Cristo Redentor, Volcán Tupungato, and other peaks. Also contactable through Hostería International Campo Base (see Accommodation, below).

Ascensiones & Trekking
S. Castellani 370
Godoy Cruz
Mendoza
☎ (0261) 4 245865
email: ascensionesytrekking@arnet.com.ar
Trekking, paragliding, photography safaris, overlanding, and fishing trips in the Malargüe district of southern Mendoza. The price for the fishing tour depends on the number of days and people—e.g., per day for 5 people is around $140.

Aymára Turismo y Aventura
9 de Julio 983
Ciudad
Mendoza
☎/**Fax:** (0261) 4 200607, (0261) 4 205304, or (0261) 4 202064
email: aymara@satlink.com

Organizes adventure activities, such as rafting (from $30), mountain trekking (from $70), hiking, mountain biking (from $35), horse riding (from $70), paragliding (from $70), visits to wineries, and bus excursions to Alta Montaña and around Mendoza.

Betancourt Rafting
Ruta Panamericana y Río Cuevas
Bo Trapiche
Godoy Cruz
Mendoza
☎ (0261) 4 390229 or (0261) 4 391949
Rafting on the Río Mendoza. For beginners, trafting along a 15-km (9-mile) stretch, including Class I–III rapids (from $30). For experienced rafters, there is an intermediate tour along a 20-km (12-mile) stretch, with Class III–IV rapids (from $40), plus an action and technical rafting day along 35km (22 miles), with Class III–IV rapids (from $70). Equipment and transport are included. There are also 2- and 3-day excursions. Betancourt also organize mountain biking, trekking , and horse riding.

EcoAventuras
Inti Wayra Camping
Ruta Prov. No. 173, about 25km (15 miles) from San Rafael
☎/**Fax:** (02627) 4 20216 or cellular phone (0666) 81470
email: salinasp@formared.com.ar
Caving, rafting, rappelling, trekking, photo safaris, mountain biking, paragliding, and four-wheel-drive overlanding.

Escuela Are-Auca
Mendoza
☎ (0261) 4 440996 or cellular phone (0660) 63884
Fax: (0261) 4 227976
email: areauca@lanet.losandes.com.ar
Offers short and multi-day tuition in paragliding and hang-gliding in the Andes region (from $70 per session). Also hang-gliding tuition and courses. Maximum of eight per group. All equipment is provided.

Maxim Tours
50 Cutler St.
Morristown
NJ 07960
U.S.A.
☎ 973/984-9068 or toll-free 1-800/655-0222
Fax: 973/984-5383
email: maximtours@earthlink.net
website: www.maximtours.com
Arranges skiing tours in Mendoza, *estancia* stays,and cross-Andes boat trips. Also tours to Tierra del Fuego, Patagonia, Torres del Paine, and Península Valdés.

SKI OPERATORS
Ineltur
9 de Julio 936
Mendoza
☎ (0261) 4 297256 or (0261) 4 297257
Buenos Aires office:
Paraguay 93
Buenos Aires
☎ (011) 4 326 1351 **Fax:** (011) 4 393 2568
email: ventas@badino.com

Los Penitentes
Paso de Los Andes 1615
2o Piso "C" Godoy Cruz
Mendoza
☎ (0261) 4 271641 or (0261) 4 285922
Tickets for ski-lifts cost about $10 per day.

Scandinavian
Ave. San Martín 69
Mendoza
☎ (0261) 4 241920
Hires out ski equipment.

INFORMATION
Centro de Información y Asistencia al Turismo
Garibaldi, off Ave. San Martín
Mendoza
☎ (0261) 4 245353
Open 9am–9pm.

Subsecretaría de Turismo
San Martín 1143
Mendoza
☎ (0261) 4 202800 **Fax:** (0261) 4 202243
Ask for the "Mendoza Aventura" leaflet, which lists Mendoza's adventure-tourism agencies.

ACCOMMODATION
Hostería International Aconcagua $
Las Cueva; book through Hostería Campo Base (see below).Housed in an old building ,but its position on the main road from Mendoza to Santiago, Chile, is good for hiking to Cristo Redentor and for visiting the Parque Provincial Aconcagua.

Hostería International Campo Base $
Mitre 946
Ciudad
Mendoza
☎ cellular phone (0666) 96036
Seconds away from Plaza Independencia, with its nightly fountain display and craft stalls. Also close to the pavement cafés and restaurants along Sarmiento (see Food and Drink, below). Offers 35 beds, a kitchen, hot showers, email, laundry, and occasional

barbecues in the outdoor garden area. A young atmosphere, with great cooking by the host Silvia, who also possesses a good knowledge of Mendoza. From here it is possible to organize many activities.

Hostería International Puesta del Sol Hostel $
Dean Funes 998
San Rafael
Mendoza
☎ (02627) 4 34881 **Fax:** (02627) 4 30187
email: puestaso@hostels.org.ar
Meals and transport available. Can also organize activities.Rooms are basic but comfortable.

Hotel Laerte $
Leonidas Aguirre 198
Mendoza
☎ (0261) 4 230875
Just around the corner from busy Avenue Las Heras, where you can book excursions, buy souvenirs, and eat out. Rooms have bathroom, T.V., and ceiling fan.

FOOD AND DRINK
Pizza, pasta, and *parrillas* (barbecued meats), together with early morning breakfasts, are available from the bars that line Sarmiento, a bustling pedestrianized street in downtown Mendoza. Street cafés and bars are packed after 9pm.

La Marchigiana
Patricias Mendocinas 1550
Mendoza
☎ (0261) 4 200212 or (0261) 4 230751
A spacious restaurant that gets very busy after 9:30pm. Serves a wide choice of pastas, with different fillings and sauces.

Perín Heladerias
Sarmiento y Belgran
Mendoza
For totally delicious ice-creams, served in either buckets or cones, which can be taken home or eaten outside.

IN THE FOOTSTEPS OF DINOSAURS PAGES 224-231

OPERATORS
Aquatours—Aventur
Muelle Piedra Buena
Puerto Madryn
☎ (02965) 4 51954
Organizes the 2-hour overland Safari

Paleontólogica excursion to Punta Loma, near Península Valdés, in the province of Chubut, to observe sedimentary formations and marine fossils (from $20 per person).

G.A.P. Adventures
See page 282.

Hill Station/Los Pozos
Río Gallegos
☎/Fax: (02966) 4 23897 or (02966) 4 23970, or mobile ☎ (068) 221783 (it is best to fax as this a working *estancia*)
The Hallidays welcome visitors for lunch, dinner, a look around the farm or museum, or for overnight stays and horse riding along fossil trails. For experienced riders, 3-day trails are available (from $140 per day, including four meals, plus accommodation at the farm or in tents).

Journeys International
See page 265.
Tours to Patagonia and other destinations.

Latin America Travel
Guardian House
Borough Rd.
Godalming
Surrey GU7 2AE
U.K.
☎ (01483) 860088 **Fax:** (01483) 860180
The 15-day Argentina Explorer tour covers the whole country from north (Iguazú Falls), through the heart of Patagonia and its glaciers, to the south at Tierra del Fuego. Personalized itineraries also arranged.

Parque Provincial Ischigualasto
☎ (02324) 4 20511
Open all year 8:30am–5pm, but during the winter heavy rain fills the rivers and makes some routes impassable, so there are no tours. No one is allowed to tour the park alone; you must be accompanied by the resident guide..

Turismo Vittorio
Sarmiento 189 Sur
San Juan
☎ (0264) 4 212823 or (0264) 4 221732, or ask for Rodrigo Rodriguez on (0264) 4 228770
Arranges day excursions to Parque Provincial Ischigualasto. A full day (6am–8pm) costs about $55 per person, plus $5 park entrance fee. The minimum group is three; if there are fewer, you may have to makeup the difference. Overnight excursions, staying at Hostería Valle Fértil (see Accommodation, below)must be booked in advance

MUSEUMS
Museo Argentino de Ciencias Naturales "Bernardino Rivadavia"
Ave. Angel Gallardo 470
Capital Federal
Buenos Aires
☎ (011) 4 982 0306 or (011) 4 982 5243
A fine collection of fossils and bones; giant reptile displays. Closed national holidays.

Museo de Ciencias Naturales
Paseo del Bosque
La Plata
Buenos Aires
☎ (0221) 4 257744
website: www.museosargentinos.org.ar
Mummified bodies, dinosaurs, mammals, minerals, notable fossils, and an excellent selection of books (in Spanish) about palaeontology and finds from around Argentina. Guided tours at noon and 2pm.

Museo de Ciencas Naturales de la Universidad Nacional del Comahue
Buenos Aires 1400
Ciudad de Neuquén Biblioteca
Neuquén
☎ (0299) 4 490393
A palaeontology collection, plus minerals and archaeology exhibits.

Museo Paleontologico Egidio Feruglio
Ave. 9 de Julio 655
Trelew
☎ (02965) 4 35464 or (02965) 4 20012
website: www.webs.satlink.com/usuarios/m/muspal
Dinosaurs, marine fauna, site visits, and a chance to see craftsmen making replica dinosaur bones.

INFORMATION
Centros de Información Turística
Güemes y San Martin
Caleta Olivia
☎ (0297) 4 851101 or (0297) 4 851071
Provides information on El Bosque Petrificado.

Dirección Municipal de Turismo
Ave. Perón 715
La Rioja
☎ (03822) 4 28834 or (03822) 4 28839
Provides information on Talampaya.

Ente Provincial de Turismo
Sarmiento 24 Sur
San Juan

☎ (0264) 4 210004 or (0264) 4 222431
Fax: (0264) 4 225778
email: enprotur@ischigualasto.com
website: www.ischigualasto.com
Provides information on Parque Provincial
Ischigualasto.

ACCOMMODATION

Reasonably priced hotels in Buenos Aires
can be found along Ave. de Mayo, in the centre of a bustling area. Expect to pay $20–40
per person per night, which sometimes
includes breakfast.

Hostería Valle Fértil $–$$

Rivadavia s/n
San Augustín del Valle Fértil
San Juan
☎ (0264) 4 620015, (0264) 4 620016, or
(0264) 4 620017
Well-decorated rooms with private bathroom, T.V., and views of the surrounding
desert valley. Tasty food.

Residencial Hispano Argentino $

Estados Unidos 381
San Juan
☎ (0264) 4 225520
Some rooms have private shower, otherwise
it's a shared bathroom. No breakfast. Close
to the main bus terminal.

FOOD AND DRINK
Hostería Valle Fértil

See Operators, above.
An ideal stop for breakfast on the way to
Parque Provincial Ischigualasto.

La Nonna María

Ave. San Martín y Perito Moreno
San Juan
☎ (0264) 4 262277
A bit of a walk out of town, but the pasta is
recommended.

FISHING, CYCLING AND HORSE RIDING IN PATAGONIA
PAGES 232-239

OPERATORS
Airwaves World of Discovery

10 Bective Place
London SW15 2PZ
U.K.
☎ (020) 8875 1199
Fax: (020) 8871 4668
website: www.vjv.co.uk/airwaves

Offers a 13-day tour of southern Argentina,
including Península Valdés, observing
whales and other wildlife before flying to
Tierra del Fuego for catamaran trips on the
Beagle Channel. Also tours to Patagonia and
the Moreno Glacier.

In the Saddle

Laurel Cottage
Ramsdell
Tadley
Hampshire RG26 5SH
U.K.
☎ (01256) 851665 **Fax:** (01256) 851667
email: rides@inthesaddle.cix.co.uk
website: www.cix.co.uk~inthesaddle
Riding holidays lasting up to 13 nights,
based on a working *estancia*, or pack trips
into the wilderness of the Lanín National
Park and Lake District.

Jorge A. Bisso

C.C.10 (8370)
San Martín de Los Andes
☎ (02972) 4 21453
Jorge is a fly-fishing guide available for hire
by the day or on longer trips. Fees depend
on the number of people (up to a maximum
of three). Take your own equipment. He also
does spinning fishing. Fishing permits (the
season runs from the second Sat in Nov to
Easter) are available from fishing stores in
both Junín de Los Andes and San Martín de
Los Andes, or from national park offices.

Latin America Travel

See page 286.

Lihui Expediciones Paraguay

880 Floor 7
Room 52
Buenos Aires
☎ (011) 4 315 0906
Fax: (011) 4 311 0238
Organizes tours to Península Valdés,
Patagonia, and other destinations.

Patagonia Travel Adventures

P.O. Box 22
Ben Lomond
CA 95005
U.S.A.
☎/**Fax:** 831/336-0167
email: patadur@aol.com
Organizes tours to Península Valdés, Los
Glaciares, Parque Nacional Nahuel Huapi,
and Tierra del Fuego. The company's
owners were born in Patagonia.

Sendero Sur Patagonia Adventures

Perú 359

Office 608
Buenos Aires
☎/Fax: (011) 4 244 0473
email: sderosur@ssdnet.com.ar
Organizes cycling tours with lodgings to suit time and budget in both Lanín and Nahuel Huapi parks, including excursions to Volcán Lanín, Mount Tronador, and Ventisquero Negro. Cycle excursions, using top-quality mountain bikes, can be combined with hiking and rafting, and are accompanied by a shuttle service. Run by the friendly, English-speaking Jorge Barcelo, who has a real enthusiasm for the area. Fishing and horseback riding, plus cross-overs into Chile, can also be integrated.

INFORMATION
Dirección Municipal de Turismo
Padre Milanesio 590
Junín de Los Andes
☎/Fax: (02972) 4 91160
Provides information on climbing Volcán Lanín, fishing, walking, and horse riding in Parque Nacional Lanín.

Secretaría Municipal de Turismo
Centro Civico
San Carlos de Bariloche
☎ (02944) 4 23022 or (02944) 4 23122
Fax: (02944) 4 26784
Provides information on activities in Parque Nacional Nahuel Huapi.

Secretaría Municipal de Turismo
Juan M. de Rosas y San Martín
San Martín de Los Andes
☎ (02972) 4 25500, (02972) 4 27347, or (02972) 4 27695
email: munitur@smandes.datacop8.com.ar
website: www.smandes.gov.ar

CAR HIRE
ICI Rent a Car
Villegas 590
San Martín de Los Andes
☎/Fax: (02972) 4 27800
From $90 per day.

ACCOMMODATION
La Casa de Eugenia $$
Coronel Díaz 1186
San Martín de Los Andes
☎ (02972) 4 27206
Typical of the town's high-standard *hosterías*, and also doubles as a tea-house, serving pastries and afternoon teas. You can organize horse riding, rafting, kayaking, mountain biking, trekking, and fishing from here.

Hostería y Cabanas del Chapelco $$
Alte. Brown y Costanera
8370 San Martín de Los Andes
☎ (02972) 4 27610
Fax: (02972) 4 27097
This *hostería* fronts Lago Lacar, and is the first hotel you see when you arrive in San Martín from one of the Bariloche roads. The owners can organize horse riding, trekking, rafting, four-wheel-drive safaris, photography safaris, fishing, and skiing.

Hostería "Los Lagos" $
Ruta de Los Lagos
Villa La Angostura
☎ cellular phone (0683) 06274
Set on the banks of Lago Correntoso, this Mapuche-family-run overnight stay is on the Seven Lakes Road, 32km (20 miles) from Villa La Angostura. If you catch a trout the owners will cook it for your dinner. Rates include breakfast.

Hostería Pampa Linda $
Parque Nacional Nahuel Huapi, near San Carlos de Bariloche
☎ Radio Llamada (02944) 4 23757 or (02944) 4 2218, or **☎/Fax** (02944) 4 27049
A wooden chateau-style hotel within sight of Mount Tronador—an excellent location, that gives you the feeling of beingout in the wilds. Bedrooms (some overlooking the mountain and a spectacular morning sunrise) are well decorated, warm, and have ensuite bathroom. Organizes horse-riding tours up to Glaciar Castaño Overo, towards the base of Mount Tronador.

Hostería Posta del Caminante $
Salta 514
San Carlos de Bariloche
☎ (02944) 4 23626
An exceptionally helpful and friendly couple runs this small but welcoming place, which has a dining room with wonderful views over the lake. Rooms have ensuite bathroom.

FOOD AND DRINK
Bianchi
Villa La Angostura (on the Seven Lakes Rd.)
Recommended for delicious *tortillas* (chunky pancakes, fried with eggs, onions, potato cubes, and meat if you wish), served with salad and local wine.

Café Peumayen and Delicatessen
San Martín de Los Andes
For half a dozen facturas, you can buy pastries filled with lemon cream, chocolate, syrup, or fruit, together with *medialunas*

(filled mini-croissants or with a transparent sugar coating), all fresh baked.

Deli
Overlooking Lago Lácar, San Martín de Los Andes
For barbecued chicken, sandwiches, and bottles of local Quilmes beer or the even better Isenbeck beer, brewed in Germany.

Mi Viejo Pepe
San Martín de Los Andes
A multitude of pasta varieties is served, which you match with a sauce chosen from another long list. Recommended are the regional specialities of trout, deer, wild boar, and ham.

S.M.A. Charlotte Ice Cream Parlour
San Martín de Los Andes
Try the white chocolate flavour, which contains solid chunks of creamy chocolate.

WATCHING THE WILDLIFE PAGES 240–247

OPERATORS
Buceo
Blvd. Brown 893
Local 1 y 2
Puerto Madryn
☎ (02965) 4 52699
Arranges scuba-diving trips (for certified divers only) that include a 2-hour boat excursion and diving, with equipment provided. Trips are usually in the morning to avoid the wind, and travel to one of two underwater parks: one is artificial, with sunken cars and ships; the other is a natural reef, with good opportunities for sighting fish, seals, and colourful marine plants. It is best to book a day in advance.

City Service Travel Agency
Florida 890, 4th Floor
1005 Buenos Aires
☎ (011) 4 312 8416
Fax: (011) 4 313 9407
email: estravel@starnet.net.ar
Organizes internal travel to Península Valdés, Nacional Parque de Los Glaciares, and other Argentine destinations.

Hydro Sport
Balneario Rayentray
Blvd. Brown 6ta Rotonda
Puerto Madryn
☎ (02965) 4 95065 or (02965) 4 95055
Fax: (02965) 4 95016

Whale-watching and other excursions; an English-speaking guide is available. Tours can also be booked in the Bar El Salmon in Puerto Pirámide.

South American Experience
47 Causton St.
Pimlico
London SW1P 4AT
U.K.
☎ (020) 7976 5511
Fax: (020) 7976 6908
email: sax@mcmail.com
Tours take in Península Valdés, and can feature trekking, skiing at Bariloche, trips to the Moreno Glacier, and horse riding in the Andes from an *estancia*.

Sur Turismo
Ave. Roca 109
Puerto Madryn
☎ (02965) 4 50966
Fax: (02965) 4 55714
Full-day tours to Península Valdés, plus whale-watching, Punta Tombo, Trelew, and Gaiman Welsh town. Offers an excellent service, a commentary on the way to the sites, and English-speaking guides or translators. Let them know beforehand if you don't speak Spanish.

Union-Castle Travel
86–7 Campden St.
Kensington
London W8 7EN
U.K.
☎ (020) 7229 1411
Fax: (020) 7229 1511
email: u-ct@u-ct.co.uk
Tailor-made itineraries and special-interest tours, including cattle and horse breeding, freshwater and deep-sea fishing. Tours to Península Valdés and glaciers, skiing in the Lake District, horse riding from an *estancia*.

Wildland Adventures
3516 N.E. 115 St.
Seattle
WA 98155
U.S.A.
☎ 206/365-0686
Fax: 206/363-6615
email: kurt@wildland.com
website: www.wildland.com
Tours to Península Valdés, Patagonia, Los Glaciares, and Torres del Paine.

CAR HIRE
Hiring a car is economical if there are four or five in your group, and is more convenient if you want to stay longer at the wildlife sites to avoid the crowds or photo-

graph at sunrise or sunset. Both Ave. Julio
A. Roca and Blvd. Brown in Puerto Madryn
have many hire companies. Prices are per
day for a minimum of 250km (155 miles).

Puerto Madryn Turismo
Ave. Julio A. Roca 624
Puerto Madryn
☎ (02965) 4 52355 **Fax:** (02965) 4 52371
email: pmyturis@satlink.com
Free kilometres, and a 10 percent discount
if you pay in cash.

INFORMATION
Sectur
Ave. Julio A. Roca 223
Puerto Madryn
☎/**Fax:** (02965) 4 73029
email: sectur@madryn.gov.ar
website: www.madryn.gov.ar
Buenos Aires office:
Casa de la Provincia del Chubut
Sarmiento 1172
Buenos Aires
☎ (011) 4 312 2340
The Puerto Madryn office is open 7am–9pm
in summer, and shorter hours at other times.

A map of Península Valdés, featuring lodg-
ing, shelter, camping, and wildlife sites, is
available from shops in Puerto Madryn and
Trelew; alternatively, buy one direct from
the publisher:

Zaiger & Urraty Publications
See page 283.

ACCOMMODATION
Camping $
There are two campsites along Blvd. Brown:
Municipal Atlántico Sud, ☎ (02965) 4
55640; and Automóvil Club Argentino, ☎
(02965) 4 52952. Both charge $3 per person.
Camping is also available at Puerto Pirámide
and Punta Loma.

Hostelling International $
25 de Mayo 1136
Puerto Madryn
☎/**Fax:** (02965) 4 74426
email: madrynhi@hostels.org.ar
A typical Argentine hostel, with 25 beds.
Clean and attractive. Services, include
tours, trekking, barbecues, bicycles, airport
shuttle, and laundry.

Hotel Bahía Nueva $$–$$$
Ave. Julio A. Roca 67
Puerto Madryn
☎/**Fax:** (02965) 4 51677, (02965) 4 50045,
or (02965) 4 50145
Mid- to upper-range hotel; the rates include

a splendid breakfast. The lounge faces the
sea and has a superb collection of marine
reference books (all in Spanish), as well as
National Geographic wildlife videos.

Paradise Pub Hostería $
Ave. J.A. Roca s/n
Puerto Pirámide
☎ (02965) 4 95030
Fax: (02965) 4 95003
Handy for whale-watching trips and walks
along the beaches of Puerto Pirámide.
Hospitable, warm, and traditional, and with
a restaurant that serves excellent food (see
Food and Drink, below).

Residencial Santa Rita $
G. Maíz 370
Puerto Madryn
☎/**Fax:** (02965) 4 71050
email: augustoc@cpsarg.com
A 10-minute walk from the seafront. Clean,
tidy, and traveller friendly accommodation,
with kitchen, T.V., local information, and
breakfast.

FOOD AND DRINK
Puerto Madryn has a number of *parrilla*
restaurants, where beef, chicken, and lamb
are barbecued and served with all manner of
sauces, vegetables, and salads. There's also
a string of cafés on the seafront, where you
can sit on terraces facing the waves and
order crunchy mixed *ensaladas* served
with a basket of bread, oil, and vinegar.

Estela
R.S. Peqa 27
Puerto Madryn
Parrilla restaurant.

Halloween
Ave. Roca 385
Puerto Madryn
Recommended for its pizzas.

Hotel Bahía Nueva Bar
Ave. Julio A. Roca 67
Puerto Madryn
Try a *submarino*, a mug of steamed milk
served with chocolate bars and a long
spoon—particularly warming after a whale-
watching trip.

Paradise Pub Restaurant
Paradise Pub Hostería, Puerto Pirámide
(see Accommodation, above)
Three-course meals or snacks are available.
Specializes in locally caught seafood,
including white salmon. Also pastas, beef,
soups, and salads, as well as the popular
Quilmes beer.

Patio de Asado
Mitre 868, Puerto Madryn
Parrilla restaurant.

ADVENTURES ON ICE
PAGES 248–256

OPERATORS
Most operators in El Calafate line the main
tourist thoroughfare, Avenida del Liberator
General San Martin, and its side streets, and
offer excursions to the glaciers, horse riding, trekking, and trips to El Chaltén and the
Fitzroy mountain range.

Cabalgata en Patagonia
Julia A. Roca 2063
El Calafate
☎ (02902) 4 91203
email: cabalgataenpatagonia@
cotecal.com.ar
Gustavo Holzmann runs 2-hour horseback
rides, all-day rides that include lunch, and
5-day rides into the mountains, with meals
and tents (book well in advance). Beginners
welcome.

Cal-Tur
Terminal de Omnibus
El Calafate
☎/**Fax:** (02902) 4 91842
email: caltur@cotecal.com.ar
website: www.cotecal.com.ar/caltur
Runs a regular bus service from El Calafate
bus station to Fitz Roy Inn at El Chaltén, a
distance of 220km (137 miles), departing
7am and returning at 4:30pm. It is best to
book in advance as the journey is popular.
Cal-Tur Promotion is a handy deal that
includes a return ticket plus dinner and
breakfast for 1–3 nights.

Ecology & Adventure Argentina
9 de Julio 41
El Calafate
☎ (02902) 4 91587
Fax: (02902) 4 91796
Offers tours to both Glaciar Perito Moreno
and Glaciar Upsala. Also trekking, wildlife
and special-interest tours, horse riding, and
visits to an *estancia*.

El Galpón/Alice Estancia Tours
For reservations:
Ave. del Libertador 1015
El Calafate
☎/**Fax:** (02902) 4 91793
email: info@elgalpon.com.ar
website: www.elgalpon.com.ar
Evening visits include a welcome tea, a

sheep-gathering demonstration, sheep
shearings, a walk through the bird lagoon,
and an optional traditional lamb dinner.
There are all-day horse-riding excursions to
Cerro Frías for views of the Torres del Paine
in Chile and the Fitzroy range.

Fitzroy Expeditions
El Chaltén 9301
☎/**Fax:** (02962) 493017
Organizes the "Trekking Glaciar" trek in the
Fitzroy mountain range every day from
Cerro Torre Base Camp, an excursion of 8
hours, 5 of which are spent on the glacier.
Only for those aged over 15 in good physical
condition. The guide demonstrates basic
ice-climbing techniques before you set off.

Interlagos Turismo
Ave. del Libertador 1175
El Calafate
☎ (02902) 4 91179 **Fax:** (02902) 4 91241
email: interlagos@cotecal.com.ar
Organizes mini-treks on Glaciar Perito
Moreno and tours to Perito Moreno with an
English-speaking guide, plus Glaciar Upsala
tours. In addition, there are 2-hour horseback rides to Bahía Rondoda and all-day
rides to the Walichu Caves. Late-afternoon
visits to El Gapón/Alice Estancia (see
above) involve touring the sheep farm, with
live shearing and an *asado* barbecue.

Lost World Adventures
See page 258.
U.S.-based operator that arranges tours to
Los Glaciares, as well as to Patagonia, Tierra
del Fuego, Torres del Paine, and other
South American destinations.

INFORMATION
National Parks Offices
Ave. del Libertador 1302
El Calafate
Also at:
Entrance to El Chaltén
Maps, plus local information and details of
camping and accommodation.

Subsecretaria de Turismo
Julio A. Roca 1551
Río Gallegos
☎/**Fax:** (02966) 4 22702
Has information for Santa Cruz province.

Terminal de Omnibus
Julio A. Roca 1004
El Calafate
☎/**Fax:** (02902) 4 91090
email: secturelcalafate@cotecal.com.ar
Provides information on bus routes.

ACCOMMODATION

Aside from hotels and hostels, there are several campsites (the tourist information office has a list of 18) both in and around the Parque Nacional Los Glaciares. Some are in prime locations—for instance, Camping Bahía Escondida, just 7km (4 miles) from Perito Moreno Glaciar, and Camping Rio Mitre, in a beautiful setting amidst forest and by the lake shore.

Albergue & Hostal del Glaciar $

Calle Los Pioneros s/n
El Calafate
☎/Fax: (02902) 4 91243
email: alberguedelglaciar@cotecal.com.ar
website: www.glaciar.com
An official youth hostel, with cooking facilities and a separate restaurant, laundry, and bag storage. Just 5 minutes' walk from Ave. Libertador. Free shuttle service from the bus station. Excursions to the glaciers and El Chaltén/Fitzroy can be organized.

Bahía Redonda Hotel $$–$$$

Calle 15 No. 148
El Calafate
☎ (02902) 4 91743
Fax: (02902) 4 91314
email: hotelbahiaredonda@cotecal.com.ar
Upper-range hotel, although the price includes breakfast. A 5-minute walk from the main thoroughfare of banks, shops, restaurants, and tour operators. The dining room and some bedrooms overlook Lago Argentina. Facilities include room service, laundry, fax, and T.V.

Camping Lago Roca $

C.C. 49
El Calafate
☎ (02902) 4 99500
Facilities include showers, radio-telephone, restaurant, provisions, trekking, information, and mountain-bike hire.

El Galpón/Alice Estancia $$$

See Operators, above.
An upper-range hotel, where trekking, horse riding, and glacier trips can be organized. Traditional lamb dinners are also provided.

Fitz Roy Inn $–$$

Ave. San Martín
El Chaltén
☎ (02962) 4 93062
Set at the foot of the traditional trekking trails. In the upper price range for a private room with breakfast, and in the budget range for a shared room. The dining room is open all day for snacks and drinks (see Food and Drink, below).

FOOD AND DRINK

Albergue & Hostal del Glaciar Restaurant

See Accommodation, above.
Serves daily three-course set meals, plus à la carte meat, fish, and vegetarian dishes, the latter including a delectable vegetable stir-fry served with seaweed. Also wine, coffees, and full breakfasts.

La Cocina

Ave. del Libertador 1245
El Calafate
☎ (02902) 4 91758
A family-run restaurant specializing in pastas, pizzas, and salads, served in cosy, candlelit surroundings. Good house wine.

Fitz Roy Inn

See Accommodation, above.
The dining room of this inn is open all day for snacks and drinks, including thick *submarino* (hot chocolate), and toasted cheese, ham, and tomato sandwiches. A three-course evening dinner with wine is also available.

Restaurante del Club Británico

Ave. Roca 935
Río Gallegos
☎ (02966) 4 27320
A former gentleman's club (it was founded in 1911, and has an impressive visitors' book), which today has 300 Anglo-Argentine and Spanish members. It is open to tourists who book in advance. Oak-panelled walls, chintz sofas, and a tartan ceiling over the bar area remind British expats of home. Lunch and dinner are excellent three-course meals chosen from a menu that includes *purille à la Gran Britain* (tenderloin of beef) and *roballa grille* (a succulent local white fish). The bar has several speciality drinks, including Vaina Chilena (port wine, the white of an egg, and mixer), plus a top range of wines from Argentina's great wine-producing province of Mendoza.

INTRODUCTION

This book has, we hope, whetted your appetite for adventure, and the Activities A–Z is intended to supply a useful, if not comprehensive, list of as many adventurous activities as the authors could discover within an area.

The activities vary from volunteer work, cultural, and language opportunities to really intrepid sports. Most of the experiences call for interaction with local people and many are directly connected to ecotourism—where strict controls are applied to guarantee the benefits to the environment and to minimize the damage caused by the impact of increasing numbers of visitors to sensitive areas.

We have supplied the names and addresses of organizations that can help the traveller to achieve these challenging pastimes, but they have not been inspected or vetted by us in any way. Even where the authors have used a company to organize their own trip, this is no guarantee that any company is still run by the same people or to the same degree of efficiency.

Bear in mind that many of the regions covered can be volatile both climatically and politically. Weigh up all the factors first, get a feel for your chosen destination, and let us guide you towards the outfits that can help.

BIRD-WATCHING

South America is a bird-watchers' paradise, and supports one of the largest concentrations of avian species on Earth. The region's variety of ecosystems, including rain forest and rare tropical cloud forest, increases the likelihood of sightings of a large number of birds. If you hire a guide, try to make sure he or she is an ornithologist; general guides may show a frustrating lack of knowledge. Be aware also that facilities vary greatly, and that hides are rare. It is advisable to take binoculars (7x magnification is adequate) and a camera with a telephoto lens.

BirdLife International
Wellbrook Court
Girton Rd.
Cambridge CB3 ONA
U.K.
☎ (01223) 277318 **Fax:** (01223) 277200
email: birdlife@birdlife.org.uk
Birdlife International is a global partnership of conservation organizations and is the leading authority on the status of the world's birds. It can provide details of birding associations worldwide.

PARQUE NACIONAL HENRI PITTIER, VENEZUELA
Over 1,200 species of birds have been recorded in Venezuela, more than in the whole of Europe and North America combined. The rare cloud forest of the 107,800-ha (266,400-acre) Parque Nacional Henri Pittier on the north coast supports around half of this number alone. It includes Paso Portachuelo, which is a favourite bird-watching spot throughout the year.

Escuela de Agronomía (School of Agronomy)
Universidad Central de Venezuela
El Limón
Maracay
Venezuela
☎ (043) 450153
The School of Agronomy runs the biological station on the reserve. Professor Alberto Fernandez Badillo can arrange permits and basic accommodation.

MAQUIPUCUNA BIOLOGICAL RESERVE, ECUADOR
Ecuador is recognized worldwide for its biodiversity, while ornithologists rate it for its 1,500 species of birdlife. The 5,700-ha (14,000-acre) Maquipucuna Biological Reserve, near Quito, supports over 300 species. The reserve (entry fee) has a number of trails; guides are available and it is possible to stay overnight.

Fundación Maquipucuna
Baquerizo 238 y Tamayo
Quito, Casilla 17-12-167
Ecuador
☎ (02) 507 200 **Fax:** (02) 507 201
email: root@maqui.ecx.ec
This local foundation can arrange permits, guides, and accommodation on the reserve, and can provide advice.

MANU BIOSPHERE RESERVE, PERU
The 2,233,694-ha (5,519,681-acre) Manu Biosphere Reserve is one of the largest

conservation areas in the world. Its 850 species of birds are found within the drainage area of the Río Manu, where giant otters, monkeys, and ocelots can also be seen. One part of the reserve is accessible only to biologists, and another only with a guide and pre-arranged permit; a third part is open to all visitors, and contains accommodation lodges.

Manu Expeditions
Ave. Pardo 895
Cusco
Peru
☎ (01) 226671 **Fax:** (01) 236706
email: adventure@manuexpeditions.com
website: www.manuexpeditions.com
This tour company is owned by an ornithologist, and specializes in bird-watching trips in the area. It has English-speaking guides.

Chaco, Paraguay
The vast area (24 million ha, or 59 million acres) of marsh and farmland known as the Chaco is home to a huge number of birds and to very few people. A single paved road cuts through the region where isolated Mennonite and Indian populations live. There is very little accommodation, although camping is permitted.

Intertours/Natur
Ave. Perú 436 y España
Asunción
Paraguay
☎ (21) 27804 **Fax:** (21) 211870
A small, efficient agency that runs tailor-made trips to the Chaco. It is one of the few outfits offering trips to this region.

BOAT TRIPS

The region's vast rivers and accessible coast make for an inspiring choice of sea and river trips, allowing you to enjoy spectacular scenery, photograph marine life, or observe local Indian farmers. You can take a trip down the Amazon, or sail between awesome glaciers. Boat trips on smaller rivers allow you to see more wildlife and scenery , but be prepared for basic, even cramped, conditions, and if you are going on a trip that will last several days, take supplementary food and water supplies. Insects are likely to be voracious, so insect repellent is essential, and possibly a mosquito net too.

Puerto Callao, Peru
Motorized canoes known as *peki-pekis* can be hired from Puerto Callao in the Amazon Basin by the hour, or for overnight trips to visit the beautiful Yarinachocha Lake and Indian villages (where local crafts can be bought); you are likely to see river dolphins.

Laser Viajes y Turismo
Jr. 7 de Junio 1043
Pucallpa
Peru
☎ (064) 571120 or ☎/**Fax:** (064) 573776
This company offers good boat trips and advice, with experienced guides.

Lake Titicaca, Peru
On Lake Titicaca—the world's highest navigable lake—you can visit the Uros people living on their famous floating islands made from tortora reeds, and even take a trip on a reed boat.

Río Amazon, Brazil
The mighty Amazon can be explored on a voyage that takes you from the jungle town of Manaus out to the Amazon delta, and then down the coast to Salvador and the lively city of Río de Janeiro. There are many opportunities for wildlife-watching and for exploring more inaccessible reaches. For details of operators that offer boat trips along the Amazon, see pages 269–270.

Worldwide Journeys and Expeditions
8 Comeragh Rd.
London W14 9HP
U.K.
☎ (020) 7381 8638 **Fax:** (020) 7381 0836
email: wwj@wjournex.demon.co.uk
A 2-week trip in boats that have limited passenger numbers and provide cabin accommodation. Offers other tours in small groups throughout South America.

Iguaçu Falls, Brazil/Argentina
The scope and beauty of the Iguaçu Falls can be appreciated at close quarters by taking one of the thrilling boat trips to within nerve-wracking distance of their thundering walls of water.
For details of operators that offer boat trips to the Iguaçu Falls, see pages 272.

The Pantanal, Brazil
The vast, watery landscape of the Pantanal is one of the world's richest nature reserves, and its rivers and *baias* are made for

boating. For the wildlife-watcher, the area offers some of the best boat trips any-where.For details of operators offering boat trips to the Panatal, see pages 273.

PATAGONIA, ARGENTINA/CHILE

This remote region has some fascinating geology, plus huge glaciers and high mountain peaks. It also features varied wildlife and many islands. Cruises are available from Oct to Mar.

Abercrombie and Kent

1520 Kensington Rd.
Oak Brook
IL 60523-2141
U.S.A.
☎ 630 854 2944 or toll-free 1-800/323-7308
email: pr@abercrombiekent.com
website: www.abercrombiekent.com
Organizes a 12-day trip, including a 3-day cruise through the Strait of Magellan from Buenos Aires. There are excursions to Torres del Paine and Bariloche in the Lake District. Other luxury tours include the Galápagos Islands and Machu Picchu.

PUERTO MONTT, CHILE

The 4-day voyage from Puerto Montt to the Puerto Natales in the south takes you through a glacier-filled landscape populated by whales, sea lions, and a variety of birds. The journey is dramatic, but it can be rough, with basic conditions. Book well in advance.

Navimag (Naviera Magallanes SA)

Terminal Transbordadores
Angelmó 2187
Puerto Montt
Chile
☎ (65) 253318 **Fax:** (65) 258540
One of the largest cruise companies in the country, with several sailings each month. It offers economy class or superior cabin class.

Passage to South America

Fovant Mews
12 Noyna Rd.
London SW17 7PH
U.K.
☎ (020) 8767 8989 **Fax:** (020) 8767 2026
email: psa@scottdunn.com
Aspecialist in holidays to South America since 1989. It offers a 6-day cruise from Puerto Montt along the coast to remote fish-ing communities, numerous islands, and San Rafael Lagoon. Other tours on offer include fishing, skiing, rafting, riding, and trekking in every country in South America.

TIERRA DEL FUEGO–ANTARCTIC PENINSULA, ARGENTINA

Most cruise ships depart for the Antarctic Peninsula from the port of Ushuaia on Tierra del Fuego between Oct and Mar. For the rest of the year, ice makes voyages impossible. Several landings a day are usually scheduled, but weather and sea conditions may affect itineraries. Huge icebergs, whales, seals, giant petrels, and king penguins are some of the sights.

Journey Latin America

See page 282.
Offers 11-day trips to the Antarctic Peninsula. Also arranges longer voyages that take in the Falkland Islands, Chilean fjords, and South Georgia.

CANOEING AND KAYAKING

Gliding serenely through deserted jungle or battling against rushing white water— canoeing allows you to enjoy isolated landscapes, possibile close encounters with wildlife, and has minimal impact on the envi-ronment. If you plan on going independently, you need to be experienced, and you must have at least two other people with you. You will need a buoyancy aid and warm, waterproof clothing for whitewater canoeing (only during the rainy seasons) you also require a helmet. The International River Grade is a global rating for river diffi-culty: categories range from I (gently flowing) to VI (the fastest white water).

International Canoe Federation

Dózsa György út 1-3
1143 Budapest
Hungary
☎ (01) 363 4832
Fax: (01) 221 4130
email: icf_hq_budapest@mail.datanet.hu
website: www. datanet.hu/icf_hq
An umbrella organization that provides information on national bodies worldwide, and advice on safety and destination.

RÍO MARONI, FRENCH GUYANE

Terre Rouge, 7km (4 miles) south of St.-Laurent du Maroni, is an Amerindian set-tlement where canoes can be hired for day trips up the Río Maroni. Apatou can be reached on an overnight trip.

Youkaliba Expeditions
3 Rue Simon
Terre Rouge
Guyana
☎ (34) 1645 or (31) 2398
This specialist company has a range of
canoeing packages between 1 and 10 days.

Río Futaleufú, Chile
Chile has some of the longest continuous
stretches of white water anywhere in the
world; the Río Futaleufú in the Lake District
has a very high concentration of Class V
rapids. Paddlers should be able to run 2km
(1 mile) without stopping.

Adrift
P.O. Box 310
Queenstown
New Zealand
☎ (03) 442 1615 **Fax:** (03) 442 1613
email: raft@adrift.co.nz
website: www.adrift.co.nz
Adrift UK:
Collingbourne House
140–2 Wandsworth High St.
London SW18 4JJ
U.K.
☎ (020) 8874 4969 **Fax:** (020) 8875 9236
email: raft@adrift.co.uk
This specialist canoeing and rafting
operator offers an 8-day trip from Santiago
to Río Futaleufú, with additional activities,
such as trekking and fishing. It can also
arrange departures to Chile from other destinations worldwide.

Chiloé, Chile
The beautiful, rural island of Chiloé offers
sea-kayaking opportunities among the many
tiny islands to the east, such as Isla
Butachauques and Isla Mechuque. Darwin
travelled the width of the island from
Chonchi to Cucao by canoe over 150 years
ago, describing the scenic journey in detail.

Paralelo 42
Latorre 558
Ancud
Chiloé, Chile
☎ (65) 622 458
This local agency offers a 2-day kayak trip to
the Río Chepu area on the north coast of
Chiloe, near Ancud. The river and its
tributaries are rich in birdlife.

Río Cañete, Argentina
Lunahuaná's Rio Cañete, 180km (112 miles)
south of Lima, offers Class IV–V waters from

Nov to Apr for kayaking and rafting, and
professional championships are held here
every February. At other times of year, only
boat trips are possible.

Apumayo Expediciones
Emilio Cavencia 160
Oficina 201
San Isidro
Lima
Peru
☎/**Fax:** (01) 442 3886
A range of canoeing and rafting trips in the
region, lasting from several hours to several
days, are available.

Patagonia, Chile
A tour trekking through Torres del Paine
National Park and sea-kayaking among the
fjords, waterfalls, and hot springs of the
Lake District is available from Nov to Mar.

Outer Edge Expeditions
45500 Pontiac Trail
Walled Lake
MI 48390-4036
U.S.A.
☎ 248/624-5140 or 1-800/322-5235
Fax: 248/624-6744
email: adventure@outer-edge.com
Arranges a 17-day trip to the region.
Also offers multi-activity trips, including
rafting, riding, and trekking in Chile,
Patagonia, and Peru. The company (in operation since 1988) caters for small groups
and gives a proportion of its profits to conservation and research.

CLIMBING

The Andes form one of the world's longest
mountain chains and contain some of the
highest peaks outside the Himalaya,
offering impressive climbing prospects,
from volcanoes to snow-covered cordillera.
Operators offering organized tours will
provide all the necessary equipment, but if
you are undertaking a trip independently
seek advice. Mules can be hired in some
places to carry your gear. You must consider
the climbing season when planning your
trip, also weather conditions as, like altitude
sickness, they can kill. Make sure you are
fully prepared for sudden weather changes,
and allow enough time to acclimatize.

International Mountaineering and Climbing Federation (UIAA)

Monbigoustrasse 61
Postfach
3000 Berne 23
Switzerland
☎ (31) 370 1828 **Fax:** (31) 370 1838
email: uiaa@compuserve.com
website: www.mountaineering.org
Provides an address list of all UIAA member associations in its website under the heading "National Federations;" contact these direct for information.

South American Explorers' Club

República de Portugal 146
Lima
Peru
☎ (01) 425 0142
email: explorer@samexplor.org
A membership organization providing maps, travellers' and climbing information.

CORDILLERA REAL, BOLIVIA

In the Cordillera Real, the intrepid climber will find the challenging summits of Huayni Potosí and Illampu, the infamous Mapiri Trail and, some fascinating remnants of the Inca's empire. For details of operators that arrange trekking and mountaineering trips in the region, see pages 275–278.

TUNGURAHUA, CHILE

Tungurahua, in Parque Nacional Sangay (entry fee), is a 5,016m (16,457ft) volcano, best climbed between Dec and Mar. You don't have to be experienced to make the 2-day ascent with crampons, but it is advisable to hire a guide. Check any equipment thoroughly and consult other travellers. Guides and equipment (rope, crampons, and an ice-axe are essential), plus mules, are available fromthe numerous travel agents in Baños—not all are reputable.

Expediciones Amazónicas

Oriente at Halflants
Baños
Ecuador
☎ 740506
Has good rental equipment and guides who are experienced in climbing.

HUAYNA POTOSÍ AND OLLOMANI, PERU

Climb the mountains of Huayna Potosí and Illimani in the High Andes on a trip including a cultural trek to the birthplace of the Inca Empire. Beginning in La Paz, highest capital in the world, and exploring high-altitude ice fields and corniced ridges.

Colorado Mountain School

Estes Park
P.O. Box 2062
CO 80517
U.S.A.
☎ 970/586-5758 **Fax:** 970/586-5798
email: cms-climb@sni.net
Here you'll find individual instruction and guided climbs, with flexible scheduling and small teams. Also ascents of Cotopaxi in Ecuador and Aconcagua in Argentina.

HUASCARÁN, PERU

Huascarán (6,768m, or 22,205 feet), in the spectacular Parque Nacional Huascarán (entry fee), is part of the Corderilla Blanca, Peru's climbing centre. The season runs from May to Sep. A full range of equipment, maps, and guides are available on Ave. Luzuriaga in Huaraz.All accredited operators and guides have an offical photo I.D.

Augusto Ortega

Jr. San Martín 1004
Huaraz
Peru
☎ (044) 724888
The only Peruvian to have climbed Everest, this reputable guide can be hired by the day.

Casa de Guías

Plaza Ginebra
Huaraz
Peru
☎ (044) 721811
This is a good place to meet climbing partners and to get advice. Maps and information are also available.

RÍO DE JANEIRO, BRAZIL

Río de Janeiro is a mecca for rock-climbing enthusiasts, with hundreds of climbs available within easy reach of the capital. Climbing is best in the cooler season from Apr to Oct. The famous Sugar Loaf is 400m (1,300 feet) high, and its summit can be reached in about 2 hours.

ECA

Ave. Erasmo Braga 217
Room 305
Rio de Janiero
Brazil
☎ (021) 242 6857 or (021) 571 0484
The company has an English-speaking owner and guides.

CERRO ACONCAGUA, ARGENTINA

The 6,962-m (22,841-foot) Cerro Aconcagua is the highest peak in the Western hemisphere, and it is surrounded by the wilderness of the Parque Provincial Aconcagua. The ascent is not technically difficult,but bad weather and the altitude affect many climbers, and so undertake the trip only if you are experienced. The best time to make the ascent is between Dec and Feb, and allow a fortnight to reach the summit (includes acclimatization). Below the snow line are base camps for those without the experience to climb further.

Exodus

9 Weir Rd.
London SW12 0LT
U.K.
☎ (0181) 675 5550 **Fax:** (0181) 673 0779
email: sales@exodustravels.co.uk
website: www.exodustravels.co.uk
Ireland contact:
Silk Road Travel
64 South William St.
Dublin 2
Ireland
☎ (01) 677 1029 **Fax:** (01) 677 1390
Arranges discovery holidays to take in Patagonia. A guided ascent of Aconcagua, the highest peak in the Americas, plus trekking in the Fitzroy and Paine mountain regions of Patagonia, biking adventures, and overland expeditions.

Parque Provincial Aconcagua

Reached by bus from Mendoza to Puente del Inca and Las Cuevas. A 3-day walking permit costs around $15, while 21 days' climbing costs around $80 (you must have a permit). The ranger station is open Nov 15–Mar 15 7:30am–9:30pm, but offers no search and rescue.Outside the climbing season, the park provides no service.

Servicios Especiales Mendoza

Annette Schenker
c/o Hotel Cervantes
Amigorena 65
Mendoza
Argentina
Fax: (0261) 4 244721 or (0261) 4 240131
Multi-lingual guides are available for climbing Aconcagua and other Andes peaks. Also arranges trekking.

Subsecretaría de Turismo

Ave. San Martín 1143
Mendoza
Argentina
☎ (0261) 4 202800
This office is the only place to obtain the required permit for Aconcagua.

CONSERVATION PROJECTS

Conservation programmes offer you the chance to interact closely with your environment and carry out what is often groundbreaking research for scientific and educational use. Tasks may involve anything from working with Peruvian craftspeople to monitoring monkeys in the rain forest. No particular skills are usually required, although you must be willing and able to work hard and as part of a team. Food and accommodation are as varied as the programmes themselves. Although you will be acting as a "volunteer," the fee to cover costs usually works out more expensive than a standard holiday.

CHIRIJE, ECUADOR

Chirije, on the Ecuador's central coast, is an important archaeological site. Once a seaport of the Bahía people, remains of pre-Columbian architecture and ceramics have been found in this spot, which is surrounded by a vast private beach and more than 160ha (400 acres) of tropical forest.

Bahía Dolphin Tours

Calle Salinas
Edif. Dos Hemisferios
P.O. Box 25
Chirije
Ecuador
☎ 692 097 or 692 086 **Fax:** 692 088
email: archtour@srv1.telconet.et
website: qni.com/~mj/bahia/bahia
A 21-day archaeological dig in Chirije . Bird-watching, whale-watching, and other wildlife tours are available.

NORTHERN RAIN FORESTS, ARGENTINA

This project aims to conserve black howler monkeys (*Alouatta palliata*) and their habitat. Work involves closely observing groups of these monkeys in the rain forest of northern Argentina. Sexual and aggressive behaviour is monitored, and selected animals are captured for tagging, weighing, etc. Accommodation is in dormitories, with shared cooking and washing facilities.

Earthwatch Institute

Headquarters:
680 Mt. Auburn St.
Box 9104
Watertown
MA 02272-9104
U.S.A.
☎ 617/926-8200 **Fax:** 617/926-8532
email: info@earthwatch.org
Earthwatch Europe:
57 Woodstock Rd.
Oxford OX2 6HJ
U.K.
☎ (01865) 311600 **Fax:** (01865) 311383
email: info@uk.earthwatch.org
website: www.uk.earthwatch.org
Earthwatch offers a wide range of projects throughout the world. It also has offices in California, Japan, and Australia.

COLONIA DEL SACRAMENTO, URUGUAY

Colonia del Sacramento, south of Montevideo, has been continuously inhabited since Roman times. There is only fragmentary evidence available of the early periods, so volunteers are analysing and organizing archaeological collections.

Earthwatch

See above.
A 20-day trip. Mostly laboratory work, but some excavation work and assembling of museum exhibits , with training provided. Hotel accommodation and meals.

CULTURAL TOURS

The region has a rich history, and a culture as varied as the landscape. The culture is evident in the archaeological remains of famed civilizations such as the Incas, in the many indigenous groups, and in the lives of its contemporary inhabitants. Many of the archaeological sites are in remote places, reached only after a trek of several days, although the journey can be as rewarding as the destination. Don't travel to remote areas alone, and be alert to thieves and bandits, who are not uncommon. If you come into contact with indigenous peoples, respect them and their traditional way of life.

SAN AGUSTÍN, COLOMBIA

San Agustín is one of South America's most important archaeological sites. Its 500 or so ancient stone statues of animals and figures are spread throughout the isolated Magdalena Valley. It is possible to hike around the more accessible statues, but jeep tours are available. For those deeper in the spectacular countryside, it is advisable to hire a horse and guide. The "dry" season runs from Nov to Mar, although it rains almost every day.

World Heritage Travel Office

Calle 3
No. 10-84
San Agustín
Colombia
☎ (988) 373940
The owner is multi-lingual and is the ex-head of the tourist office. He can provide maps and arrange tours.

OTAVALO, ECUADOR

A tour of the villages of Otavalo will offer the traveller a genuineinsight into the uncomplicated lifestyle and the well-preserved traditions of a people famous for their exceptional craftsmanship.

HISTORICAL SITES, PERU

From Lima's ancient buildings and interesting musuems to the Inca sites around Cusco and the nearby colourful Indian markets, Peru offers a varied cultural experience.

Mila

100 S. Greenleaf Ave.
Gurnee
Il 60031
U.S.A.
☎ toll-free 1-800/367-7378
email: milalatin@aol.com
website: www.a2z.com/mila
A 9-day tour takes in the main sites, plus a visit to the Lord of Sipan and the Nazca Lines. A 14-day tour also includes artesan studios in the region, the ruins of Sacsayhuaman, Urubamba's pottery workshops, and a jungle option from Iquitos.

KUELAP, PERU

Kuelap, at an altitude of 3,000m (9,800 ft) in northern Peru, is the Inca equivalent of the Great Wall of China. It is much older than Machu Picchu ,but relatively few tourists visit the site. Horses and guides can be hired by the day in Tingo, from where it is a 4-hour steep walk. Don't descend the same day (you can camp at the top).

Oscar Acre Cáceres

"El Chillo"

Near Río Utcubamba, 4km (6m) outside Tingo, Peru
Oscar is knowledgeable and helpful, and can arrange both guides and accommodation on his farm.

INCA SITES, BOLIVIA

The Andean culture is best experienced by visiting ancient Inca sites, the Aymara people who still live on the shores of sacred Lake Titicaca, and pilgrimage centres such as Copacabana.

Fremen
See page 275.
A 12-day Genesis of the Andean Culture tour. It also has tailor-made tours and business tours, plus bird-watching excursions and trips to the Bolivian Amazon.

BUENOS AIRES, ARGENTINA

The lively and sophisticated city of Buenos Aires has a rich cultural heritage, including numerous museums, churches, cultural events, and tango bars.

Centro Cultural de Buenos Aires
Junín 1930
Recoleta
Buenos Aires
Argentina
☎ (011) 4 803 1041
The Office of Culture can give information on cultural events, which are often free.

Maxim Tours Ltd.
See page 284.
Customized tango workshops and tango city tours are available, as well as the Faces of Buenos Aires, Jewish Heritage, and Eva Peron's Buenos Aires tours.

EASTER ISLAND

Easter Island, 4,000km (2,500 miles) west of Chile, is famous for its 600 or so giant stone figures, or *maoi*, built on family burial grounds. There are daily flights from Santiago, Chile. It is possible to walk to all the island's major sites in about 2 days, but provisions and shade are scarce so it is best to hire a jeep, motorbike, or horse.

Maxim Tours Ltd.
See page 284.
Custom-made trips to Easter Island from Santiago. Also offers wildlife, scenic, and cultural tours in all the countries of South America, including wine tours and skiing trips in Chile. Local guides are used, and

background information and suggested reading are provided to each destination.

Passage to South America
See page 295.
Offers 4-day tours to Easter Island from Santiago, Chile, which can be combined with any of the company's other tours, such as the Patagonia Adventure.

CYCLING

Cycling through a country allows independence and full interaction with your surroundings. A cyclist can cover up to 80km (50 miles) a day, and many cyclists in South America report that they rarely have to pay for accommodation. The main hazard is the strong wind, but you can always stick your bike on a train, bus, or boat when you've had enough. On organized tours, you will have booked accommodation, and usually a vehicle to carry your luggage. Hire shops are usually found only in established tourist spots, and are for fixed-centre hire. For longer tours take your own bike with you (few airlines charge extra if you are within your luggage allowance). Take a full repair kit— inner tubes, tyres, and spokes. Ecuador, Chile, and Colombia are the only countries in South America that have any decent cycle shops.

Cycling Touring Club
Cotterell House
69 Meadrow
Godalming
Surrey GU7 3HS
U.K.
☎ (01483) 417217 **Fax:** (01483) 426994
email: cycling@ctc.org.uk
website: www.ctc.org.uk
Provides members with information sheets for independent travel in specific countries, and trip reports with detailed practical information. It also has details of cycling-holiday operators worldwide.

Touring y Automobile Club del Peru
Ave. César Vallejo No. 699
Lince
Lima
Peru
Mailing address:
P.O. Box 2219 , Lima, Peru
☎ (01) 403270
This is essentially a motoring organization

that prepares routes, provides information on road conditions, and sells maps.

MÉRIDA, VENEZUELA

Mérida, on the snow-covered Sierra Nevada de Mérida range, is the tourist base for exploring the surrounding Andes, an increasingly popular location for mountain biking. From here it is possible to hire bicycles and so visit isolated villages such as Pueblos del Sur.For details of operators offering c ycling in Venezuela, see page 260

Guamanchi Tours

Calle 24
No. 8-39
Mérida
Venezuela
☎/Fax: (074) 522080
email: geca@bolivar.funmrd.gov.ve
website: www.ftech.net/~geca
A specialist it can recommend independent tours. Bike rentals. Also offers riding, climbing, hiking tours, as well as information.

QUITO–MANCHILILLA NATIONAL PARK, ECUADOR

A tour that follows the country's quiet rural roads and trails from Quito, on the Andean *altiplano*, through the Cotopaxi National Park to Baños and the Machililla National Park, taking in a variety of landscapes, Indian villages, and the coast.

High Places

Globe Works
Penistone Rd.
Sheffield S6 3AE
U.K.
☎ (0114) 275 7500 Fax: (0114) 275 3870
email: highpl@globalnet.co.uk
A 20-day, mostly downhill, trip, with sightseeing detours and a support vehicle. Trekking and climbing tours are also possible.

Pedal Andes

P.O. Box 17-12-602
Quito
Ecuador
☎ (02) 228 465 Fax: (02) 566 076
email: pedal@explorer.ecx.ed
This specialist company arranges cycling trips around Quito and beyond, with all equipment provided. It also offers a general information service to cyclists.

LA PAZ–LAKE TITICACA, BOLIVIA

A trip from La Paz to Lake Titicaca and pre-Inca sites, through the peaks of the Cordillera Real and the Condoriri Massif, to the subtropical valleys of the Yungas and the Amazon rain forest. Follows good tracks and covers a huge altitude range, and takes in a variety of landscapes and local cultures.

KE Adventure Travel

32 Lake Rd.
Keswick
Cumbria CA12 5DQ
U.K.
☎ (01768) 773966 Fax: (01768) 774693
email: keadventure@enterprise.net
website: www.keadventure.com
The trip lasts 22 days. Also arranges a 21-day trip along the Inca Trails of Peru, with a support vehicle plus trekking and general adventure tours.

THE YUNGAS/COROICO, BOLIVIA

The hair-raising bike ride from La Paz to the Yungas takes you from high altitude to sultry jungle, and includes a road reputed to be the most dangerous in Bolivia. For the faint-hearted rider, their are easier routes. For details of operators that offer cycling in Bolivia, see page 275-278.

ATACAMA DESERT, CHILE

The Atacama Desert of northern Chile features salt flats, sand-dunes, volcanoes, and some of the biggest downhill runs in the world. Old mine tracks climb to over 6,000m (19,700 ft) on the mountains of Aucanquilcha and Ollague, giving easy access for an ascent of the peaks on foot; you then make dramatic bike descents of over 3,000m (10,000 feet)—all in one day.

Andes

93 Queen St.
Castle Douglas
Kirkcudbrightshire DG7 1EH
U.K.
☎/Fax: (01556) 503929
email: john@andes.com
A pioneer of mountain-bike trips to the Andes. It also arranges mountaineering, trekking, and skiing holidays in the region.

OSORNO, CHILE

The snowfields on Osorno (2,669m, or 8,725 feet), the Petrohue Falls, Puyehue National Park, and the nearby hot springs are explored on foot and by bike. The Casablanca Volcano (2,240m, or 7,350 feet), with its breathtaking views of the area, beautiful Pucón in the Lake District, and Huerquehue National Park are some other highlights of the region.

Southwind Adventures
See page 258.
A 10-day van-supported trip is available from Oct to Feb, starting in Santiago. The company also offers cruises, plus trekking, cultural, and climbing trips from deluxe tours to rugged expeditions.

PATAGONIA, ARGENTINA
Various cycling tours, via minimum-traffic roads and backroutes, and range from the easy going to the challenging, you can explore the forests and glassy lakes of Patagonia's fascinating landscape.
For details of operators that offercycling in Patagonia see page 287–289.

FISHING

There are some world-class fishing spots in South America, whose coasts, lakes, and rivers all teem with potential catches. Chile and Argentina have some of the best trout fishing in the world, where the trout season starts just as the one in the U.S.A. comes to an end. Check on seasonal differences and any legal restrictions (for example, a "catch-and-release" policy operates on all Agentina's rivers). Arrangements can often be made to enable you to take your catch home with you. When travelling independently, outside an organized group, make sure you have a valid licence. Tourist offices can usually provide information on licences and where to fish.

LOS ROQUES, VENEZUELA
The archipelago of Los Roques, 150km (90 miles) north of Caracas, make up a national park of fish-filled water, with miles of remote white flats.

Cutting Loose Expeditions
Fishing Connection!
P.O. Box 447
Winter Park
FL 32790-0447
U.S.A.
☎ 407/629-4700 **Fax:** 407/740-7816
Specializes in fishing trips around the world. Also offers packages to the Río Orinoco.

RÍO NEGRO, BRAZIL
The black waters of Rio Negro, 320km (200 miles) from Manaus at the confluence with the Amazon, are home to world-record-sized peacock bass. Many anglers manage to catch fish weighing over 6.8kg (15lbs).

Trek International Safaris
1503 The Greens Way
Jacksonville
FL 32250
U.S.A.
☎ 904/273-7800 **Fax:** 904/273-0096
email: trek@treksafaris.com
Offers 8-day trips on board the luxury *Amazon Queen*, as well as land-based tours in lodges or tents.

MALDONADO, URUGUAY
Maldonado, at the mouth of the Río de la Plata, is a good place for fishing from boats at sea, along the coast, or off the nearby islands. The tourist office can provide a map of the best spots (☎ (042) 21920).

Tuttie
Local 1 de Servicio de Tráfico de Lanchas
Punta del Este
Maldonado
Uruguay
☎ (042) 44352
Offers a variety of boat fishing trips, lasting for a day or longer.

LAKE DISTRICT, CHILE
Puerto Montt, in Chile's Lake District, is surrounded by sea, lakes, and rivers. Río Maullin to the west has good salmon fishing, while Río Petrohué has fishing for rainbow and brown trout (Nov–Mar).

Turismo Cocha
Ave. El Bosque Norte 0430
Santiago
Chile
☎ (02) 230 1000 **Fax:** (02) 203 5110
email: cocha@cocha.com
This local agency offers 3-day fishing trips in selected spots from Puerto Montt to Puerto Varas.

NAHUEL HUAPI NATIONAL PARK, ARGENTINA
The Nahuel Huapi National Park is home to a 500-sq-km (190-square-mile) glacial lake that contains both native and introduced fish, including trout (rainbow, brown, and brook). The season runs from Nov to mid-Apr, but the best time for fishing is in Nov

and Dec. A permit is required to fish anywhere in the country.

Club de Caza y Pesca
Costanera 12 de Octubre and Onelli
Bariloche
Argentina
☎ (02944) 4 22403
Provides information on licences and rents out fishing equipment.

Last Frontiers Ltd.
Fleet Marston Farm
Aylesbury
Buckinghamshire HP18 0PZ
U.K.
☎ (01296) 658650 **Fax:** (01296) 658651
email: travelinfo@lastfrontiers.co.uk
Fishing, photography, riding, and wildlife tours. Also arranges occasional specialist small-group tours for painters and photographers.

Villa La Angostura
Parque Nacional Nahuel Huapi
Neuquén
Argentina
☎/Fax: (02994) 4 494308
email: balsas@sutlink.com
Offers fly-casting or trolling trips from mid-November to mid-April. Half- or full-day excursions and tailor-made programmes. Also sailing, trekking and skiing trips.

HORSE RIDING

Whether you want to follow in the footsteps (or rather the hoofprints) of the gauchos—Argentina's cowboys—or just want to explore some of the region's vast open country, riding allows you to appreciate the landscape while covering up to 30km (20 miles) a day. Trips may be based at a centre, returning each night, but more often they involve staying in luxury ranches or in camping along the way. Many operators will take novices and children. Be aware that Western-style saddles may not ber used, and that the horses may be a bit wilder than at home. The "gaucho gait" is a South American trot, faster than the Western style, and requires a particular saddle. You will need footwear with a 5-cm (2-inch) heel to stop your foot from slipping out of the stirrup.

BAÑOS, ECUADOR
The popular resort of Baños in the Central Sierra is a good starting point for trips into the foothills of Tungurahua in Sangay National Park.

Hotel Isla de Baños
Halflants 1-31 y Montalvo
Baños
Ecuador
☎/Fax: 740609
Good horses to rent by the day, along with a guide who has a thorough knowledge of the surrounding area.

SAN ALFONSO, CHILE
San Alfonso, near Santiago, is the starting point for horseback trips into the central Andes. Local herdsmen known as *arrieros* lead trips across the rugged terrain, where there are no marked trails.

Cascada Expediciones
Orrego Luco 054
Santiago
Chile
☎ (02) 232 7214 **Fax:** (02) 233 9768
email: cascada@ibm.net
website: www.cascada-expediciones.com
Arranges various riding trips in Chile and Argentina. Also diving, mountaineering, and trekking throughout South America.

Centro de Turismo Ecuestre Huepil
Casilla 16
Pucón
Chile
☎ (09) 453 4212
Rodolfo Coombs, a professional showjumper from Argentina, and his partner, Carolina Pumpin, run this homely equestrian centre in the beautiful Liucura Valley, some 30km (19 miles) from Pucón. There's a 3-day option in the summer to ride across the mountains into Argentina and back.

TORRES DEL PAINE, CHILE
The Torres del Paine is probably the world's finest national park, and horse riding through its fascinating landscape is a memorable experience. For though the terrain makes for difficult going, the horses are born to it and the spirited rider will find it a thrilling alternative to trekking.
For details of operators that offer riding in Chile see page 280-282.

NORTHERN PATAGONIA, ARGENTINA

The vast expanse of Northern Patagonia's pampas meets the Andes in a varied landscape of snow-covered mountains, clear lakes, and dense forests. Day trips and longer tours are possible.
For details of operators offering riding in Patagonia, see pages 287.

Blue Green Adventures

2 Priory Cottages
Parsonage Lane
Lamberhurst
Kent TN3 8DS
U.K.
☎/Fax: (0181) 947 2756
Specializes in horse-riding trips in southern Chile. Also hiking and kayaking packages in the country.

Ride World Wide

58 Fentiman Rd.
London SW8 1LF
U.K.
☎ (020) 7735 1144 **Fax:** (020) 7735 3179
email: rideww@aol.com
Horseback excursions (based at a working *estancia* in northern Patagonia), exploring the Lake District and Lanín National Park. Also camping trips and the opportunity to join gauchos on a working cattle drive.

Travel South America

Trinity House
Market Place
Easingwold
North Yorkshire YO61 3AD
U.K.
☎ (01347) 822235 **Fax:** (01347) 823336
email: tvisa@aol.com
Arranges 6-day horse treks in the Argentine Andes, with whitewater rafting, trout fishing, and cattle ranching options.

JUNGLE TOURS

The tropical rain forest in the centre and north of South America teems with unusual wildlife and exotic plants. Tours are available year round, but the best season is between Jul and Oct, when the drier weather means there are fewer insects to contend with. To allow time to reach your lodge, a minimum 3-day trip is recommended. Perhaps more than other types of tour, jungle trips are prey to unscrupulous operators; don't go for the cheapest guide and choose carefully as there is no turning back once you've started. Humidity can be a problem, because, apart from the personal discomfort it causes, it can affect camera film and energy levels. Accommodation is in makeshift tents, or in lodges of varying degrees of comfort.

LETICIA, COLOMBIA

The town of Leticia is a good gateway to the Amazon Basin. It is advisable to take a trip of at least 3 days to reach the real wilderness and more remote Indian settlements.

Amazon Jungle Trips

Ave. Internacional No. 6-25
Leticia
Colombia
☎ (9819) 27377
This popular and reputable agency runs trips into the remote regions of the country. Book in advance if possible.

COCA REGION, ECUADOR

The Coca region is mostly made up of the Yasuní National Park and Huaorani Reserve, which require a trip of at least 5 days if you are to appreciate them to the full. To visit the Huarorani territory you must first obtain special permission from the Ministerio de Defensa (Ave. Maldonado, Quito). The wildlife here is under threat, and you can help matters— insist there is no hunting on your trip and take all litter away with you.

Pankitour Alternativo

6 de Diciembre y Garcia Moreno
Coca
Ecuador
☎ 880405
This local company has extensive knowledge of the area and maintains good relationships with the Huaroni people.

PUERTO MALDONADO, PERU

There are several jungle lodges near Puerto Maldonado, overlooking the Tambopata and Madre de Dios rivers in one of the least developed regions of the Amazon, all of which can be reached in a few hours by motorized canoe. Numbers and species of animals spotted vary, as do the standards of accommodation. Colpa Lodge is the best place for seeing wildlife, but it is both remote and expensive.

Peruvian Safaris

Ave. Garcilaso de la Vega 1334
Lima
Peru

☎ (01) 313047
Takes bookings for the Explorers Inn jungle
lodge, which employs naturalists as guides
and is in a great location for wildlife.
Accommodation is in traditional cabins.

MANAUS, BRAZIL
Manaus, in the north of the country, is a
good starting point for Amazon trips into a
quiet, beautiful region, and allows plenty of
opportunity for activities such as trekking.

Swallows and Amazons
See page 270.

RURRENABAQUE, BOLIVIA
Rurrenabaque, on the Río Beni, offers
jungle trips that give you a full experience
of the local people, wildlife, and scenery.
Trips (usually 4 days) can be tailor-made to
include a motorized canoe journey, rainforest walks, river swimming, or even playing
football with the local Indians.

Agencia Fluvial
Hotel Tuichi
Calles Avaroa y Santa Cruz
Rurrenabaque
Bolivia
☎ c/o ENTEL office, Rurrenabaque (0832)
2205
Inclusive and tailor-made tours are available
from this local company, which also offers
pampas trips in the region (see Wildlife
Safaris, pages 313–314).

SCUBA-DIVING

South America's Caribbean coast and
national marine parks are popular with divers
from all over the world. Sub-aqua clubs at
home offer courses that can be taken before
you leave, but take evidence of any certification with you. Some operators may require
experience, but it is normally possible to
become certified as a diver once you reach
your destination. This sport is particularly
dangerous for the inexperienced, so do not
choose the cheapest operator as it may be
saving money by having a high pupil-to-
instructor ratio and unsatisfactory
equipment. Ask to see the instructor's dive
book to check his or her experience, and
make sure he or she has a valid instructor's
card. Check any equipment carefully before
you go out on the dive. Snorkelling is a good
introduction if you have never dived before,
and is especially suitable for children.

British Sub-Aqua Club
Telford Quay
Ellesmere Port
South Wirral
Cheshire L65 4FY
U.K.
☎ (0151) 350 6200 **Fax:** (0151) 350 6215
website: www.bsac.com
Offers information about diving abroad, and
runs diving courses in the U.K.

National Association of
Underwater Instructors (NAUI)
NAUI Worldwide
9942 Currie Davis Dr., Suite H
Tampa
FL 33619-2667
U.S.A.
☎ 813/628-6284 or toll-free 1-800/553-6284
Fax: 813/628-8253
website: www.naui.org
Provides training and certification to high
standards.

Professional Association of Diving
Instructors (PADI)
PADI International Ltd.
Unit 7
St. Philips Central
Albert Rd.
St. Philips
Bristol BS2 0PD
U.K.
☎ (0117) 300 7234
Fax: (0117) 971 0400
website: www.padi.com
PADI certifies 55 percent of all divers world-
wide, and is recognized for its promotion of
safety and training supervision.

SAN ANDRÉS, COLOMBIA
San Andrés, one of a group of islands off the
country's northwest coast, has extensive
coral reefs, a varied marine life, and an
established tourist infrastructure.
Snorkelling equipment can also be hired.
There is an entry fee to the island.

Buzos del Caribe
Centro Comercial Dann
San Andrés
Colombia
☎ (9811) 23712
This local agency has equipment for hire
and offers reef trips.

LOS ROQUES, VENEZUELA
The archipelago of Los Roques, north of
Caracas, is a spectacular national park

(entry fee) that offers good diving and snorkelling. The sand is white and the water clear, although the area can be crowded with Venezuelans during weekends and holidays. For details of operators that arrange diving and snorkelling trips in Los Roques, see page 261.

GALÁPAGOS ISLANDS, ECUADOR

In the crystal-clear waters of the Galápagos archipelago, the experienced diver can embark on an exciting adventure into a world of spectacular colour and marine life that only the privileged few can explore.

Galápagos Scuba Iguana
See page 265.

FERNANDO DE NORONHA, BRAZIL

The Fernando de Noronha Marine National Park is an archipelago off the north-east coast of Brazil, with only one inhabited island. It is very popular with Brazilian divers, who come to see the shipwreck sites and the variety of marine life, including dolphins, turtles, eagle rays, and barracudas. The numbers of tourists are restricted, and there are many rules to protect the park's fragile environment. There is also a visitor tax of about $15 a day.

Gigaturismo
Rua México 21/402
Centro - Rio de Janeiro - RJ
CEP 20.031-144
Brazil
☎ (021) 524 1028 **Fax:** (021) 240 3183
website: www.gigaturismo.com.br
Offers diving and sailing packages, with some of the profits going to conservation programmes. It also arranges other diving and adventure trips in Brazil.

PENÍNSULA VALDÉS, ARGENTINA

The two underwater parks in the Península Valdés—one artificial and the other a natural reef—offer the qualified diver the opportunity to explore one of the world's most important marine wildlife reserves.

Buceo
See page 289.

SKIING

South America provides the skiing opportunities of most European and American destinations, yet its slopes are often uncrowded. And when the snow has melted in the Alps and Rockies, the Andes is preparing for the start of the season. Chile and Argentina have resorts to match those of established Western skiing spots, while Peru, Ecuador, Colombia, and Venezuela offer ski-touring experiences that allow you to see more of the wildlife and scenery. Heli-skiing gives you the thrill of untouched mountains, but requires special equipment and at least 3 years' experience. Snowboarding can be done in most places that offer skiing facilities. The ski season varies from country to country, depending on the weather. The price structure for ski passes is often complex, and there is also a great deal of variation in standards of facilities and equipment, although skis and boots are available at all resorts.

CHACALTAYA, BOLIVIA

The basic facilities at Chacaltaya, 35km (22 miles) from La Paz and at an altitude of 5,200m (17,000 feet) make it the world's highest "developed" ski resort; it is suitable for experienced skiiers only. A wooden hut acts as a ski lodge, and ascents depend on a rope cable tow. Limited equipment is available, but it is much better to take your own. The season runs from Feb to Apr, and the high altitude makes acclimatization essential.

Club Andino Boliviano
Calle México 1638
Casilla 5879
La Paz
Bolivia
☎ (02) 324682 **Fax:** (02) 329119
Runs weekend excursions and can arrange mid-week skiing, the latter permitted only if you book in advance.

PORTILLO, CHILE

Chile is said to have the best skiing in the southern hemisphere. Portillo, at 3,350m (10,985 feet) and 145km (90 miles) north of Santiago, is its most traditional resort. The season runs from late Jun to early Oct. It is a scenic spot, with good runs down to a lake, off-piste facilities, and a snowmaking system. There are 12 lifts, 23 runs, and a ski school, and the resort is suitable for families.

Hotel Portillo
Roger de Flor 2911
Santiago
Chile

☎ (02) 231 3411 **Fax:** (02) 231 7164
Most visitors to Portillo stay here, and
packages can be arranged. It is expensive,
but is the most convenient hotel for the
resort.

LAS LEÑAS, ARGENTINA

Las Leñas, 445km (276 miles) south of
Mendoza, attracts wealthy skiiers from all
over the world, but is within the budget of
most travellers. The resort covers a huge
area at an altitude of 2,250m (7,380 feet),
and has 41 pistes, 11 lifts, and (expensive)
accommodation. The season runs from early
Jun to early Oct.

Badino Turismo

Perón 725, 6th Floor
Buenos Aires
Argentina
☎ (011) 4 326 1351 **Fax:** (011) 4 393 2568
Arranges tailor-made trips to the resort and
can also organize ski-only options, without
accommodation.

SURFING

South America's many miles of coast have a
number of internationally renowned surf
breaks, although Brazil is probably its
surfing mecca. Be aware that some
beaches, particularly in Peru, suffer from
pollution. It is advisable to take a
wetsuit as the water can be cold even
when the weather is warm, and not all
places have them for hire. Try to avoid
beaches that are crowded with swimmers
as you are more likely to cause injury.
Take note of any local conditions: there
may be dangerous currents and
undertows. Particular regulations may
apply for ecological reserves, nautical
routes, and places where there are
recreational vessels.

Surfer Publications

P.O. Box 1028
Dana Point
CA 92629
U.S.A.
☎ 714/496-5922
Fax: 714/496-7849
Publishes the *Journal of International
Surfing Destinations*. A list is available on
request, and trip reports of interest can be
ordered for a fee.

ILHA DE SANTA CATARINA, BRAZIL

Ilha de Santa Catarina has, among its
42 beaches, some of the continent's best
surfing spots. Joaquina, on the island,
hosts the Brazilian professional surfing
championships each Jan. Between Apr 30
and Jul 30 surfing is prohibitedto protect
the migrating tainha fish, and in Jan and Feb
the beaches can get very crowded.

Tourist Office

Portal Turístico de Florianópolis
Ave. Engenheiro
Max de Souza 236
Coqueiros
Florianópolis
Brazil
☎ (0482) 244 5822 or (0482) 244 5960
Can provide up-to-the-minute information
on the best places to go, and can give details
of where to hire equipment.

MAR DEL PLATA, ARGENTINA

Mar del Plata, on Argentina's Atlantic coast,
is a popular resort with 8km (5 miles) of
beaches and good surfing. It is necessary to
book accommodation in advance between
Dec and Mar.

Tourist Office

Ente Municipal de Turismo
Blvd. Marítimo 2267
Emtur
Mar del Plata
Argentina
☎ (02293) 4 21777
Provides information on surfing spots and
where to hire equipment.

HUANCHACHO AND PUERTO MALABRIGOL CHICAMA, PERU

Huanchacho is a fishing and surfing village
northwest of Trujillo, where fishermen
battle with the strong surf on narrow reed
rafts, called *caballitos* (meaning "little
horses"), as if on surfboards. These can be
hired from the beach. Nearby Puerto
Malabrigol Chicama beach, 70km (45 miles)
north of Trujillo, may have the longest left-
hand break in the world. Boards can be
hired in Lima. The water is cold in Peru, and
sometimes these beaches are polluted.

O'Neills

Ave. Santa Cruz 851
Miraflores
Lima
Peru

☎ (01) 445 0406

Rents out boards and equipment, and has knowledgeable staff. *Tablista*, a surfing magazine, is available in kiosks in Lima.

TREKKING

The vast tracts of wilderness in the region provide for excellent hiking. The Inca roads of the Andes and the local Indian trails of Ecuador and Bolivia lead through spectacular landscapes, while in the south, many national parks have a high standard of facilities for the visitor. The high altitudes of the Andes make acclimatization essential. Extremes of weather in mountain areas also make it important to be prepared for both sunburn and frostbite. In remote areas, robbery and attacks are not uncommon, especially around volcanoes; travelling with guides and as part of a large group is therefore advisable. Reliable maps are best obtained at home, although decent ones are available from the Institutos Geográficos in capital cities. The South America Explorers' Club (see Climbing, pages 297–298) can provide maps, guides, and travel information.

SIERRA DE LA CULATA, VENEZUELA

The Sierra de la Culata, near Mérida, offers good trekking opportunities in a desert-like landscape with mountain lakes and hot springs. There are various day treks that do not require guides, and it is possible to camp overnight.

Bum Bum Tours

See page 260.

Guamanchi Tours

See page 302.
Can provide information and maps for independent treks. Also offers cycling, riding, and climbing trips.

RORAIMA, VENEZUELA

Bordering Venezuela, Guyana, and Brazil, 810-m (2,660-foot) Roraima is one of the region's highest *tepuis* (mesas), and is believed to have been the inspiration for Sir Arthur Conan Doyle's *The Lost World*. The ascent takes 2 days (a guide is recommended), but allow at least 2 days on the top (camping overnight) for exploring the unusual cloud forest, wildlife and plant life. The best time to go is between Dec and Apr.

Roraima Tours

San Francisco de Yuraní
Roraima
Venezuela
☎ (088) 951283
Fax: (088) 951339
This agency specializes in trips to the *tepui*, and offers all-inclusive tours as well as the day hire of guides (recommended) and equipment.

CERRO GOLONDRINAS CLOUDFOREST, ECUADOR

Treks through ecosystems that are as fascinating as they are pristine take you across the high-altitude wilderness of the paramo, into the mystical cloud forest of Cerro Golondrinas, and down to the sub-tropical forest of the lowlands.

Golondrinas Foundation

See page 263.

CORDILLERA BLANCA, PERU

Cordillera Blanca is the most popular area for trekking in Peru, and offers circuits of various lengths plus mountain scenery to rival that of the Himalayas. It can be wet even during the dry season, so go prepared for all weather. Trails are well defined, but because of the altitude you must acclimatize properly. The Cordillera Huayhuash circuit takes a demanding 12 days, starting from either Chiquián, Cajatambo, or Oyun; part of the circuit, to Laguna Jahuarcocha, takes 5 days.

Safaricentre

3201 N. Sepulveda Blvd.
Manhattan Beach
CA 90266
U.S.A.
☎ toll-free 1-800/223-6046 or 1-800/546-4411
email: info@safaricentre.com
Knowledgeable guides with experience of the area. Overland jeep safaris in Bolivia are also available.

PARQUE NACIONAL DA CHAPADA DIAMANTINA, BRAZIL

The 1,599-sq-km (580-square-mile) Chapada Diamantina National Park offers good walking among waterfalls, mountains, and large caves. There are a number of short excursions from Lençóis, the park's head-quarters, for which a guide is not necessary.

Agency Saturno

Olivia Taylor
Pousada dos Duendes
Rua do Pires
Lençóis
Brazil
☎/Fax: (075) 334 1229
This agency is run by an English woman,
who arranges treks in the area of any length
up to 11 days.

TORRES DEL PAINE, CHILE

On the trails though the park beneath the
towering granite pinnacles of the Torres del
Paine, the trekker will find the blue lagoons,
shimmering glaciers, and grassy valleys of a
dramatic, ever-changing landscape.

Amerindia Concept

See page 282.

See also Patagonia, Argentina, below.

PATAGONIA, ARGENTINA

The wilderness of Patagonia includes a
number of national parks whose remote
areas are home to guanacos, eagles, silver
foxes, and elephant seals. Mountain peaks,
icebergs, and exotic birdlife are all encountered on a trek in this region, best
undertaken between Nov and Mar.
For details of operators that offer to
Patagonia, see page 282.

Butterfield and Robinson

70 Bond St.
Suite 300
Toronto
Ontario M5B 1X3
Canada
☎ 416/864-1354 **Fax:** 416/864-0541
email: info@butterfield.com
website: www.butterfield.com
A 9-day trip with accommodation in
luxury lodges, including a boat trip to
Moreno Glacier and a fly-fishing option.
This specialist operator offers treks around
the world.

Explore Worldwide

1 Frederick St.
Aldershot
Hampshire GU11 1LQ
U.K.
☎ (01252) 319448 **Fax:** (01252) 343170
email: info@explore.co.uk
A 22-day trip from Buenos Aires or the U.K.,
with whale-watching and boat-trip options.

Trekking trips in other South American
countries are also available, along with
wildlife, cultural, and rainforest trips.

LOS GLACIARES NATIONAL PARK, ARGENTINA

In the Los Glaciares National Park you can
actually walk on the crunchy surface of
glaciers. You need crampons strapped to
your walking boots for making your way up
slopes and straddling the deep fissures.

Fitzroy Expeditions

See page 291.

WHITEWATER RAFTING

The clear waters of South America's fast-
running rivers are ideal for this exhilarating,
often hair-raising sport, available only
during the rainy season. No previous
experience is necessary, although there may
be fitness requirements. There are two
styles of rafting: "paddle rafting," in a team
with a guide, when everyone uses their
paddles to steer; and "oar boating," when
a guide directs the raft without any
assistance. There is an internationally
recognized grading system for rivers on a
scale of I (slow-moving current) to VI
(unsafe to run commercially). Helmets and
safety equipment should be provided. It is
recommended that you take waterproofs as
you will get wet.

COLCA CANYON, PERU

Trekking through the variable altitude of the
Colca Canyon is a challenge, but magnificent views, soaring condors, and the warm
welcome that awaits the visitor to its remote
villages, makes the effort well worth while.
For details of operators that offer
whitewater-rafting tours in the region, see
pages 269.

RÍO ALLO NAPO, ECUADOR

Río Allo Napo is an unpolluted river
(the Chambo, Patate, and Pastaza are all
polluted) on the edge of the Amazon Basin,
south of Quito. Most tours start from Baños.

Explorandes

Wilson 537 y Diego de Almagro
Quito
Ecuador
☎ (02) 222 699, (02) 556 936,
or (02) 556 937
Fax: (02) 556 938

email: explora@hoy.net
This is the longest-established rafting company in the country, and has been operating for over a decade. It offers various river-rafting trips that start from Baños.

Julio Verne

Oriente 11-69 y Alfaro
Baños - Tungurahua
Ecuador
☎/**Fax:** (03) 740249 or (03) 740253
This part Dutch-owned company provides tailor-made rafting, climbing, and trekking trips in the area around Baños.

Río Urubamba, Peru

The beautiful Urubamba river in the Sacred Valley, northwest of Cusco, has the best whitewater rafting in Peru. Class IV and V waters occur only between Nov and Apr. Day trips are possible (Ollantaytambo and Huaran are recommended), but the best rapids are reached on a 3-day trip.

Worldwide Journeys and Expeditions

See page 295.
A 17-day trip, including 4 days river-running. Offers tours in small groups throughout South America.

Río Trancuro, Chile

Chile has some of the world's best whitewater-rafting. Río Trancuro, in the Lake District, is popular from Dec to Feb, when there is the best white water. Most agencies in Pucón offer all-day or half-day trips that can include Class IV and V rapids and a waterfall, or lower-grade waters.

O'Higgins

No. 211 Calle
Pucón
Chile
☎ (045) 441189 or (045) 441959
Fax: (045) 441959
This pioneer of rafting trips in the Pucón area also runs similar trips down the Río Bió Bió and Río Futaleufú

Río Manso, Argentina

The Río Manso, in Parque Nacional Nahuel Huapi on the border with Chile, has Class III whitewater rafting against a backdrop of scenic lakes and glaciers. Most tours start from Bariloche, at the park's centre.

Expediciones Náuticas

Rolando 268
Local 4
Bariloche
Argentina
☎ (02944) 4 27502
Knowledgeable, local guides can be hired for day trips or longer.

Río Mendoza, Argentina

For sheer, adrenalin-pumping fun there can be little to beat the whitewater rafting on the Río Mendoza, whose gurgling waters spin you through dry-bone canyons from one set of thrilling rapids to the next.

Betancourt Rafting

See page 284.

WILDLIFE SAFARIS

The region that inspired Darwin's *Origin of the Species* supports a large number of exotic animals, such as spectacled bears, iguanas, tapirs, armadillos, and even pumas (see also Bird-Watching, pages 293–294). To appreciate fully the wildlife and environment, a trip of at least 3 days is recommended. Generally, it is best to go in the dry season when creatures come out to search for water and there are fewer insects. Jungle areas support a dense population of fauna (see Jungle Tours, page 305), but the thick vegetation does not always allow for the best viewing opportunities. Flat, open landscapes such as Argentina's pampas and the Llanos in Venezuela can provide animal-studded views stretching as far as the horizon. Try to minimize impact by leaving the wildlife undisturbed, taking litter away with you, and checking that tours do not include hunting.

Los Llanos, Venezuela

Los Llanos is a vast area of plains that is home to cowboys, cattle, and a large number of exotic animals and birds (see Bird-Watching, pages 293–294). In Oct and Nov the plains are flooded and particularly large numbers of dolphins, capybaras, caiman crocodiles, and birds can be seen. It is advisable to go as part of a tour and to stay on a ranch as the area is very remote. For details of operators that offer wildlife safaris to Los Llanos, see pages 260–261.

Turismo Aventura
Caracas
Venezuela
☎ (02) 951 1143
Arranges trips lasting from 3 days to Hato
Cedral, a ranch where hunting is banned
and where there is a swimming pool.

Cuyabeno Wildlife Reserve, Ecuador
East of the Andes in Ecuador is the
600,000-ha (1.5 million-acre) Cuyabeno
Wildlife Reserve, a beautiful area of remote
rain forest. Anacondas, pink dolphins, and
other mammals thrive around the many
lagoons of the national park, and most trips
(lasting between 3 and 6 days) are by boat
or motorized canoe. It is advisable to hire a
guide. There is hotel accommodation and
camping on the reserve.

Jungletur
Amazonas 854 y Veintimilla
Quito
Ecuador
☎ (02) 571098
Offer 6-day tours to Cuyabeno, plus other
wildlife tours in the country.

Galápagos Islands, Ecuador
For the nature lover, the Galápagos
archipelago is one of the world's most
rewarding destinations. Here, in this living
laboratory, an awe-inspiring ecology and
close encounters with exotic fauna
guarantee you the experience of a lifetime.
For details of operators that offer wildlife
safaris to the Galápagos, see pages 265–266.

Abrolhos Archipelago, Brazil
The Abrolhos Archipelago, in Bahia, was
Brazil's first national marine park. It is
located off the coast of Caravelas, and is
made up of five islands; its clear waters
support an enormous variety of fish and
corals. Whale-watching is also possible from
Jul to Nov.

Gigaturismo
See page 307.
A 2-night sailing package around islands,
with bird-watching and diving options.
Gigaturismo is a conservation organization,
with some of its profits going to charity.

Rurrenabaque, Bolivia
Rurrenabaque is the start of tours into the
pampas (for jungle trips see page 305).

Because there are fewer places for animals
to hide, pampas tours offer the best sightings of animals such as snakes, dolphins,
capybaras, and many bird species. Trips
normally involve taking a motorized canoe
along the network of rivers, camping along
the way.

Agencia Fluvial
See page 306.
Offers 4-day jungle tours and 3-day pampas
tours with knowledgeable guides.

Patagonia, Argentina
In the vast, scarcely populated, semi-desert
plain of Patagonia is a richly diverse range
of fauna and flora—some in danger of
extinction—waiting to be discovered by
the adventurous wildlife-watcher.

Wildlife Worldwide
See page 265.

Península Valdés, Argentina
At the marine wildlife reserve on the
Península Valdés, you can take boat trips
into the ocean to watch cavorting whales,
mingle with penguin colonies, and enjoy the
antics of the seals and sea lions.
For details of operators that offer
wildlife safaris to the Península Valdés,
see pages 289.

Tierra del Fuego–Antarctic Peninsula, Argentina
Tours depart to the Antarctic Peninsula, a
remote, scenic area with extraordinary
wildlife. There are penguin rookeries, seal
colonies, whales, and albatross amongst the
many glaciers and fjords. Return voyages
(possible only between Oct and Mar) from
Ushuaia, Tierra del Fuego, take at least 4
days, and include days ashore and visits to
scientific stations. Sightings of wildlife
cannot be guaranteed.

World Expeditions
4 Northfields Prospect
Putney Bridge Rd.
London SW18 1PE
U.K.
☎ (020) 8870 2600
Fax: (020) 8870 2615
email: worldex@dircon.co.uk
An 11-day voyage from Ushuaia, with an
option to camp ashore.

WINDSURFING

There are a number of windsurfing spots both on the coast and on South America's many inland lakes that often offer the ideal conditions of strong, consistent winds and reasonably calm water. It is advisable to get some instruction first as the sport (sometimes known as sailboarding) is deceptively difficult to master. Always check the weather forecast before setting out, and even if it is warm consider wearing a wetsuit if the water is cold and the wind strong. Even if you are experienced, wear a lifejacket as there is a risk of being knocked out by the mast. Ideally, sail in pairs and inform someone where you are going. Where there are windsurfing facilities, other watersports and activities are often available for non-surfers.

International Board Sailing Association

The Race Office
P.O. Box 1439
Kings Norton
Birmingham B38 9AU
U.K.
☎/Fax: (0121) 628 5137
email: jim@bsa.demon.co.uk
An umbrella organization that can advise on windsurfing courses and organizations worldwide.

ISLA MARGARITA, VENEZUELA

Isla Margarita, off Venezuela's north coast, is possibly South America's most-visited spot and is a watersports mecca. The winds here are strong and consistent, and at their ideal in Jun and Jul, also the hottest months in terms of water temperature. El Yaque is a particularly popular beach for windsurfing.

Sailboard Vacations

193 Rockland St.
Hanover
MA 02339
U.S.A.
☎ 617/829-8915 **Fax:** 617/829-8809
email: sby@sailboardvacations.com
This operator specializes in all-inclusive windsurfing holidays, but also offers snorkelling, sea kayaking, and other water-based activities.

SAN ANDRÉS, COLOMBIA

San Andrés is an 11-km (7-mile) long coral island off Colombia's northeast coast. Diving and most watersports, from pedaloes to boat trips, are available here.

Windsurf Spot

Hotel Isleño
San Andrés
Colombia
☎ (9811) 23990
Both equipment hire and windsurfing lessons are available here.

JERICOACOARA, BRAZIL

Jericoacoara, in the northeast of Brazil, is one of the country's best-known beaches. It offers several windsurfing options, and boasts a year-round strong wind. For beginners and those who prefer a calmer sail, there is the nearby lake of Jijoca.

Pousada Casa do Turismo

Jericoacoara
CE Brazil 62.598-000
Brazil
☎/Fax: (088) 621 0211
email: email@jericoacoara.com
Rents windsurfing equipment and provides a daily wind report by email.

LAKE NAHUEL HUAPI, ARGENTINA

Lake Nahuel Huapi, 100km (60 miles) from Bariloche in the Argentine Lake District, lies within a national park where there are snow-capped volcanoes, serene lakes, and dense forests. It offers opportunities for windsurfing, as well as sailing, water-skiing, and non-water-based activities such as riding and walking.

Last Frontiers

See page 260.
This specialist in South American tours arranges tailor-made trips throughout the region.

GENERAL INDEX

ACKNOWLEDGEMENTS

Guy Marks would like to acknowledge the following for their assistance in the course of research-ing this book: Avianca for providing flights to South America; Angermeyers for their kind hospitality on board the yacht *Sulidae* in the Galapagos Islands; Piet Sabbe and the Golondrinas Foundation for taking me on an excellent trek through the cloud forest in Ecuador; Manu Expeditions for their continued support in making local arrangements in Peru.

Lee Karen Stow would like to thank: Jorge Barcelo of Sendero Sur Patagonia; mountain guide Adrian Cangiani; Silvia at Hostel International Campo Base, Mendoza; Aerolineas Argentinas; Betancourt Rafting, Mendoza; Airwaves World of Discovery; Latin America Travel; Pauline Young of G&O Associates representing LATA (Latin America Travel Association); Museo Argentio de Ciencias Naturales 'Bernardino Rivadavia', Buenos Aires; Museo de Ciencias Naturales, La Plata; the Hallidays of Hill Station.

Steve Watkins would like to thank the following for their support and advice during his work for this book:
British Airways, Tom and Raquel Evenou at Bum Bum Tours (Merida) and Sehis work for this book:

Abbreviations for terms appearing below: (t) top; (b) bottom; (l) left; (r) right; (c) centre.

Cover acknowledgements

Front cover (t): Bruce Coleman Collection
Front cover main picture: Guy Marks
Front cover (b): Colin Monteath/Mountain Camera
Spine: Bruce Coleman Collection
Back cover (t): Image Bank
Back cover (ct): Steve Watkins
Back cover (cb): Tony Stone Images
Back Cover (br): Guy Marks
Inside flaps: (t): AA Photo Library/Guy Marks; (ct): AA Photo Library/Steve Watkins; (cb): AA Photo Library/Steve Watkins; (b) AA Photo Library/Steve Watkins

The Automobile Association wishes to thank the following photographers and libraries for their assistance in the preparation of this book:

Bruce Coleman Collection 46(c), 150/151, 151, 163(t); **Cascada Expeditions** 198; Sue Cunningham/SCP 46(b); **Gravity Assisted Mountain Biking** 182(t); **Simon Richmond** 14a, 15c,130/131, 134/135, 134, 138, 139, 143, 146/147, 146, 150, 154/155, 154, 155, 158/159, 158, 162/163, 163(b), 166/167, 170/171, 174(t), 174(b), 178, 182, 183, 186/187, 190(c), 190(b), 191, 194, 194(b), 199, 199(t), 202(t), 202(c); **South American Pictures** 15b, 107,138/139, 142/143, 178/179, 179 (Tony Morrison); 174 (Kimball Morrison); 242/243 (Frank Nowikowski)

The remaining photographs are held in the Associations own library (AA PHOTO LIBRARY) and were taken by the following photographers:

Guy Marks 2/3, 3, 7, 14/15, 15a, 66/67, 67, 70/71, 70, 71, 74(c), 74(b), 75, 78, 78/79, 82, 83, 86/87, 86, 87, 90/91, 90(tl), 90(tr), 94/95, 98/99, 98, 102/103, 102, 103, 106(cl), 110/111, 111, 114/115, 115, 118/119, 118, 119, 122, 123, 126/127, 126, 127;
Lee Karen Stow 6/7, 14b, 206, 206 (b), 207(t), 207(c), 210, 211(t), 211(b), 214/215, 218/219, 219, 222(t), 222(b), 223, 226(t), 226(b), 227, 230, 230(t), 231, 234/235, 234, 235, 238(t), 238(b), 239, 242(c), 243, 246(t), 246(b), 250, 251, 251(b), 254/255, 255;
Steve Watkins 18/19, 22/23, 22, 23, 26, 27(t), 27(c), 27(b), 30, 31, 31(t), 34/35, 34, 35, 38/39, 38, 39, 42/43, 42, 43, 47, 50, 50/51, 54, 55, 58/59, 59, 62, 63(t), 63(b)

SOUTH AMERICA

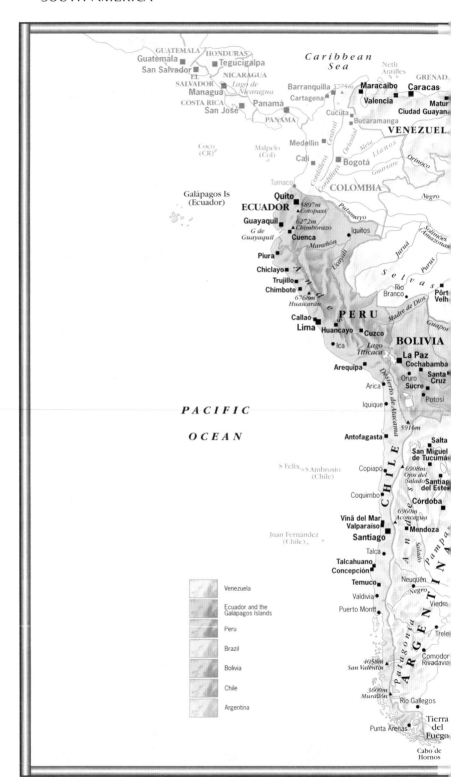

GUATEMALA HONDURAS
Guatemala ■ ■ Tegucigalpa
San Salvador ■
EL
SALVADOR NICARAGUA
Managua ■ Lago de
Nicaragua
COSTA RICA
San José ■ Panamá ■
PANAMA

*Caribbean
Sea*
Neth
Antilles
GRENAD

Barranquilla 5775m Maracaibo ■ ■ Caracas
Cartagena ▲ Valencia ■ ■ Matur
Cúcuta ■ Ciudad Guayana ■
Bucaramanga ■
VENEZUEL
Medellin ■ Meta
Cali ■ ■ Bogotá *Llanos*
Guaviare *Orinoco*
Tumaco *Negro*
COLOMBIA

Galápagos Is
(Ecuador)

Quito ■
ECUADOR 5897m
▲ *Cotopaxi*
Guayaquil ■ *Putumayo*
6272m
G de ▲ *Chimborazo* Iquitos ■
Guayaquil Cuenca ■ *Solimões*
Marañón *Amazonas*
Piura ■ *Juruá*
Chiclayo ■ *Ucayali* *Purus*
Trujillo ■ *A* *Selvas*
Chimbote ■ Rio
6768m Branco ■ Pôrt
Huascarán Velh
Callao ■ PERU *Madre de Dios*
Lima ■ Huancayo ■ ■ Cuzco *Guapor*
Ica ■ BOLIVIA
Lago
Titicaca La Paz ■
Cochabamba ■
Arequipa ■ Oruro ■ Santa ■
Arica Sucre ■ Cruz
Iquique *Desierto de Atacama* Potosí ■

PACIFIC 5916m
S Félix ○S Ambrosio Antofagasta ■ ■ Salta
OCEAN (Chile) San Miguel ■
de Tucumá ■
Copiapó ● 6908m
▲ *Ojos del*
Salado Santiag ■
del Este ■
Coquimbo ● *C* Córdoba ■
H 6960m
Viñā del Mar ■ ▲ *Aconcagua*
Juan Fernández Valparaíso ■ *I* ■ Mendoza *Pampa*
(Chile) Santiago ■ *L* *Salado*
Talca ● *E*
Talcahuano ■ Neuquén ●
Concepción ■ *Negro*
Temuco ■ Viedm
Valdivia ● *A* Trele
Puerto Montt ● *R*
G
E
4058m *N*
San Valentín *T* Comodor
Rivadavia
3600m *I*
Murallón Rio Gallegos ● *N*
Tierra
Punta Arenas ● del
Fuego
Cabo de
Hornos

Venezuela

Ecuador and the
Galápagos Islands

Peru

Brazil

Bolivia

Chile

Argentina